Gardner, Virginia.

"Friend and lov-
er"

DATE DUE			
NOV 1			

"Friend and Lover"

THE LIFE OF
LOUISE BRYANT

"Friend and Lover"

THE LIFE OF
LOUISE BRYANT

VIRGINIA GARDNER

HORIZON PRESS NEW YORK

Library of Congress Cataloging in Publication Data

Gardner, Virginia.
  "Friend and lover."
  Bibliography: p.
  Includes index.
  1. Bryant, Louise, 1885-1936. 2. Reed, John, 1887-
1920. 3. Communists—United States—Biography.
4. Journalists—United States—Biography. I. Title.
HX84.B73G37   1982   070'.92'4 [B]   82-80433
ISBN 0-8180-0233-6

Manufactured in the United States of America

To my son
John Marberry

Contents

Photographs

John Reed, 1920

John Reed, the Second Congress of the Comintern

John Reed, the Oriental Congress in Baku

Acknowledgments

More than a decade has passed since my first interviews with men and women who knew Louise Bryant; many of them knew John Reed as well. What seems amazing is how clear the recollections of most were, how alive and keen they themselves were. Kitty Cannell was about eighty when I last saw her, in 1972—gay, intrepid, vivid. Both Conrad Aiken, at eighty-two, and Floyd Dell, at eighty-one, were masters of the spoken word. Vincent Sheean, one of the youngest of those who knew and cared about Louise, was unfailing in writing from Italy, even from China, in reply to my letters of inquiry. Then I saw him and his wife, Diana Sheean, when they came here in 1975 before they went back to Italy, he to die among the hills he knew so well, at seventy-five. I think of those who were tireless in their reminiscences whenever I went to see them: Dorothy Day, an old friend, and the painter George Biddle.

I feel sad that both Andrew Dasburg, that great artist and Louise Bryant's lover, and his son, that wonderful man Alfred Van Cleve Dasburg, are not here to see the book to which they gave so unstintingly—Andrew, of memories; Alfred, through his mother's and father's letters, checking dates and places. Alfred read most of an earlier draft, and Andrew, those chapters in which he figures. Because he was so upset and indignant over certain biographers' accounts of Louise, I had hoped to get the book out before Andrew died. To Anne Dasburg of Santa Fe, New Mexico, Alfred's widow, I am indebted for generous hospitality and spirited comments as she and Alfred and I spoke of Andrew and his life and loves.

Among those who knew Louise, I also want to thank Mura Dehn, still vibrant and creative; Lucia Moore of Eugene, Oregon, Hugo

Gellert the artist, and George Seldes. I want to remember the editor Charles A. ("Cap") Pearce, who in a discussion of this historic period urged me to write this book, shortly before he died suddenly of a heart attack.

Early on, I received a Rabinowitz Foundation grant for research into Louise Bryant's background and youth.

Many individuals have helped and encouraged me for long years, first of all the editor of Quadrangle Books in Chicago, Ivan R. Dee, presently director of the Department of Public Affairs, Michael Reese Hospital and Medical Center, Chicago. It is impossible to say how often and generously he has helped me.

In 1975, after failing to obtain information from the King Features Syndicate, I wrote The Hearst Corporation in an attempt to trace Bryant's movements and to pin down the dates of her employment. Later I reached by telephone Ralph E. Mahoney, national editor, Hearst Newspapers. Many letters and phone calls were exchanged between us after his retirement, and his reading of four chapters of the manuscript led to Mr. Mahoney's providing a means of finding still missing articles written by Louise. Through the late John Ely, first secretary to William Randolph Hearst Jr., arrangements were made at the Humanities Research Center, The University of Texas at Austin, to make accessible to me Bryant's by-line articles and any stories about her in the Hearst Archives there. The entire reference library of the *New York Journal-American* after the combined papers folded was deposited in the Research Center.

I want to thank Clifford S. Gardner, professor of mathematics at the University of Texas, for his painstaking work on my behalf, and Mrs. Charlotte Carl-Mitchell, Humanities Research Center librarian who searched out the missing Bryant articles one summer. Without this help I could not have presented excerpts from Bryant's interview with Mussolini or her series on Kemal Pasha, among other stories.

I am also indebted to the Humanities Research Center Library, The University of Texas at Austin, for the use of the lovely frontispiece photograph of Louise Bryant.

Among the different libraries where I worked in years past, my warmest recollections go to the once frequently visited Houghton Library at Harvard, presided over by Miss Carolyn Jakeman when I first went there, and later, Miss Marte Shaw, with the inimitable Joe McCarthy, keeper of the archives in those years, an indispensable and cheerful purveyor of lore. I also am grateful to Corliss Lamont who maintained contact with the Houghton staff and deposited many letters from Louise Bryant and other memorabilia in the John Reed Collection which I have examined.

I am indebted to the present staff of the Newspaper Annex of the New York Public Library for assistance in obtaining copies of Bryant's stories in the *New York American*, and to Arthur Spencer of the Oregon Historical Society. The full list of libraries which were helpful over the years is given in the Bibliography.

My thanks to Julia Ruuttila for the Oregon interviews called for by the Rabinowitz grant, and to Margaret Bome of Reno, Nevada, for research on Louise's background. Evelyn Averbuck, a dear friend, not only put me up when I went to California for my earliest research but continued interviewing Californians who had known Louise.

William A. Reuben read chapters of the book and was most helpful. I want also to thank Svend Hoiberg for years of assistance.

I am especially grateful to Ben Raeburn of Horizon Press, and to Mary Newman for her thorough copyediting.

Old friends who read a number of chapters in early drafts include Sara Gauldin, Isabel Grossner, and Maurine Green; recently Judith Evans, Vivian Cherry, and Blanche Wiesen Cook read a number of chapters. Close friends whose encouragement was unflagging from the start include Nancy Sullivan and Esther Unger; with Esther, a running course of discussion about Louise went on over the years. My son John Marberry gave careful attention to many chapters in the early years, and throughout, cheered me on.

1.

The Village

WHEN LOUISE BRYANT's train pulled into Grand Central Station in New York City on January 4, 1916, John Reed was waiting for her.[1] Two days before the New Year's eve when she left her husband, Paul Trullinger, and Portland for John Reed and New York, she wrote her lover, ". . . the night is so empty without you. Wonderful man—I know there isn't another soul anywhere so free and so exquisite and so strong!"*[2]

If Bryant loved him because he was so free, he was drawn no less to similar qualities in her, writing a friend while he was visiting his mother in Portland: "I have fallen in love again, and . . . think I've found her at last. . . . She's wild and brave and straight, and graceful and lovely to look at. . . . And in this spiritual vacuum, this unfertilized soil, she has grown (how I can't imagine) into an artist . . . a poet and a revolutionary. . . . I think she's the first person I ever loved without reservation."[3]

Without compunctions for her undemanding dentist husband, Bryant had become Reed's lover and agreed to follow him to New York within days. Seeing Reed again, it was as if the six years spent as the wife of Paul Trullinger had never been.

In the taxi bearing them to his apartment at 43 Washington Square South, Reed told her he had rented a room for her nearby but wanted her all to himself for the moment. Once at Number 43, she was

---

*Throughout this and other chapters all letters will be quoted or excerpted as written, without correction of words, names, or punctuation, and without the use of *sic*.

welcomed rapturously, and had no desire to go elsewhere. He agreed there was no need to. She never even went to look at the room he'd engaged. The unhappiness and loneliness she had known with Trullinger fell away from her.

At Number 43, she wrote, each of them had a separate work room, which she called a studio, a hallway dividing them. He wrote until four o'clock usually, then came across to her domain. They would have tea. "We had a habit of taking long walks after tea to different parts of New York, going over bridges, to the East Side, Harlem, anywhere. . . . Jack at that time was one of the most popular writers in America. Also, I suppose, one of the highest paid. . . . We used to spend it as he made it. There was a common [familial] purse. I could always go to it and take what I wanted and no questions were ever asked. I had lived that way in my grandfather's house, so it was easy to fall into it again."[4]

Reed took pride in introducing her to his friends and people on the celebrated *Masses* magazine. He took her to a *Masses* ball and noted with pleasure that others too found her attractive.[5] He boasted of her beauty and promised friends they would hear from her talents. Together they visited the Liberal Club, where occasional one-act plays by Floyd Dell, managing editor of *The Masses*, and others were performed, and dancing to a gramophone was usual on Friday nights. She was tireless, endlessly curious as he introduced her to the city with its myriad cultures, all enhanced for her by Reed's poetic love for the discoveries he'd made. In between more distant excursions there was Greenwich Village itself, with dinner at the old black brick Brevoort Hotel at Fifth Avenue and Eighth Street or the Hotel Lafayette, a block away on University Place.

The Washington Square Book Shop on Macdougal Street, next door to the Liberal Club, was the hub of Village literary-social life. Of course Reed took Bryant in to meet Albert Boni, who, with his brother Charles, ran it. Reed had known him at Harvard where Boni was three years his academic junior. From the first Boni thought her "a lovely, attractive person."

"I used to drop in on them, in Washington Square South. I'd go in and find them in bed and I'd just pull up a chair and we'd talk. Jack and Louise had a lovely relationship."[6]

At times Reed and Bryant would meet Jim Larkin, the Irish labor leader, at Three Steps Down, 21 West Eighth Street, run by the famous Strunskys. (Papa Strunsky also was a landlord and never could bring himself to evict artists.) Larkin and Bryant cottoned to each other; Louise was passionately Irish, and at times when Reed was at work she met Larkin at lunch there. That's where Hugo Gellert, the youngest of *Masses* artists, first met her; he was introduced by Larkin and joined them briefly at their table.[7]

It was also at Three Steps Down (three steps down led to the entrance) that the poet Conrad Aiken first met her. He had come from Boston with a Boston newspaperman, Julius Clark, on one of Aiken's periodic visits to New York. They no sooner sat down and ordered than Clark spotted "a very pretty girl seated alone" a few tables away. "I think she can be made," Clark confided, to the shy poet's embarrassment. The newspaperman began his silent overtures and continued to ogle and leer at the woman, when the door opened and Jack Reed burst in. The two poets had been closely associated at Harvard, Aiken on the *Advocate* and Reed on the *Harvard Monthly* with adjoining offices on the top floor of the Union Building.

"Oh, Conrad," Reed cried gaily as soon as he entered, "come over and meet my wife!" and proceeded to seat himself by the side of the object of Clark's conquest. Aiken and Clark joined them and were introduced to Louise Bryant, Reed beaming as he showed her off. They remained only a few minutes: Aiken was glad enough to get his ambitious friend away from the scene.[8]

A vivid description of Bryant as Villager was supplied by one who, though a confirmed Villager, drew a distinction between himself and the Bohemians. Said Roger Baldwin: "Louise was striking. Of course young, and beautiful in a very pure sort of way—not made up at all. Her hair was dark, her eyes gray-blue—Irish, changing. If I recollect rightly, her coloring was quite on the light side. There was a quality of light to her face—no high color, but very fresh. She was eccentric, of course, but her eccentricities fit right in with the period.

"She had a lot of courage, was a flame in the protest socialism of the day. She was on her way, although she didn't know where she was going. That, too, was typical. There was a lot of feeling, a lot of talk about socialism, but no one seemed to know what kind of socialism they were for. You felt she sensed what was stirring, and was ready to take off in the wind. It was an exciting period and Louise was a dramatic figure. By 1918–19 she had made a definite contribution."[9]

For Bryant to live openly with her lover conformed with the prevailing canons of the Golden Age of America's Bohemia, and she felt largely at home in the mores of the Village. John Reed was still the Golden Boy in Villagers' eyes, the radiant troubadour of Pancho Villa's men and their exploits in the Mexican revolution, the reporter who had aroused them regarding the silkworkers' strike in Paterson, New Jersey, and produced the magnificent pageant of the strike in Madison Square Garden. His was the quintessential voice of *The Masses*, and the periodical, the conscience of the Village. While the *Metropolitan, The World,* and other publications paid for his journeys, the magazine that couldn't pay got his most colorful reporting.

Villagers were jealous of their bright star, moreover. ("Jack, big Jack, beloved by all," Konrad Bercovici wrote of him, while Van Wyck Brooks later called him "the wonder boy of Greenwich Village.")[10] There had been minor carpings when he and Mabel Dodge cohabited at 23 Fifth Avenue and elsewhere, but the Village was proud of the famous salon she ran. Even so, the archetypal Villager Hutchins Hapgood wrote that "Reed, emerging from the jail at Paterson, was put in jail by Mabel—a far more difficult prison to escape from."[11]

But Bryant was an unknown. She had friends among the younger women, staunch feminists all: Madeleine Z. Doty, writer for popular magazines; Inez Haynes Gillmore, a *Masses* contributor who also wrote for *Harper's Bazar;* Crystal Eastman, brainy and beautiful (the black poet Claude McKay wrote of her as the loveliest white woman he ever saw);[12] Doris Stevens, for a time married to Dudley Field Malone, lawyer; and Inez Milholland, said to be the most beautiful woman who ever bit a policeman's wrist before landing in jail. But among the Village notables there were older women who felt something like outrage that Reed had picked such a provincial.

Publicly Bryant was made much of, and before the year was out she became a sort of reigning queen of Bohemia.[13] Privately, many women intellectuals felt superior to her. Nor was it unknown for men's views of her to be tinged with resentment. When Dorothy Day became assistant to Dell on *The Masses*, most of the staff were men. "The *Masses* people didn't like Louise," she said. "I think it was jealousy. She had no right to have brains and be so pretty. They were constantly minimizing her."[14]

Bryant on her part was puzzled by one aspect of Villagers. In some of the talk across the wooden tables in Polly's Restaurant beneath the Liberal Club, a certain earnestness in discussing freedom bordered on the fanatical. To hear a woman confide in another that when she suspected she was falling in love, "of course I told George about it," made her uncomfortable. However much she honored freedom she never trusted it enough to desert discretion.[15] Freedom was nothing new to her but confession reminded her of the Catholic Church she had long ago put behind her.

Not only women but men told about their lovers, and those who had nothing to confess kept silent; it was their apologia. "I have been busily engaged all my life in confessing to my friends, especially my wife, and, as far as I could, the world," wrote Hutchins Hapgood, who tirelessly searched for a woman who could understand his soul.[16]

Reed was a confessor, too, though less relentless than Hapgood. In Portland he had told Bryant of experiences in love that had shaken him, none so much as the two-year intermittent intimacy with Mabel Dodge.[17]

Late one afternoon at 43 Washington Square South the doorbell rang. The door was opened by Bryant, holding a lighted candle in her hand. "Is Jack Reed here?" a woman's voice asked. Reed then appeared, with tousled hair, behind her, saying gravely, "This is Louise Bryant."

"How do you do?" the visitor asked. "Reed, I came to ask you for your old typewriter, if you're not using it."

"Louise is using it," he said.

"Oh, all right. I only thought. . . ." The voice faded and the visitor was gone. (In her account of the incident, Mabel Dodge Luhan described her successor as "a very pretty, tall young woman with soft, black hair and very blue eyes.")[18]

In her jealousy of Reed, Bryant may have felt that the Dodge of formidable reputation had employed an obvious ruse in order to make another overture to Reed. If she fleetingly thought of the pact she and Reed had made, she remained wary. Whatever she agreed to, she was never magnanimous concerning Jack Reed and other women. Max Eastman described it as "a kind of gypsy compact" that would allow each to "live life," which meant "to live it in freedom and stark reality and immense honesty."[19] Eastman wrote a lot of mush about the supposed pact. He seemed to assume that Louise would be the only one called on to forgive.

Early in their association Bryant discovered that life with a hard-working reporter bore little semblance to her dream of "somebody who wouldn't care what hour you went to bed or what hour you got up"—unless you wanted to sleep alone. She also found that his two trips to the European war zones still were very much with him. He had never been very well since the Serbian retreat, and in 1915 had suffered terribly with his weak kidney. "Jack was war weary, while I wanted adventure," her memoir records.[20]

She also found herself alone a good deal. When out of town he

wrote her longingly, as he did on the *Palm Beach Limited* on his way
to interview, and cruise the St. John River with, William Jennings
Bryan for *Collier's:*[21]

"Dearest sweetheart—I've just had a bum dinner in the dining-car,
and am trying to write you to the juggling of the train. . . . My little
lover, I become more and more gloomy and mournful to think I'm not
going to sleep all over you in our scandalous and sinful voluptuous
bed. All my enthusiasm begins to run out of my toes when you get
farther and farther away, and I can't go rushing into your room and
kiss you four or five hundred times. Old darling, what are you doing
now, I wish I were around—that's all."[22]

A letter of Reed's to Bryant in 1917, after eighteen months of
cohabitation, wrestled with his problems with women and declared
contritely, "I've had four or five of these things that have worn you
down. Still, my darling, *you've* got to make up your mind to trust me
to a certain extent, or our life together will be a farce."[23]

No record is known as to when the first of "these things" took place.
Whether Bryant was acting in retaliation or merely because of her
desire for adventure, one cold day she boldly knocked on the door of
the painter Andrew Dasburg, a few doors from 43 Washington Square
South. She knew little about him except that he had come home from
a 1909–10 stay in Paris to herald the work of the late Cézanne and
proclaim the new age in art celebrated by Picasso, Matisse, and others
he had met. She had been introduced to Dasburg and many other
artists by Reed. Strong and agile despite his lameness, he had an
unaffected, even modest, manner, dry humor, guileless blue eyes,
and a broad open face that appealed strongly to women, judging from
his history.[24]

The door was opened by an unsmiling and surprised Dasburg; it
was plain he had been painting. He asked what he might do for her.
She laughed and said he might ask her in. As he himself laughed, she
grew serious. She was, she said, curious about his work. Since she'd
already interrupted it, might she just see some of it? Of course he had
a right to throw her right out.

Dasburg said he had little there, but she was welcome. He asked
after Jack. Oh, she replied, he was out of town on some story.

She wanted to know how long he had been painting. He suggested
they talk about herself. There was nothing to say, she hadn't done
anything—yet. She returned to her query. At last some of the story
came out, so persistent was her questioning.

Dasburg had come with his mother from Europe when he was five years old. They were very poor. His mother made sleeves for a French dressmaker, and while she was away (from seven in the morning until seven at night) he was alone in their Hell's Kitchen room. Before he reached school age, he fell into an excavation, and a tubercular hip developed. At the Crippled Children's Hospital he got what care they could give—not much, for there were many crippled children to serve.

Eventually Dasburg went to an industrial school for the lame; two teachers discerned talent and got him into the Art Students League at an early age. Later the League gave him a scholarship to its classes in Woodstock, New York. But he wanted to know more about her.

Wild horses couldn't have dragged from Bryant a confession of her old hope of being an artist; suddenly she knew her talents were small. She was trying to write, she said, and had had some experience on a weekly paper. Oh, that's how you could be so expert at giving me the third degree, remarked Dasburg; and what else? She told him she had a husband in the West; whether he would ever give her a divorce she had no idea. Now, that's enough confessing for one day, yes?

Before she left him Bryant asked if he liked to take walks; when Jack was away she went alone and more than once got lost. He did, adding that it would be good for his leg.

She had not asked about his marriage.

After that Dasburg saw Bryant with Reed on occasions, and never alone unless Reed was out of town. Once in the spring of 1916, according to the painter's memory, she visited him at Woodstock for a weekend. Neither realized that what was at the time only a delightful interlude would be repeated in Woodstock more than once in the coming four years—"although never for more than a weekend."[25]

Bryant may have heard that Dasburg and his fiercely independent, attractive feminist wife, the talented sculptor of animals Grace Mott Johnson—she wanted to be called "Johnson"—were separated. It was not quite that way. Each found the other fascinating, but life together for two full-time artists was hard (and probably for their very young son, Alfred, whose care they shared).[26]

Who was this Louise Bryant? The third child of Hugh J. and Anna Louisa Mohan, she was born in San Francisco December 5, 1885, and christened Anna Louisa in the Roman Catholic Church.[27] Mohan was a roaming newspaperman with a colorful background. How much of it was ever known to his youngest child is uncertain. Apparently she believed he was born in Ireland, and that her mother came from

Louisiana and was a Say, although she was a Flick. Throughout high school and college Bryant invented careers for him as a mine owner, a lawyer, or a politician.

The reality was more interesting. Hugh Mohan was born in Minersville, Pennsylvania, in the heart of the anthracite region, on March 9, 1858, and as a boy worked in the coal mines. He attended public schools there, and early was known as the "Orator of the Day" in St. Patrick's Day rites in various towns in the region. In nearby Pottsville, seat of Schuylkill County, he obtained his first newspaper job, reporting for the *Standard,* later becoming editor of the *Free Press.* (Pottsville was the rallying ground for the so-called Molly Maguires.)[28] In 1876 he was secretary of the Workingmen's State Anti-Monopoly convention in Harrisburg.[29]

It is easy to believe that Louise Bryant knew none of this history of the father whom she continued to adore, nor of his years spent in working for three Catholic Congressmen in Washington City, as it was then called, while he continued as a journalist, writing for the *Irish World* and other pro-labor organs. For when she was three years old her mother, an energetic woman who before her marriage had worked as a dressmaker in San Francisco,[30] obtained a divorce from Mohan in Reno, Nevada, where the family had gone to live. District Judge R. R. Bigelow found that he had left the state and was "of drunken and improvident habits, and of wandering and migratory disposition."[31]

A fragmentary memoir by Louise Bryant pictures her as often in tears or seated disconsolately in a corner listening to her mother play the piano at this time. She was grieving for her father. On June 11, 1892, when she was six years old, her mother married Sheridan Daniel Bryant. A brakeman and later a conductor on freight trains, he worked for the Southern Pacific throughout a long life, providing the home-staying traits so missing in the footloose newspaperman Mohan.

For the child Anna Louisa to have invented her father's death at the time was an understandable fantasy: an insupportable burden had been placed on her, a father who betrayed her by his absence. More surprising is the fact that Louise Bryant never climbed out of her fantasy. Writing her memoir as she approached fifty years of age, she maintained her father had died and that her mother was "grief-stricken beyond all recovery," while she found herself "a very, very lonely little child."

"I *had* a father!" she wailed when her mother's new husband asked her at age six to call him "father."

"Everything went very wrong with me. I was nervous and often ill," she continues. "Then one night my grandfather, a tall, thin, handsome Irish-Englishman, arrived. . . . 'How would you like to come and live with me?' he asked me. 'You must decide it for yourself.' "

Only after she deliberated and said, "Well, sir, I think I'd like to come," did he smile and say: "Very good, on the day you arrive you shall have a white horse. Remember, I always keep my word." The difficulties of finding a white horse "gentle enough for a child to ride" did not occur to her.

When she at length arrived at his combination cattle ranch and mine called "The Mines," on the Nevada desert near Carson Sink, it was late at night. But the next morning as she was breakfasting he came in, asked if she remembered their bargain and led her to the stables—and the white horse, "a horse out of an Arabian dream, with a long tail, long mane, and gentle as a lamb. For years I lavished all my starved affection on that animal."[32]

"Grandfather Say" was English, not an Irish-Englishman. Nor was he related to her by blood, but was her step-grandfather, a search of obituaries in old newspaper files and other scattered documents indicates. Her mother was a Flick, whatever Bryant believed.[33] It was after the mother's mother became a widow in the Nevada Territory that she married James R. Say. He was thought to be a descendant of the Lords Say.[34]

The grandfather had his own ideas about how to bring up a young girl. "I was taught never to cry in public, to go to my room at night all alone and stay there. To be devoid of superstition or prejudice." Combined with the individualism of the frontier and her idealization of her own father in defiance of his errant ways, the plainly aristocratic teachings of "Grandpa Say" would be translated by Bryant later on as "make your own rules" in behavior and the public be damned. It also had its good points: keep a stiff upper lip, eschew prejudice and cant, and keep your troubles to yourself (although the last carries a risk).

Her education Say relegated to a Chinese overseer, Yeegee, "a very scholarly old man." When she was 14, however, Mrs. Bryant wrote to Say that her daughter was not getting a proper education. On the day fixed for her departure she was admonished by the old gentleman not to forget that she was the daughter of her father, Hugh Mohan. Apparently he had been charmed by the young man, as no doubt many were, such as the important Californians who had recommended him for a position with the government,[35] for Say told her: "And whatever the family may say about your father, I always liked him better than any of them."

Returning from her desert life of freedom to a stable, comfortable home life, Anna Louisa was subjected by her mother to a "very systematic, almost Germanic, training . . . she had been trained by Germans to play the piano."[36] In these few words she suggests the value placed on education by her mother, who with her railway worker husband sent four of the five children of the combined family to college. These included Bryant's brother, Louis Parnell, who like all the Mohan children adopted their stepfather's name, and her half-brothers, Floyd Sherman, born in 1894, and William Philip, in 1896. Floyd became a Rhodes scholar. William dreamed of becoming an architect.

Silas E. Ross of Reno remembered Louise Bryant as "bright, vivacious, well-groomed, a very independent thinker."[37] After attending Wadsworth High School she enrolled at the University of Nevada in Reno as Anna Louise Bryant, saying she was born in San Francisco December 5, 1885. (So far as is known, it was the last time she revealed the accurate date.) For a year she took a commercial course, and to make up requirements also attended classes at University High School. This was not unusual: Nevada, still frontier country, had a dearth of good high schools and the university, in order to obtain students, had to create them.

High school and colleges shared campus and even buildings and the students mingled socially. Only in 1904 did she enter the Liberal Arts College, sharing a room in Manzanita Hall with Millie Hunewill of Bridgeport, California.

Both young women were on the women's basketball team, and Bryant was on the staff of the *Student Record,* editing its Young Ladies' Edition of December 17, 1905. She was also on the staff of a short-lived literary magazine, *Chuckawalla,* and both she and Hune-will wrote short short stories for it.

"We surely were morbid," Mrs. Millie Hunewill Hamblet reflected cheerfully, many years later.[38] Her own lone character dies in the desert of thirst, crazed by a mirage, while a coyote howls in the distance. Bryant's story, "The Way of a Flirt," ends with the flirt's death by drowning after a gay excursion party comes to grief on a lake. It is interesting for other reasons. The flirt, "beautiful, carefree Lenore," seems to be following the precepts laid down by Grandfather Say. When Lenore is jilted she hides her grief, acts the clown, lightheartedly flirting with many. The author obviously identifies with the fickle Lenore, despising both the non-hero who chooses "quiet little Sybil" and Sybil herself, "just an ordinary girl" who thinks "as most people do."

Occasionally Millie and Louise took the streetcar to visit the Bryants, first to Wadsworth, Nevada, and then to Sparks, after the Southern Pacific moved the western terminal of its Salt Lake division there. When she wasn't busy in the kitchen, Mrs. Bryant played the piano; at times Barbara, five years Louise's elder, who had her own piano, played duets with her. The mother also made most of Louise's clothes, which appeared professionally turned out. Louise played only a little. "Her real talent was art, and both *Artemisia* and *Chuckawalla* used her signed sketches."

To help out on finances one year, Louise taught in Jolon, California, a predominantly Mexican-American community, living with a family and learning a little Spanish.

To Millie Hunewill Hamblet, Bryant was attractive rather than beautiful: her eyes and hair were beautiful but she had crooked teeth. "Still, I'd say the word 'glamour' was just made for her."

She felt Louise "got her good looks from her mother, but it was clear that her father meant a lot to her. I remember she said he died young, and that he'd been a lawyer, with connections in Denver, and was known as 'the silver-tongued orator.' "[39]

In September 1906 Anna Louise Bryant was registered as a student at the University of Oregon at Eugene, listing as parents only her mother, Mrs. S. D. Bryant of Sparks, Nevada, and giving her own date of birth as December 5, 1887. At 21 she was thus thought to be 19. She had exchanged the lavish sunsets and star-filled night skies of the desert for the cloudiness, the fogs, duller skies, and lush green of the Willamette valley. Instead of barren distant hills there were thickly forested buttes hemming in Eugene.

Seen in the foreground of old Deady Hall with its Virginia creeper, in her tailored light blue suit, fitted jacket and long pleated skirt, her "rosebud mouth always a little open," her green-blue eyes open wide, her pigeon toes planted firmly on the ground, she seemed fully at home in her new surroundings. Showing beneath her hand-stitched jacket was the invariable white silk shirt. She had a look that was "a little floaty."[40]

To wear stiff petticoats underneath contributed to the look, and Bryant wore three: on the outside, her cleanest; beneath it, last week's, and closest to her skin, week before last's. They were starched, white and embroidered, and they really made a skirt stand out.[41]

For all her "floaty" look, she was down to earth. Eugene had no dormitories, living costs were high. In the spring she and four others formed a sorority and by the next fall had acquired a house, spacious and with fireplaces. She was the first president. They employed a cook, Bertha Barrett, and set a good table. Meanwhile they applied for a charter from Chi Omega.

Her sorority sisters on the whole were amused and rather proud that their Louise created a scandal as the first to use rouge on campus. "It never caused criticism—just envy maybe," according to Lucia Wilkins Moore. "I loved Louise Bryant. As far as I was concerned, she could do no wrong. I just adored her."[42]

But perceptions of Bryant differed widely on the campus. With an entire student body of less than five hundred, everyone knew everyone else—or thought they did. In this atmosphere, friendly on the surface, the puritan moralism in which Eugene was steeped spawned endless gossip. Perhaps it was Bryant's disinclination to confide her own affairs or discuss others' that somehow whetted the curiosity she inspired.

A shrewd observer, Bertha Dorris Carpenter, suggested such an analysis, as she spoke of her sorority sister in laconic sentences that had a true ring. "Louise was very circumspect, she did not talk. She always kept her own counsel. She was very smart." Oh, she talked about her family, or the wildly popular professor, Herbert Crombie Howe. "But in matters more personal, such as how serious she was about any of her beaus, she was discreet. Even a sorority sister would not have thought of asking her, either."[43]

It was all in keeping with the teachings of Grandfather Say and with the code of the frontier prospector after gold: play your cards close to your chest.

Speaking more in amusement than condemnation, a woman recalled: "The men buzzed around Louise, and we were so very moral in those days that we had no use for her: she was 'different.' "[44]

The only serious charge came from Miriam Van Waters, a noted penologist, who also had high praise for Bryant. As editor of the *Oregon Monthly,* Van Waters had accepted numerous poems with pen-and-ink sketches signed "A. Louise Bryant" or "A. L. Bryant," as well as essays and reviews, and declared she had "recognized Louise Bryant's genius." She also accepted Bryant as "a delightful personality, refreshing and always at work on creative thinking in various fields [but] unconcerned with what today we call 'social issues.' "

But Van Waters, a confidante of Luella Clay Carson, dean of women, charged that Bryant, in opposing Dr. Carson's injunctions, "openly flaunted drinking, smoking and flashy dressing, in cafés in the town and neighboring towns. I know the dean was deeply hurt."

All this she placed in the context of a critical time for the university when future legislative appropriations were at stake. A Professor Hawthorne, head of the anthropology and psychology departments, had published a paper on his find: the bones of the three-toed horse, genealogical ancestor to the camel, in the bottom of an old well. Newspapers had picked up the story, and this confirmation of the theory of evolution had the hard-shell Baptist farmers up in arms. To soothe them, some sixty teams of students, each with a professor accompanying them, were sent into the hinterlands to speak before Grange locals.[45]

As Floyd ("Squee") Ramp, the campus radical, said, however: "Sixty years is a long time to remember. I was not aware that Louise Bryant was among those picked to lecture the Grangers. I wasn't—too radical. If I am not mistaken, Louise was a sort of doll—and no doubt did dress in a way that Dr. Carson would find objectionable. She objected to everything—she was really Victorian."[46]

Bertha Dorris Carpenter had the utmost respect for Van Waters. But, she said firmly, "I don't think Louise ever drank in Oregon. For that matter, I think that any girl who was pretty and vital was suspect in Dr. Carson's eyes and to most of the older deans."[47]

August 1908 found Bryant in San Francisco. She wrote a friend of meeting many newspaper editors; they were crying hard times and not hiring people. She felt discouraged, but the letter was decorated with sprightly drawings of the Merry Widow hats they were wearing. She had not graduated with her class, and expected to return to Eugene soon.[48]

When the Chi Omegas obtained their charter in 1909, Bryant was "teaching school somewhere in Washington; she came hurrying back as soon as she was free. It was in May or June; she was initiated by herself. She seemed just the same—our merry Louise."[49]

After secretly marrying Dr. Paul Trullinger, a Portland dentist, in Oregon City on November 13, 1909, Louise Bryant retained not only her own name but her own studio, at 415 Yamhill.[50] She had stayed with Eugene friends, the Wold sisters, in the same building before she obtained the studio, and through them met Trullinger, "a very pleasant, even handsome, man, outgoing and with a sense of humor."[51]

A small circle of dissidents revolved around Clara and Jean Wold, joined now by Bryant and Trullinger. "We were belligerents—we'd be called hippies in another period," said Marguerite Dosch Campbell. "Dr. Trullinger trailed along behind Louise. He was charming, but had no spark. Portland was a very small place."[52]

Bryant began placing sketches and occasional articles with the

Spectator, a weekly tabloid of society, sports, and comment. In early 1913 she became its society editor, continuing to contribute sketches and occasional political cartoons.

For several years the Trullingers lived in a houseboat in the Oregon Yacht Club harbor. Dances took place frequently in the clubhouse, an advantage in a city with no night life. Bryant learned to swim and, like all Portlanders, to love the Willamette River, which curves through the town in a great S and provides Portland's harbor. "The water was clean and pure: there was a grove of oaks on the bank."[53]

Stern-wheelers still plied the Willamette (until 1914), and the Trullingers could take one to Astoria, where Paul was born, to be the weekend guests of Grant and Adele Trullinger. This was where Grandfather John Trullinger operated a prosperous mill, owned lumber tracts, and on Christmas eve 1885 turned a switch and viewed his handiwork: electric lights blazed forth, product of the first plant west of the Rockies.

When Adele Trullinger, Paul's aunt, was an alert ninety, she said: "Louise is very vivid in my memory—extremely bright, but more, wise and intelligent. Beautiful, too. Paul's mother told me she thought Louise must rouge her cheeks, but they were natural. I can attest to that."[54]

Trullinger was a gentle person. Together the couple raised pedigreed Persian cats and were quite foolish about them. The cats often shared their bed, especially when kittens were imminent.[55]

The cats figured importantly in a memory Brownell Frasier had of the day she and her sister Janet were taken by their mother, Jennie Lee Frasier of Eugene, to have tea with Bryant. "She wore a long smoke-colored chiffon hostess dress and a bunch of fresh violets which matched her eyes. Her two large gray Persian cats matched the dress. I was only a child, but went away with the impression that Louise was very different, very romantic."[56]

In the 1912 Oregon crusade which won the state for woman suffrage, Bryant was encouraged to become active by the principal mover and shaker of the campaign, Sara Bard Field, then the wife of the Rev. Albert Ehrgott. "I found her living kind of a dull life for a woman like that," she said when she was eighty-eight and long the widow of C. E. S. Wood. "She was a sort of protégée of mine." She felt that she had helped Bryant to be aware of her own talents, but it was Wood who aroused her as to the Industrial Workers of the World (I.W.W.), she said.[57]

Through Wood, Bryant met Emma Goldman, who once was a guest

in the Trullinger home.[58] A part of the ruling hierarchy of Portland, attorney Wood contributed to *The Masses*, took I.W.W. cases for nothing, bailed out and defended Margaret Sanger and Goldman, and on the whole "shocked—stimulated—enraged—enchanted."[59]

When Jacob R. Proebstel met Louise Bryant in 1914, he saw her as serious, alluring and rather grave, "one of the thinkers of Portland." He was a member of a group who met twice a week in late afternoon to study French under a tutor, in either Trullinger's office or that of Dr. Thomas Ross, physician, both in the Selling Building. Others included Bryant, Kina McKelvey Ross, and Ross Trullinger, Paul's brother.

At times they went after class to the house on Riverwood Road that Trullinger had bought for Louise. To be a guest in their home was to feel "an indefinable distance between them, possibly a division of interests." Trullinger, genial, often witty, took over as host; Bryant was withdrawn, rather like a guest in her own home. "Something in the marriage was wrong. But a story originating outside the group that Louise had turned to Ross Trullinger I did not believe."[60]

Other stories about Bryant included one told secondhand but with élan. One wintry day she was nearing the Morrison Street bridge when she saw the driver of a beer wagon mercilessly beating his dray horses who had slipped on the ice. Bryant ran up to them, put a hand on one horse's flank, laced into the driver, bade him to put away his whip—and herself led the horses over the slippery bridge.

"I didn't know Louise, but when I heard that story from Carl and Helen Walters it endeared me to her forever," said the sculptor Marie Louise Feldenheimer. "I thought, 'Oh, God, I wish I had done that!' "[61]

Chafing at the trivia she turned out for the *Spectator*, for some time Bryant had worked hard getting subscriptions for *The Masses*, often using Jack Reed's pieces as a selling point.[62] In December 1915, hearing Reed was in Portland, her spirits soared. Floyd Ramp has said that he saw them together in 1912 at a political meeting and spoke to them afterward.[63] However that may be, one thing is undeniable: in 1915 she scurried around to friends who knew Reed, making sure that on this occasion she surely would see him.

"I brought Louise and Jack together," Sara Bard Field Wood said. She felt responsible, and at the only time she saw Trullinger, "my heart ached for him. A nice but unintellectual man, not the kind of man to hold a woman like Louise. He did love her, poor man. He took it very hard, but did nothing to prevent her going."

Asked if she felt that Louise loved Jack, her answer came at once: "Passionately."[64]

Others also claimed to be the initiators of the Reed-Bryant meeting, or to have witnessed it.[65]

When a small group of friends went to the depot to see her off for New York, she wore a bunch of fresh violets Paul had sent.[66] He then quietly had a nervous breakdown. He never spoke ill of her nor did any of the Trullingers.[67] .

The peppery Mrs. Linley Crichton, a second cousin on his mother's side, scorned such tolerance. "Louise was a fascinating person, and exotic—but no morals, no morals whatsoever. And that Reed was no good. Look where he was buried!"[68]

2.
Provincetown

IN THE SPRING REED'S weak kidney was troubling him; he was told by physicians that he should rest. He had long wanted to write a novel; perhaps he and Louise both could have a quiet, productive summer in Provincetown.

The writer Mary Heaton Vorse had invited them to stay at her place, but when they arrived she greeted them rather absently, as if she really hadn't expected them. They went house-hunting and Reed found one he thought very nice, but Louise took one look at the wallpaper and said she could never live with that. The search continued—until they found another, all furnished, on the seashore with its own little beach. They moved in immediately.

Late in the day they called on the columnist Hutchins Hapgood and his writer wife, Neith Boyce. Seeing them approach, a familiar figure ran out to meet them, asking, "Jack, don't you want a cook?" It was Hippolyte Havel, a scholarly man, long an anarchist editor. "You don't want to be a cook, Hippolyte," Jack said. "Yes, I do," Havel replied, "and I am a very good cook, too." So Havel was hired at about eighty dollars a month, and went to live with them.[1]

The summer of "rest" began auspiciously. Settled in the white clapboard cottage, they spent most of their days outdoors. Reed, a prodigious swimmer and diver, took long swims daily. They spent blissful hours on long walks, sunned themselves in the nude in the shelter of the dunes. Evenings they visited the early arrivals at the Cape, or played host to Mary Vorse, the Hapgoods, or others. But in a week's time Reed departed on assignments that would spell a three-week jaunt for the *Metropolitan*, with stories for *The Masses* an adjunct. With Art Young to illustrate his pieces, Reed set out for Chicago and St. Louis to cover national political conventions and for Detroit to interview Henry Ford.

Whenever he ran into friends he invited them in his casual way to stay with him and Louise. Or he remembered David Carb, whom he worried over, and wired him to spend the summer in Provincetown's healthy climate. Bryant received a telegram, "Please meet David Carb. He arrives at three this afternoon." She went to the station, saw the train from Fall River disgorge its passengers, and when one lone figure remained, guessed that it was Carb. Before Reed's return, others arrived: the painters Marsden Hartley and Charles Demuth; Robert E. Rogers, like Carb a Harvard classmate, who taught English at the Massachusetts Institute of Technology; and later his brother Merrill, business manager of *The Masses*.[2]

To Max Eastman, *Masses* editor, who with Ida Rauh and their infant son Daniel lived almost directly across the street, the home made by Reed and "his red-cheeked, freckled, grey-eyed Irish bride from Oregon . . . never seemed to draw me in except as to a spectacle. . . . Louise herself was no housekeeper, and their place was barnlike in its physical aspect. A large assortment of interesting males was provided with abundant nutrition, however, and beds to sleep on. . . ."[3]

Stopping in New York, Reed was told by physicians that his condition was improved, or so he assured Bryant in a telegram and a letter written on the train June 6. "That's wonderful isn't it?" she replied. "I feel perfectly elated—of course this summer will do it all right." She wrote daily, at times twice. She fretted that "it seems absolutely absurd without you and I can't get adjusted to it." The second night of his absence she "didn't sleep one minute." She added with pride that "we have *four* tableclothes and 24 napkins and I have holes all over my fingers."[4]

"I have eaten my dinner in 'solitary confinement' and Hippolyte called me Marie-Antoinette-in-Prison," she wrote one evening, closing with "I love you with all my heart." In this letter she enclosed a little snapshot of herself in the nude. Half-reclining, her hair long, her slender body is faintly etched against the white sand, a dune in the background. She wrote on the reverse side, "This is to remind you of 'the Dunes' & all the nice months after the Convention—Please, Honey take good care of yourself out there—"[5]

After hearing from Reed that he didn't feel well, she urged, "If you *really feel* ill, Honey, run away from the silly Conventions . . . the most important thing in the world to us is your health now." She had written Fred Boyd, his sometime secretary, "to *be here* when you arrived"—after a letter from Boyd saying that he might not come to Provincetown right away.

"Oh, darling, you'll be so busy you won't have time for all this chatter but I want to *visit* with you so much and I miss you so dreadfully."⁶ This was a refrain that would sound again and again in her letters to Reed from now on.

She had written him that various people had asked her and Hippolyte over for meals, and now wrote that the sociability was continuing. Before the summer was over it would give way to barely concealed hostility.

Reed had written that he had met the poet Edgar Lee Masters, and she responded: "I'm so glad you met *Masters*. I *knew* he'd be great." Everyone was talking about his Bryan story. She concludes: "Dearest, I love you so much and I need you so greatly and that's all I really want to write now. Please hurry home."

But a postscript added a recurring complaint as to Provincetown, where she was a teetotaler and few were: "Neith Hapgood is coming tomorrow—of course with a bottle—as is the custom. I'm sort of sorry. I hope it isn't too large a one—but after all it's none of my business. . . ."⁷

On June 11, a Sunday, Reed wrote her from the Hotel Sherman in Chicago, addressing her, "Dearest darling":

"I have had the most terrific time since last night. Roosevelt sold out his party and the delegates wept and went to pieces—many of them broken men, men without anything left. Leaving in half an hour for Detroit, then back again to St. Louis, where I'll be Wednesday. I was around with Sara [Bard Field] last evening—Art Young, Doris Stevens, Amos P. [Pinchot], Fuller [probably Walter, artist and an English impresario, newly married to Crystal Eastman] & ex-Congressman Bill MacDonald of Michigan, who'se one of the finest people I ever heard of. O I wouldn't have missed this for the world! But O I wish you were with me. It's an awful story, & a magnificent one. . . . All my love, my darling. Have had no sleep but feel *wonderful*. Jack."⁸

From Detroit he wrote her: "I have had two glorious interviews with Ford, and am putting up to him the most magnificent scheme ever conceived. I haven't time to tell you about it now, but if it goes thru, *you and I may come to live in Detroit for a while*. It would cost Ford more than a million dollars. . . . No sleep for weeks, feeling fine. All my best love, your loving Reed."⁹

Bryant longed to know what "your grand scheme" was, but above all she wanted him back home. When she'd thought he would return the next day she had bought marigolds and cornflowers in town, "and on the way back I got buttercups in a field. When the house was all dressed up I got your letter, saying you might not be back for more than a week."

She had run into Grace Potter and insisted on her leaving her hotel and staying with them. "Lucy Huffaker and Eddie Goodman came down yesterday with a suitcase full of booze. They have most everyone drunk by this time. Hippolyte is just able to fry fish tonight . . . but tomorrow he will not be able to tell a fish from a brown-tailed moth."[10]

Reed had hoped to persuade Ford, who had financed the quixotic Peace Ship and still opposed the war, to finance a daily antiwar newspaper. By June 18 Reed's burgeoning hope was evaporating but he remained cheerful, writing Louise from Detroit:

"Dearest darling: Damn my luck at having had to come back here—and for the purposes I was secretly after, all for nothing, too, I'm afraid. But anyway I shall have a better article on Ford now. It is going to be a world-beater.

"But O how I wish I was in my sweetheart's arms in bed together!

"I've had a glorious trip; the wonder of it lasted about eight days, and then I began to want to get back to you. But I'm glad I came away alone, and left you there. It gave me a new perspective on us, darling, and a new view of myself, and I think a vacation from each other every now and then is wonderful for two lovers. Now I know still more and in many new ways how much I love you, and how. I love to think of coming back to you. I saw Sara again in St. Louis, and she sent her love to you a hundred times."[11]

Provincetown in that period before the invasion of tourists was a place of serenity and beauty. Governor William Bradford, landing there with the Pilgrims in the *Mayflower* in 1620, wrote of the harbor and Cape Cod Bay: "It is a good harbor and pleasant bay, circled round, except at the entrance, wihch is about four miles over from land to land, compassed about from sea to sea with oaks, pines, juniper, sassafras, and other sweet woods; it is a harbor where a thousand ships may safely ride."[12]

Despite the lure of the outdoors and the various diversions—drinking, making love, bathing in the nude by moonlight, marathon swims, hunting wild flowers—a lot of hard work was done in the summer of 1916. Bryant, too, was working on a play, and had sent six poems to Floyd Dell, who wrote her:

"Those poems hit me hard. I think they are almost terribly beautiful—like Greek fragments. They go in the next issue unless something
extraordinary happens to stop them." He asked her to write a review
for the coming issue or to keep it in mind for the next. He had hoped
to get to Provincetown that summer, "but can't pay the r.r. fare!"[13]

Bryant's most ambitious journalistic attempt to date appeared in
The Masses that summer, an essay on the Easter Rebellion under the
title "The Poets' Revolution," which begins:

"The Irish Revolution is the most hopeful thing that has happened
since the world went war mad. Ever since August, 1914, we have
been asking one another why the Socialists didn't do more. . . . The
revolutionary spirit seemed dead.

"Everytime we read in the British controlled papers how the Irish,
the Hindoos, the Canadians and the Australians were rallying to the
aid of England we felt sick. We saw a carefully fostered Pro-ally feeling
growing up in this country. . . .

"Then suddenly came the splendid revolt of the Irish—a revolt led
by poets and scholars—a revolt which actually lasted but a few hours
and which was doomed to defeat from the start, yet which won the
greatest victory of the whole bloody war."

At the time of her writing, fourteen Sinn Fein leaders had been put
to death, all signers of the declaration of the Irish Republic, and more
than 1,500 other Irishmen arrested and, without a trial, kidnapped to
England and jailed.

"The immediate cause of the revolt," wrote Bryant, "was the
discovery of an order which had been sent to the military authorities
in Dublin, authorizing the arrest and imprisonment of all the principal
Sinn Feiners. This order was stolen from Dublin Castle by one of the
rebels, and that was why they struck when they did, knowing well
that it meant the end for them."[14]

In regard to the background of the revolt, Bryant would have done
well to flesh out her analysis, and to make the whole less of a paean to
Jim Larkin than it is. But she had tackled a big and rich subject.

For a time after Reed's return he was indeed too busy to do much
about letting Bryant "*visit* with you." He and Boyd worked on his
convention stories while his many guests frolicked on the beach.
Eventually, however, he too was infected by the play fervor around
him.

The previous summer had seen the conversion of an old fish-house
at the end of Mary Vorse's wharf into a rough theater. They had
written and produced their own plays, and the audience brought its

own chairs. Now they hoped to improve the theater—and the fare. Reed offered his *Freedom*, a prison one-acter spoofing the romantic; it was decided it should be on the first bill, on July 15, with Neith Boyce's *Winter Night* and a revival of *Suppressed Desires*, aimed at devotees of psychoanalysis, by George Cram ("Jig") Cook and Susan Glaspell. Bryant's play, *The Game: A Morality Play*, had been accepted.

The exciting event of the season was the discovery of a new talent, Eugene O'Neill. The poet Harry Kemp has one version of the coming of O'Neill, Susan Glaspell another.

Kemp said O'Neill first read a play, at Jack Reed's place, that was "frightfully bad, trite and full of the most preposterous hokum." It was "something about an American movie man who financed a Mexican revolution for the sake of filming its battles. . . ." But at the next meeting of the group O'Neill, motionless in a wicker chair, looking like a sailor who had just jumped ship, read a one-act play about seamen in a ship's fo'c'sle, the death of one in his bunk forming the climax.

"We heard the actual speech of men who go to sea; we shared the reality of their lives; we felt the motion and windy, wave-beaten urge of a ship. This time no one doubted that here was a genuine playwright."[15]

They were on the lookout, wrote Susan Glaspell, for a strong play to balance *The Game* and Wilbur Daniel Steel's domestic comedy *Not Smart* on the second bill, and were to take it up at a meeting that night, when she caught sight of a familiar figure walking along Commerce Street. It was Terry Carlin, elderly Irish anarchist, a beautiful man with long silver hair. A day or so earlier he had stepped off the gangplank of a ship arriving from Boston with a young companion, darkly handsome.

"Terry," Glaspell asked, "haven't you a play to read to us?" Carlin said he didn't write, just thought and at times talked. But his friend O'Neill had a whole trunkful of plays. Jarred by the idea of so many, Glaspell said cautiously, "Well, tell Mr. O'Neill to come to our house tonight at eight and bring some of his plays."

O'Neill was too shy to read aloud his *Bound East for Cardiff*, but Frederick Burt, a professional actor, did so, while O'Neill kept out of sight in the dining room. When the reading came to an end, Glaspell wrote, "We knew what we were for."[16]

With the new play and its author the center of excitement, O'Neill and Carlin were persuaded to move closer by, taking the old sail-maker's loft opposite the Reed house. Jig Cook had depended on Reed's return for support and enthusiasm in keeping his group in harmony, and was not disappointed, however busy Reed was with his own work.

The entire community worked, creativity blossomed. Reed even found time to write the first poem he had written in months, his by now celebrated "Fog," its first line "Death comes like this, I know—." Reed was often buoyant but moods were not unknown to him. He knew a medical examination in the fall might mean surgery for the removal of his weak kidney. But it was not considered a dangerous operation even then. Death fascinates most poets as an experience to contemplate. Granville Hicks is apologetic that a lapse in his "fiery vitality" allows Reed to sense the dark of dying.[17] But perhaps nothing more was needed to provoke his mood than for the poet to watch the fog creep in and over that harbour "where a thousand ships may safely ride."

Reed was to play Death in Bryant's play and create a rakish, jaunty Death. Bryant was the Dancer in another O'Neill play now in rehearsal: *Thirst*, the title play in his only published work to date, *Thirst and Other One Act Plays*, its publication in 1914 subsidized by his father, the popular actor James O'Neill, Sr. O'Neill played the mulatto seaman in *Thirst*. He and Bryant were seeing a good deal of each other. To all appearances it was a mutual fascination. They sat together on the sand deep in talk, unmindful of others and apparently of the gossip swirling about them.

The surface cordiality toward her that prevailed in Reed's absence was giving way to intolerance, with undercurrents of petulance and backbiting. Few felt happy about Bryant's *The Game*, and now one woman, "envious of Louise's looks and her having a lover such as Reed, complained to intimates: 'Just because someone is sleeping with somebody is no reason we should do her play.' "[18] Added to this resentment now was the double affront: having ensnared the adored Reed, this unknown from Portland, Oregon, without any background of European education such as Vorse had, or European travels and intimacy with Gertrude Stein such as Dodge and Boyce experienced, was endangering their newfound genius. Despite all his dourness, the young genius was attractive to women, too.[19]

Eastman was convinced there was nothing more between Bryant and O'Neill than her earnest desire to get him off the bottle.[20] It was said that she told him her father drank; she even saw his "death" (she clung to the fantasy) as caused by drinking. If so, it was probably the first time in her life she ever admitted that the father she so adored was less than perfect. It was recognized that she did get O'Neill to stop drinking; but to keep him off the bottle required constant effort.

The playwright and the poet—for Reed was a poet before he ever was a reporter—liked each other. Two more unlike temperaments would be hard to find: the open, boyish-looking Reed with an irrepressible sense of humor, and O'Neill, withdrawn and shy, intense and humorless. Reed envied the other his experience: after Princeton, O'Neill had been a sailor, prospector, salesman in South America, and reporter in New London. O'Neill on the other hand was impressed with Reed's knowledgeableness as to publishers, editors, and the writing business and opened up a little before his ease of manner.

Known for his generosity since Harvard days in reading and encouraging other writers, Reed read some of O'Neill's poems and liked them. It was just a matter of walking over to Eastman's place to assure publication of his "Submarine."[21] One evening at Reed's place with Carlin, O'Neill showed him his play *Tomorrow* and was advised to make a short story of it; Reed would submit it to Carl Hovey of the *Metropolitan*.

All this made for mixed feelings on O'Neill's part. He was alternately melancholy, seeing Bryant in this setting, and fired with excitement—over the forthcoming premiere of his *Bound East for Cardiff*—and over Louise. Only to Terry Carlin could he talk about his dilemma. "When Louise touches me with the tip of her little finger it's like a flame," he confided.[22]

Wary, he was nonetheless fascinated by the situation. Because it had the makings of tragedy, it took on added attraction for him: Bryant without Reed would not have affected him so strongly.[23] Three days before the premiere of his play he wrote Beatrice Ashe of New London, urging her to visit him in Provincetown, assuring her it would be quite respectable, for she could stay with "Jack Reed and his wife" or "a dozen other households with females presiding." His biographer Louis Sheaffer felt that he "wanted Beatrice around to spur their flagging romance and save him from falling in love with Reed's girl."[24] Ashe did not come and O'Neill was not saved.

Bryant wrote many poems that summer, among them "Dark Eyes," which *The Masses* published.[25] The Bryant-O'Neill legend has it that she wrote a note, "Dark eyes, What do you mean?" and left it in a book she gave O'Neill one night at the Reed house, and that this was her initial ploy for O'Neill.[26] It may have been the poem—not a very good poem.

It was not difficult for many of the women summering in Province-town to feel protective toward O'Neill as well as Reed. Reed they sincerely loved. As Mary Vorse once said in the most succinct of tributes, "He was a poet and he hated cant."[27] So, virtually all united in feeling critical toward Bryant. They could even feel for the moment sympathy for Mabel Dodge—not always easy.

Not long after Hutch Hapgood wrote Mabel Dodge about the crowd of guests at the Reed house, she came to stay with the Hapgoods. She apparently was not slow to ferret out the scandal, and had envisioned a Reed happy and eager to see her again. "When I saw Reed on the street, he steeled himself against me," Mabel Dodge Luhan re-counted. "Though I wanted to be friends, he wouldn't. People said Louise was having an affair with young 'Gene O'Neill . . . and I thought Reed would be glad to see me if things were like that between him and Louise—but he wasn't."

She found a little house on the edge of town: "I wanted to get outside Provincetown where Reed lived with Louise Bryant a little way up the street in a white clapboard cottage that had a geranium in the upstairs window."[28]

Actually not only Mabel Dodge but many another illustrious woman on the Provincetown cultural front had proved herself fully able to cope with the double standard—without, it is true, making a frontal attack as Bryant seemed to be doing.

3.
Reed Writes a Farce

MUCH INSENSITIVE, UNCOMPREHENDING speculation has been written about Reed's attitude to the unfolding triangle that so engaged Provincetown that summer. An early biographer of O'Neill, for example, states: "O'Neill and Louise became lovers. What Reed's position was no one could quite understand, but all three seemed to find the arrangement satisfactory and they continued to work amicably together that summer."[1]

Despite his openness, a careful study of Reed's correspondence, works, and memoirs of others about him, especially that of Albert Rhys Williams,[2] leads to the conclusion that Reed was far more complex than he was ordinarily thought to be, and in matters that counted deeply with him, given to self-examination and searching introspection. His honesty has been often noted, and rightly, but the self-critical moods rarely suggested.

A letter Louise Bryant wrote late in life and close to twenty years after these events throws some light on Jack Reed's thinking at the time. It concerns the tale-bearer, Fred Boyd.

It is not irrelevant to consider how patient and loyal Reed had been to Boyd over a period of several years, however trying he found Boyd. Boyd had made an indiscreet speech to workers during the strike in Paterson that was too close to urging sabotage and landed him in jail.[3] In the hope of a pardon he then recanted, renouncing his association with the I.W.W. When Reed returned from an assignment in the war zones, he made inordinate efforts for Boyd and finally obtained his release. He never blamed Boyd for his turncoat act as Boyd claimed it was all due to his disillusionment over the surrender of European socialists to the war.[4] Eastman also was an admirer of Boyd, whom he described as "the dry, precise litle English Marxist."[5]

But Boyd was far from being either dry or precise when drink flowed freely, and in the summer of 1916, as in earlier times in Provincetown, there were too many people who liked to drink with Boyd. He had now been banished from the Reed home as his services were needed no more, Reed having completed his convention stories, and had ample time to hunt up drinking pals.

Brooding over the talk about Bryant and the diffident playwright described as "that wide-mouthed, anguished, sunburned boy,"[6] Boyd was seized with an inspiration one night. He himself would administer justice, and with a simple act: he would kill Eugene O'Neill.

But he had no revolver. He had too little money to get one. He got into the Reed cottage and made his way to the upstairs bedroom where Reed and Bryant slept. He stumbled, they awoke—it was four o'clock in the morning—and the weaving figure of Boyd was discernible. He demanded forty dollars.

"Jack asked him what he wanted it for," Bryant wrote. "He said that he had to kill Eugene O'Neill because I was untrue to Jack and Gene was the culprit." At that point Reed leaned over to kiss Louise, then told Boyd to go home and to bed.

"Early in the morning," the letter continues, "Jack went to Gene's little shack. . . . He said somewhat this to Gene, 'Boyd was drunk last night and shooting off his face around town. If you hear any stories don't pay any attention to them. And I wish you and Terry Carlin would take all your meals with us for a while.' "[7]

The letter is self-serving, explaining at one point, "Gene and I were working day and night in the theater," but it has the ring of truth insofar as the Boyd escapade goes and suggests that Reed would react publicly to all the gossip with his usual insouciance.

O'Neill and Carlin did continue to visit the Reed house and Reed to all appearances was his usual affable self. Nor did there seem to be any abatement in Bryant's assiduous efforts to wean the playwright from whiskey—or her maneuvers to relieve his conscience of guilt toward Reed. To this end she supposedly assured him that she and Reed lived as brother and sister.[8]

This allowed the so-reluctant O'Neill, as pictured by biographers and memoirists, to take heart.[9] Reed's precarious health lent some verisimilitude to the story, and was a sombre note irresistible to O'Neill. The situation was almost worthy of Strindberg, his favorite dramatist. O'Neill's partiality for what he termed "the impelling, inscrutable forces behind life"[10] helped him see all of them as players in a drama of tragic undertones, and Bryant became for him "a great woman, something out of the old Irish legends, betrayed by life . . . always the pivotal person, beautiful, passionate and strange."[11]

The cop-out which O'Neill supplied Bryant (and himself), waiving responsibility in the name of fate or mysterious forces, was dramatized in 1928 in *Strange Interlude,* whose central character, Nina, inspired by Bryant, gets away with everything.

The theme of Bryant's play—the validity of risking all for love and measuring it not in terms of durability or how it conforms to bourgeois norms, but its creativity—is found in writings of other feminists of the day. Emma Goldman in "Love Among the Free" celebrates Ibsen's Mrs. Alving and others who repudiate marriage, and declares, "They know, whether love lasts but one brief span of time or for eternity, it is the only creative, inspiring, elevating basis for a new race, a new world."[12]

In Mabel Dodge Luhan's memoirs her discussions of sex generally rely on even more mysticism and talk of the soul than Goldman's. It should be "a means to . . . the growth of the soul." "Margaret Sanger made it appear as the first duty of men and women . . . not promiscuity, for that defeated its own end if pleasure were the goal; not any man and any woman, but the conscious careful selection of a lover that is the mate, if only for an hour—for a lifetime, maybe."[13]

Jack Reed too spoke of the soul and felt that the man-woman relationship required freedom, especially for the artist. In a 1914 letter he told of an evening with a 22 year-old violinist, Virginia Bean, and her mother. "Virginia asked me what I thought of her playing. I told her if she could get a soul, she would be a real artist. But, she said, I don't see how one can get a soul without letting go all the ideals and standards of life one has set before oneself to hold one to the right. There isn't any other way, I told her. There isn't any law you have to obey, nor any moral standard you have to accept, nor in fact anything outside of your own soul that you have to take any account of."[14]

By the time of the second bill at the theater in Provincetown, which opened July 20, the call had gone out for a play for the third bill, and Reed eventually let himself be pressed into supplying it. He dashed off an hilarious, outrageous, hyperbolic Shavian farce in one act. But some keen thinking went into it—and possibly some inner fury, aimed not at Louise or even O'Neill but at talebearers and prying gossips.

Jack Reed had long been loved by the men and women in the avant garde for his personality and the talent that, when a subject moved him, glowed into genius. Some of them in this period might be foolish enough to long to extend their sympathy, to take his side. Those who knew him best would never do so. Possibly the play was written nonetheless precisely to discourage any such attempt. It seems to be saying to his well-wishers, "Get off my back."

Perhaps he felt that to bring the theme into the open would be therapeutic. Until the advent of O'Neill and his plays suggesting the tragic, it was standard for the players to keep a light tone in their plays about one another or about their own foibles. It is a broadly funny play but it shows the banality of the preoccupation with adultery in the Broadway theater (and now seemingly among the Provincetowners). It was a familiar posture of his to war against cant.

It is even possible that he wished to remind himself of what he had told the young violinist Virginia Bean, and to remember that Louise Bryant belonged to herself, too. Meanwhile he gave her and the lovesick playwright every chance to be together. Reed had a marked degree of self-esteem: doubtless he felt that as the better man of the two, he would outlast O'Neill. Basically he felt secure about Louise. In contrast to the gloom-ridden O'Neill, his was primarily a joyous nature—but with undertones of darkness.

The play bears the title *The Eternal Quadrangle: A Farce Adapted from the Wiener-schnitzler*. To poke fun at marriage and the double standard was proper in Bohemia. Like his friend Emma Goldman, Reed believed that a relationship between a man and a woman must be voluntary to be valid. Even in Bohemia, however, one subject was approached obliquely if at all: the traditional masculine fear of being cuckolded. Reed's farce turns upside down the perennial nervousness over cuckoldry and all the hallowed criteria for male and female roles as well. It is a subversive play.

Jig Cook played Robert Fortescue, a magnate wedded first of all to the stock market. Marsden Hartley created a stock ticker which occupies a prominent position in Fortescue's Fifth Avenue drawing room where the action takes place. The one thing Fortescue cannot afford is to have to bother with the undivided attentions of his wife, Margot (Louise Bryant). He is only too happy to have her lovemaking propensity at least partly taken care of by others.

Estelle, Margot's maid, who is paid to spy on her and report to Fortescue, warns the master that she has tired of her recent lover, and this makes for a crisis. Estelle, the only intellectual in the play, was played by Ida Rauh, acknowledged the best actor among the nonpro-

fessional players. Reed played Archibald, the butler. With no ready
replacement for the departing lover, Eddie Temple—a nonentity—
Fortescue suggests Archibald. Estelle and Archibald are married, but
Estelle promptly agrees. Archibald asks about his pay and when he is
assured he will get a slight raise, nobly says he will even take less,
which charms Margot, a romantic soul, so that she begins to see his
possibilities. Estelle declares: "Mrs. Fortescue is just the kind of
woman Archibald needs, and I think he ought to suit her perfectly.
He's shallow, clever with a sort of Broadway cleverness, rough with
women, and has a kind of barbaric rhythm about him like ragtime."
She had thought he needed psychoanalysis, but this might be even
better for him, and cheaper.

As for Temple, Estelle recognizes him as a man who wants to be
molded. As she has read her Bernard Shaw and lets them know it, she
says majestically in her last line: "It is for us Superwomen to make
men what they will be."

Fortescue thereupon comments on Estelle's last declaration in his
sole moralizing remark, on which the curtain falls. "Now this is the
real danger. The first since the beginning of the world. Masculine
dominance totters on its throne. I'm glad I am protected from you."[15]

Whether or not the play had a chastening effect on the prurience
abroad in the Provincetown colony, or whether it made men ponder
on what the anthropologist Elsie Clews Parsons called American
husbands' "indifference to women,"[16] is not known. But it should have
put to rest any idea that any of the players might dare to patronize
Reed.

For *The Game* the sculptor William Zorach and his wife, the artist
Marguerite, designed a stage setting along formalized lines suited to
the Greek costumes worn. For *Thirst,* another O'Neill play of the
season, they wanted to repeat the almost abstract genre that had
proved so successful for the Bryant play.[17] But Cook and Reed
objected on the premise that O'Neill was a "realistic playwright."[18]
The Zorachs yielded and produced a crumpled, if not exactly choppy,
sea. Bryant played The Dancer, Cook was Gentleman, and O'Neill
was the largely silent mulatto seaman.

To the twelve-year-old drama critic Heaton Vorse the play was
"horrible" and his worst fears were justified as to Bryant's acting. He
had felt "that she would be too conscious of her good looks to be able
to act well. The thing that struck me was her amazing complexion and
brightly colored cheeks. She was a perfectly beautiful person." As for

O'Neill, he looked the part, Vorse agreed, and even to appear on stage he must have had a battle to overcome his shyness—although the precocious Heaton figured it was "a shyness mixed with a defensive sort of arrogance."[19]

Actually, for O'Neill it was an exultant summer. Except for a few lapses into heavy drinking, largely as an antidote to nervousness brought on by contact with people, he was working well. He had found recognition for the first time—and from superior people whose achievements he respected. Then there was Bryant, and he was "in the throes of falling in love more deeply than ever before."[20]

Unquestionably Bryant was more and more emotionally involved with the playwright, too. Eastman, whose memoirs are studded with accounts of his own amours, interpreted the "compact" between Reed and Bryant in chauvinist terms. He praised Louise Bryant as a woman who "stood sufficiently upon her own feet to become the mate of an impressionable and absolutely forthright man, without lies and without any dissimulation between them."[21] He saw Jack Reed as always forthright, and Louise as forbearing, presumably to accommodate Reed's inevitable sexual transgressions. He failed to see the pact would be a greater test for Reed.

When Cook first told his wife, Susan Glaspell, of his daring plan for the players to continue in New York in a theater of their own, she disagreed, considering that they were not ready. He sought out Reed, and returned to tell her, "Jack Reed thinks we can make it go."[22] Others, too, agreed that if Reed, who had produced the great drama of the Paterson silk weavers, using the strikers themselves, in Madison Square Garden, thought so, it was possible. On September 5 they met, Bryant taking minutes as secretary pro tem, and a formal resolution was passed establishing the Provincetown Players. A constitution they adopted set forth their primary object: "to encourage the writing of American plays of real artistic, literary and dramatic—as opposed to Broadway—merit." A roster of twenty-nine names as members was recorded, each giving what he could, some as little as two dollars; eight gave thirty dollars each, and O'Neill, who was penniless, was listed as honorary member. With a total of $320 in his pocket, Cook set out for New York to rent a theater.

Most of the other players began straggling home then, but Reed and Bryant stayed on the Cape throughout September. In nearby Truro they found a house with a big tree close by; Reed made a down payment on it, located a local carpenter, and bargained with him to have it shipshape by the next summer. They were even more charmed by Truro than Provincetown, and often hiked there and back. Reed was busy much of the time on potboilers. He regularly sent his mother money, and needed extra sums now in the event an operation would be necessary.

So even though they had no guests or plays to worry over, there still was not a lot of time in which she could "*visit*" with him. Time enough, however, to settle one thing. Dr. Trullinger had been awarded a divorce in Portland July 7, a matter they had kept to themselves. The complaint charged cruel and inhuman treatment; he said his wife had told him she did not love him and loved another and wished to marry him.

O'Neill or not, neither Louise Bryant nor John Reed was about to abandon the other.

4.
They Marry

BACK AT 43 WASHINGTON Square South, Bryant plunged into activities around the theater. Reed went with her to inspect the new premises Cook had acquired—an old bottling works that previously had been a stable, at 139 Macdougal Street, next door to the Liberal Club and around the corner from their apartment. He saw the hitching ring imbedded in the wood now part of the right wall of the auditorium and suggested a motto that was later painted around it: "Here Pegasus stood."[1] But he had other things on his mind.

His physicians had scheduled his admittance to Johns Hopkins Hospital in Baltimore for November 12. Although not at all well, he was anxious to make money against the expenses of possible surgery.

Without turning sombre, he was proceeding on the basis that he might die. He selected his best poetry and turned it over to his friend and fine printer, Frederick C. Bursch of Riverside, Connecticut, to be made into a volume, dedicating it to his mother.[2] He decided to buy a second house, which would make up to Bryant for the home she had left so readily in deserting Trullinger for him.

The charming little Sharkey cottage, once a farmhouse, on hilly Mt. Airy Road in Croton-on-Hudson, a village some thirty miles from New York, was vacant. Situated far up on the hill, the house and its garden, though somewhat neglected, at once appealed to Bryant, the double fireplaces, back to back and solidly built, she found attractive. She knew that Mabel Dodge had once rented it and that it was the scene of one of the many leave-takings between her and Jack, but that did not bother her. Caught in a trap of her own making (even if

O'Neill's helplessness was a trifle overstated—after all, he had been married and had had ample sexual experience in his sailor's life), she was haunted by many things, but not by ghosts. Reed made a down payment in October and put the title in Bryant's name.

Two new actors had to be recruited for *The Game* and rehearsals scheduled. Reed did what he could to help Bryant before he got an assignment from the *Tribune* that engrossed him full time. They were told that Kitty Cannell, educated as a dancer in Paris, and her husband Skipwith Cannell, a poet, were recent refugees from the war and living on Twelfth Street, and sent word asking her if she would like to play the role of Life. She and Skip went to see them at their apartment, which already was in the process of being stripped for the move to Croton.

"There was only one bed there, and not much else," Kitty Cannell said in later years. "John kept walking around and quoting lines from the play, while the rest of us sat on the bed. We all fell in love with each other. It was a slight play, not terribly good, but what made it different was that John as Death was awfully jolly, while Life was austere, in classical robes, not jolly at all."

She felt the ebullience of Reed and liked the way Bryant's laughter sounded even as he clowned and acted the ham with her cherished lines.

"All of us connected with the Players lived *La Bohème*," Cannell reminisced. "We were all poor, and looked out for one another. Like everyone else—really just *everyone*, it seemed—I believed in the revolution and thought it was just around the corner. But we all were convinced we would not live long, that we would die young. And of course some of us did. After those five days when we played *The Game*, I never saw John Reed again."[3]

O'Neill had taken a room at 38 Washington Square South, just doors away from Reed and Bryant. He was not more upset than Reed when Hovey of the *Metropolitan* wrote Reed rejecting the O'Neill story "Tomorrow," which he had converted, at Reed's suggestion, from a play by that title, and which had been submitted with a strong letter of recommendation by Reed, the magazine's foremost writer at the time.[4] Reed, furious, vowed he would place it elsewhere. But then he became too involved, so that it was Bryant who sold it to *Seven Arts* while Reed was hospitalized; the playwright would receive fifty dollars for it, his first pay for any creative work.[5]

Everything seemed to be closing in around Bryant, building up to some unguessed and frightening climax. O'Neill's dark intensity was beginning to be threatening to her. She was in love with both men, but at times had the feeling she was no longer in control. Nothing would ever induce her to forsake Reed—but she was aware that that was precisely what O'Neill expected her to do. She tried to put off the whole question.

Both Reed and Bryant, in different ways, brought to their relationship something from recent wounds or deprivations. Had Bryant had a less arid life with Trullinger in their six years, she would not have been so voracious for life now. Reed had released her from her bondage, given her her freedom, and, taking it, she had run the risk of endangering her relationship with him. Reed, rebelling again and again against Mabel Dodge's efforts to cabin his spirit, reveled in Bryant's responsiveness to the things that most deeply excited him, like the Bayonne strike of Standard Oil workers he now was working on. From Dodge he once had fled, leaving for her this note:

"Goodbye my darling. I cannot live with you. You smother me. You crush me. You want to kill my spirit. I love you better than life but I do not want to die in my spirit. I am going away to save myself. Forgive me. I love you. I love you."[6]

Reed came to Louise with a great capacity for forgiveness, fortunately for her and not always emulated by her. Her inability to forgive Jack's indiscretions would come near to tearing their marriage asunder before another year was out.

But with all the elements involved that, from a reasonable view, would combine to make the coming marriage ill-starred, it was possessed of some remarkable ingredient for viability. It endured. Always stormy, it prevailed even beyond a test neither foresaw that would soon present itself, and many future tests. Friends of Reed, such as Boardman Robinson, who thought it was a mistake,[7] were not reckoning with a number of factors, chief of which was that Reed knew his own mind. He wanted her and his belief in her rode out the storms. As for Bryant, she was—as Eastman told Dell—hard to take,[8] but she had within her a sterner mettle than any but Reed guessed, and in the coming years fulfilled his judgment.

The great night arrived when the Provincetown Players, thanks to Cook's miracle of patience and work, opened to a New York City season on November 3. The theater had no dressing rooms, but several players lived on Macdougal in adjacent houses (Reed's place was but minutes away), and the actors used them as dressing rooms. After those in *The Game*, which was the first on the bill, were dressed in their Roman sandals, wigs, and classical drapes, Cannell and Reed discovered there were no footlights.

Putting on raincoats, "John and I fled like lightning to Fourteenth Street for footlights. Then we ran back, slowing down at one point—as John felt sick; his kidney bothered him.

"Toward the end he completely forgot his lines, I think because he was ill. It was all he could do to act jovial and rakish as Death, and the words fled. It didn't matter, as I knew all the lines in the play, having that type of memory. So whenever it was his turn to speak, I simply turned my head toward him, in the formal stylized motions we adopted, and gave him his lines," Cannell related.[9]

The others in the cast were Bill Zorach as Youth and Martha Ryder Fuller as The Girl. It made a hit, according to Cannell, the setting by the Zorachs (who were given credit on the program) adding much. Floyd Dell's *King Arthur's Socks,* in which Eastman acted, also was on the bill. But none of it mattered once O'Neill's *Bound East for Cardiff* was staged. Even without the sound of the water lapping Mary Vorse's fish-house, it still was absorbing drama. With O'Neill's more universal and powerful themes, the little plays with which the Villagers had amused themselves at the Liberal Club and then the Wharf Theater on the Cape, which developed into the Provincetown Players, became only historical footnotes.

O'Neill's *Emperor Jones,* as staged by Cook, pushed him into the ranks of the great, and later O'Neill would graduate from the Provincetown Players to Broadway. The Provincetowners struggled on for a number of years. "But the Provincetown Players died a premature death," wrote Albert Parry. "It was a pity because they were doing the great and necessary work of discovering native American playwrights and producing their plays in the freshest native manner." Parry felt that O'Neill's plays eventually lapsed into "blundering psychologizing void of any native heartiness or deep heartbreak that distinguished his earlier work."[10] Although Dell felt that O'Neill "broke George Cook's heart," he had little patience with Cook's flight to the peasants of Greece.[11]

Reed played Death in *The Game* for five nights. On November 9 he and Louise Bryant went to Peekskill, obtained a license, and were married, Bryant insisting on secrecy as she had done when she and Trullinger were wed. This time, though, it was slightly more logical, as the divorce from Trullinger had not become final.[12] Not introspective, she was unaware then of how deep her love for Reed would prove. But she was temperamentally closer to Reed, whose predominant mood was buoyancy, than to O'Neill, for whom her love was mixed with compassion.

Increasingly, too, what she felt for O'Neill was marked by a curious foreboding. Whether rationally or not, she had looked on her mother as victim (not of her father, in whose passionate defense she never wavered except to impress O'Neill on the need to quit drinking, but of her exceptionally kind stepfather). The vision of becoming a victim made her perpetually reluctant to marry, and all her feminist ideology only fitted in with this approach. When O'Neill proclaimed that once Reed was well she must let him have it out with him,[13] she saw his mouth turn cruel. She had never been drawn to a man whose sense of possessiveness was prominent, and now she felt the violence that lay so close to the surface.

She tells of the marriage in the following passage, forgetting the name of the city, calling it Poughkeepsie: "[Jack] had never been very well after the Serbian retreat. That year (1916) he suffered terribly. He was ordered to go to Johns Hopkins. . . . He said to me, 'Well, honey, I think we'll have to get married, because I might die, and there seems a very good chance that I will, and I want you to have everything I've got.' We took a train one morning for Poughkeepsie. There we were married at the little city hall. . . . [T]he clerk, sitting in his shirt sleeves, called to someone in the other room, 'Come in here, Bill, and get another witness.' So they all stood up and mumbled a few words, we signed our names, and the clerk handed me my wedding certificate, [saying] 'Hang on to this, lady, you may need it some day.' "[14]

One of her minor deceptions was to say she was twenty-six years old, when she was thirty-one. She gave her name as Ann Louise Mohan, and he gave his as John Silas Reed, his age as twenty-nine. She said her father, Hugh J. Mohan, was born in Ireland—which she apparently believed. (Had she known he was born in the anthracite region and as a boy worked in the coal mines, she would have said so, confident that this would only enhance her in Reed's eyes.) Her mother's name, she said, was Louise Say; she was a native of Louisiana. She noted her divorce from Trullinger.

Three days later Bryant saw him off on the train headed for Baltimore and Johns Hopkins. Both were ill, and she clung to him as she told him she would come down to be with him if it was decided to operate—and wondered to herself if she would be well enough. She had complained of having "crazy sick-to-my-tummy spells" and had on Reed's insistence gone to a doctor, reporting that it was an abscess.

Certainly there were enough real worries all around, but before his train came he gave her a note to give to the lead in a play by Padraic Colum, *The Betrayal,* and various instructions to people: he was afraid the Players might not do well by Colum and that anything might happen to the play while he was in the hospital. Her heart sank as she saw the big man swing up the steps of the train.

She went at once to the theater, then home to write him reassuringly:

> Darling:
>   Please don't worry about Column's play any more. It is going fine. . . . Elsie Sloane almost wept over your note and showed it to Column. He said, "Poor Jack Reed it's a shame he's been worried over my play and you just go home and write him it will be all right and I will coach Elsie Sloane." . . .
>   O, I hope you are feeling cheerful. I had a lump in my throat as big as the Woolworth Tower when I left the Station and it still comes back any moment. The old faithfuls Nonnie [Nani Bailey, whose restaurant The Samovar was around the corner from the playhouse] and Gene are taking me to dinner. I'll weep in the middle of it if they aren't careful. . . .
>   Oh, honey-heart—everyone's been pouring out love over you all day long and it's nice to have the little secret about us when they do. Please write. Please be careful.
>
> All my love to you—
> Louise[15]

Reed answered her joyously the day her letter reached him. That he could not resist making a pun on her condition was with Reed no sign that he was not concerned. Out of sheer exuberance he often made inappropriate remarks. At Harvard, Conrad Aiken was walking down the street with a classmate, Harold Pulsifer, a poet, who had only one ear and to cover the hole wore his hair long; Aiken liked him very much. "We met Jack, and as he passed he called out, 'Hello, Repulsifer.' He went on and left me to handle it. All of us felt that way about Pulsifer but no one else would have had the nerve to say it. Once he did, it got around, and whenever anyone saw him he thought of it.

"Jack was a forthright, ongoing, semi-wild man. It was terrible of him, but I could understand it. I have said occasional cruel things. I think it was said in sheer joy; Jack just thought of it and it was irresistible," said Aiken.[16]

Reed's letter was typed:

Your letter just came—at five in the afternoon, and I've been reading it over and over and over, deary honey. You got to stop having lumps all over the inside of your throat (It isn't abcesses, is it?) Do write me right away and tell me all about how your insides are doing. I'm really worried about them. You must spare no expense and pains to get that fixed up—*at once*. . . .

I just got my typewriter fixed, as you see, and am starting to work tomorrow to write some stories. . . .

He had been promised by a doctor that if they had to cystoscope him it would certainly be with anesthetics. He was "awfully touched by everybody's affection in New York," and didn't see why, "or what it all means." But Colum's play being off his mind, he said, "thank God for them all."[17] His letter ended:

For two or three days yet I won't know how long I must stay. But if it is any great time I am going to send for my honey, for without her it is getting to be almost impossible.

Your loving hub
Jack[18]

Bryant wrote him daily, at times twice a day, in an effort to keep up his spirits—and her own. The letters are a medley of endearments, theater gossip, humorous accounts of Village life—with acerbic asides on the drinking, requests for advice on her writing, muted but never misleading reports on her condition, and carefully casual allusions to "Gene." For all the dissimulation she employed, they breathe warmth, genuine concern over Reed, and a naturalness. Reed wrote lovingly and found her descriptions of Village goings-on hilarious.

Yet surely he was not deceived by the rather simplistic attempts of his darling to persuade him it was a dreadful bore to have to see so much of O'Neill. She wrote regarding O'Neill's new play: "I'm prompting *Before Breakfast* tonight. If I do it every night—well, I can think of something pleasant like Croton—that's the only way I'd get through."[19]

Seeing through his bride's clumsy effort to reassure him, Reed's way was to treat it lightly, nor is there any indication in his letters that, away in distant Baltimore, he worried over Eugene O'Neill as a serious rival. He replied that of course he would love to see the new bill, adding: "But let me tell you a secret—If I were to come home tomorrow afternoon I'd go off somewhere with my honey and let the theater go to hell."[20]

In *Before Breakfast* O'Neill had joined Reed in writing a play expressing his scorn of the marriage rites, but the difference between the two plays is profound. In O'Neill's bitter one-acter his essential hatred of women is revealed. It is a monologue throughout, by the nagging slattern of a wife, who derides her husband for his dreams of a literary career. A totally unseen character is the other woman, whom the husband now loves and who is pregnant with his child. The suicidal husband is visible only in his sensitive long-fingered hand, which reaches through a doorway to receive a bowl of shaving water from his spouse. The hero's voice is heard only once, in a fine agonized death gurgle as the razor supposedly does its work and releases him from the complexities with which his two women will have to cope alone. The beautiful red-haired Mary Pyne, who in real life was miserably treated by her husband Harry Kemp, poet and poseur, somehow transformed her appearance utterly as the slattern; O'Neill himself played with gusto the man so ignobly trapped by matrimony—his last "appearance" on any stage.

Two days after Reed entered Johns Hopkins, Bryant wrote her "Dearest Lover" that "Becky" had gone with her to the doctor's. This was Beckie Edelson, young anarchist leader, who was living with Charles Plunkett, a writer for Emma Goldman's *Mother Earth*.[21] The doctor, Bryant continued, found that the abscess had broken and was better, but he had applied another poultice as pus still remained. She quoted the doctor indirectly as thinking that this would be the end of the matter.[22] Doubtless the doctor was well aware that she had much more serious trouble to come, as what she had was a tubo-ovarian abscess, but in that period it was the custom to tell patients only what was necessary; the amount of covering up by the profession was enormous, and questions by patients were just not asked.

Beckie Edelson would continue to be a friend in need when a crucial stage was reached. The doctor was Harry Lorber, physician and surgeon, a great favorite in the Village.[23]

Reed wrote her he'd had the cystoscopy, "besides X-rays, functional tests, and a whole crowd of strangers sticking their fingers up my insides. No anaesthetics, either. I came back here in a wheelchair."

Bryant was well enough to make the trip to Baltimore for the surgery that had been decided on. She arrived in the station about nine and at the hospital was told she could not see Reed that night. The operation was to be the next day, November 22.

After four days there, Bryant returned, and it is evident in the letter she wrote the following day that while in the hospital she had told Reed that O'Neill had moved into 43 Washington Square South. She wrote that she arrived to find "everyone in the world living in my room and kicked them all out—pleasantly, my dear—no harsh words." Then she went on to say quite casually:

> What I'm really writing you in haste about, nice old darling, is to say a telegram came for you yesterday from that lawyer in Provincetown saying that the Express Co. will pay $100. If that suits you wire him. Gene can't find the telegram, of course, so I can't send it to you.

Her last paragraph comes through with genuine concern for Reed:

> Oh, darling, the hospital was so white and cold and efficient I hated to leave you there. Please be good and take care of yourself. I'll send you books on China very soon and write later today. Best, best love[24]

Early in December Bryant wrote Reed that she thought his last plan, for her to come in a week's time, very good. She went on:

> It's pretty dismal camping out in my studio with a chair and a cot but I don't mind anything in the world if you love me and understand all about everything. When we get back to Croton I hope we can have many long talks. We never really did this summer except once and we were too busy when we came back. It's the best way to keep close to each other and I want to be very very close.[25]

At one point Reed wrote his wife, "My dearest, your descriptions of life in the Village are *wonderful*. I almost busted when I read about Gibbs Mansfield, Gene, Nani, etc."[26]

Writing of parties, Bryant told Reed:

> You know I said they were to have one here. Only *twenty* people came and stayed until four. At two I went to sleep. When I woke up I was all alone with many empty bottles and a terrible stale smell of booze hanging around the room. I don't know why this studio has suddenly became the centre of the Village but it has. People like Dudley Tucker and Marcell Du Champ [Marcel Duchamp][27] and Adele and Alan Norton and [Charles] Demuth and God-knows-who. I'm wondering if it wouldn't be a good plan to give this up too on the 15th because we can get along some way without it. What do you think?[28]

In the same letter she told Reed in a postscript that O'Neill was excited about her play *The White Rose*, or at least its concept. He wanted her to rewrite a portion of it, and proposed that he then

should read it at a meeting of the Players and not say whose it was.
"What do you think?" she asks. "I'd have to get someone to produce it.
Tell me what you would do."

Without doubt Bryant and O'Neill, working on *Before Breakfast*
together at the theater and going back to 43 Washington Square
South, each agonized over Reed in very different ways. Doris Alexander sees him as at times "wishing that Jack would die, only to be
overwhelmed with self-loathing, for Jack had given him nothing but
affection."[29] According to Boulton, O'Neill had "almost loved" Jack
Reed.[30] It could not have been a happy time for either, and Bryant was
far too ill for lovemaking. Some lines of a poem in the making, in her
hand, penned on the reverse side of one of the envelopes that
enclosed a letter from Reed in this period, suggest that she found
O'Neill's presence, however compelling, largely demanding and un-
fulfilling. "And oh, that you had never been/ Some of yourselves, my
love, that some/ Of your several faces I had never seen!" Other
fragments faintly legible were: "I suffocate in this intimacy" and "Back
from my beautiful, lonely body/ Tired and unsatisfied."

Meanwhile, if Reed felt any emotional conflicts he kept them to
himself. It would be years before O'Neill used as "copy" the experience of being lover to a woman whose husband was his friend and
benefactor. *Strange Interlude* appeared in 1928 and became the
greatest success of O'Neill's career and one of the most profitable
plays in the Theater Guild's history.[31]

In a letter from Croton to Reed, although she is not well, Bryant is
in a different mood from any others she wrote in the month Reed was
in the hospital. It is as if the trees and hills, the work she did in their
new home there, bring a singleheartedness to her, and peace. Suddenly she can talk lightheartedly about news from Portland; forgotten
is all the bickering among the Players, and gone is the proximity to the
tense and handsome dark-eyed man, so lately a victim of tuberculosis,
who would begin drinking violently if she threw him over. In this
letter she feels really at one with Reed; she speaks seriously of their
need to work, like a character in a Chekhov play; work and China
would save everything.

She tells Reed that in all the weeks before his operation, afraid for
him, she kept thinking to herself, "the pity the unpardonable pity that
you had always to *waste* yourself with Greenwich Villagers, family and
all that. Oh darling, I mean this in the broadest sense. We never,
never can take a chance like that again. That's why I think it will be so
fine to do *work* out here, uninterrupted, and play in town. We can't

put off real work year after year. I think China is going to be a splendid thing for both of us."

She suggested that she come to Baltimore to make sure she was getting the right treatment, "because I do feel that thing inside me a little now. . . . I'm not at all worried, though, because I am really much better. I feel so sure that we will both be all well again if we stay out here for a little while. It's *so* quiet and peaceful and happy." She closed sending love and "everything that's best in me."[32]

Bryant had stayed with Boardman and Sally Robinson while she fixed up their place. In two days, however, it was clear that she was very ill indeed, despite efforts to write soberly and factually, as she did, and not alarm him:

> Dearest—
> Please don't let anything I tell you upset you. I'm *all right* but I'm in bed. You remember I told you that I began to feel my insides again, well I got really ill out in the country so I came in and Dr. Lorber examined me and ordered me to bed under special care or in a hospital. I couldn't go to a hospital. . . . I sent for Noni but she . . . had a party on and here I was with a high temperature and the Dr. threatening a serious operation. Then good old solid Becky arrived and took the situation in hand so I'm to stay in bed at her house under Dr. Lorber's care. I go up there in a taxi tomorrow. I'll be there when you come back. It's as good and better than a hospital because while I need special care and ice bags and douches and enemenas, the *principal* thing is quiet and rest. It's the *only* way I can keep from having an operation. I don't have the abscess any more but my whole left insides (overies etc.) seem to be inflamed and infected.

Dr. Lorber, she said, was very pleased with the arrangement with "Becky"—who would be with Louise constantly—because he insisted Bryant be "under his observation all the time."

At this point Bryant, involved in two great love affairs with two of the leading talents of the day who apparently loved her madly nonetheless could not rise above the feeling of being trapped, of having become what she did not want to be, a victim. The woman who without a qualm took a lover almost before the eyes of her husband and left the husband to travel across the continent to the lover, who had then dared to take as lover, covertly, the attractive blue-eyed Andrew Dasburg, only to become the lover of the playwright with the dark magnetic eyes, was now overawed, stunned, by her predicament. All her efforts to be cheerful now spent, all her brave inconsequentialities and chatter at an end, feeling only dull, unreasoning and misplaced resentment, she wrote: "They think maybe that I got it from your condition, anyway it's a lot better than a growth. . . . Dr. Lorber . . . says he'll do his *damndest* to keep from operating and he thinks it can *really really* be done."[33]

With her world crashing in on her, Bryant packed an overnight bag and waited for Beckie Edelson to come by or call. All the foreboding she had felt of late in this association with O'Neill now was real. She had not heeded it, because she always made her own rules—Grandfather Say had taught her to, and to learn not to cry when she was hurt, and to hold her head high.

The next morning she went to 72 Morningside Avenue and gratefully received the ministrations of Beckie Edelson, who had Plunkett's apartment there. Edelson had been Alexander Berkman's companion for some years after he got out of prison. But according to Agnes Boulton, Beckie too "loved Gene."[34] Shortly before O'Neill had gone to Provincetown with Carlin, he had taken Edelson, "dark and vital-looking," with him to visit his friends Harold and Helen DePolo at their rented cottage by a lake in New Jersey. He had spoken proudly to them of her thirty-day hunger strike when she was sent to jail for organizing a labor protest.[35]

It is entirely possible that Bryant believed that Reed's kidney had caused her infection, that she understood Dr. Lorber as saying so. In all likelihood Dr. Lorber at the time did not suspect that there was not only a husband but a lover in this case. Perhaps Bryant did not guess the potentials in the etiology of the infection that gripped her. In use in the doctor-patient relationship at the time was a language highly colored with euphemism.

Doris Alexander evolved a theory that Bryant was deceiving Reed not only about O'Neill as lover but about the nature of her illness, and introduces it with an assumption about Dr. Lorber: "Dr. Lorber knew all about her relationship with Eugene O'Neill. . . . Why did she tell Lorber? Perhaps she just needed a confidant. Or perhaps, her illness was not an infection as she had told Jack. It is significant, perhaps, that Nina, in *Strange Interlude,* tells Sam [her husband] that she has 'some woman's sickness' in order to hide from him the fact that she has had an abortion."[36]

"Various things suggest that her 'illness' was an abortion," wrote Sheaffer. Villagers in times of trouble turned to Dr. Harry Lorber: he was known to be discreet. Louise had turned to him, "but perhaps more conclusive evidence as to her illness may be found in *Strange Interlude*. . . ."[37]

It was a literary theory, so appealing that neither Alexander nor others bothered to check excerpts of letters with a medical authority or to read the literature on tubal abscess. Had they done so they would have found that the symptoms she described were typical: pain in the lower abdomen, fever, occasionally high fever. They also would have found that the treatment she said Dr. Lorber prescribed was standard for the ailment: the patient, who is wracked with pain upon motion, must lie flat on her back, usually for some weeks, with icebags on her abdomen and very warm douches and enemas given regularly.

The threat of operation was also real. It was at the time the usual sequel to the bed rest and douches to remove both tubes and ovaries after the inflammation subsided. Only a physician and surgeon like Lorber, who was in addition a canny diagnostician, would dare trust his precision of diagnosis enough to risk omitting the surgery; if he did, he would keep a close watch on the patient, as Bryant described his supervision of her. As an experienced gynecologist Dr. Lorber knew that surgery might prolong the illness, and that if the diagnosis was definite, and no diverticulosis or acute appendicitis was involved, waiting would do no harm.

It was certainly a letter bound to unnerve Reed, and it did. It almost brought his precipitate return. He answered at once in longhand. Beginning "O my sweetheart—," Reed now spoke of his alarm over the nature of her trouble, told her that he would be breathlessly awaiting word and that he was at least relieved that she was able to write:

> But if you hadn't told me everything or even if I think you aren't telling me, I'll leave here on a stretcher if necessary, and get carried to New York. You mustn't hold anything back from your honey. You ought to have told me when you first got sick. I was afraid you were ill, & worried a good deal about you from the time you went back.
>
> But honey—it's awful to remove your ovaries, isn't it? Doesn't it make you incapable of having children and everything like that? I never heard of that being done to anybody but dogs, cats and horses. You remember you promised to let me know *immediately* they have decided what to do. I'm waiting for word.

After reproaching her for having waited so long to see a doctor ("That wasn't fair to me!") and saying they "must do something handsome for Becky," only then did Reed take up her accusation—not to express indignation but to reassure her, as well as to pose a fresh worry:

> I didn't mind what you said about my infecting you—if it were true—but I had been awfully careful to find out about that, and was

naturally alarmed. Are you *sure* the abcess isn't tuberculous, or that it isn't a tubercular infection? That's what scares me.

He added that he should surely leave Baltimore by Wednesday morning (the letter was headed "Sunday"), possibly earlier, and that he would then have to rest a couple of weeks, and signed himself "Your lover, Jack."[38]

Bryant doubtless did not miss his emphasis on a tuberculous infection. O'Neill was an arrested tuberculosis victim—and unless he had been for a checkup there was the danger of a recurrence. Reed may have spoken to Dr. Carl Binger at Johns Hopkins, whom he'd known at Harvard, after Binger's overtures, and thus learned that a tubal infection could be caused by tuberculosis. But for her to have been subject to a tubercular infection of the tubes through coitus would have been very unlikely.

Over the years the inflammatory disease of alpingo-oophoritis, or tubo-ovarian abscess, was thought to be caused by gonorrheal infection in a large majority of cases, but recent bacterial studies have thrown great doubt on its generality. Difficulties in proving any given case of gonococcal origin even with good culture techniques have made it a controversial subject in medical literature. Other causes are post-abortal infection, tuberculous infection, or the infection may be caused by streptococci, staphylococci, E. coli, or other organisms.[39]

But O'Neill, an autobiographical writer, had lived a vagabond existence for a time as a sailor, and later as a sort of waterfront derelict in the New York area, drinking to excess. The bums and prostitutes he associated with were to prove a source of rich material for him and populate such plays of his as *The Iceman Cometh*. It is possible that he repaid Bryant's devotion in a way he did not intend.

If she had had an abortion before she went to Dr. Lorber and an infection arose, she would have been very sick indeed, and she would not have written as she did after seeing him in mid-November: "I really feel quite good and think I may be all over that other business." It was only on December 7 that she wrote that she had become "really ill in the country." Of course the entire treatment of such abscesses was drastically altered with the advent of the sulfonamides or, even better, the later penicillin, and it then became a horrendous mistake to operate.

Reed's letter may have irritated Bryant inasmuch as she *had* told him she was sick, and not once but a number of times. It's unlikely that she herself knew earlier how sick she would be. But his letter let her know that whatever imponderables were implicit in their marriage, as long as he had anything to say about it, it could withstand all sorts of shocks and endure.

There would be other times when they both seemed to skate on very thin ice indeed, but, against all odds, it did endure.

5.

Reunion and Flight

REED HAD ACQUITTED HIMSELF with both sense and sensibility in his
response to his wife's shocking plight. Before the coming summer was
over he would be assailed by doubts. But when he finally brought
himself to question her, he was at once repelled by that hateful role
and turned his questioning inward, fiercely, moodily, demanding an
accounting of himself rather than Louise. In the same period she
would be plunged into despair, loneliness, and the beginnng of self-
doubt as to how she had treated him. It yielded no confession, but left
her shaken—yet aware it was Reed, not the demanding O'Neill and
not the undemanding Dasburg, whom she needed.

For the time being, however, she was far too sick for any emotional
flights. Her illness seemed to have reduced her to a state of infancy in
which she was utterly dependent upon Beckie Edelson and existed
only in dread of another onset of pain. Still flat on her back, she rather
crossly set out to answer Reed's somewhat heavy letter. The result was
a terse note in ink, unlike her warm, carelessly penciled notes and
long letters written over the past month.

> Dear Jack:
> The doctor has just been here. Please don't worry. There *could* be
> no operation at present or probably ever. I just have to get well by
> myself. He thinks I can go to the country in ten days or two weeks if I
> improve as I should. Don't hurry down. Stay there as long as you
> ought to. Wednesday I'll look for you—be *sure* to let me know when
> you are coming. Surprise parties won't do for me darling—not now.[1]

Her "or probably ever" may have been only a wish and seems a bit wavering. But it was factually true that no operation could have been performed at the time. It was standard practice to wait until the inflammation receded; and if in the meantime Dr. Lorber's instructions were carried out and his watchful eye detected no complication, none would be necessary.

On December 12 Bryant had a telegram from Reed: "Caught slight cold must stay day or so why dont doctor write me whats the matter with you love Jack."[2] In reply, Bryant wrote she was all set to see him walk in the door, and "could have wept" with disappointment at his wire; she urged him not to come one minute before he was well enough as that would be "mad and silly." She went on: "There isn't any use for the doctor to write—there's nothing to tell. I'm just the same—a little better maybe they have to wait and watch developments. There will be no operation."[3]

On December 13 Reed wrote her a special delivery letter, to let her know he might see her the next day, adding, "I wrote Gene to send all my mail to the Harvard Club. Hastily, Jack."[4] But before she could receive it another wire told her he would be there about five-thirty.[5]

Reed put up at a hotel where Edelson had engaged a room for him; he visited Bryant daily but also went to the Harvard Club each day for his mail. Recuperating or not, the gregarious Reed couldn't resist certain happenings, and attended the *Masses* ball three nights after he left Johns Hopkins. Early in January Dr. Lorber gave his permission for his patient to go to Croton, and Reed took her to the little house for which she had been longing. On January 4 he wrote Eddie Hunt they were at Croton-on-Hudson, "living very happily out here, with all our plumbing burst, but both about entirely well."[6] They expected to leave for the Orient in about a month, he added. The *Metropolitan* was sending Reed to China; Louise was to go, too—thanks to the generous *Metropolitan* expense allowances.

They sent in resignations to the Provincetown Players. It was a loss Cook expected, as he knew of the China assignment. Cook was beset by troubles of late, jealousies among his actors, a lack of good plays, and the continued lack of productivity in his star playwright. Without Bryant to steer O'Neill away from the bottle, he was now drinking heavily, spending most of his time in the Hell Hole, the tough saloon at Sixth Avenue and West Fourth Street and a favored spot among the Bohemians. Its proper name was the Golden Swan, but no one ever spoke of it as anything but the Hell Hole. A hangout for the Hudson Dusters (one of several Village gangs), thanks to its underworld connections the Hell Hole never closed its doors.

For O'Neill "the whole affair was agonizing. The year of his first real success was embittered by his torment over Louise and Jack Reed," Alexander wrote. "Later, in *Strange Interlude*, he would depict the anguish of sharing a woman with a friend."[7] But when, in 1928, Lynn Fontanne played the part of Nina in the play, she came to hate *Strange Interlude*. "I didn't ever feel O'Neill made her a tragic figure. I don't think he knew the first thing about women," she told Sheaffer.[8]

Bryant's recuperation was helped along by the appearance of her nine-stanza poem "Lost Music" in the January issue of *The Masses*.

For a short time Reed and Bryant were the envy of their friends as they prepared to go to China. Then the China dream exploded. Just before this happened, the *Metropolitan* ran in its January 1917 issue a plug for Reed's expected series, proclaiming in part: "He will hold up the mirror to this mysterious country, and we shall see its teeming millions and the big forces at work there. Imagine Reed in this rich 'copy' empire—the man of whom Rudyard Kipling said, "His articles in the *Metropolitan* made me see Mexico.' "

But on January 22 Wilson, the President who won reelection with the slogan that he had kept America out of war, made his "peace without victory" speech, stating the essential terms of peace in Europe. On January 31 Germany announced that unrestricted submarine warfare would begin the next day, and on February 3 Wilson declared diplomatic relations with Germany severed. Sniffing war and realizing that with America in the war Reed's usefulness to the magazine was at an end (since he was sure Reed would not change his anti-war position), Hovey of the *Metropolitan* wrote Reed that it was now deemed unwise to spend money on a trip to China. He went through the motions of asking him if he could suggest any assignment connected with "the new situation."

Reed had none. Hoping to make a little money before a final break, he wrote a few things at the editor's request, including an article on the A.F. of L.'s Samuel Gompers. But although it was a carefully documented and objective piece of work, it was rejected. Reed was made aware that the *Metropolitan's* policies would be trimmed to fit the demands of a nation at war, its mild pro-socialist stance at an end. Shortly afterward the break was complete. Suddenly the best-paid reporter in America, whose Mexican revolution articles made him in wide demand, began looking for a job. But he was not done with fighting the warmakers.

For all committed radicals the spring of 1917 was a sad and terrible time, for the United States entered the war on April 6. For Bryant and

Reed there was deep gloom and bitterness on that score; they were both below par physically and Reed was having no luck in finding work. Bryant took pride in his refusal to knuckle under, and indeed Reed took every opportunity to make known his opposition.

On the evening of April 2, when the President addressed both houses of Congress asking for a declaration of war against Germany ("The world must be made safe for democracy"), Reed was a scheduled speaker at a pacifist meeting in Washington. When the chairman proved reluctant to call on him, he stood up and declared: "This is not my war, and I will not support it."

He hung around the capital to testify, first against the espionage bill, and then to tell the House Judiciary Committee considering the conscription bill: "I am not a peace-at-any-price man, or a thorough pacifist, but I would not serve in this war. You can shoot me if you want. . . ." This was enough for two members of the committee, who wanted him silenced at once. But he was allowed to go on and was asked if he had any objection to fighting. He did not, he said, "I just think that the war is unjust on both sides, that Europe is mad, and that we should keep out of it."

In the very month that war was declared, Reed's voice sounded loud and clear in *The Masses* in his article "Whose War?" with these lines: "I know what war means. I have been with the armies of all belligerents except one, and I have seen men die, and go mad, and lie in hospitals suffering hell; but there is a worse thing than that. War means an ugly mob-madness, crucifying the truth-tellers, choking the artists, sidetracking reforms, revolutions, and the working of social forces. . . . Whose war is this? Not mine."

Bryant passionately believed every word of it. Just the same, when her half-brother Floyd Sherman Bryant came to visit them in uniform, on his way to France, she would not stand for any patronizing remarks aimed at him by Villagers (who generally opposed the war, although soon many would keep quiet). The elder of two half-brothers, Floyd Bryant was then twenty-three. He had gone to England as a Rhodes scholar from the University of Nevada and took an A.B. in jurisprudence at Oxford. From Oxford he went with Herbert Hoover on the American Commission for Relief in Belgium and became his good friend; later he drove a Red Cross ambulance in France. Shortly before the United States entered the war he underwent Army officers' training in the Presidio in the San Francisco area.

Young Bryant knew that his older sister Louise was married to the writer John Reed, but when he stepped up to the entrance of 43

Washington Square South (where they stayed on frequent trips into town), he was taken aback on seeing the name plate, which read, "Louise Bryant and John Reed." Nervously pressing the bell, he thought, "Oh, my Lord, they're not even married."

Louise kissed him, introduced Reed, who greeted him warmly, and other guests—a number of artists and writers, both men and women—and after some talk they all trooped out to have dinner in a Village spot. At dinner there was some general talk of the war. But when disparaging remarks were aimed at his being in uniform, Louise flared up and said feelingly to the mockers: "You can think anything you want, but you are not to criticize my brother. He is doing what he believes in."

It was the last time he saw his sister, but in after years he read about her with interest.[9]

At home in the Croton cottage, Bryant planted shrubs and bulbs and flower seeds, trying to stave off depression over the war and the collapse of Reed's plans to go to China, and when Reed was home he helped her. The garden is still there, and the house, in a part of Croton-on-Hudson seemingly little changed, and a tiny studio can be seen some distance in back of the house.

O'Neill had left his Washington Square rooming house owing rent, forfeiting a trunk of clothes and books to his landlady as a result. Despite his success he was still living on a few dollars a week doled out by his father, staying with friends or at the Hell Hole. O'Neill went to Provincetown but only after he was successful in getting Harold DePolo to go with him: he did not like to be alone. While there he received word that his story "Tomorrow" had been accepted by *Seven Arts* if he would make some minor changes. He did so, and was thrilled when he was asked if he had a play to submit. Waldo Frank of *Seven Arts* also accepted *In the Zone* for publication, for another fifty dollars, and O'Neill moved into the quarters the grocer John Francis had made ready for him. By this time DePolo had gone and he had sent for Carlin to stay with him.

In May Bryant visited O'Neill. A telegram from Reed, addressed to her in care of John Francis, Provincetown, said more eloquently than any plea, "Come back." It read: "Peach tree blooming and wrens have taken their house."[10] It was Reed at his tenderest—a Reed irresistible to Bryant. As Aiken said, "Jack did have a tenderness, a gentleness, with all his brashness."[11]

Writing of her visit some eighteen years later, Bryant said: "When early spring came I went to Provincetown to see [Gene]. . . . I took a room in a house nearby and stayed a week, till I got a telegram from Jack saying 'The fruit trees are in bloom.' When I arrived in the morning I found that Jack had gone out at dawn to pick wood violets and put them all around the house."[12]

What Bryant told O'Neill in farewell she does not say. It is clear that she was dealing with two men, each with a strong egocentric drive. O'Neill's spirits had so soared with her arrival that he "began to believe that only pity had bound her to Jack and that now, inevitably, she must leave him."[13] But all the poetry in Reed, his essential gaiety, spoke in that telegram, and Bryant found it a relief to be hurrying back to him, putting a distance between herself and O'Neill's possessiveness. If O'Neill could even imagine her cleaving to Jack out of pity, Reed, far more self-possessed than the playwright, was for his part supremely confident that she *would* return.

She could not have admitted to herself that she found O'Neill disappointing. She was able to defy conventions and mores only in the name of real love. Nor was she given to rationalizing her impulsive acts by means of definition. It was a period when many of the couples in the avant garde were caught in the crosscurrents of an evolving momentous change (so they thought) in woman's societal position, and problems of definition were not unique to her.

What she had not counted on, however, was that shortly after her return she would be jolted out of all thoughts of O'Neill. She and Reed quarreled—not over O'Neill; Reed refused to be jealous of him. But Bryant was exceedingly jealous when it came to Reed, and she soon learned of a sexual experience he had had that spring. It was not the first such occurrence, as their letters later in the summer would show, and she reacted as she always did—with fury, a scene, tears and voice raised high. It was not unusual among the men in Bohemia to approve verbally of the single standard but to ignore it when it conflicted with their own sexual appetites, which they always assumed were peculiar to men.

If on this occasion Reed had been caught up in something serious, Louise liked to think she would have reacted soberly, contained her anger, and sat down to discuss it with him. But she knew that Reed got carried away by all sorts of things other than love. She could see all too readily how with his genius for enthusiasm, sexual intercourse might be merely the logical extension of a good conversation. That she found altogether too casual to forgive.

She could tell herself that her feeling for O'Neill was based on love, with a strong admixture of unhappiness and concern, and that for

Dasburg she would always feel a quiet trust, a pervasive happiness without any self-laceration over fear of hurting anyone. At one point this spring she saw Dasburg when Reed was out of town. They met in the Sharkey cottage, now hers, and when they returned to Washington Square she found her canary dead and wept bitterly.[14]

Still, from any viewpoint, Bryant's unbounded rage on learning of Reed's experience must seem totally irrational. Perhaps it was a reflection of her own vacillation, her failure to understand intellectually her own position vis-à-vis two men, Reed and O'Neill, both of whom loved her without any visible understanding of her own wants, so that she briefly turned again to Dasburg in her quest for certitude. Basically she had not found herself or her own identity. She was on the defensive.

In the ensuing turmoil of scenes with Reed over his admission, she heard someone suggest Europe—"Mike" Robinson's idea. Gratefully she seized on the idea, only wanting to be as far away as possible. All at once Reed was busy obtaining press credentials for her, and it seemed to her she was going away involuntarily, "as the heart beats."[15]

On May 26, about a week after his wire to her at Provincetown, Reed wrote his friend Hunt: "Louise is going abroad with some friends. After she gets over she is going to quit them and travel around a bit. Is there anything possible she could do for the Red Cross over there which would pay her—no matter how little; or do you know any other organization, public or private, which could use her? Anything but nursing. Please write me at Croton quick."[16]

But then his attempts at press credentials for her turned successful. John N. Wheeler, who was just organizing the Bell Syndicate, supplied the credentials that Reed himself, with all his experience, could not obtain because of his well-advertised attitude towards the war.

There was one last visit to O'Neill, at the home of his parents, James O'Neill and Ellen Quinlan O'Neill, in their summer place at New London, Connecticut. There she let O'Neill know she approved of his efforts to avoid being drafted, which his father found distressing. And then she was off.

Bryant sailed on June 9 on the *Espagne*. In this impulse-ridden, not very sensible way she was launched on her first trip abroad, in wartime, part of it through submarine-infested waters, to take her first tentative steps as war correspondent. In a long personal and stock-taking essay Reed soon would begin, he wrote: "Whenever I have tried to become some one thing, I have failed; it is only by drifting with the wind that I have found myself, and plunged joyously into a new role."[17] This was about what Bryant was doing now. Drifting with the wind, but not so joyously, she would experience only an introduction to her new role; only with the help of Reed to shape her stories and send them to Wheeler, to the *New York American*, and elsewhere. Only later, without him, would she master her craft and become an outstanding foreign correspondent.

6.
Paris Without Reed

No SOONER HAD THEY parted on board the ship than both Reed and Bryant were assailed by misgivings. An outpouring of letters from either side of the Atlantic followed. Both were suffering, both were confused, lonely, and miserable. Their letters reveal not just remorse, often an easy indulgence, but very real struggles to assess their relationship, and where they had failed. Above all the letters are human, touching, their inner turbulence set against the background of a world at war, and proof of the basically strong bond that held the two, the poet-reporter and social critic and the erratic, appealing woman he had rescued from the banality of middle-class existence in Portland.

"It took incredibly long for the ship to leave. . . ." As soon as they passed the Statue of Liberty a woman bustled up to where Bryant stood talking to a sculptor and his wife, telling them importantly, "John Reed is on board." "I said I didn't think so. She said 'My dear child,' in a very haughty manner, 'I saw him with my own eyes, and I know him very well.' I said, 'I know him rather well myself, he's my husband.'"[1]

Bryant had written Reed unhappily while the ship still lay in harbor, a note he received two days after she sailed:

> Please believe me Jack—I'm going to try like the devil to pull myself together over there and come back to act like a reasonable human being. I know I'm probably all wrong about everything. I know the only reason I act as crazy is because it hurts so much, that I get quite insane, that's all. . . . If this thing ever happens again *don't don't* get despondent.[2]

In the last awkward sentence (which will be matched by some of Reed's, for both seem unable to speak clearly about anything sexual), she probably envisioned some repetition of Reed's occasional, apparently almost accidental, sexual contacts. It is quite obvious that she drew a distinct line between them and her own interest in Dasburg or O'Neill, considering his mere casual encounters without a basis of love, empathy, or, for example, the compassion she had felt for O'Neill.

Reed's first letter to her, headed "Saturday" (June 9), on Harvard Club stationery, begins:

> Well dearest, you're gone, and I've got a big lump in my throat—and I feel awfully lonely. I met Dudley Malone & he said he had been on board to tell them how important you were, etc. He seemed quite overcome with emotion, somehow, & so was I, so we had a terrible trip uptown in his machine. I dropped off here to just write this line and then I'm going out to desolate Croton. I feel very shaky, my dearest far lover.

Inside the fold was a penciled note, dated Monday, June 11 (two days after she sailed):

> Dearest of honies—Got here to find your pitiful little note—it isn't you who must learn, my honey, but me. In lots of ways we are very different, and we must both try to realize that—while loving each other. But of course on this last awful business, you were humanly right and I was wrong. I have always loved you my darling ever since I first met you—and I guess I always will. This is more than I've ever felt for anyone, honestly. I know that the one thing I cannot bear any more is consciously to hurt you, honey.[3]

Reed had taken a job on the New York *Mail*. It was a comedown, and he was unaware that the paper was subsidized by German money. He wrote a daily signed feature story, and as usual wrote his best stuff for *The Masses*, which was staunchly battling away as its enemies began efforts to shut it down. *The New Republic* was supporting the war but the men and women writing and drawing for *The Masses* kept on telling the truth bravely. As Floyd Dell described it:

> The "Renaissance" . . . begun in 1912, was still—fantastically!— going on. The war did not stop it. The war only made it bloom more intensely. And *The Masses* became, against that war background, a thing of more vivid beauty. Pictures and poetry poured in—as if this were the last spark of civilization left in America. And with it an incredible joyousness, the spirit of man laughed and sang in its pages.[4]

Shortly after Bryant sailed Reed took a room on Fourteenth Street, put a Yale lock on the door, bought window screens, and arranged for a cleaning woman. He told no one where he was. It was not the old gregarious Reed. He missed Louise. Some of the stories he wrote for the *Mail* he enjoyed doing. He covered the invasion of the Village by renegades with a gaudy pageant, the Alley Fiesta, staged right on Macdougal Alley where artists and writers sold Liberty Bonds and berated the Huns. Society women came, the novelist Gertrude Atherton played fortune teller, and there was much martial music.

After writing the Alley Fiesta story, he told Louise, he dropped into the Brevoort and saw the writer Djuna Barnes accompanied by Courtenay Lemon, drama critic Benjamin De Casseres, Emma Goldman and Alexander Berkman. Except for that, "I haven't seen a soul, hardly." Padraic Colum, who had given Bryant a list of Irish revolutionary leaders to see, as she hoped to get to Ireland, had phoned and finally reached him. "He said he wanted to see you, to tell you how you would be identified by his friends. He will tell me, however, and I shall write you in some way or other."[5]

He added to the letter the next day at the *Mail*, telling her of meeting an old acquaintance who was on the stage. She looked "shockingly old and sick" and he asked her what was the matter, at which "she drew me into the back room of a saloon and told me her lover had ditched her." She had had the operation Louise had escaped, "and she was going to kill herself." He called Harry Lorber and sent her to see him.

"I just tell you all this stupid history, my honey, so you may know all that I've been doing, and that you may believe that nevermore is there going to be any chance of any girl coming between me and my honey, and that I'm perfectly tranquil about how I shall be, waiting for you, old lover," he concluded.[6]

Reed was working on his long autobiographical essay, "Almost Thirty," getting his bearings, sorting out what he still believed now that he was twenty-nine years old in a world drenched with blood. He reviewed his life from childhood on. In the past ten years he had "gone up and down the earth drinking in experience, fighting and loving, seeing and hearing and testing things."

And now, almost thirty, some of that old superabundant vitality is gone, and with it the all-sufficient joy of mere living. A good many of my beliefs have got twisted by the Great War. I am weakened by a serious operation. Some things I think I have settled, but in other ways I am back where I started—a turmoil of imaginings.

He had no idea what he would be doing a month from then. "I must find myself again." He wished with all his heart that the proletariat in America would rise and take their rights, but while once confident, he no longer was sure it was "capable of revolution."

> As for me, I don't know what I can do to help—I don't know yet. All I know is that my happiness is built on the misery of other people, that I eat because others go hungry, that I am clothed when other people go almost naked through the frozen cities in winter; and that fact poisons me, disturbs my serenity, makes me write propaganda when I would rather play—though not so much as it once did.[7]

He was still at work on the essay. He also was hard at work on an ambitious piece for *Seven Arts*. Up to then it had published nothing of his and when it did it would help close the magazine.[8] The crucifying of the truth-tellers he had warned against in April would be going at a furious pace by year's end.

Except for the note written on the day she sailed, he had received no letter or cable from Louise. One afternoon, "just a week since you went away from me," he wrote to her; he was not sure of the date, only that it was Saturday, and he was "very very lonesome as I sit here in my darkish room trying to work and trying not to think." He again mentioned Dr. Lorber, whom he had gone to see that morning. The physician told him that the "poor girl" was "alcoholically poisoned & undermined" and for that he had recommended a sanitarium.

But he refrained from telling what he would in time write Bryant: that he and Dr. Lorber also discussed Louise. He ended: "O my dear lover, I wish we could have gone together! I don't suppose I'll ever be convinced that you had to go so far away!"[9]

Finally he had her cable that she had arrived safely and was relieved. He had "worked myself up to such a pitch of worry that I couldn't sleep—although I oughtn't to have, as the French line said they had word the boat was out of all possible danger."[10]

On the sixth night at sea Bryant tried to persuade herself that her going was not a mistake. "I can't get back for awhile at least," she wrote Reed sensibly. "Something has to be settled by that time." But then she recalls something he wrote her "early in our companionship," saying it as if recalling something long ago, though they had been together only a year and a half. He had told her "that people seldom find the lovers they dream about. Oh my darling, I think they seldom *know* when they *do* find them—they let them slip away. My deepest belief is that . . . from now on we *will know*." If left alone, that very effective paragraph would have suggested self-criticism in addition to some reproach. But a tone of self-righteousness now creeps in. "I always *knew* but you didn't. It seems to me that I loved you before I was born, before I can remember & noone else—ever. No one else *could* love you as I do!"[11]

Remaining at Bordeaux two days to rest, she wrote a story of the events of the passage and mailed it to Reed with letters. He combined her story with more vivid bits in her letters, sent it to Wheeler, who sold it to the *New York American*. He told her:

> Somehow or other Heywood Broun's story beat yours here by one day—and the Tribune published it; otherwise I would have done better with yours. It was news, and perishable news, so I had to act quick. I enclose herewith the story I got up for Wheeler. . . . I did another one, too, for Every Week.

The *American*, he said, "will use more of your stuff." He had gone to the Brevoort briefly the night before and there saw Nani Bailey, Edna Kenton (who wrote about the Provincetown Players), Harry Kemp, Bobby Rogers, and Dave Carb. "Everybody asked eagerly for news of you—Harry Kemp was actually lyric about you."[12]

In a later letter headed "After midnight," in which he again wrote of her U-boat story, Reed explained, "When I say I've 'finished a story,' don't imagine I am rewriting it; I'm using your words, only in some cases editing a little." He ended by urging her not to go to England if it were dangerous but to come home when she felt she wanted to. The following lines, written in weariness, suggest poignantly the void left by her journey to France, to finance which he borrowed money and was repaying it with his hated job:

> Of course I want you to come all the time. I am quite lost without you. I have never I think been so moved as I have been today, reading your letters. I certainly do awfully feel my roots in you, honey.
>
> I'm so tired. Love
> Hon[13]

One unexplained fragment of a letter without a beginning or a date, found among Reed's letters to her, written in a big scrawl, has a provocative phrase, "repeating that you don't care if you die or not?" It continues:

> I ask you in all wonder, for the first time in my life I have been feeling the same way.

There is with me—and I suppose with you too—a kind of incurable bitterness running through my veins, & a taste of ashes in my mouth.

Come home soon!

Jack

In the days before any of Reed's letters had reached her, Bryant started out by writing him a humorous account of two very middle-class women she met on shipboard who clung to her after landing, and their insistence, because they could order lavish and terribly expensive meals, that the French people must have all they wanted. But there are days when, waiting for her credentials to be validated and sent to the Maison de la Press and unable to work until then, she is melancholy and at sea. Wandering in the Tuileries Gardens, she sits alone on a stone bench and watches the swallows flying, smells the flowers and observes old men picking their way with care along the garden paths, sees widows nearby gazing vacantly into a little pool and, as always, the mutilated veterans of the battles. She talks to a big jolly Frenchwoman who had once spent some time in America only to find on her return that all her friends thought her American clothes strange. But, Bryant told her, she never seemed to be regarded as different, or even noticed. "She looked at me almost in pity. 'Ah, Mlle., *you* do not look strange in Paris, you are so little and so sad,' she said."

This day was, she wrote, the first time since leaving home that she had really "broken down." She remembered how when they first found each other he used to say, "Oh, Louise, how lonesome I've been." "Now we are separated again and I cannot bear it. I wonder why such terrible torture doesn't actually kill one," she wrote. [14]

From then until his first letters reached her, she wrote cheerful accounts of whom she met, especially writers who admired Reed, and others marked by a rising crescendo of loneliness for him. Meanwhile there was a sorting out and reexamination of old attitudes for each of them, mixed with a wartime boding of violent changes, unquiet, and possible loss of the other. Uncertainties of shipping and the long delays before letters reached their destinations added to their tension. When correspondents were taken to see the arrival of American troops, Louise met Floyd Gibbons, who boasted that he looked like Jack Reed (and he did, she added). With others she listened to the two commanders of troop ships tell about the journey; she was seated next to Paul Rainey, official photographer for the Army, and as she hadn't slept much in three nights, she fell asleep. Later he wrote her a note,

"I like you. You not only fell asleep, but you snored. What confidence!"[15]

At one point she wrote she could not stand it any longer.

> The only thing I want to live at all for is to be with you—*if we can be happy* again. Otherwise—*I'm sick of the whole thing* . . . I've tried to be interested & hopeful over here but I can't! I can't! I've walked the streets for hours trying to pull myself together. I'm so *awfully* alone and I can't bear it. I'd much, *much* rather be dead.

She had cabled him that day and as soon as she heard she would begin to get ready to go home.[16]

A long letter from her outlines possible stories she might do, then admits that she wants to come home more than anything else. "I guess I needed a little education. I'm awfully sorry I had to be such a dam fool to get it. I'm awfully sorry that I haven't been more decent to you, honey. . . . I've been just an ass about it all & I know it. . . . Always I love you over and above all this jealousy a million times. The trip has done at least *that* for me."

She tells him of a frightful nightmare: he seemed to be in trouble. With the dream over, she remembers "something very terrible you said about getting out of my way if anything happened to you."[17]

But if this moment in Paris, the dream and his real words locked in some fearful symmetry, was the first time that she could even visualize the ebullient, the insouciant Jack as concerned about her relationship to O'Neill, it would not be long before he suggested that he had some knowledge he had not had earlier. On July 2 she wrote him:

> My darling:
> Two of your letters have just reached me. I almost wept at the sight of them. O, dearest, I *could* talk to you now. I *could* air every part of my heart and brain. I understand you and I understand myself better than you think. We would be happy—more deeply happy than we have ever been—this just *had* to happen—not this particular little miserable mess but *something* to make us find each other. I love you with all my heart—I can never love anyone else. I want everything about you to be beautiful and fine. You are essentially so wonderful and so big. Artists you do not know at all love you over here. I will tell you all that when I see you—I hope to God it is soon.

This is one of several letters in which she hints of new developments. Censorship allows her only to say to Reed that "everything over here has changed—the whole aspect *has within the last three months*" changed, and to urge him, as if that were at issue, to trust her vision. [18] These would lead, on her return, to a story under a joint byline which *The Masses* played as its leading story. [19]

She had spent one evening with John Storrs, the American sculptor, and his French wife, Marguerite; after a happy return visit when they talked about Reed and his book *The War in Eastern Europe*, she was moved to offer what was to Louise the ultimate sacrifice:

> Oh, sweet old honey, you are all over Paris, all over the world and you *must* go on with your work and not wear yourself all out too long with the Mail job. I'm quite well now and I don't need anyone to cook at Croton when I come back. Couldn't we be awfully economical and quiet so you could do more work—so you could begin your novel? [20]

From her letters it appears that Bryant's emotional state continued even after Reed's letters began arriving. She met a correspondent, a Miss [Esther] Andrews, who appealed to her as equally lonely, and they planned a visit to the devastated region together. [21] But she feels that she is treated queerly by Inez Haynes Gillmore, well known author and feminist and *Masses* contributor, and her husband, the popular writer Will Irwin, and that they avoid her. "They all handle me with gloves as if I would bite."

Before the week was up, however, she and Gillmore "had it out" at dinner, and she finds that Gillmore "really *is* all right":

> She tells me that she has never been emotional but that she spends a third of her time weeping . . . she thinks you are the greatest writer we have.
>
> "No one, *no* one at all can write as he does and he ought to be in France right now . . . writing the truth about France." She was crying. . . .
>
> . . . I can't imagine why people *make* me cruel and hard before they act naturally—before they pour out their souls. . . . *I* don't want to be hard but I hate them to pretend. . . . I don't! Why should *they*?

This passage provides a possible clue to the hostility many women felt for Bryant. It is possible that she was as direct and without pretenses as she indicates here—Roger Baldwin found her so. George Biddle and Vincent Sheean in subsequent years found her straightforward, although a little theatrical. Perhaps because of her good looks women did not expect this of her.

In her next dramatic paragraph in the same letter she takes advantage of her situation—her impending departure in submarine-infested waters—to deliver a thrust: "Oh, my dear, if I can only get home to you! even for a *little* while! If anything happens that I don't you will always know that I loved you with all of my being. I know you don't think that's as fine as the love that's scattered but, dearest, it's the best thing, the deepest thing in my life. It would be infinite peace to go to sleep once again in your arms—Goodnight my dear lover—"[22]

Reed meanwhile was in Washington covering the scene for the *Mail* and by June 28 still had had no letter from Bryant. On that date, after a laconic recital of the day's events (he met George Creel, was offered and promptly refused a job in the censorship office, he spoke with the President, who was very cordial), he continues:

> I took to dinner last night a little girl 19 yrs. old here, a friend of Nina McBride's, who is going to leave her family to go to N.Y. Her name is Isabel Middleton, and she is just a kid busting loose from everything and feeling so adventurous, etc. It did me good to talk with her and tell her about life in Wash. Sq.
>
> That has been my only feminine diversion, except for the drunk girl, since you went away. . . . But the fact of the matter is I'm awfully lonely, and sort of depressed all the time. . . .
>
> However, honey darling, dont you get the least bit worried about me. Nothing will happen to me under any circumstances.

His old friend the writer and publicist Lincoln Steffens had blown in from Russia, and asked how it was "between us," and Reed told him he had been "a fool and a cad, & he just told me most people were at some time, in some way." Then he adds:

> Sweetheart, I do hope you're going to get all over your awful feelings by the time you come back. I had a long talk with Lorber about you, which I'll tell you sometime. Think about you and me a good deal, will you? It is not worth keeping going if you love someone else better. Yours
>
> Jack[23]

In his words about her "awful feelings" (inspired by his inconstancy) he refrains from reminding her, Look at the awful fuss you raised, while all the time—. He does not even ask that she abstain from loving someone else, only that she think over whether she loves anyone *more* than him. By the time he wrote the letter he had had almost two weeks to think over the talk he had with Dr. Lorber. Certainly that final paragraph had been carefully thought out. It is tempered, controlled—and is a reaffirmation of his commitment to her, but only in the event that he comes first.

But before she could receive the letter, he wrote her again, on July 5, when the first packet of her letters reached him. This remarkable letter shows that for Reed, however forbearing his earlier letter, it was not enough. It is evident that with the receipt of her warm letters, for him to remember the punch line he delivered was to recoil from it, asking himself if he were not being pharisaic.

The letter evokes a Reed unlike the legendary Jack Reed pictured by memoirists—fun-loving, lusty poet, boisterous man of action, to Hapgood irritating in his "Gargantuan gall, and his three-dimensional self-confidence."[24] It is also different from the other letters of this period, although none is far away from his brooding depression.

It is no more nor less than his confession. Nowhere in it is even a hint of Louise's inconstancy. No one can say exactly what Dr. Lorber told him, but if the doctor were asked what was the cause of her illness of the previous winter, and if he replied that the causes might have been many, but listing as a possible cause a gonorrheal infection, and Reed was taken aback, by the time he wrote the letter he had rid himself of resentment. It was to be expected that to Steffens he would declare he had been "a fool and a cad." But this long, thoughtful letter is another matter. With candor and without mercy he reviews not Louise's but his own past over the years, and especially the year and a half they have been together, and condemns himself. He does so not in formal terms but in human, often confused, and frequently touching words.

Implicit in the letter is the superior assumption that a wide gulf divides men and women in sexual feelings, but he was a product of his culture. What is more surprising is his ignorance about his own sexuality.

"I have been reading your very heart from the time you left me," he said at the outset, and was feeling "sick to my stomach, with relief, and love and shame and all kinds of terrible emotions." It is hard to write, as he has felt "frozen." One night in Washington, after Nina McBride[25] introduced him to the 19-year-old Isabel Middleton, he "thawed out" enough "to be able to control myself: and I burst out and talked of you and what you meant to me for about an hour—why, I don't know."

> That's all, my darling. I was decent and nice to a girl and pitied her—she wanted to make love. I didn't and couldn't. But I think perhaps there's something terribly wrong about me—that I may be a little crazy, for I had a desire once, just the other day. I can't tell you how awful, how wretched that made me feel—how I have looked into myself and tried to know why those things happen.

So exaggerated is his guilt over a desire suppressed that it might be concluded he was being sarcastic. But he is in deadly earnest:

> I told you once, my darling, that this had all done something to me. It has, O it has. I am awfully tired a good deal of the time, lonely, and without much ambition or much incentive. I feel pretty dull and old. I don't know why all this is.
> But I know why it is that people run to vice when they feel loss—I know that—I can imagine it—I should do it.

It is doubtful that Reed knew anything about prostitutes if he thought men sought them out "when they feel loss." It is more likely an idea culled from reading a not very good French novel. He seems to be only petulant when he adds "I should do it," as if to say, "since at your insistence I am foregoing any response to nice young things who throw themselves at me." But the balance of the letter is on another level, and is more telling on the same subject—his struggle against the fetters involved in being faithful to one woman:

> You see, my dearest lover, I was once a free person. I didn't depend on anything. I was as humanly independent as it is possible to be. Then along came women, and they set out deliberately, as they always instinctively do, to break that armor down, to make the artist a human being and dependent upon human beings. Well, they did it, and so now without a mate I am half a man, and sterile.

As the letter on the whole makes clear, Reed's trouble was not that he was "sterile," whose meaning he seems woefully ignorant of, but that he was a very normal, if confused, man. He continues, now accusatory in tone against his would-be jailer:

> I am under repression a good deal of the time in late years. I dare not let myself go. I feel that I am always on the verge of something monstrous. This is not as bad as it seems, dear—it is just that no one I love has ever been able to let me express myself fully, freely, and trust that expression.

In subsequent paragraphs the complaining tone is replaced: he is here not answering the reproaches that rang in his ears before Louise's ship sailed, but his own, painfully developed in his weeks of self-searching:

> You will remember that among other things I told you in Portland, I said that I had reached the limit of my fighting strength, and that one more combat would bust me. Well, it has. I've had four or five of these things that have worn you down. Still, my darling, *you've* got to make up your mind to trust me to a certain extent, or our life together will be a farce.

In effect he is saying here that what is of great importance to one person, in any partnership, has to be acceded to by the other if the relationship is to prevail. Thus, however irrational he might consider her attitude toward his undoubted proclivity for "promiscuity"—if four or five side-interests in a year that she knew about add up to that—he agreed he must make an effort not to succumb to this urge. Reed goes on in a self-lacerating passage that reveals that the laughing troubadour who rode with Villa's men and danced with their women and wrote sheer poetry about their revolution has no idea of how to assess himself as a sexual human being in America: "In other words, you've got to recognize the fact that I'm defective (if that is it) or at any rate different, and though I won't do anything you ask me not to, you must accept a difference in my feelings and thoughts [from her own]."

But he rallies at the recollection of a Louise raising hell on one or another of "these things that have worn you down." Now he admonishes her: "It would be intolerable to both of us if you felt you had to direct and censor my thoughts, my actions—as you have in the past—as you did even in your letter telling me not to drink."[26]

This letter of Reed's has been widely misconstrued. Max Eastman,[27] Granville Hicks,[28] and Robert Rosenstone[29] all comment on it with varying interpretations, none of them convincing.

Bryant, in comparison with her agonized earlier letters, seems relatively serene in her reply to Reed's letter asking that she "think about us" and alluding to the talk with Dr. Lorber.

"This will probably be the last letter I'll write before I come home," she wrote, addressing him as "Dearest." She would leave the last part of July, she said. She had "lots of material," and to write it there was "the only possible way." She continued:

> Now, honey dearest, I am feeling *very calm* as I write this. Nothing matters so much as my love for you—I don't know what you have said to Lorber or he has said to you—I *don't* love any one *else*. Im *dead sure* of that I just love you.
> I can talk every thing out now with you.[30]

On July 8 Reed wrote her asking, in the event he had a chance to go to Russia by way of Vladivostok, if she could go to Petrograd and wait for him, adding, "We'd come back, of course, by China." But a letter followed in which he felt there was little likelihood he would have a chance to go. If he did, he would go only "if you can be there. Staying home alone is bad enough—but of late years travelling alone has been the worst torture." *Seven Arts* had accepted a short article of his, so that he was "beginning to feel as if I could do something again." The letter ended with a touching paragraph:

I am finding out things about myself, dearest, in all this loneliness; I have discovered, with a shock, how far I have fallen from the ardent young poet who wrote about Mexico. As Bobby Rogers phrased it, I had "let myself go." I cannot help admitting that all this sex stuff is a symptom of that, perhaps. But please god I intend to get back to poetry and sweetness, some way.

> Your very loving
> Hon[31]

Jubilant over her cable that she would be home in August, he knows this letter might never reach her but declares:

I must write anyway from my full heart, to tell you how glad I am you are at last coming home. It will be wonderful, my own sweetest, to see you again and hold you in my arms. I do love you very much, no doubt about that. I love and need you. I don't mind saying that it has been a pretty terrible summer for me. And it is probably going to be hard still for a while; but when you are here I won't mind so much.[32]

Reed met the boat, claiming his friend and lover, but their travels had only just begun. Within days, at most a fortnight or so, they were off to Russia.

According to Bryant, Reed changed the closing paragraph of his long moving essay, "Almost Thirty."[33] This is the ending that would appear when many years later the essay was first published:

In thinking it over, I find little in my thirty years that I can hold to. I haven't any God and don't want one; faith is only another word for finding oneself. In my life as in most lives, I guess, love plays a tremendous part. I've had love affairs, passionate happiness, wretched maladjustments; hurt deeply and been deeply hurt. But at last I have found my friend and lover, thrilling and satisfying, closer to me than anyone has ever been. And now I don't care what comes.

7.
Into the Whirlwind

WRITING OF IT ALMOST two decades later, Louise Bryant said she returned from France in August in the midst of a heat wave and was met at the dock by Reed, wearing a shantung suit and Panama hat. "You got home just in time, in four days we're going to Russia," he told her.[1] It was longer than that, but they did sail August 17, 1917, for Russia by way of Stockholm, on the Danish steamer *United States*.

In February 1917* the Russian masses had overthrown their tsar in favor of peace, land, and bread.[2] But the Provisional Government composed of moderates had provided none of these, seemingly more interested in keeping Russia in the war to satisfy the Allies. Now all signs pointed to the overthrow of the Provisional Government and to what Reed had called "the establishment of a new human society upon the earth."[3]

Ironically, Bryant was going to Russia armed with far more imposing credentials than her famous husband: the Bell Syndicate, which had given her credentials for her Paris journey, renewed them without objection. *Metropolitan* magazine, having sorrowfully severed relations with its star reporter, gladly extended credentials to Bryant, whose name was unknown to the public. *Seven Arts* and

*By the Julian calendar then in use in Russia, dates were thirteen days behind the Western (Gregorian) calendar. In this and the next two chapters Old Style will prevail for events taking place in Russia; events in the United States will carry New Style dates, but for major events familiar to both countries both dates will be given, e.g., October 25/November 7. In January 1918 the Soviets adopted the Gregorian calendar, effective on their February 1, which became February 14.

Every Week also accredited her, although both would cease publication before long.

Reed was accredited only to the radical *Masses* and the Socialist daily, the *New York Call*. He had spoken out too emphatically against the war. The whole venture—passage for Bryant as well as Reed—was made possible when Eugen Boissevain raised money for it from friends of *The Masses*.

It was a long journey for Bryant and Reed. Their ship provided passage for numerous Russian émigrés joyously returning to their homeland; at Halifax, Christiania (Oslo), and Stockholm, the Russian-Americans were examined and reexamined fussily by officials. Finally the émigrés "were in a state of nervous terror; Russia was so near and yet so far," Bryant later wrote.[4] From Stockholm a train took them through vast forests of northern Sweden; a little ferryboat gliding over dark waters finally deposited them and their baggage on the edge of Finland. Through intermittent rain, Bryant saw Russian soldiers with every emblem of tsardom—epaulettes, decoration, buttons—removed; each wore an armband or a bit of red cloth. None saluted. A white-bearded émigré ran about speaking to one soldier and then another, expressing his joy to be back, asking where they were from. At first the soldiers smiled indulgently, but at last one said to the irrepressible greeter that there were other things to think about in Russia now than family reunions. "The old man appeared bewildered. He had been a dealer in radical books in London for many years and . . . he was coming home to a millennium to die at peace in free, contented and joyful Russia." Clutching at the soldier's arm, he asked, " 'What else begins now, save peace?'

" 'Now begins work,' shouted several soldiers. 'Now begins *more fighting and more dying! You* old ones will never understand that the job is by no means finished.' "[5]

The old émigré seemed suddenly shrunken and tired. He asked in a whisper what was wrong: they pointed to a large new proclamation posted nearby. Signed by Aleksandr Kerensky, the head of the Provisional Government, it declared martial law in Petrograd and announced the removal of General Lavr G. Kornilov, commander in chief of the army. It was a long, rather muddled statement appealing for peace and order on the part of citizens and for the defense of the nation by officers of the army and fleet. From United States and British consulate officials the Reeds learned that Kornilov had ordered the Cossacks to advance on Petrograd and overthrow the regime. Picturing Petrograd as under siege, the officials urged Reed and Bryant to turn back.

It was three o'clock in the morning when they arrived at the Finland Station in Petrograd (formerly St. Petersburg, and, after Lenin died, Leningrad). Several soldiers in greatcoats stood about, showing no interest in them whatsoever. Otherwise the great station was deserted. The square in front, where Lenin on his arrival in April had addressed a large crowd from atop an armored car, was empty. Bryant felt confused. The Kerensky proclamation was already two days old when she saw it. What had happened meanwhile? A young soldier came running toward her, asking "Aftmobile?" and she nodded consent. Following him, she and Reed came to a gray motorcar, another soldier at the wheel. Reed gave them the name of the Angleterre and they whirled off through deserted streets. Here and there a sentry called out sharply, received the proper word, and the car swept on. As they approached the Angleterre, "Mysteriously out of the darkness the bells in all the churches began to boom over the sleeping city, a sort of wild barbaric tango of bells, like nothing else I had ever heard."[6]

The next day they learned that the Kornilov revolt had been defeated without a single shot fired. It was now August 30 or 31/ September 12 or 13. They had been away from home four weeks.

On waking, Bryant glimpsed through the faded gold and blue draperies of a window in their large unfriendly room the high, gilded dome of St. Isaac's, supported by red granite pillars. It was across the street from the Angleterre. As she saw the source of the music, she watched fascinated. Bellringers, with bell ropes tied to elbows, knees, feet and hands, performed high in the ponderous cupolas—great bells and little bells, all being sounded just as they had been for generations. People hurrying by glanced up at the bellringers; only an occasional man or woman made the sign of the cross. To Louise the ex-Catholic this was of interest, and as she later observed the ordinary people of Petrograd and Moscow passing by the many churches she felt that this occasional gesture of respect was made absentmindedly, "like an old courtier bowing to a dead king."[7]

At breakfast in the hotel dining room she wondered at a hand-printed sign on each table, and on learning the translation, decided that the waiters were the new order of citizenry. The notice said curtly: "Just because a man must make his living by being a waiter, do not insult him by offering him a tip."[8]

Some time that afternoon or the following day, Bryant was typing in the hotel room, seated before the big typewriter Reed had brought from home, when a visitor came looking for him. He said he was a

friend of Jack's and had been sent by Bill Shatov. Once she had
traveled to a New Jersey town with Reed to hear Shatov speak for an
anarchist cause. The caller introduced himself: he was Manuel
Komroff, a newspaperman. Bryant cut short his apologies for inter-
rupting her, said Jack would soon return, waved him to a chair, and
went on typing away. Recalling the scene, Komroff, writer and
novelist, described the big tin typewriter top with a handle which lay
on the floor, and "Louise's sort of innocent blue eyes."

"Now how in hell," said Jack when he came in, "did you know we
were here?" Komroff told him. But first he delivered his message.
"Shatov wants you to talk to nobody till you see him." Komroff had
been asked to stop by on his way to work as editor of an English-
language morning newspaper. He told Reed that Bill would come by
that night.

He explained how Bill Shatov knew about their arrival, a tale that
might have seemed odd in any place but Petrograd. Earlier that day
Shatov had been called in by the police, ushered into the office of the
chief, and asked whether he had brought any firearms into Russia. Bill
told him no, he had brought in matrixes. Shatov, a linotype operator
in New York on the Russian-language newspaper *Golos Trudo*, knew
they used the Mergenthaler linotype machine in Petrograd—and that
they needed matrixes. He had invested in Russian type, packed in
boxes, which he stuffed in pockets and carried on his person. They
were in no danger of being dropped or mutilated that way, but his
appearance had aroused suspicions and the police chief found it
convenient to question him at this time. He nodded, and then,
looking at the I.W.W. button worn by Bill, reached into his vest
pocket and showed Shatov his own. He had worked in Chicago. As
Bill rose to depart, the chief said casually, "Oh, by the way, do you
know a fellow by the name of John Reed? You do? Well, I just received
his passport." (On checking into a hotel a new arrival in Petrograd had
to yield his passport, which was immediately sent to police headquarters for clearance.) Shatov was told where Reed could be found, and
the two Wobblies, chief of police and recent suspect, parted amiably. [9]

That night Louise and Reed strolled back and forth on the Nevsky
Prospekt with Shatov and learned a great deal. They were told that
Petrograd had but three days' supply of bread on hand. It was a fact
hard to reconcile with the scene before them, for as Louise noted, the
Nevsky Prospekt was as crowded and lively at midnight as Fifth
Avenue on a sunny afternoon. Cafés were filled, and not by the

bourgeoisie alone. The menu was unvarying: weak tea and sand-wiches. But the range of costumes was infinite, for men as well as women. Bryant described the men at one table:

> . . . a soldier with his fur hat pulled over one ear, across from him a Red Guard in rag-tags, next a Cossack in a gold and black uniform, earrings in his ears, silver chains around his neck, . . . a man from the Wild Division, recruited from one of the most savage tribes of the Caucasus, wearing his sombre, flowing cape.

She added rather patronizingly: "And the girls that frequented these places were by no means all prostitutes, although they talked to everybody." Having introduced the topic, she proceeded to tell her readers, nor can her sincerity be doubted: "Prostitution as an institu-tion has not been recognised since the first revolution. The degrading 'Yellow Tickets' were destroyed and many of the women became nurses and went to the front or sought other legal employment."[10]

From Shatov, Bryant and Reed learned something of what had happened in the abortive Kornilov revolt. The only ammunition used by the Red Guards who streamed out of the shops to meet the Cossacks sent to do Kornilov's bidding consisted of words. Kerensky at the moment was in such a weak position that he was forced to appeal to the Bolsheviks, who sent their best agitators on this mission of radicalizing the Cossacks (historically the most anti-revolutionary force in Russia) and it worked. For the time being the Cossacks had retired.

When Shatov arrived from the United States, the Bolsheviks were a persecuted minority, but already they had a majority in each of the largest Soviets, in Moscow and in Petrograd. Kerensky had thrown open the doors of the jails at the Kornilov threat: he needed the Bolsheviks' help as the moderate Socialist parties had dwindled swiftly in the last month. As for Shatov himself, he apparently found nothing disconcerting in still being a loyal Kropotkin man, handing out books and pamphlets by the anarchist Prince Peter Kropotkin while also working amicably with the Bolsheviks in the shop commit-tees that were of ever-increasing importance. He greatly admired Lenin, who was at the time still in hiding in Finland, and was convinced, as others have been, that Lenin had a sneaking affection for anarchists because of his older brother Aleksandr (Sasha), hanged when implicated in a tsarist assassination plot.[11]

Before he left them for the night Shatov told Bryant she should visit Viborg, the great industrial center located across the Neva River from the city proper, and take a look at the Red Guards and the guns stacked alongside their benches or in committee rooms. Then she would get the feel of the coming revolution—for come it would, whether or not the Bolsheviks decided on it. This time he hoped they would move in time. In the July Days, as they were termed, the Bolsheviks were divided; they tried too late to join and control the uprising, and failed. Then bloody repression reigned and there were massive arrests of Bolshevik leaders on charges of being German agents, or without any charge at all placed against them.

Within a few days of their arrival Bryant and Reed met Albert Rhys Williams, a Boston minister and Socialist whom Reed had known. He too had missed the Kornilov revolt, as he had been journeying in the provinces. Williams had been in Russia since June, and although his specialty was the peasantry, he had opinions on everything Russian, and Reed sounded him out tirelessly. Questioning him, Jack and Louise learned that the already shaky Provisional Government was greatly weakened by the Kornilov events. The demands of the people still went unsatisfied. The makeshift Provisional Government, first under Prince Lvov and Miliukov, then organized and reorganized until Kerensky replaced Lvov, had elected to keep the armies on the front and Russia in the war. Kerensky was still trying to do so by persuasion alone, visiting the front and exhorting the soldiers to fight, while thousands of the peasant-soldiers continued to leave the front unceremoniously and return to their villages. Russia was still in the war despite the spectacular failure of the last offensive, and nothing that was promised had been effected. To the peasants' cry for land the answer was, "Wait. Wait until the Constituent Assembly gives it to you." The Constituent Assembly was to be elected and draw up a constitution, but the elections were repeatedly postponed by the moderate parties backing Kerensky. These included the Social Revolutionaries and the Mensheviks. When the Social Democrats had split over methods of organization they became Mensheviks (minority) or Bolsheviks (majority).

Bryant and Reed had come at a fateful hour in the revolution. Two months earlier, after the disaster of the July Days, Bolsheviks were held in low esteem and, with Lenin in hiding and Trotsky in jail, were leaderless. By now workers and most of the garrison were listening to no one but the Bolsheviks. At this time, on September 4/17, the exciting news was that Trotsky, Aleksandra Kollontai, and the talented agitator Anatoly Lunacharsky had just been released from jails. (The three were kept as prisoners after other Bolsheviks were released at the time of the Kornilov affair.)

Reed and Albert Davidovich, as some of the Russian-Americans called Williams (giving him a Russian patronymic), were forever articulate, and forever arguing issues. Bryant shared unquestioningly Reed's dream of a coming revolution that would signify the birth of a new world. But now, hearing the two chew over some newly acquired knowledge, she gathered with some dismay that Marx and Engels specified there must be a bourgeois revolution before there could be a trained proletariat capable of making a social revolution, or, for that matter, a modern industrial plant to sustain it. Russia had its industry, much of it foreign-owned, but was still largely agricultural, with a backward peasantry. The bourgeois revolution was still unfinished. Even Lenin, said Williams, when he got to Russia in April and startled Mensheviks and Bolsheviks alike by telling them to get on with the revolution, did not claim that the bourgeois revolution was all complete, signed, sealed and approved by Plekhanov, the early Marxist theoretician.[12] Lenin merely asked that all power should lie *only* with the Soviets: no more support for the Provisional Government, but "Councils of Workmen's, Laborers' and Peasants' Deputies throughout the country and from top to bottom." Of course, the program Lenin outlined implied the end of capitalism; at the same time he made it clear it could not be achieved all at once. Just the same a beginning must be made.

But who said that one revolution had to end before another began? Bryant was impressed when she found that of all the top Bolsheviks present in April, it was the brilliant Madame Kollontai who alone had the daring to back Lenin when he enunciated his program. Kollontai had long been a Menshevik before turning fiery Bolshevik, and never had set much store by what she regarded as Menshevik passivity— which she first noted when fighting for a program to activate women. This cultivated, widely read woman and expert linguist, daughter of a tsarist general and former wife of an apolitical engineer, could quote chapter and verse of Marx and kept abreast of fiction in other lands.

Bryant went to Viborg with Reed and Williams, hugging her coat around her in the chill air as the old steam tram chugged across the Liteiny Bridge, swaying and creaking. On a Sunday she breathed in the air still redolent of smoke and chemicals and heard Jack remark that it smelled more like Pittsburgh than "feudal Russia." Plekhanov's theories that Russia was still a pre-capitalist state were the basis of the Mensheviks' difference with the Bolsheviks, out of which flowed the passivity to which Kollontai had objected. The three Americans approached a massive unfinished plant and found waiting for them a translator sent by Shatov. The meeting had begun, and on the platform was Lunacharsky, a poet, delicate of face and figure. All the same Louise recognized the effective mass orator in the poet. In this setting of bare brick walls the thousands of men and women packing the area, standing or seated on lumber or piles of brick, maintained an almost unbroken quiet as he spoke and, as he finished, gave an ovation to the man just out of jail.

Louise went everywhere, covered Duma meetings filled with Menshevik forebodings and laments, interviewed leading figures, not forgetting the many fascinating women revolutionaries; at night she went to the theaters, opened several nights a week and crowded with workers and soldiers. She wondered at the Russians' "patience" as she observed long lines of women waiting to buy bread, milk, sugar, or tobacco. One quarter of a pound for two days was the usual ration of the black peasant bread which was for Russians literally the staff of life. She saw the great ballet artist Karsavina dance before an audience that had gone without bread to buy the cheap tickets, an audience that could not let her go, so that she returned again and again "until she was wilted like a tired butterfly." But Louise missed many artists— notably the singer Chaliapin, and the dramas staged by Stanislavsky's actors—in order to attend meetings at Smolny.

The Smolny Institute contained more than a hundred rooms and now furnished headquarters for all the political parties, for the All-Russian Central Executive Committee of the Soviets of Workers' and Soldiers' Deputies and the Petrograd Soviet, as well as the Factory Shop Committees, the Central Army Committees, various unions, and the Military Revolutionary Committee which met in Room 17 on the top floor, "a throbbing room," Bryant wrote, with couriers coming and going. The Smolny lay on the bank of the Neva, the broad river which joins the Gulf of Finland, and could be reached by a lumbering tram so long as street cars ran. More and more Bryant was drawn to the Smolny, where she sensed the pounding heart of the revolution. There, as a reporter and respected internationalist, she came to know the various militants who, hunted and accused a bare two months ago, now were recognized as leaders, or at the least agitators with influence in Viborg. As she would so perceptively write, they were activists borne along on the whirlwind gathering force, "and they themselves did not know how long or how well they would be able to ride that whirlwind."[13]

At one time girls of noble birth came from throughout Russia to the Smolny to be educated. Now the polished white floors of long dark corridors, punctuated at rare intervals by electric lights, echoed to the tramp of factory workers, soldiers from the trenches, and sailors from the naval base at Kronstadt. Bryant found she could buy a ticket for two rubles that paid for a meal in the huge ground-floor mess hall. She lined up with the rest and ate many meals alongside soldiers at wooden tables set with wooden spoons such as they carried in their boots. The menu of cabbage soup and black bread was as unfailing as the friendliness on all sides. All who were poor and hungry were treated as comrades. Waiting in line, she was asked by big burly men in greatcoats, "So, Tovarish, how does it go in America now?" Tea was served upstairs in a small room at all hours in the Bolsheviks' quarters, and Bryant could usually find someone newsworthy there. At times Trotsky, whom she described as always approachable, was there; at others, Kollontai, with whom she was becoming friends, or Leo Kamenev, Trotsky's brother-in-law. Or she might find V. Volodarsky, an activist who, like Kollontai, Bukharin, and Trotsky, had lived in New York and worked on *Novy Mir*, the Russian-language daily. Increasingly, all of them and all the Russian-Americans who had come flocking back after the February revolution, a number of whom she knew, looked drawn, tense, terribly weary.

Many a night Bryant and Reed sat in the great white hall, a former ballroom with graceful columns and silver candelabra, where delegations from the front, representing soldiers' committees, gave vent to their fury. Occasionally peasants from nearby provinces also brought their grievances. They had overthrown the tsar to get peace and land, and had neither. Since there was no legislature or congress to take their misery to, they came to the Petrograd Soviet. In more and more provinces, peasants did not bother to complain, but simply took the landlord's land. Bryant was moved by a soldier from the front, obviously making his first speech of a lifetime, who blurted out:

> *Tovarishi! I come from the place where men are digging their graves and calling them trenches!* We are forgotten out there. . . . *We are forgotten while you sit here and discuss politics!* . . . the soldiers are starving. . . . *I tell you something's got to be done or the soldiers are going home!*

Nor were the men of Viborg silent. Some told of sabotage by the managers; aware that a Bolshevik takeover was imminent, some managers "were shutting down the mills so [the workers] would starve." And, "over and over and over like the beat of the surf came the cry of all starving Russia: *'Peace, land and bread!'* "[14]

Bryant always was stirred by the nobility of people who go to jail for their beliefs.[15] Thus she was rather awed by anyone who had been banished to Siberia. Among these martyrs was old Katherine Breshkovsky, known as the "Grandmother of the Revolution." A veteran Social Revolutionary, she had been condemned to long exile in Siberia. Since her return she was a voluntary captive of Kerensky and a rather diffident resident of the Winter Palace. Bryant found her after climbing a tortuous spiral staircase—the elevator in the Winter Palace like all other elevators in Petrograd was not working—tucked away, by her own choice, in a small room on the top floor, though she could have had any of a number of lavish suites. She was miserable, but less so than she would have been in comfortable, spacious rooms.

She complained to Bryant: "There is something about palaces that makes me think of prison . . . I stay here because 'this man' wants me to." When the 80-year-old woman confided that she expected the Constituent Assembly to elect Kerensky president of Russia, and that she herself would soon embark on a tour of Russia campaigning for him, Bryant told her that she'd like to go along, as well as meet Kerensky.

"You're very naive," replied the old Social Revolutionary who sought to help the young Social Revolutionary, Kerensky.

"So were you," Bryant replied, "when you smuggled bombs across the country." Babushka, as she was called, an old-time terrorist like many a Social Revolutionary, laughed with delight and agreed, "That's right." Thereafter she welcomed the reporter whenever she climbed the twisting iron stairs to Babushka's strange little nest, crowded to bursting with all her possessions. In turn she received compassionate treatment from Bryant, who wrote of her:

> There is nothing strange in the fact that Babushka took no part in the November revolution. History almost invariably proves that those who give wholly of themselves in their youth to some large idea cannot in their old age comprehend the very revolutionary spirit [with] which they themselves began; they are not only unsympathetic to it, but usually they offer real opposition.[16]

Increasingly now, in province after province, the "Red Cock" was crowing, as the peasants said: the manor houses of the *barins* and the landlords were set afire. It was the peasants' way of revolt, as it had been in other crises in other generations. But this time they were seizing the land, too. Time and again Bryant made her way to Number 6 Fontanka Street where Maria Spiridonova was to be found sur-

rounded by her followers among the Left Social Revolutionaries.
Maria spent many hours acquainting Louise with what went on in
farflung provinces, and with the main issues in the thorny subject of
the land. At the time the Bolsheviks were still calling for the convening of the Constituent Assembly, not fully realizing that if the Soviets
did in fact seize power, the Soviets themselves would be the legislative power and a Constituent Assembly would be merely redundant.
Two rival governing apparatuses would mean confusion. It was bad
enough to have a Provisional Government which took its power from
the elected Soviets but was not accountable to them. Maria, however,
was more critical of the Social Revolutionaries (of the Right) than of
the Bolsheviks.

At least the Bolsheviks did not say to the little peasants—wait, do
not seize the landlord's property, wait until laws will be passed by the
Constituent Assembly. The Social Revolutionaries did say just that:
they were part of the Coalition Government (meaning the representatives of the moderate socialist parties and the bourgeoisie) and were
stuck with its policies. Nothing escaped Maria Spiridonova's observation. She had been aware since Lenin's talk at the Peasants' Congress
back in May that the Social Revolutionary intelligentsia, the party
hacks, could not hold the semi-proletarians or poor peasants—and
maybe not the little *muzhiks* either—and now she was helping direct
them toward the Bolsheviks.

Maria assured Louise that Lenin, underground in Finland, received reports from trusted couriers, including his wife Krupskaya,
and that he would be carefully watching for signals of the gathering
momentum of the peasants' revolt. He must know by now that as for
the most revolutionary sector in Russia, the Viborg workers, he could
be sure. They were ready, and becoming restive. As soon as he felt
the peasant revolt was pervasive, watch, he would get things moving.
Maria made Louise aware of the tremendous importance of the
peasant question to the revolution. Lenin's position ever since 1903
was that while factory workers would be the shock troops of the
revolution, they would in time need the support of the poor peasants.
Otherwise a revolution could not be maintained in backward Russia
where more than eighty percent of the populace was a primitive
peasantry. (Nor was this deemed to be obvious; Lenin in those early
years was considered a bit odd among the Social Democrats for his
absorption in the conditions of the poor peasant.) Such were the
dynamics of the time, in the autumn of 1917, that Maria Spiridonova,
long associated with the Social Revolutionaries, now saw Lenin as a

prophet of the peasant—at least the poor peasant. It was with rather notable acumen, nevertheless, that Lousie wrote:

> Lenine objected to elaborate legal plans for transferring either land or industries into the hands of the proletariat. He believed that the central authority should have nothing to do with this transference, that it should be accomplished by direct revolutionary action on the part of the local workers and peasants.[17]

To pick this out as a key element in Lenin's thinking in this early period illustrates Bryant's knack for getting to the heart of an issue. This was the touchiest problem relating to the land, for it involved what Lenin had defined since 1905 as the second stage of the revolution in the countryside, "when the urban worker would march with the poor peasant against the *kulak* oppressor." Writing in early 1918, Bryant could not know that this fond dream of Lenin's only began to resemble some reality in May 1918, and at such a late hour this Bolshevik "going to the people,"[18] as the old *Narodniki* had done, was in for particularly hard sledding.[19] What Bryant gleaned from Maria Spiridonova, however, was that agricultural production was the largest problem the Bolsheviks would face—a problem to this day but imperfectly solved after a course of action the reverse of that which Lenin advocated.[20]

For Maria Spiridonova, Bryant entertained a virtual heroine-worship. She was, she wrote, the most powerful woman in all Russia, but she admired her primarily as a martyr. Long before Bryant went to Russia, Spiridonova was a heroine to the militant feminists of America. Her courage, and presumably her marksmanship, were celebrated in a poem in one of the first issues of Margaret Sanger's *The Woman Rebel*. At the age of 17, still a student, Spiridonova became a terrorist and, stalking her quarry—the peasant nemesis, Governor Luzhenovsky of Tambov—took aim and shot him dead with one bullet. (Bryant declared that Spiridonova first fired a shot in the air as warning; Luzhenovsky was flanked by his Cossacks, who, once the fatal shot rang out, seized Maria.) Spiridonova was tortured in jail and sexually assaulted, and the barbarity of her treatment was matched only by the incredible dignity with which she met it. Bryant wrote:

> First the Cossacks beat her and threw her quite naked into a cold cell. Later they came back and commanded her to tell the names of her comrades and accomplices. [Spiridonova] refused to speak, so bunches of her long, beautiful hair were pulled out. . . . For two nights she was passed around among the Cossacks and the gendarmes. . . . When they sentenced her to death she knew nothing at

all about it, and when they changed the sentence to life imprisonment she did not know. She was deported to Siberia in a half-
conscious condition. [21]

On her return after the February revolution, the celebrated terrorist was 29, five feet tall and weighed about a hundred pounds. The
face that looks out severely from the pages of Bryant's book *Six Red
Months* is as ascetic as a nun's and her dress as plain. She was a
revolutionary of the old Populist or *Narodnik* type, and as revered by
the peasants and the soldiers as the great peasant revolutionaries,
Stenka Razin the Cossack and the Don River Cossack Emilian Puga-
chev, each of whom in bygone eras swept up the Volga inciting serfs to
revolt. The rebel in Bryant, and the romantic, responded to the
firebrand in Spiridonova.

Up to the time Bryant departed for home, the Bolsheviks had been
wooing the Left Social Revolutionaries and had entered finally into a
trial marriage with them. But after the Brest-Litovsk peace with
Germany, the Bolsheviks were left waiting at the altar, while the all-
but-spouse joined the Right Social Revolutionaries in an attempt to
overthrow the regime. As a signal for the putsch, the German
ambassador was murdered. The putsch narrowly failed, but other
assassinations and attempted assassinations would follow, including
the shooting and wounding of Lenin. The killing of the German
ambassador had been ordered by Spiridonova. [22]

As Bryant told a Senate hearing, Spiridonova was "a very belliger-
ent person . . . a terrorist," but she herself would never denounce
her. "I like her better than any other woman I know." [23]

Aleksandra Kollontai, about whom Louise wrote and spoke even
more extensively, presented problems of another kind. With all her
revolutionary experience, Kollontai retained the intransigence and
the fiery determination of her youth. The human dimension was
never secondary to the politically expedient with Kollontai. Though
she fought through in political terms all causes important to her, until
she was removed from Russia and the inner party struggle to assume
diplomatic posts abroad, it was what she called "the unfinished task,"
the liberation of the working woman, that was her highest goal, her
chief aim in life. For years before the October Revolution, she was a
spokesman for Lenin and the Bolsheviks in many lands of exile
including the United States and the recognized propagandist for
Bolshevist views on the problems of the family.

Once the Bolsheviks seized power, Kollontai was made People's
Commissar of Social Welfare, the only woman in the cabinet, and as

she had long been a member of the Party's powerful Central Committee, she helped formulate and effect the immediate reforms in marriage and divorce laws. Bryant also attributed to her the regulations for maternal and infant care, a law giving mothers a total of sixteen weeks' leave from factories with pay before birth and afterward, when they were expected to nurse their infants, and a provision that recognized no child as illegitimate and stipulating the same advantages for all.

In March 1918 Kollontai resigned from her post as Minister of Social Welfare. But she continued active political work, and with Inessa Armand and others in the Coordinating Office for Work Among Women, which the former minister directed, she organized the first Congress of Women Workers and Women Peasants, with 1,147 delegates.[24] In 1920, largely through this bureau's work, the sweeping law ensuring freedom of abortion was passed.

On the whole it is a too subdued, too well-laundered profile of Kollontai that comes through in this first book of Bryant's. Instead of the stormy petrel that she was, she is shown as a patrician who forsakes her class to side with the workers but is "never an extremist." Neither Lenin nor Trotsky would have recognized the latter description. Bryant, who says in passing, "She often disagrees with Lenin and Trotsky,"[25] returned from her first stay in Russia convinced that there was complete equality of the sexes there. She did not see the nature of the struggle Kollontai, Armand, Krupskaya, and others faced in encouraging women in backward Russia to liberate themselves, nor did she know then that Kollontai felt herself thwarted in her chosen efforts.

In one of her writings Kollontai recognizes that in the night sessions of the Bolshevik commissars under Lenin, working in a small room with only one secretary, resolutions were passed in those "first months of the Workers' Government" which "changed Russia's life to its bottommost foundations." Kollontai's passionate nature demanded a faster, more sweeping breakaway from old institutions than she saw occurring. She declared rather sadly:

We, the women of the past generation, did not yet understand how to be free. . . . It is certainly true that we, myself as well as many other activists, militants and working women contemporaries, were able to understand that love was not the main goal of our life and that we knew how to place work at its center. Nevertheless we would have been able to create and achieve much more had our energies not been fragmentized in the eternal struggle . . . against the intervention of the male into our ego.[26]

The 1908 *Artemesia,* University of Nevada annual, carried this photograph of Louise Bryant, referring to her as "ex-'08 Literary and Art Contributor to the *Artemesia.*"

Sara Bard Field and Col. C. D. S. Wood, at "The Cats," their California home. Wood had been close to John Reed in Portland, and Field regarded Louise as "a sort of protegée of mine."

John Reed and Louise Bryant at their cottage in Croton-on-Hudson, New York, about 1918. (John Reed Collection, Houghton Library, Harvard University.)

Andrew Dasburg, the artist, 1914, when he visited Mabel Dodge and Reed in Provincetown. Snapshot provided by Andrew's son, Alfred.

Eugene O'Neill, 1916. One of several Provincetown snapshots in the John Reed papers.

John Reed, Provincetown, 1914, while visiting Mabel Dodge. The man in the hat is believed to be Robert E. Rogers, a classmate of Reed's at Harvard.

Bryant at Provincetown. In sending this photograph to Reed, 1916, she wrote on the back: "This is to remind you of 'the Dunes' & all the nice months after the Convention" (which he was then covering). (John Reed Collection.)

Maria Spiridonova, who at 19 killed the notoriously cruel Governor of Tambov and was sent to Siberia. On her return she was a leader in the Left Social Revolutionaries. This photo in Bryant's book *Six Red Months in Russia* is captioned: "Spiridonova. This is the only photograph she ever gave to anyone. She tore it off her passport the day I left Russia."

Aleksandra Kollontai. She inscribed this photograph "To dear comrade Louise Bryant from her friend Alexandra Kollontay [then so spelled in the West]." The only woman in Lenin's cabinet, she survived Stalin's purges later by abstaining from her old role as political fire-brand.

Louise Bryant. Photograph from the Louis Shaeffer Collection.

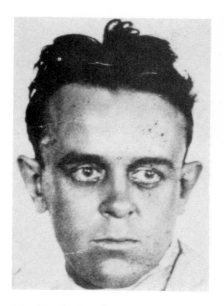

John Reed, after his imprisonment in
Finland. (John Reed Collection,
Houghton Library, Harvard Univer-
sity.)

Louise Bryant. This photograph is believed
to have been made when her second book,
Mirror of Moscow, was published in 1923,
three years after Reed's death.

This photograph, from the John Reed Collection at Houghton Library, Harvard Univer-
sity, is believed to have been taken at the Second Congress of the Comintern in Moscow.
Reed, standing, shows the ravages of his jail experience in Finland. Seated, center, is
Angelica Balabanov; the woman at right resembles Kollontai, but is not identified.

John Reed at the Oriental Congress in Baku, second from the top, left of center, in a collarless white shirt, his face still revealing the effects of his recent imprisonment and near starvation in Finland. He died within a month after this photograph was taken.

Because Kollontai considered that the double standard in sex mores held back women's liberation, she constantly raised it politically, drawing the ire of many men—and women—comrades. As for the men leaders, they differed openly on many pressing issues and engaged in sharp dispute—expected in the early Bolshevik period—but at the very words "free love," or anything bordering on them, they became as one, stuffy moralists all.

Bryant tells her readers that she met Kollontai about a fortnight after her arrival in Petrograd, and "as I watched her work in the months that followed I came to admire her more than any other woman in Russia, except Spiridonova." She continues:

> She is a slim little person, whose age is hard to determine; sometimes she looks twenty and again much, much older. She works untiringly and, through persistence born of flaming intensity, she accomplishes a tremendous amount. She is one of the best women orators I ever heard. . . . Kollontay [an early spelling of her name] dresses very well, which is exceedingly unusual in Russia among women interested in revolutionary ideas.[27]

According to Bryant, Kollontai lived in only one room, fashioned new clothes out of old, and on the standard commissar's salary of fifty rubles a month managed to achieve an air of elegance—in which the reporter delighted. This daughter of an old general of mildly liberal persuasion had been exiled under the tsarist regime, arrested at the Russian frontier on her return, and accused of being a German spy.

> She was let out again because they could not bring her to trial without any evidence whatsoever. She was re-arrested and imprisoned by Kerensky after the July uprising for having openly said that the Soviet government was the only form for Russia, which was the belief of all the Julyists.[29]

Kollontai was not tortured, as Spiridonova had been by her jailers, but two secret service men who had served under the tsar were told to keep their eyes on this dangerous subversive woman; so literally did they follow Kerensky's instructions that "for a month she could not even bathe without the solemn scrutiny of these individuals."[28]

In her theses and pamphlets Kollontai is always pleading with women to put work ahead of love. In her novels, which she began writing only in the period when she served as diplomat, her heroines find it hard advice to follow; they are as human and vulnerable as Kollontai. But Bryant, naturally unaware of the novels to come, simply says she is the author of "many books on mothers and children and on sociology in general." Kollontai was especially endeared to Bryant precisely because in the midst of herculean work and pitiless hours as Commissar of Social Welfare, she found time for a lover. Her beloved was Pavel Yefimovich Dybenko, a former Kronstadt man, a common sailor who, after the Bolsheviks seized power, was made commissar of the Red fleet; he was then 28. Louise wrote happily that theirs was one of the few romances among the leading revolutionaries. When Commissar Kollontai lost her post, it was "because she was a woman and allowed her love for her husband to interfere with her political judgment." Dybenko, Bryant explained, was arrested soon after the marriage. As head of the fleet he had hired some former officers of the old regime, as was done, she wrote, in the Red Army under Trotsky; but the naval men, pretending loyalty to the Soviets, had turned certain ships over to the Germans. While he was in prison awaiting trial, Aleksandra Kollontai made "rather violent and conspicuous protests" and was removed from office. "Revolutionists have no tolerance for romance among their leaders during critical moments. . . .," wrote Bryant. "From the beginning they looked with disapproving eyes upon Kollontai's infatuation for Dybenko."[29] By the time he was released, Kollontai had been sent to Sweden on a mission. When she returned, the Germans were approaching Petrograd.

In this early period of Bryant's Russian experiences, these two remarkable women, Kollontai and Spiridonova, influenced her strongly. She received their friendship and warm support. In a note in faulty English (she translated brilliantly in many languages but had difficulty in writing English), Kollontai calls Louise "dear comrade Bryant." She reminds her that "the Russian revolution of November" is "the first step to the worlds revolution for socialism. But our victory depends [on] the help and solidarity of all comrades and friend all over the world. Marching together against war and empiricalism, we shall have the victory![30]

Old Breshkovsky, too, treated her with affection. In spite of her occasional naive or romantic queries, these various revolutionary women respected her as an able, serious worker. By taking her seriously, they gave her further self-assurance. In their presence she emerged from the shadow of her famous poet-reporter husband. She felt that she was on the way to being a professional writer herself, as indeed she was.

8.
Red Petrograd

BRYANT DELIGHTED IN THE physical aspects of the city built by Peter the Great as his "window looking on Europe." She found it "impressive, vast and solid." Compared to its buildings New York's had "a sort of tall flimsiness." "The rugged strength of Peter the Great is in all the broad streets, the mighty open spaces, the great canals curving through the city, the rows and rows of palaces and the immense façades of government buildings," she wrote. "Even such exquisite bits of architecture as the graceful gold spires of the old Admiralty building and the round blue-green domes of the Turquoise Mosque, cannot break that heaviness."

She saw irony in the metamorphosis of "this huge artificial city," built against all reason in marshland, "over the bodies of thousands of slaves" into "the heart of world revolution . . . *Red Petrograd!*"[1]

The spacious city with its classical architecture designed for Peter by the finest French and Italian architects had cradled as old St. Petersburg the finest music, theater, and ballet in Europe, as well as a lavish, glittering social life. Peter's dream capital nonetheless embodied a booby trap for the autocracy. Contained in its suburbs was the furnace of the revolution stoked largely by foreign capital—steel, armaments, fine machinery, textiles—whose long restive and highly articulate proletariat, having deposed the tsar in February,[2] now in the autumn of 1917 was beginning to call the shots as to where Russia was going.

By a curious inversion the city designed as a showpiece to prove to the world that backward Russia could rival the West was now making the crowned and uncrowned heads of Western nations shiver in their collective boots lest it lead Russia into Bolshevism—a contagion that borders might not contain. Peter had decreed that the city be built only of stone; apparently the monarch believed in the immutability of things. But in the Petrograd of September 1917 nothing appeared changeless save change itself. "Happily no matter what changes may come the churches will remain a striking part of the Russian landscape," and "it was impossible not to get spiritual inspiration by merely looking at the beautiful exteriors," wrote the former Catholic Louise Bryant.[3]

Certainly all was in flux on September 14/27 when the so-called Democratic Conference was convened. It was the brainchild of the Mensheviks and other moderate Socialists who, alarmed that they were becoming a minority in the Soviets of both Petrograd and Moscow, sought to gather strength outside the Soviets. Delegates were not elected but drawn from carefully prepared lists. All popular democratic organizations were represented, as well as various apolitical groups such as the prerevolutionary *Zemstvo,* but the delegation as a whole was "so devised as to secure in advance an anti-Bolshevik majority."[4]

Bryant begins her account of the Democratic Conference:

> It was a cold mid-September evening, and the rain glistened on the pavements and splashed down from the great statue of Catherine in the leafy little square before the entrance of the Alexandrinsky Theatre, as the delegates filed past the long line of soldiers, solemnly presented their cards and disappeared into the brilliantly lighted interior of the immense building.
>
> Our little army of reporters, of [whom] about six spoke English, went around to the stage door at the back, climbed up many dark stairs, down many more, tip-toed behind the wings and finally emerged into the orchestra pit, where places were arranged for us.[5]

If the Democratic Conference were to carry out the aims of its planners, it was necessary to shore up support for Kerensky and refurbish his tarnished image. The Mensheviks and Social Revolutionaries who had quit his cabinet were uncomfortable in the face of evidence that Kerensky himself had initially intrigued with General Kornilov. An investigation of the whole Kornilov business had been demanded in the Petrograd Soviet by Trotsky and Kamenev. Almost daily new strands were developing in the unraveling of the conspiracy—or conspiracies?—surrounding the Kornilov revolt. A rumor persists, Bryant hears, that Kerensky might even fail to show up at the Democratic Conference.

She describes the scene: 1,000 invited delegates, among them Cossacks, Ukrainians, Georgians, Letts and Lithuanians; members of Jewish groups, doctors, lawyers, and landowners from the old *Zem-stvo;* labor groups, members of Cooperatives, twenty-three women. The boxes formerly kept for members of the tsar's family are occupied by foreign diplomats and others, and hung with flaming revolutionary banners. Boyce Thompson and Raymond Robins of the American Red Cross were in one. Mrs. Kerensky, dressed in black, "pale and wistful," sat in the first gallery. Madame Lebedev, Prince Kropotkin's daughter, sat in one box, using the only lorgnette in evidence.

Soon after the conference is opened by Nikolai Chkheidze, a Georgian Menshevik and head of the Central Executive Committee of Soldiers' and Workers' Deputies, Kerensky appears, despite the rumors. Tall, slender, the 34 year-old premier wore a plain brown uniform bare of insignia. Scorning the rostrum, he strode instead to a ramp leading from the main floor to the stage, facing his audience. Bryant saw it as a gesture that momentarily created an intimacy between speaker and audience. At the outset he referred to the Moscow Conference, held earlier (from which the Bolsheviks were excluded), a gathering arranged to be a credit to Kerensky that wound up more as a forum for Kornilov's supporters.

" 'At the Moscow Conference,' he began, 'I was in an official capacity and my scope was limited, but here I am T[o]varish—comrade. . . .' " The audience stirred restlessly. " 'There are people here who connect me with that terrible affair. . . .' [referring to the Kornilov counterrevolution].

"He was interrupted by shouts of 'Yes, there are people here who do!'

"Kerensky stepped back as if struck, and all the enthusiasm went out of his face. One was shocked by the extreme sensitiveness of the man after so many years of revolutionary struggle. Deeply conscious of the coldness, the hostility even of his audience, he played on it skillfully—with oratory, with a strange unabated inward energy. His face and his voice and his words became tragic and desolate. . . ."

In the end, radiating triumph, he received an ovation. But the Russian temperament soon exerted itself in his audience, for Russians "are never convinced by phrases." Although Bryant's reporting of the Democratic Conference as a whole leaves much to be desired, she is at her best in these passages on the young premier.

"They were disappointed in Kerensky's speech. He was charming, but he had not told them anything. There were many details about the Kornilov affair which they wished straightened up in their minds, they also wanted desperately to know . . . about a conference of the Allies to discuss war aims, and he had not mentioned it. An hour after his departure his influence was gone." It was, she wrote, the last ovation Kerensky received on Russian soil.[6]

Bryant, Reed, Albert Rhys Williams, and Bessie Beatty attended all the sessions of the conference, which often lasted until four in the morning. The speeches, about which Bryant was euphoric, seeing all the speakers as poets, were punctuated by recesses announced from the podium, when "we would all rush out into the corridors and eat sandwiches and drink tea."[7] The reporters would compare notes and occasionally wander in search of some Russian-American friend for behind-the-scenes tips or to verify translations.

After one such foray Reed and Williams returned with exciting news. Two letters from Lenin in his underground hideout that sounded the alarm on the need for insurrection had been received by the Central Committee of the Bolsheviks. Something of their contents had been leaked to the two by some of their Bolshevik Russian-American friends. Certain of Lenin's dramatic phrases now rolled off Reed's tongue or Williams's.

"There is no middle course. Delay is impossible. The revolution is dying."[8]

Lenin also objected to the presence of Bolsheviks at the Democratic Conference. The Aleksandrinsky parley did not reflect the revolutionary elements as a whole, but rather, the "compromising upper strata of the petit bourgeoisie." Getting arrested would be none too good for them. Even if the Conference declared itself a permanent revolutionary parliament, that would "decide nothing."

The Bolsheviks there should remain only long enough to prepare a Party program, announce it to the Congress, and when it was not accepted declare a complete break with the bourgeoisie and depart. One of the fiery letters then advised that "our entire group" should repair to the factories and the barracks and put the question. To them they should explain their program and the alternative: either the Democratic Conference should adopt it entire, or the people adopt insurrection.

"By putting the question in this way *we shall be able to determine the right moment for launching the insurrection. . . .*"[9]

The little group of reporters was now restless and both excited and puzzled. They asked each other what it meant. Reed wanted to get the letter. "I wouldn't use it now." Williams laughed. "Try telling that to Voskov or Volodarsky or Jake Peters or anyone we know." Someone wanted to know whether this meant that the revolution all had been expecting was only days away? No, said Reed, not necessarily. Lenin had not said *when* the uprising should be; *that* was the answer that the men and women in the plants and the soldiers in the barracks would decide by their responses. [10]

Their questions and surmises were brought to a sudden end for the moment when the Bolshevik delegates, after caucusing during the recess, trooped back into the assembly room, Kollontai among them. All the reporters had been looking forward eagerly to hearing Trotsky speak. As an orator he was said to be without peer. Now with the leaked report on Lenin's letters they were even more eager to hear him. But other parties' speakers took precedence, and the nervous Americans, afraid to leave the auditorium for a moment lest they miss him, sat through every speech.

At long last Trotsky was on the podium. All eyes were riveted on him, for this would be the first time that the former Menshevik, who with Lunacharsky and others had joined the Bolsheviks while in jail, was heard as official spokesman for the party whose label he "had so long considered as little better than a slur."[11] For many of the bourgeois gentlemen present (who suspected that Kerensky had first encouraged, then betrayed Kornilov), Russia now had two choices, Lenin or Kornilov. Naturally they opted for Kornilov. Now they gazed, most of them for the first time, at the man they considered as, next to Lenin, the most wild-eyed evil genius in all Russia. Bryant wrote, rather sensationally:

> Flashing out of that remarkable gathering was the striking personality of Leon Trotsky, like a Marat; vehement, serpent-like, he swayed the assembly as a strong wind stirs the long grass. No other man creates such an uproar, such hatred at the slightest utterance, uses such stinging words and yet underneath it all carries such a cool head.[12]

But despite all of Bryant's metaphors she gave no inkling as to what Trotsky *said*. Nor did Reed in *Ten Days*, although the entire speech he made at the forthcoming Pre-Parliament is in an appendix. Neither did Williams, although he remarked that throughout the speech he and Reed, keyed up by the import of Lenin's letters, were "simply straining to catch the word *vostravat* (insurrection)." It was not heard.[13]

According to his biographer Isaac Deutscher, Trotsky scored irrepressible laughter even from his hostile audience when he replied to a speaker who argued that the entire Cadet party should not be blamed for the Kornilov mutiny; the questioner pointed out that the Bolsheviks had not liked it when their party was held accountable for the July Days. Trotsky found a "small inaccuracy in the comparison." When the Bolsheviks were arrested and charged with fomenting the movement of July 3/16–July 5/18, said Trotsky,

> there was no question of your inviting them into the ministry—they were being invited to the Kresty prison. There is, comrades, a certain difference here. . . . We say: if in connexion with the Kornilov movement you want to drag the Cadets to prison, then, please, do not act indiscriminately. Examine the case of every Cadet individually, examine it from every possible angle!

When he demanded arms for the Red Guards against a threatened new and more powerful Kornilov movement, the laughter was silenced.[14]

Bryant wrote that a resolution in favor of another coalition government—meaning it would include once again the bourgeois elements—won by a slight majority. But then, she wrote, a resolution proposed by Trotsky for a "coalition of all democratic elements" but not including the Cadets "carried overwhelmingly." This was indication enough that however imposing the panoply at the Aleksandrinsky Theater, the heretofore ruling groups in the Soviets were in disarray. Many of Kerensky's own supporters among the moderate Socialists had joined forces with the Left Social Revolutionaries led by Kamkov and Spiridonova, as well as the Mensheviki Internationalists under Martov, and were bitter in their denunciations of the Cadets and the insistence by Kerensky in maintaining the coalition.

And now Kerensky exerted his control, making a farce of the Democratic Conference. He sent word, shortly after the Trotsky resolution passed, Bryant wrote, that he was "about to announce his new cabinet containing representatives of the Cadet party." Tseretelli hurried to the Winter Palace to plead with him, for "the formation of such a cabinet would lead directly to civil war."

But the next morning Kerensky appeared before the presidium and threatened to resign; the presidium fell in line and urged the gathering at the Aleksandrinsky to immediately form a Pre-Parliament. Tseretelli, Dan, Lieber, Gotz, and others spoke repeatedly for the resolution, Tseretelli engaging in a shouting match with some Bolsheviks. Bryant wrote further:

"When Spiridonova arose and told her peasants that this measure [coalition with the Cadets] cheated them out of their land, a sullen, ominous roar followed her words."[15]

At long last the Bolsheviks bolted the assembly. The next evening coalition passed by a small majority and the delegates filed out into the rain.

The same day, making the goings-on at the Aleksandrinsky all the more insignificant and unreal, the Bolsheviks won a majority in the Executive Committee of the Petrograd Soviet. Trotsky was now president, and the count was thirteen Bolsheviks, six Social Revolutionaries, and three Mensheviks. The Pre-Parliament, with consultative status only, opened, and Bryant faithfully attended its sessions, all boring.

Other letters from Lenin from his Finland retreat were arriving, some addressed to various Party groups other than the Central Committee and some to regional conferences or such that were not even under the aegis of the Russian Social Democratic Workers' Party, Bolshevik. Certain letters were published in part or fully, others reported by the friends of the American reporters.

In turn elated and depressed, Reed intoned such phrases as "History will not forgive us if we do not assume power now."[16] He could understand less than ever why the Bolshevik faction at the Democratic Conference had not heeded Lenin's words and walked out at the start. The new shift of forces in the Petrograd Soviet showed that at a nod from Trotsky the workers would arise. Yet there was no hint of any armed uprising in Trotsky's speech. Bryant too became affected by the general restiveness of Reed and Williams. Kerensky, shakily presiding over the fifth coalition provisional government in seven months, was said to be preparing to redistribute the troops, with those garrisons inclined to support the Bolsheviks sent to the front. So what were the Bolsheviks waiting for? They could miss out if they were not careful. The American reporters, who had become quite proprietary over the Revolution, asked this of one another.

It occurred to Bryant that Jake Peters, the Latvian-Englishman who was friendly with all the American reporters, especially friendly with Bessie Beatty, must be rather close to Lenin. Beatty had told her once that Peters had confided in her that he on occasion acted as a courier to Lenin in hiding. Reed and Williams brightened at her suggestion now that they go see Peters. Maybe he could tell them why Lenin's drumfire of alarms seemed to go unheeded.

They found him—weary to the point of exhaustion, as were all their friends among the activists—and not a little annoyed by their questions. What were they worried about? Williams, Reed, and Bryant all talked at once. They were not coming as reporters but as friends. Wasn't it dangerous to wait longer? Hadn't Lenin been saying just that? Peters heard them out, then made his reply.

What did they want, a copy of their secret plan? There wasn't any. They might have saved themselves the trouble of placing such significance on Trotsky's talk if they had recognized one thing. He said that "only a Soviet government" could meet the needs of the people. That, today, meant insurrection. To the workers the slogan "All power to the Soviets" now meant insurrection. The old-line Mensheviks and the Right Social Revolutionaries, the whole Kerensky gang of compromisers who stood by the Dual Power (of bourgeoisie and Soviets, or as Trotsky called it, Dual Powerlessness), were fully exposed by now. Moreover, agitators were busy nightly speaking at the plants. Yes, Peters said wearily, what they had been told by their Russian-American friends could be true: certain people in the leadership were dragging their feet. But pressure was building from below. The trio left Peters, sobered, hardly satisfied, still apprehensive but willing to practice patience. At least they had some basis on which to believe that it was coming![17]

Everyone seemed to be waiting: the tension was palpable. Reed and Williams indulged in verbal horseplay with each other to let off steam. But Bryant had glimpses of built-up tensions that lay beneath the jests and abrasive remarks the two exchanged at each other's expense.

Bryant, knowing the deeper undercurrents in her lover, aware—as she had not been before the painful months spent apart in the summer—that in moods of introspection he listened to a stern self-judge within, was apprehensive over his swift changes of mood. On one occasion she saw him lapse into a sombre, self-taunting vein, saying: "What counts is what we do when we go home. It's easy to be fired by things here. We'll wind up thinking we're great revolutionaries. And at home? Oh, I can always put on another pageant!"[18]

Bryant knew from talks with Mary Heaton Vorse how effective was the silk strikers' pageant in Madison Square Garden which Reed had directed, how important as a symbol, to Glaspell and Jig Cook. Bryant also knew the Paterson strike ended in defeat, and that news of its failure reached Reed when he was happily (and unhappily) ensconced at the side of Mabel Dodge in her luxurious Italian villa.

She suspected that in these moods he was being needlessly hard on himself, as if to goad himself on to some action or goal he pondered over, wondering whether he would be equal to it. It was an additional impetus to her longing for the storm to break. When it did, she felt, Reed would spring into activity and the introspection give way to his usual self-confidence.

It was a period of acute tension and excitement for both Reed and Bryant. For Reed, whatever the momentary depressions or more complex struggles he underwent, it was the affirmative answer to the question he had put to himself the previous summer when he wrote "Almost Thirty": *what was left to believe in after every Socialist party in Europe abandoned all principle in the rush to support the bloody carnage engulfing the world?*[19]

For Bryant, after a long, uncertain quest, with changing goals, with her attempts at self-realization often ending in blind alleys of personal attachment, it was self-discovery—and the promise of fulfillment. It is doubtful that she believed in herself as journalist when she entered Russia, but as the results show, she must have each day gained confidence in her craftsmanship.

What was happening to Bryant was not measurable; it is impossible to say that at any specific point her career took on form and character. It was more basic. Those critics who saw her in Provincetown and in later years merely as a beautiful woman who manipulated talented men to advance her career were wide of the mark. She was, in Andrew Dasburg's words, "serious about living." ("It had nothing to do with a career. It was that she lived in the Russian Revolution, till it became a part of her.")[20]

A debate raged among the Bolshevik delegates to the Pre-Parliament (or Council of the Republic) on whether to participate or to boycott it. At length they agreed to boycott, and on the first evening of the parley, Bryant wrote, the Bolsheviks through their spokesman Trotsky

> hurled a bomb into the gathering from which it never recovered. They accused the *sens* element—propertied classes—of being represented out of all proportion to their numbers . . . and charged them with the deliberate intention of ruining the Revolution; appealing to the soldiers, workers, peasants of all Russia to be on their guard, the Bolsheviki left the council never to return.[21]

It is no small wonder that Lenin greeted with relief Trotsky's stand on the boycott. For although they were agreed on the need of armed insurrection, they differed on tactics. Trotsky, according to his biographer, took less seriously than Lenin the threat of an immediate counterrevolution. As Deutscher points out, it was not a principled difference; but he pictures Lenin as viewing Trotsky's approach with uneasiness, especially as he was new in the Party.[22] Thus Lenin wrote the Central Committee: "Trotsky was for the boycott. Bravo, Comrade Trotsky!"[23]

Meanwhile, despite the division and paralysis of the Central Committee, Trotsky and other agitators well known in Viborg, among them Lunacharsky, Kollontai and Volodarsky, addressed factory meetings, going to the largest industrial plants, from the Obukhovsky to the Trubochnyi, from the Putilovsky to the Baltiisky, and from the Cirque Moderne to the barracks. And on October 16 the regiments of the garrison declared they would refuse to obey Kerensky's marching orders: they would remain in Petrograd. This was a great victory for Trotsky and the Bolsheviks. At a session of the Executive of the Soviet, a Military Revolutionary Committee was formed, on the motion of a Left Social Revolutionary, Lazimir, who headed it. But Trotsky as president of the Petrograd Soviet was *ex officio* its head. Podvoisky, Antonov-Ovseenko, and Lashevich, future commanders of the insurrection, were members.

Day after day Bryant covered sessions of the Pre-Parliament, now held in the Maryinski Palace. Because the Cadets were so numerous, she wrote, "the vote on every important measure was a tie." Every few days Kerensky would appear and make an impassioned plea:

> He would be received coldly . . . the Cadets often choosing this particular time to read their papers. During one of the last speeches he made . . . he was so overcome with the hopelessness of the situation that he rushed from the platform, and having gained his seat, wept openly before the whole assembly . . . he had been betrayed by the very Cadets he had worked so hard to keep in the government . . . and the people were going over to the Bolsheviki.[24]

Bryant and Reed went back and forth to Smolny, they rode the lurching steam tram to Viborg, boiling with huge meetings, and they saw queues of women waiting to buy bread—no longer patient but grim and angry. They read reports of entire villages taking matters into their own hands, dividing up estates, slaughtering or driving off herds, burning manor houses or "nests of the gentry." The latest coalition government ordered troops everywhere—Cossacks preferred. Riots were reported in Zhitomir, Tambov, Orel, Kharkov, Odessa. The government ordered repressions, shootings. There were hunger riots, and savage pogroms in the provinces. In Petrograd there was hunger, and waiting, and hunger. People no longer argued on street corners; the Russian passion for discussion seemed to have played itself out. Violence hovered over the city, its very atmosphere drenched with it. But everywhere, save in the Smolny itself, there was a marked stillness—the tension in the eye of the hurricane.

Going from the Astoria hotel to the Pre-Parliament, and from the Maryinski Palace to the white-hot vortex of revolution that was Smolny, Bryant and Reed were aware that the betrayed people of Russia, peasants and peasants-become-proletariat or soldiers, were at the point of explosion. It was a harrowing time, yet they rejoiced that they were there, whatever the circumstances. In a few days John Reed would be thirty, and he no longer asked what meaning life held. Alongside the black-bloused workers, Reed and Bryant were ready to be counted. No longer merely witnesses, they had made the Revolution their own, nor stopped to reckon the possible cost.

9.
A Strange Revolution

SO FREELY HAD IT been discussed and for so many weeks, that when the Revolution actually took place in Petrograd October 24–25/November 6–7 few were surprised. Only with such a widely accepted scenario would it have been possible for stray American reporters to be so frequently on the scene of action as it unfolded.

Ironically, one of the few taken by surprise when it finally began was Lenin. Isolated and largely ignored in his hiding place in a Viborg flat, he spent the day of October 24/November 6 doubting that the Central Committee had acted but resolved that, come what may, the insurrection must begin that very day. No one had bothered to inform him that the committee that morning had set a date: it had voted to proceed at once with the insurrection.

For weeks Lenin had been in a state of tension, mistrusting the Central Committee and never wavering in his conviction that the masses were only awaiting a signal to act. On September 29/October 10 he had written angrily to the Central Committee from his Finland hiding place that, as they had left unanswered his persistent demands ever since the Democratic Conference, while the editor of the Party's newspaper (then Stalin) had deleted from Lenin's articles all references to "such glaring errors on the part of the Bolsheviks as the shameful decision to participate in the Pre-Parliament," he took this as "a 'subtle' hint to keep my mouth shut.

"I am compelled," he continued, "to *tender my resignation from the Central Committee*, which I hereby do, reserving for myself the freedom to campaign among the *rank and file* of the Party and at the Party Congress."[1]

From then on he wrote letters and articles to be distributed among Party and non-Party groups suggesting military tactics for seizure— and building support for his proposal. On October 7/20, wearing the wig with curls down his forehead in which he fled to Finland, clean-shaven as then and with spectacles, he took up quarters in a flat on the Viborg side of Petrograd. On October 10/23 he attended a ten-hour meeting of the Central Committee, and although few spoke with any optimism on his proposal, the vote for insurrection was 10 to 2. (For armed uprising: Lenin, Sverdlov, Stalin, Dzerzhinsky, Trotsky, Uritsky, Kollontai, Bubnov, Sokolnikov and Lomov. Opposed: Kamenev and Zinoviev.) But no date was set!

Secreted in the flat of Marguerita Vasilievna Fofanovna, Lenin was visited by his wife Krupskaya, his sister Maria Ilyinishna, and at times by Eino Rakhya, a militant Petrograd Bolshevik who was by birth a Finn—and by almost no one else. On October 24/November 6 he wrote a letter to the Central Commitee urging the necessity of taking power that very day. After directing Marguerita Vasilievna to take it to the Smolny, he changed his mind, overtaking her and relieving her of the letter, saying she should return home and not expect him.

Rakhya accompanied him. They found a streetcar and crossed the Liteiny Bridge. Getting off, they saw a quarrel between soldiers and workers and slipped past. But as they started into Shpalernaya Street they were stopped by two mounted Junkers (military cadets) who demanded their passports. Rakhya whispered to Lenin, "Go on, I will deal with them," and faked a noisy quarrel over passports: no one knew they had been distributed, and how could they manage to provide themselves with such documents at a time like this? Lenin meanwhile was not to be seen. Rakhya caught up with him.[2]

That same night Krupskaya, after hearing from Fofanovna that Lenin had started for Smolny, climbed with a woman comrade onto "a lorry that our people were sending to Smolny. I was anxious to know whether Ilyich had reached Smolny in safety. . . . I do not remember now whether I actually saw Ilyich in Smolny or only learned that he was there."[3]

A strange revolution. An even stranger conspiracy. For weeks a varied mass of the population had waited for it and complained that the Bolsheviks couldn't seem to make up their minds. United States Ambassador David Francis was heard to scoff at the Bolsheviks for playing at insurrection. In the lobby of the Astoria an old landlord type, prowling the drafty cavern, was overheard to say the Bolsheviks must be getting cold feet: they had their chance now—were they yellow?

Louise Bryant and John Reed, leaving the Smolny at three in the morning of October 24/November 6, saw shop chairmen lined up and getting slips of paper from the Military Revolutionary Committee that would entitle them to guns. The garrison at the Peter and Paul Fortress had come over after a speech from Trotsky, and the guns could be picked up there now. As Bryant and Reed went out the door they ran into Bill Shatov, who sang out, "We're off!" Kerensky had had the Bolshevik newspapers closed down and sealed, but the seals were smashed. "And now we're sending detachments to seize the bourgeois newspapers!"

As Shatov left them, they looked at each other, eyes alight. The Revolution had begun.

Later that morning Bryant was at the Maryinski to hear Kerensky's last speech. Reed, who as yet had no idea that *The Masses* had folded under government pressure, went to file a dispatch, then joined her at the Maryinski. That evening they were at the Smolny for the meeting of the outgoing All-Russian Central Executive Committee. The Congress was to open the next day. As expected, a bitter wrangle was in progress. Then Volodarsky, one of the Russian-Americans and a fire-eater, shouted that the old *Tsay-ee-kah* (for the initials of the outgoing body) was virtually dead and had no right to assume the functions of the forthcoming All-Russian Congress of Soviets; on that note he led out the Bolsheviks.

Bryant and Reed stayed on, making their weary exit at four in the morning of October 25/November 7. In a corridor, heading for the stairs, was Zorin, with a rifle across his shoulder. They called his name and hurried to him. Zorin reported jauntily that two ministers had been arrested and were at the moment locked in the cellar. A regiment was on the way to capture the Telephone Exchange and Telegraph Agency and another would head for the State Bank. The Red Guard was out, on duty. "We're moving!" he cried, and rushed away.

The arrest of the ministers in the early dawn on their way to answer a summons from Kerensky was an error, it was announced, and they had been released. This and other acts of leniency provoked Bryant to write, "The Bolsheviki have been so long suppressed that when it falls [to] their lot now to suppress other people they do it half-heartedly."[4] Curiously, in that period when the Revolution was new it was all true.

As Bryant and Reed made their way down the Smolny steps they saw a few workers carrying guns with bayonets, nervous and important—the Red Guards. They were so young! In the distance scattered rifle fire sounded; Lenin had specified as targets for seizure the Telephone Exchange and State Bank and above all the bridges. The Kerensky forces were closing the bridges to cut the Viborg workers off from access to the city, and the Red Guards and an advance contingent of sailors were opening them almost as fast as they were shut.

Bryant and Reed returned home and slept late, went to Williams's room to collect him, and then headed toward the Winter Palace. With advance information from Zorin, they figured their arrival would be in time to coincide with the big news of the day; if not, they would wait there. When asked later by a United States Senate committee what she was doing in the Winter Palace that day, Bryant said sweetly, "I wanted to be there when the palace fell."[5]

Within the Winter Palace she interviewed many of the beardless Junkers. She was sorry for them. One asked if it would be possible for him to work in America or join the American army. More than one showed her the final bullet he was keeping for himself. Short of ammunition, they expected an attack any minute. Throughout the palace there were about 1,500 Junkers and 200 women soldiers. Presumably the palace was cut off from all outside help. Where would help come from? Kerensky had worked through the early morning hours in vain trying to find it.[6] Now the ministers crouched somewhere inside, hiding and waiting for what each expected to be his end, while below were the young men trained in officers' schools, for whom Bryant felt pity; they seemed so young and so frightened.

The interlopers seemed to have the run of the palace, but however much they explored, they failed to find the ministers' hiding place. Near Kerensky's office a young officer paced back and forth. Reed asked if they might see the minister-president. The reply was in French, which Reed understood: "Aleksandr Feodorovich is extremely occupied; in fact, he is not here." Nor was he. He was on his way to the front. As his car was short of gasoline he had sent to the English hospital for some. (They were to learn that he fled in his own car, followed by a touring car flying a small American flag contributed by the American Embassy.)

After several hours the Americans left the palace and its unhappy occupants: obviously the seizure of the Winter Palace had been deferred. They saw a cordon of soldiers, Red Guards, and a few sailors who paced slowly around in an oval encirclement. It was about five-thirty. The three ate a hurried meal at the nearby Hotel France and returned to the palace. Only a few faint lights were visible. The cordon without was slightly augmented by soldiers. They stopped to talk to a few Red Guards and soldiers standing beneath the Red Arch. None of the three spoke Russian as well as they understood it by now, but with gestures they made their questions clear. When would the attack take place? At first no reply was forthcoming. Then a Red Guard said sorrowfully that the Women's Battalion was protecting the ministers. It would not look nice if they fought them, and if they did attack the women they would be called cowards. The Americans walked on, puzzled, wondering if revolutions turned on such nice points of gallantry.

They walked to the Smolny, where the Second All-Russian Congress of Soviets was to open that night. In a square across from the pale yellow Smolny Institute stood an armored car with engine running, a Red Guard at the wheel. Nearby were a cannon and large piles of firewood for use as barricades in the event of attack. At the entrance was a mounted machine gun, the only one possessed by the Red Guards at the time, [7] and Guards on either side clutched rifles.

Entering, they met Kamenev and Lunacharsky coming down the crowded stairway and learned from them that the Petrograd Soviet had just met. Both men looked so exhausted that they did not burden them with questions. When told later that Lenin had made a surprise appearance there they cursed their luck.

The Congress had not opened on time, but that was hardly cause for alarm. Few meetings in Petrograd ever did. They saw Bessie Beatty coming their way, deep in conversation with Alex Gumberg. One or the other may have been present when Lenin spoke, Williams said, adding pointedly that he'd tackle them when they came alongside the trio.

Gumberg, a former business manager of *Novy Mir* in New York, was a man of mystery in Russia, a translator for the Americans at the embassy and so knowledgeable that his functions were many. Immensely able, shrewd, respected, and feared, for his sardonic humor spared no one, it was well known that he and Reed invariably clashed, and Williams wanted to head off any confrontation. Brother to the red-haired, blue-eyed, attractive Zorin (revolutionaries often had two or more names), Alex affected a dour impassivity in contrast to Zorin's bold and cheerful personality. Whatever the original difficulty was between Gumberg and Reed, it had escalated, and for this Reed bore his share of responsibility. It may have been that the cautious Gumberg mistrusted Reed's candor and his capacity for getting into trouble.[8] Or he may have held Reed's class origins in contempt. He got along admirably with a capitalist like Raymond Robins and in time would be, with Ambassador Francis's approval, the back-door go-between for Robins with Lenin and Trotsky. But a Harvard man in the revolutionary camp triggered the parochial in Alex. Bryant, fierce in her loyalties,[9] reflected Reed's bias against Gumberg.

Williams asked Beatty and her companion if either was present when Lenin addressed the Petrograd Soviet, and if so, could he get a fill-in. Before Beatty could answer, Gumberg took over and related in his sarcastic vein that Trotsky opened the meeting and very generously presented to the Soviet, on behalf of the Military Revolutionary Committee, the newly won revolutionary power. "Or almost won," he added quietly.

Perhaps Gumberg was just clowning. On the other hand they had just come from the Winter Palace, which was not only intact but harbored the cabinet of the Provisional Government whose premier had decamped. Perhaps Alex's gallows humor hid some real worry? After a pause he continued. Speaking of power, even as Trotsky declared the Provisional Government extinct, he admitted that one little thing was missing: the Winter Palace. And the ministers huddled within, of course—defended by a few hundred shivering Junkers and the Women's Battalion. But, said Gumberg, before the puzzled men of Viborg could begin questioning him Trotsky, master of stagecraft, brought forth Lenin and introduced him. Of course the meeting went wild. For the new members it was their first glimpse of the great strategist, and for all, a thrilling moment. The little matter of the palace was forgotten.

Then they all were talking, and among them, Reed. What did Lenin *say?* Did he *mention* the Winter Palace? So, having risen to the bait, he had to listen as Gumberg, soft as silk, wondered aloud why it was that "every time I see American reporters they want to know what took place somewhere where they weren't." He reminded them he did not take notes, and no minutes of the meeting were recorded. Then he let another bombshell fall. The Winter Palace would have been taken by now, he said, "if our friends the sailors had arrived here on time."

This was heresy to Bryant, who thought the men of Kronstadt could do no wrong. She would write that throughout the October Revolution "they moved splendidly with a fervour that created around them forever a legendary glamour." But Alex had had his fun and wandered off.[10] Beatty remained, and let them in on news she had gleaned from

Trotsky: troops were even now moving on Petrograd from the front! Reed and Williams, perturbed doubly by now, left them to try to learn more. Beatty and Bryant exchanged experiences of the day.

Beatty had been on the Morskaya when an armored car and an approaching company of military cadets shot at each other; she was saved from the crossfire when someone pulled her into a doorway. Bryant had nothing to match this. She too had heard a "shot"—which proved to be the flash gun of a photographer, a funny little man who came out of the Palace, walked across the square and set up his tripod to photograph the women soldiers building a barricade. But the shot caused "the wildest confusion" among the Junkers around her.[11]

At ten-forty in the evening of October 25/November 7 the Second All-Russian Congress of Soviets was sourly opened by Fyodor Ilyich Dan, the Menshevik editor, in the great columned hall of the Institute, lit by chandeliers. The elegant white chamber was filled with men from Viborg, roughly clad. Shabby army greatcoats were much in evidence. The hall rapidly filled with coarse tobacco smoke. Members of the new presidium were elected on the basis of proportionality: fourteen Bolsheviks, seven Social Revolutionaries, three Mensheviks, and one Menshevik Internationalist. Lenin led in votes but, still incognito, remained in a little room.

The meeting ground on, while "Lenin was cursing in his little room, 'Why hasn't the Winter Palace been taken? Do something! You all deserve to be shot!' " Between speeches Trotsky joined him, trying to snatch some sleep, but telephones and messengers made it impossible.[12]

In the chair, strangely enough, was Kamenev, although no one seemed to think it strange. He and Zinoviev had opposed insurrection until the last minute and had, moreover, polemicized against their Party's decision in favor of it in a non-Bolshevik paper.[13] It was Lenin's way first to fight them as "strike-breakers" and seek their expulsion and the next week to work with them. Trained personnel were few enough and all were needed to "ride the whirlwind," in Bryant's apt metaphor. In her book she would contrast Kamenev with Trotsky, and with a touch of malice note that Kamenev in his mild utterances reminded her of Lincoln Steffens.[14]

The first objections on procedure were being made when a deep boom shuddered through the great White Hall. "The civil war is beginning, comrades!" a mournful voice cried from the floor. It was that of Julius Ossipovich Martov, who had come out of Siberia with Lenin. Bryant described Martov as grey and worn, his voice always husky from throat trouble. He is much beloved by his constituents and is known everywhere as a brilliant writer. Exiled in France for many years, he became one of the principal figures in the labour movement there. He is a Menshevik Internationalist by politics. [15]

Martov urged that "the Congress must not sit with folded hands before the developing civil war, the result of which may be a dangerous outburst of counter-revolution"—at which point another hollow booming of cannon sounded. "Stop the bloodshed!" he demanded. "The guns are roaring."

A large sailor with a black beard arose to say that the *Aurora* was only firing blanks. It happened to be true, but Martov seemed shaken. He then proposed a delegation to negotiate with all socialist parties. After caucusing, presumably with Lenin, the Bolsheviks returned, and Lunacharsky declared they had absolutely nothing against the Martov proposal. But the Mensheviks (as far from the Menshevik Internationalists as they were from the Bolsheviks) did. A Menshevik army captain denounced the Bolsheviks for placing soldiers around the Winter Palace. Militiamen interrupted fiercely with cries of "Kornilovist!" and "Provocateur!" and, worse by far, "Counter-revolutionary!"

The battle of words went on. Mensheviki and Social Revolutionaries claimed that the Congress itself was without authority to legislate, that only the Constituent Assembly could. But now the Left Social Revolutionaries, more numerous at this point than their right-wing brothers and sisters, and the Menshevik Internationalists stood together with the Bolsheviks in opposing that contention. For a moment it appeared Martov's resolution would carry, with all the left parties united and agreeing on a conciliatory approach to all the Socialist parties. But in one of those tragic vagaries of history Martov reversed his stand, and the moment was lost. (That was among other things a blow to Lenin, who throughout his life ever since their break in 1903, whenever Martov appeared amenable, began to hope passionately that he would again work with him. [16])

Suddenly someone arose and solemnly announced that members of the Municipal Duma and delegates from the Menshevik and Social Revolutionary parties had "decided to perish with the Provisional Government." They were heading, he said, for the Winter Palace. "Unarmed we will expose our breasts to the machine guns of the terrorists." Bryant, describing the scene, added:

This came as a complete surprise to many of the delegates who were to be sacrificed, but nevertheless a number of them impulsively followed the speaker; others sat uneasily in their seats looking as if they felt this was carrying party principles too far.[17]

Trailing the would-be martyrs out of the hall were Bryant and Reed, Bessie Beatty, Williams, and Gumberg. No trolleys were running. Luckily they found a huge motor truck outside the Smolny, its motor running; hailing the jaunty driver, they showed their Military Revolutionary Committee passes (Bryant's was Number 1, the first issued) and piled into the back, joining several sailors and soldiers and a Cossack from the Wild Division (or Savage Division, made up of mountain people of the North Caucasus) wrapped in his black cape.

> They warned us gaily that we'd probably all get killed, and they told me to take off a yellow hatband, as there might be sniping. Their mission was to distribute leaflets all over town, and especially along the Nevsky Prospect. The leaflets were piled high over the floor of the truck together with guns and ammunition. As we rattled along through the wide, dim-lit streets, they scattered the leaflets to eager crowds. People scrambled over the cobbles fighting for copies. We could only make out the headlines in the half-light:
> *Citizens! The Provisional Government is deposed. State Power has passed into the hands of the organ of the Petrograd Soviet of Workers' and Soldiers' Deputies.*[18]

Gumberg, insisting that the leaflets had been ready for distribution since ten that morning, grumbled that such optimism was not reflected in the military geniuses running the show, who were so cautious that they waited for almost the whole navy to arrive. Even then, they kept sending ultimatums in to the palace that if the ministers didn't give in by zero hour, the guns would fire.

No one had believed the sailor who said those terrifying blasts from the *Aurora* heard in the Smolny, which backed on to the swollen Neva River where the *Aurora* lay, were the sounds of *blanks* being fired. The plan, it was later learned, was that if the Provisional Government ministers rejected all ultimatums, then live shells would be used, but until that time, only blanks. But a hitch developed in the plans. A red signal lamp was to be hoisted on the Peter and Paul Fortress, which would tell the *Aurora* when to fire. But no red lantern could be found. The agreed-on assault hour of nine o'clock (if the ministers had not given in) came and went, and the lantern still had not materialized. A furious search finally produced one, but the first efforts to attach it to the flagstaff failed—just one of many things that went wrong. And the guns never did fire live shells.

Meanwhile the truck in which the Americans were careening around Petrograd was stopped by Red Guards where the Ekaterina Canal crosses the Nevsky. The driver was told emphatically he could go no closer to the Winter Palace. The Americans climbed down and saw a dark mass of people facing a cordon of sailors—Bryant estimated more than two hundred. By an arc light they recognized some of the Mensheviks and Social Revolutionaries and other Duma members who were moderates, some of the men wearing frock coats, the women well dressed, a few officers among them.

"Let us pass! Let us sacrifice ourselves!" they cried to the puzzled sailors who explained they had their orders: no one was to go to the Winter Palace. Bryant was impressed because, as she wrote, "any body of unarmed people protesting against armed force is bound to be impressive." But as she listened to them, she began to suspect that

> the last thing the delegates wanted to do was to die, although they kept shouting that they did at the top of their voices. . . .
>
> Only twenty husky sailors barred the way. And to all arguments they continued stubborn and unmoved. "Go home and take poison," they advised the clamouring statesmen, "but don't expect to die here. . . ."
>
> "What will you do if we suddenly push forward?" asked one of the delegates.
>
> "We may give you a good spanking," answered the sailors, "but we will not kill one of you—not by a damn sight!"[19]

Then Minister of Supplies Prokopovich, who should by all rights have been closeted with his fellow ministers in the palace except that he was lucky enough to have been one of the ministers arrested before dawn that day, stepped forward, cleared his throat, and said in a quavering voice, "Comrades: let us return, let us refuse to be killed by *switchmen!*" Bryant had no idea what he meant by the word except that his tone implied an undistinguished category of citizen perhaps in the laboring class. But at the word the entire assemblage marched off in the direction of the City Duma.

The Americans showed their impressive passes, the sailors smiled and let them by. At the Red Arch they were told by a Red Guard in charge of a group of soldiers that the Winter Palace had just surrendered. In Bryant's words:

> We ran across the Square after the Bolshevik troops, a few bullets whistled by, but it was impossible to tell from which direction they came. Every window was lit up as if for a fête and we could see people moving about inside. Only a small entrance was open and we poured through the narrow door.

Inside the Junkers were being disarmed and given their liberty. They had to file past the door through which we had come. When those we had been with in the afternoon recognized us they waved friendly greetings. They looked relieved that it was all over, they had forgotten about the "one bullet" they were keeping for themselves.[20]

The reporters, the strangely subdued Gumberg among them, sat on a long bench by the door and watched the ministers descend the stairs, Tereschenko looking "so well groomed and so outraged." Their hiding places, first the Malachite Chamber overlooking the Neva and then a large room in the interior of the palace, where they sat around a table illumined by a single lamp shaded with newspaper, had been discovered. They could have been ousted at any time, but Antonov-Ovseenko, Chudnovsky, and Podvoisky were anxious to avoid bloodshed. As it was, Antonov-Ovseenko, a slight man with wild hair partly hidden by a black felt hat, pushed aside bayonets held by officer-cadets and informed the ministers that they were under arrest. Under ample guard they were to be taken to the Peter and Paul Fortress. The only resistance he encountered was from the crowd in the square outside, who wanted to lynch his prisoners. They would very soon afterward be released from the fortress so familiar to revolutionaries. The members of the Women's Battalion were disarmed and told to go home and to remove their uniforms. Bryant later hunted up a number of them and wrote of them compassionately.

On leaving the Winter Palace she dropped in at the City Duma about five o'clock the next morning and found those who had wished to perish, and others, calling for counter-measures and organizing the Committee for Saving the Country and the Revolution.

The singularly bloodless insurrection in Petrograd at an end (a total of six men were killed, all insurgents), Lenin made his appearance at the Second All-Russian Congress of Soviets on the night of October 26/November 8. To Bryant the short, stocky man with great bald head, eyes of Mongolian cast and penetrating gaze, speaking without gestures or oratorical flourishes, a popular hero whose simplicity was surprising, seemed cold—"sheer intellect" she pronounced him.[21]

Here is John Reed, reporting on that historic moment: "Now Lenin, gripping the edge of the reading stand, letting his little winking eyes travel over the crowd as he stood there waiting, apparently oblivious to the long-rolling ovation, which lasted several minutes. When it finished, he said simply, 'We shall now proceed to construct the Socialist order!' Again that overwhelming human roar."[22]

A sentence to be found in no record, for there were no minutes of the Congress, the stenographers having walked out along with the right-wing Socialists, but one verified by Trotsky as "quite in character with Lenin's way of thinking and style."[23]

Bryant on the other hand seems to be arguing with herself and veering from one position to another. Strangely, out of this amalgam, one thing stands clear: she is writing from conviction. She found Lenin "absorbed, cold, unattractive, impatient at interruption." Yet it intrigued her that this man who "writes treatises on philosophy and philosophic method" at the same time "appeals to the peasants with pamphlets that are marvels of simplicity."

She listens to his prosaic reading of the peace program he was urging for the "workers' and peasants' government"—as yet it had no other name—and thinks him "monotonous and thorough and . . . dogged." She sees Trotsky as "much more human than Lenine" (at the time her stories and book were published that was still the common spelling of his name in the West) and even declares, "It is not easy to write fairly of Lenine, I confess that." But she reminds her readers (and herself) that he is "an authority on economics" and "a master propagandist." And she insists:

"Lenine and Trotsky, especially Lenine, are symbols representing a new order. Lenine stands before us, spokesman of the Soviets, and the Soviets are Russia."[24]

The draft of the peace decree submitted by Lenin to the Congress proposed to open immediate negotiations for a just, democratic peace, without annexations or indemnities, to all the warring peoples and their governments, the Soviet terms to include the right of self-determination. It declared that all secret treaties signed by the old regime would be annulled and there would be no more secret diplomacy—all tsarist secret deals would be published, Lenin announced.

There were objections. The Left Social Revolutionaries and the Gorky faction of the Internationalist Mensheviks—smaller than the Martov group—had given support to the new regime the previous night but now said they had not been given time to study the document or to suggest amendments. Others felt that only a government representing *all* socialist parties could carry out such a program. Although delegates had voted that only representatives of parties might speak, one man arose and said he wanted to protest as an individual; he was allowed to and at once put his finger on the central dilemma. It was one born of Russia's present powerlessness except as a moral force or as a revolutionary propagandist. How could unjust peace proposals be resisted, with an army sick of fighting?

Lenin replied with care. What was important was that the *peoples* understand that the new Russian government would be receptive to any real peace offer. "We want a just peace, but we are not afraid of a revolutionary war. . . . If the German proletariat realizes that we are ready to consider all offers of peace, that will perhaps be the last drop which overflows the bowl—revolution will break out in Germany." For some of their terms "we shall fight to the end," but it would not be a sign of weakness to forego ultimatums to the governments which spurned their appeal.

"Our idea is that a state is strong when the people are politically conscious. It is strong when the people know everything, can form an opinion of everything and do everything consciously."[25]

The vote, called at ten-thirty-five, was unanimous. Men and women smiled, laughed, wept; caps were thrown in the air, strangers embraced. In the rear of the hall a voice began the "Internationale" and soon all joined in, including the entire presidium on the platform, headed by Lenin, all standing and singing. Bryant saw Kollontai visibly struggling to hold back tears. Reed and Bryant sang with the rest. Throughout the hall insofar as she could see, the eyes of delegates dimmed with tears, as the "Funeral March," with the words, "You fell in the fatal fight," in memory of the martyrs of the 1905 revolution buried on Mars Field, followed. Applause, stamping of feet, embraces.

Not all felt a part of the rejoicing, however. An Internationalist Menshevik editor's memoirs describe the scene vividly, after which he declares: "But I didn't believe in the victory, the success, the 'rightness,' or the historic mission of a Bolshevik regime. Sitting in the back seats, I watched this celebration with a heavy heart. How I longed to join in, and merge with this mass and its leaders in a single feeling! But I couldn't."[26]

There were others who, for a whole complex of feelings and reasons associated with long years of factional fighting, felt that way. Of these, some would actively fight the Bolsheviks for all they were worth, but many, including the memoirist Nikolai Nikolayevich Sukhanov (the pseudonym of Himmer), would work with them later. Still later perhaps they would be imprisoned as Sukhanov was in the purges of the thirties directed by Stalin.[27]

The delegates next voted on Lenin's proposed land reform decree. It provided for the expropriation without compensation of large privately owned estates and those owned by the Crown and the Church, all of which were to be handed over to peasant committees. The land "of ordinary peasants and ordinary Cossacks" would be retained by them, and freed of all taxes, mortgages, and debts. Local committees must carry out confiscation with strictest order and accounting.

This proposal written by Lenin, totaling only thirty lines, presented with the statement that it was the first duty "of the government of the workers' and peasants' revolution . . . to settle the land question . . . and satisfy the vast masses of poor peasants," was amplified by the Mandate to the Land Committees compiled from 242 demands put forward by local peasant Soviets. These had been collated by the Social Revolutionary party and published the previous August.

As the proposal was put to a vote, Williams, highly excited, demanded to know how the Social Revolutionaries could object to that one. Reed, needling him, asked why, if he was so certain, was he so worked up? Did he expect to settle there, behind a plow? Because he couldn't—hired hands were not to be allowed.[28] (A provision of the Mandate was, "The employment of hired labor is not permitted.")

The Social Revolutionaries did object, and the Mensheviks as well. Even the Left Social Revolutionaries and Internationalist Mensheviks were talking in excited groups, heads bobbing. But Lenin calmly said: "Voices are being raised here that the decree itself and the Mandate were drawn up by the Social Revolutionaries. What of it? Does it matter who drew them up? As a democratic government, we cannot ignore the decision of the masses of the people, even though we disagree with it. In the fire of experience . . . the peasants will themselves realize where the truth lies."[29]

This did not mean that Lenin had abandoned the Marxist tenet of large-scale organization of agriculture as essential to socialism. He was willing to go slow in order to rally the peasantry to the new government as a way of survival. Nor was he so far from the Marxist position as some in the hall may have thought him that night. The last word Engels had to say on the subject was that in order to enlist the small peasants in large-scale farming, not force but persuasion should be used.[30] (Such would be Lenin's position throughout his lifetime.)[31]

When at two in the morning the land decree vote was completed, only one vote was against it. Bryant wrote serenely in the coming months:

> When the Bolsheviki came into power they took over the land programme of the Socialist Revolutionists. This brought about great turmoil in the party [of the SRs.] The Right maintained that it was

their programme and no one had the right to steal it, but Spiridonova and all her wing only laughed.

"What difference does it make," she wanted to know, "who gives
the peasants their land—the principal thing is that they get it."[32]

The forces of reaction were mobilizing. Within a fortnight it became
known that Cossack troops of the Third Corps under General Krasnov
were marching on Petrograd, with Kerensky at their head. Bryant
watched the Red Guards start out to meet them:

> A cruel wind swept the wide streets and hurled the snow against
> the bleak buildings . . . they came, an amazing, inspired mass in
> thin, tattered coats. . . . They came pouring out of the factories in a
> mighty spontaneous *people's army*—men, women, and children . . .
> all out of step, in odds and ends of clothing . . . some only armed
> with spades. . . . It took infinite courage . . . to go out untrained and
> unequipped to meet the traditional bullies of Russia. . . . All of them
> expected to die. Suddenly they broke into a wailing, melancholy
> revolutionary song. I threw discretion to the winds and followed.

She was especially moved by the women, who "ran straight into the
fire without any weapons at all. It was terrifying to see them; they
were like animals protecting their young.

"The Cossacks seemed to be superstitious about it. They began to
retreat. The retreat grew into a rout. They abandoned their artillery,
their fine horses, they ran."[33]

During the fighting in the streets of Petrograd, Bryant came closer
to actual bullets than either Reed or Williams. While she flattened
herself against a doorway in St. Isaac's Square, Junkers fired a
machine gun from an armored car, killing seven in a street crowd.

A wire declaring the Kerensky forces smashed reached Smolny at
three in the morning of October 31/November 12. Kerensky fled in
disguise. Though General Krasnov was taken to the Peter and Paul
Fortress, it was not for long; he was paroled shortly and became one of
the most ruthless and ambitious of the generals recruiting counterrevolutionaries in the South.

In contrast to Petrograd, in Moscow there was heavy resistance.
The pro-Soviet forces were victors, but at enormous cost. Louise
Bryant and John Reed arrived on the first train to enter Moscow after
six days of intense fighting. Soldiers were digging an enormous trench
in frozen snow-covered ground near the north wall of the Kremlin, by
the light of sputtering torches stuck on poles. Of the total of eight
hundred dead, five hundred were Red Guards and soldiers.

The next morning, in bitter cold, Bryant and Reed stood on a mound of newly turned earth and watched wave after wave of people pouring through the white arched gateway of the old Tartar city, filling Red Square. Young soldiers bore the rough wooden coffins, painted red. Bryant would write of the solemn magnificance of the Red Burial: "Slowly, rhythmically they moved along, like a great operatic pageant symbolizing the long, bitter struggle of the masses throughout the vast intricate fabric of history."[34]

On November 18/December 1 both Williams and Reed went to work for the Bureau of International Revolutionary Propaganda for a salary of fifty roubles a month, helping get out such revolutionary newspapers as *Die Fackel (The Torch)*. Tons of newspapers and fliers went by train daily to be distributed along enemy fronts, smuggled into Germany, and circulated among prisoner-of-war camps in Russia.

When Bryant began to be trailed by spies, Reed thought it might be because of him, and was seriously worried. Bryant herself with a good deal of logic attributed the spies to her own work. She was then attending meetings of prisoners in a room next to the propaganda bureau. In her words:

> Secret meetings were held in the Foreign Office, where German and Austrian prisoners came to plot revolution in their own countries. I was the only woman ever present. We had to sign our names when we went in, as if we were making a death pact and it was truly a dangerous business. Whoever signed was somehow discovered and thenceforth marked by both the monarchists and their co-workers, the German agents.[35]

But Bryant had her own protectors who began spying on the spies. After the editor of Gorky's *Novaya Zhizn (New Life)*—that would be N. N. Himmer, although she does not give the name—told Bryant she was being followed by one of the most notorious of the tsar's secret police, she and Reed moved.[36] She was, however, followed into the Taurida Palace by two spies, who were seized, along with their notebooks filled with data on Bryant's comings and goings, and landed in Peter and Paul Fortress. A month later the Bolsheviks let them go, "as they do most every one else they arrest, on the promise to seek honest employment," she wrote.[37] She was critical but deeply understanding of this period, brief and poignant, when a climate of optimism made the Bolsheviks far more lenient than their rhetoric would suggest.

As the year drew to a close, debate over Brest-Litovsk, a town in the Polish-Ukrainian plain, now the headquarters of the eastern German armies where a Russian delegation met with spokesmen for the German high command, overshadowed all else. It was a deeply disturbed period. Passions ran high. There were powerful arguments on each side. A. A. Joffe, head of the first delegation, grappled with the big problem. In the interest of world revolution should the Bolsheviks stand on principle and refuse to make any peace that failed to observe the right of self-determination? Or would it be even more likely to serve world revolution to maintain the government that miraculously prevailed after almost two months, in a smaller area, if they accepted the loss of parts of Livonia and Estonia, as Minister of Foreign Affairs Kuhlman of Germany demanded?

In Williams's recollection, he and Reed and others in the group Kollontai called the "internationalist reporters" at first vacillated back and forth,[38] and certainly Bryant did, for not only Maria Spiridonova was strongly against making peace but also Aleksandra Kollontai—and fighting Lenin fiercely over it. It was understandable that the Americans would be swayed for a time one way, then another. Some of the finest oratorical talent of the day was supporting Nikolai Bukharin, the leader of the revolutionary war group. Trotsky was somewhere between Bukharin and Lenin; his position shifted, and eventually he supported Lenin.

The debate over a peace hard to take or a war seemingly impossible to win still raged as Bryant departed for home. Reed wanted to stay for the Third All-Russian Congress. For Christmas she had written a poem to him that ended: "I want you to know that sometimes when I am thinking/About you/I have a lump in my throat/And I am a little bit awed./You are the finest person I know/On both sides of the world/And it is a nice privilege to be your comrade."[39]

10.
Bohemia in Retreat

ON JANUARY 7/20, 1918, Louise Bryant, Bessie Beatty, and Madeleine Doty left Petrograd in a driving snowstorm, the thermometer at twenty degrees below zero, on the last train to get through Finland, where civil war raged and the Whites were massacring Red Guards. From Tornio, Finland, they crossed a frozen river into Haparanda, Sweden, borne on a Finnish sled; the three journalists lay cozily beneath heavy fur rugs while the driver was exposed to the elements.[1]

From Stockholm they went to Christiania (Oslo), Norway, where at the American Legation Bryant presented a letter of introduction from Raymond Robins to Major James Carson Breckinridge, U.S.M.C., naval attaché. Robins wrote that any assistance he was able to secure for her to depart for the United States on the first boat leaving Christiania would "be greatly appreciated by me."[2]

Only with the recent release of State Department records through the Freedom of Information Act has the attention Washington paid to the departure from Russia of Louise Bryant become known. Had it not been for the Robins letter and the swiftness with which young Breckinridge acted in getting her and her associates off for New York, it appears likely that she might have been held hostage there for weeks, as Reed shortly would be.

Major Breckinridge's outlook regarding the workers' and peasants' government, under whose aegis Louise Bryant was traveling, had much in common with that of Colonel Robins, the head of the American Red Cross in Russia. The son of a former ambassador to tsarist Russia, Breckinridge had lived in St. Petersburg with his family at the age of seventeen, studying with private tutors for a year or more, and his observations of the autocracy made for a sympathetic understanding of the Revolution.[3]

On February 7 Bryant, Beatty, and Doty departed on the steamer *Bergensfjord* for New York. On the same date a telegram in cipher marked "Urgent," signed by Secretary of State Robert Lansing, left Washington for Christiania ordering that no passport of John Reed's wife, "alias Louise Bryant," be verified without authorization from the Department.[4] It did not arrive until February 8, a day after her departure, the legation informed Washington.[5]

On the steamer with the young women was Brigadier General William V. Judson, military attaché at the embassy in Petrograd until December 19/January 1, on which date he was suddenly ordered recalled. Originally violently opposed to Kerensky's fall, Judson was won over when Colonel Robins decided the Lenin-Trotsky regime was viable and became a strong apostle of U.S. cooperation with the Soviets. Judson had interviewed Trotsky prior to the peace parleys—as an individual, unofficially, *Izvestia* reported—and Reed, Bryant knew, had blamed Edgar Sisson's indiscretion for his recall.[6]

Bryant and her companions found Judson far from crestfallen, however. Rather, he seemed to view his recall as a means of reaching ears in Washington with his assessment of the Bolsheviks.[7] Excerpts from Judson's diary made on board the *Bergensfjord* are illuminating.[8]

They arrived in New York February 18. Bryant took a room in the Brevoort Hotel and plunged into writing articles on what she had seen and heard in Russia, which she hoped to sell to newspapers. Occasionally she emerged, walking to favored haunts such as the Three Steps Down restaurant or Sari's. Villagers walked along in the cold, heads bent against the wind: if they spoke to her it was but briefly. Talk was, she sensed, dangerous these days. She felt out of touch with all about her, her mind on Russia.

Bryant felt strangely alien in the Village, more so than she ever felt in Petrograd. Even physically the old Bohemia had given way to something new and brassy. Tourists and the bourgeoisie from uptown, out slumming for the evening, poured into the quiet winding streets. Rents had gone up with wartime affluence, as had prices. Did anything remain of the Bohemian spirit that had made for an unselfish life? Many people who had been low in funds but high in humanity had either moved away or were infected by the new commercialism.

In the old days lunch at Gonfarone's, at Marie's, or Mori's, or Angelina's, still on Greenwich Street today, or Mama Bertelotti's under the now extinct Third Avenue elevated structure, cost fifteen cents; a nickel for minestrone and bread and butter, a nickel for red wine, and another nickel for a tip. All was changed. Tearooms had mushroomed, the decor was cute, and waiters and doormen in *costume* in basement restaurants justified the higher prices. Romany Marie had been so successful in providing "gypsies" that she had opened other tearooms with the same motif.

More than a few whom Bryant had known as faithful anarchists or Socialists were now shoveling in money. Romany Marie had been a follower of Emma Goldman, ushering and collecting dimes at her meetings on the East Side. Christine Ell, who fed the Provincetown Players from her kitchen at prices just above cost, now strode around the Village streets with a cub leopard on a leash. In addition there were repulsive new types such as Guido Bruno, playing up to the hick's concept of the Village; his garret on Washington Square was the first stop for tourists who paid fifty cents to see "the long-haired men and the short-haired women." He was sure to have on hand a few hungry freaks he introduced as geniuses.

So fashionable had Bruno become that Frank Harris, editor of *Pearson's Magazine*, agreed to give evening lectures where Bruno played impresario on lower Fifth Avenue. Even more surprising, he was said to have been steered to Harris by Djuna Barnes. Djuna had a commanding place in the Village. Not only was she a towering intellectual, but it was said she had not hesitated to kick a policeman in the bottom when he tried to subdue an effervescent parade celebrating the Bolshevik takeover.[9]

Before Bryant had left the Village for Paris, within the space of a single block it was possible to see Leon Trotsky taking tea in the Purple Pup, above which Emma Goldman resided and held court, Gene O'Neill hunched over a drink in the Hell Hole, and the poet Maxwell Bodenheim selling the *Little Review* on the street. Now all had disappeared from view, and issues of the *Little Review* were seized by authorities as they appeared. Not that that prevented Margaret Anderson and Jane Heap from continuing to publish another section of James Joyce's *Ulysses* in following issues.

Several new publications were both brisk and determinedly zany, but when it came to the war, sober as the *Saturday Evening Post*. Chief among the magazines was the *Quill*, started in June 1917 by Arthur Moss and, when he went off to war, bequeathed to Bobby Edwards. Edwards had not cared much for Village radicals: they were too cerebral. Now that so many had moved, or had begun to limit their protest to art, he was more comfortable. The *Quill* was a money-maker.

The theme of the day was not protest of any kind, but enjoyment. There was a mindless kind of sexiness in the new magazines. Some original verse was published by Joe Klinger's *Pagan* and the *Greenwich Village Spectator*. Bruno issued the *Greenwich Village* and *Bruno's Weekly*. None of these magazines commented that America's culture was a war casualty; they unwittingly advertised the fact. Many conscientious objectors had been sent to prison, and Roger Baldwin was soon to go, but the tone of the new Village was happiness. No space was available for martyrs.

The trend would produce shortly after the war the lavishly hand-some *Playboy* put out by Egmont Arens. Parry describes the same horseplay and crazy-cat antics evident in the *Quill* as dominating "even the beautiful *Playboy*."[10]

The war and the gathering storm of repression—soon to break in its totality—forced many Village radicals to reappraise their radicalism. Bryant heard about the various defections from the ranks of contributors to *The Masses*. The same division marked the old Provincetown Players. She was glad to learn that Max and Crystal Eastman were starting another magazine, the *Liberator*, and that they would use Reed's long piece, "The Rising of the Proletariat."[11]

Many of those Bryant knew were absent from the Village that winter. Mary Heaton Vorse had joined the Red Cross and was in Europe writing and collecting material for articles. Susan Glaspell and Jig Cook were warm in their greetings, but Cook was downcast by his problems with the feuding Provincetown Players, and Susan had her hands full building up his morale and making a living for them from her writing. She was also writing three new plays for the Provincetown, among them *The Verge*, to be condemned by the tiresome Hapgood as an "expression of half-mad feminism."[12]

Absent also was the veteran writer for *The Masses*, Horatio Winslow, now a captain; after the armistice he would go to Archangel with the American Expeditionary Forces to help the White Guards annihilate the Reds. William English Walling, Frank Bohn, and Arthur Bullard had taken flying leaps into the war camp, and George Bellows was turning out propaganda for the war.

Of more personal concern than any other absence was the Village's temporary loss of Andrew Dasburg. He and Bobby Jones were visiting Mabel Dodge and her husband, Maurice Sterne, in Taos, New Mexico.[13] Bryant especially felt his absence a loss as some Villagers seemed skittish of her, barely speaking and hurrying on. It was her initial experience with the peculiarly American virus, for such it would become, of guilt by association.

O'Neill was in Provincetown, working on *Beyond the Horizon,* although it would be two more years before it was produced on Broadway, to wide acclaim. When Bryant wrote him a few days before she and Reed sailed in August, he knew he had definitely lost her. He brooded over it unhappily and longed for companionship with a woman. He became interested in Dorothy Day, nineteen and beautiful, who wanted to be a writer. She never fell in love with O'Neill, but was spellbound by his genius, never tiring of sitting in the Hell Hole with him and hearing him recite poetry.

When O'Neill saw Agnes Boulton in the Hell Hole waiting for Christine Ell, he stared at her as if he seeing a ghost, struck by her resemblance to Louise Bryant. Often Dorothy Day and O'Neill made a foursome with Boulton and Harold DePolo. Dorothy considered Boulton "much better-looking than Louise, with more chiseled features, but without Louise's brains and sophistication." But, shown photos of Louise, she saw "a surprising vulnerability about the eyes." It occurred to her, too, that as DePolo was married, Boulton was more sophisticated than she seemed.

Basically Dorothy Day mistrusted the kind of love that O'Neill could offer anyone. She had heard him dwell on the suffering he underwent at Louise's hands and remained unimpressed. "Gene fell in love with Louise first of all because Jack loved her," she said. "Gene needed a hopeless love, Jack was more in love with Louise than Gene was or ever could be. All Gene's experiences were 'copy' to him. So I watched the Agnes-Gene association and hoped she would not be too hurt."[14]

Boulton was with O'Neill when he left the Village and settled down to writing in earnest in Provincetown. All was going well and he had finally quit telling her of his pain in losing Bryant and Reed, when he had a letter from Bryant after her arrival from Russia. She wanted to see him, and he thought he should go into the city and talk to her. Boulton was convinced that Bryant had cut short her stay in Russia because she had heard that she and O'Neill were living together.

O'Neill handed her the letter to read, but even before she read it, she wrote, "this woman was invested, in my mind, with all the wiles of the serpent." She had seen O'Neill's face as he read the letter; "I could see him remembering all the dark passionate travail of their love. . . ."

One of Bryant's letters, according to Boulton's purely undocumented account, hinted that Reed, to make her happy, had agreed to
speed her on her way. But at that point Boulton put her foot down,
declared she would not let O'Neill go to New York—and saw her lover
look admiringly at her. He did not go, and in the coming April, with a
little boost from a writer, Alice Woods Ullman, they were married. [15]

It happened that this Boulton portrait of a Louise Bryant so open
about her loves as to discuss O'Neill with Reed and tell him the
playwright needed her more does not square with the Bryant revealed
in dozens of letters she wrote Reed. Boulton herself was rather shy
and easily put upon. (When Agnes was lunching with Helen and
Harold DePolo in Provincetown, O'Neill burst in and roughly and
forcibly pulled her homeward. He could not bear to be alone for an
hour. He was, DePolo said, "the most possessive and jealous man who
ever lived.")[16] Attributing to Bryant her own docility, Boulton apparently believed that Louise was a pawn for Reed to move about and
his the decision whether she take the Russian Revolution or O'Neill.
It had no bearing on the actual Louise Bryant.

In the winter of 1927–28 when O'Neill was claimed by fame and
riches, he abandoned Agnes Boulton and their two children for
Carlotta Monterey—who, unlike either Boulton or Bryant, had a
talent for managing a husband and a husband's business affairs.

In a letter written shortly before her death Bryant remembers her
correspondence with O'Neill as having taken place when she was in
Petrograd. If she was in fact rejected by him, she reveals only scorn
for O'Neill's betrayal not of Louise Bryant but of the revolution
O'Neill once applauded—before there was an actual revolution overseas and a mounting wave of reaction at home. To her he became a
"counterrevolutionary," writing her, according to her recollection,
that he "took no interest in the war or the Russian Revolution."[17]

Bryant worked steadily on her articles on the October Revolution,
pounding out copy appealing for understanding of the gargantuan
problems facing the new regime. When she got out a book based on
the stories, she wrote in the introduction:

> Socialism is here, whether we like it or not—just as woman
> suffrage is here—and it spreads with the years. In Russia the socialist
> state is an accomplished fact . . . if it must fail because it is
> premature, it is nevertheless real and must have tremendous effect
> on all that follows. . . . The most significant fact is that it will not fail
> from *inside* pressure. Only *outside,* foreign, hostile intervention can
> destroy it.

. . . We must somehow make an honest effort to understand what is happening in Russia.[18]

With the future of the Revolution uncertain, it was not enough simply to write about it, nor would Bryant have been allowed to do so uninterruptedly. Radicals throughout the country were aroused, and Bryant, Scott Nearing, and many others sent cables pledging moral support, money, and their lives. To Boris Reinstein, who headed the International Propaganda division of the Foreign Office, she cabled:

"All American revolutionists aroused by German advance. Offer their services and their lives to the saving of the Russian revolution and world freedom. Are organizing revolutionary army. Mass meetings, tremendous sentiment. Beg Russians to hold out for original peace formula. Louise Bryant."

To Spiridonova she cabled, "All American revolutionists offer their sympathy and their lives to the Russian revolutionists in this hour of peril. . . . I will come back and fight with many American Socialists. Louise Bryant."

Crystal Eastman pledged the membership of her Women's Peace Party to work for official recognition of the Bolsheviks and expressed her Party's firm belief in the Bolsheviks' "courage, wisdom and ultimate triumph, and our horror at the brutal demands of German autocracy."[19]

It is not surprising that the radicals, Marxists included, in America were anguished and confused as to the real situation, as many in Russia also were, including fiery young Bolsheviks. None was more aware of the deep emotions of the idealists who opposed any signing of the peace with Germany than Lenin; he realized that among his fiercest opponents most were guided by principle.

Nevertheless, before her book came out Bryant changed her position and wrote: "Lenine wanted to accept the first German peace terms, bad as they were; Trotsky wanted to fight for better ones. Trotsky it was who staged the Brest-Litovsk negotiations and insisted that the negotiations be public. He played for three things: that the Allies join in, that the German revolution commence and that the aims of the Soviets be known throughout the world. Lenine believed that it was absolutely necessary to have a respite, time to firmly establish the Soviet state and to organize an army and propaganda against the German government. Everything turned out as he predicted at Brest. It was all disastrous, yet President Wilson, himself, praised the honesty of Trotsky's stand. Trotsky did not want to sign the treaty and refused to do so. . . . Both men now agree that a huge fighting force is necessary for Russia. Lenine's idea is to save as much of Russia as possible by a temporary peace and, in the meantime, to build up the army, systematically, instead of trying to fight trained German soldiers with hastily constructed forces. To use his own words:

" 'We are compelled to submit to a distressing peace. It will not stop revolution in Germany. We shall now begin to prepare a revolutionary army, not by phrases and exclamations . . . but by organised work, by the creation of a serious, national, mighty army.' "[20]

Bryant worked on her articles while her heart was torn both for the Russians and for Reed. She had heard nothing from him, and sensed some awful plight—and the German armies still marched on Petrograd.

The days were filled with tension not only for Bryant but for multitudes of men and women, foreign-born and native socialists, for whom the triumph of October had heralded world revolution. "The international party / Shall be the human race." As the German troops had advanced, the fear was great that the workers' government (at the time it was known by no other name) would be crushed. Labor and Socialist papers ran articles and even poems protesting such a disaster. The *Ladies' Garment Worker* for February 1918 carried a poem on the subject by Louis Untermeyer with the opening lines:

> God, give us strength these days—
> Burn us with one desire;
> To smother this murderous blaze,
> Beat back these flames with fire.[21]

Bryant, speaking at a meeting of three branches of the Socialist Party in New York, according to the New York *Call* of March 21, "brought home the suffering which revolutionary Russia is enduring in such a . . . forcible manner that a committee of Bolshevik relief was immediately formed." A telegram was sent that night from the meeting to the President asking that a ship be set aside for the purpose of sending food and clothing to Russia.[22]

Still Bryant had no letter from Reed. The day after her arrival a delayed Petrograd dispatch in *The New York Times* reported he had left Russia as a private citizen, his appointment as general consul canceled. Not until February 28, when Steffens appeared at her hotel with a curious proposal, did she learn that Reed was in Christiania. As she wrote:

"Steffens arrived at the Brevoort Hotel one evening with someone from the Bureau of Public Information of the State Department and told me that they wanted Jack to go back to Russia and persuade Lenin that the United States would stand by the Soviets if they were reasonable. I didn't like the idea at all."[23] She agreed to sign one cable with Steffens: "Don't return, await instructions." She refused to sign a second, which was signed by Steffens alone: "Trotsky making epochal blunder doubting Wilson literal sincerity. If you can and will change Trotsky's and Lenin's attitudes you can render historical international service."[24]

Reed's reply was sent to Bryant in care of Roger Baldwin. If a group of revolutionary leaders, he said, including Debs and Bill Haywood, asked him to return to Russia, he would; otherwise he would not.[25] Baldwin took the cable to her himself—speedily, on the insistence of Madeleine Doty (whom he would marry in 1920). He found Bryant calm and controlled. No tears, but a visible pallor. She said little, and that to the point. He came away feeling that she would do whatever needed to be done, and competently.[26]

(Ever afterward Bryant harbored misgivings about Steffens. In the same note to Granville Hicks in which she described the cables, written not long before her death, she added: "I remembered how Steffens persuaded the McNamar[a] brothers into confessing. He told them he had the word of the authorities that they would get light sentences if they confessed. They got *life sentences!* Ask Steff how many times in the last twenty years or *if ever* he went to see these two Irish boys."[27]

Bryant wrote Reed daily and, when she had it, sent money. Not a single letter reached him. She had bombarded the authorities with demands for an investigation to learn his whereabouts. Now that she knew where he was, she continued to demand the reasons for his exile but no explanation was made. A hurriedly scrawled note from Crystal Eastman to Bryant said Eugen Boissevain had had word from Secretary of State Lansing "that Jack is at Christiania and wants $300." Crystal asked Louise: "Do you suppose he's coming home? Do you think we could cable him direct? And what do you think we ought to say?"[28] What Bryant feared was that Reed might not be permitted to come. There still was no letter from him.

Worried sick over Reed, worried too over the fate of the Revolution, Bryant was forced to keep a stiff upper lip. Perhaps she was fortified by the memory of Grandfather Say's teachings. The need to complete her newspaper series gave her added discipline. To do so she had to have some faith in the essential good sense of ordinary newspaper readers. She thought of them as distinct from the government, truly believing that many average readers could still be reached.

This springtime of 1918 in the United States was a time of heightened contradictions. Openmindedness about the new Russian experiment in cities and the hinterland coexisted with the intensified patriotism of wartime. Women flocked to badly fumigated war plants to take the places of men in the training camps and trenches. Machines hummed while they sang "Keep the home fires burning/ While our hearts are yearning." In radium-dial watch plants young women, told by foremen that "it'll put color in your cheeks,"*[29] rolled the tips of their brushes in their lips (it also made their work go faster).

Vigilantes in the South and Midwest hunted out "slackers" at the same time that interest was quickening in the October Revolution. No matter what appeared on their editorial pages, newspaper editors knew that feature stories with first-hand knowledge of the Revolution sold papers. The conservative and Republican Philadelphia *Public Ledger* syndicate bought Bryant's thirty-two stories and sold them to Hearst's *New York American* and to more than one hundred newspapers over the United States and Canada.

At last Bryant had a letter from Reed, written March 27. In the entire period, more than seven weeks while he was beached in Norway, it was the only letter of his that the State Department permitted to reach his wife. It had been sent in care of Sonya Levien of the *Metropolitan*. The cartoonist Bob Minor, with Steffens's blessing bound for Russia, had stopped in Christiania to see Reed who was of course overjoyed to have direct word that Louise was all right.

"He also delivered to me," wrote Reed, "the 'instructions' concerning which Steffens and you telegraphed. I understand how they look at things over there, but really, from my viewpoint, it looks absolutely ridiculous. I cannot do what Steffens wants."

Minor, who was traveling on *Public Ledger* accreditation arranged by Steffens, had more news for him: Louise would be graciously allowed by the government to join Reed in Norway. Fearful as she was that some mysterious force might keep him from returning, this news deepened her fear. In the misery of isolation he asked:

> But how can we support ourselves here, or in Russia? Some people here are trying to make up their minds to offer me a job—and of course if they do that, we can get along all right. At present, however, the authorities don't want me to stay in this country,

---

*So it did, too, before their teeth began to fall out and they lost arms or legs and died slowly of radium poisoning.

even—so it doesn't look very hopeful that I shall be able to do much.
. . . Anyway, my dearest, don't fail to come *immediately* if you can
arrange some way of settling the money question. . . . I do so want
to see you![30]

What Bryant did not know, and Reed could only suspect, was that
his long sojourn in Norway, an archetypal sample of irrational bureaucracy, was the work of a vindictive ex-newspaperman with
power—Edgar Sisson. Years later in his account of the sleuthing he
did for George Creel's Committee on Public Information, Sisson
writes that it was he who arranged for Reed's exile.

Reed, he said, left Russia "with so much rumor circulating as to
what he was to do upon his return to the United States that it seemed
advisable that he should be received at home with some care. He was
delayed so long in Sweden [sic] that I reached the United States not
long after he did. In the State Department . . . I found waiting for me
his papers."[31]

Sisson's implication, that the reason he must keep Reed inoperable
in Scandinavia was his fear Reed would serve as consul for the
Bolsheviks, was a hoax. He knew the consulship had been withdrawn;
he had played a role in having that done.

Albert Rhys Williams, in a posthumously published book, *Journey
Into Revolution: Petrograd 1917–1918*, told the story, both why Reed
was kept in Christiania for seven weeks, and why he lost the consul-
ship Trotsky had offered. He reveals that Robins and Sisson agreed
with Ambassador Francis that for Reed to come home as an official
Bolshevik consul would not help the tenuous relations with the
Soviets which Francis had used Robins to establish. Francis left it to
Robins to decide how the Bolsheviks should be persuaded of this;
Robins asked Gumberg, who was then working with him, to take care
of it, and Gumberg was happy to oblige.[32]

Early in the morning of April 28 Louise Bryant was at the dock
waiting for Reed. But she learned that Naval Intelligence agents had
boarded the ship and seized all his papers, posters, newspaper files,
literature on the Revolution, and his notes on day-to-day events.

It was a daylong wait for her. She had summoned a Croton friend,
the lawyer Dudley Field Malone, who was with her when the agents
released Reed at nightfall. Malone assured them that he would
produce Reed in court the next morning for arraignment in the old
Masses case, although the trial had ended the previous day in a hung
jury.[33]

After the long, wearing hours at the pier, to be swept up in his arms, to cling to him in the taxi while they headed for the Brevoort, was enough for Louise. All she had to tell him and ask him could wait. He was back. Her mounting paranoia about whether they would ever be together again was dispelled. For the time being they had found each other. She knew he would not long be content to visit with her, to shut the world out and be alone with her happily. But she too had her work to do now.

They held fast to each other, rejoicing in his return. In the coming months she would help him battle discouragement as he waited for the return of his Russian materials and the chance to start his book.

11.
In Search of Revolution

BRYANT'S RECURRENTLY EXPRESSED longing for Reed to take time "to visit" with her again went unfulfilled as he began answering every request that came in to speak on Russia. She knew the need of it, both for his morale and because of the objective situation, for his was a powerful voice raised in warning against intervention. At the same time her fears of his going to prison, to haunt her so long as he lived, grew apace as his speaking led to two more indictments.

A June 1 street meeting in Philadelphia, growing out of a revocation of a permit for a hall, resulted in charges of "inciting to riot," uttering seditious remarks, and assault and battery. On September 13 he spoke on intervention, which by midsummer had become a reality, at Hunt's Point Palace in the Bronx, for which he was again charged with making seditious utterances. As the prosecution had decided in favor of a second trial of the *Masses* editors, he faced that trial in the autumn.

Despite all this activity, Reed was restive and often gloomy, for until he obtained his papers from Washington he could not begin on his book. By the time he returned from Norway, Bryant's newspaper articles had been running for two weeks and were continuing to appear daily. A letter he wrote to Steffens June 9 spoke almost wistfully of Bryant's stories:

> I started a big newspaper syndicate series, like Louise's, but the newspapers were afraid to touch them; some of them sent the stuff back after it was in type. Then Collier's took a story, put it in type, and sent it back. Oswald Villard [of *The Nation*] told me he would be suppressed if he published John Reed!

He had a contract with Macmillan for a book on the Revolution, he told Steffens, but he could not write it without his papers, and in two months' time the State Department had done nothing.

> I am therefore unable to write a word of the greatest story of my life, and one of the greatest in the world. I am blocked. Do you know any way to have my papers sent to me? If they don't come pretty soon it will be too late for my book—MacMillan's won't take it.

He felt "sort of flat—and stale." His brother was going to France in a week with the American Expeditionary Force (A.E.F.). He added that he believed intervention "will be pulled off."

> Excuse the depression. I don't see why I chose this low, grey moment in which to write you. I felt pretty good this morning, and probably will tomorrow morning.[1]

Steffens's reply tells much about the retreat of many intellectuals and liberals. It was "the Reactionaries" who prevented the war from ending "in reasonable progress," Jack was wrong "to buck this thing."

> Really, I think it is wrong to try to tell the truth now. We must wait. You must wait. . . . Write, but don't publish.

Closing, Steffens adopted his familiar stance, that of the assured, worldly-wise man who could laugh tolerantly at youngsters for their idealism. "Write again, and I will, Jack. The last letter from Louise was more like a cry than a letter. She said among other things that she didn't believe people wanted what they said they wanted! I'm afraid Louise is seeing the world."[2]

But Reed and Louise knew that it was Steffens who was daydreaming and unworldly in this time of crisis, continuing to hero-worship President Wilson. They themselves, despite Reed's occasional moods of despair or depression, were supremely sure of themselves, of the Revolution they defended. The more they spoke and traveled in the years 1918–19, the more the insatiable curiosity concerning the Bolshevik triumph manifested itself over the country. The flight of the radicals in the Village became unimportant. In less than a year's time Steffens would come under Lenin's spell and return from Russia to tell Bernard Baruch: "I have been over into the future, and it works."[3]

Obviously Reed had not forgotten for a moment what he had told Albert Rhys Williams in 1917: "What counts is what we do when we go home."[4] So he wrestled with the problem of organizing the revolutionary forces in America, although only that summer of 1918 had he become a member of the Socialist Party. Hicks declares that

Reed had "discussed plans with the Bolshevik leaders," although "exactly what form the organization should take he did not know." But in setting himself "the task of organizing Bolshevism in America"[5] it is clear that his objective was one of heroic proportions and, moreover, one to which he could bring only untried and imperfect skills. He went at it doggedly, conscientiously, to keep the faith. It weighed on him even in this summer interlude, which he conceded was not the moment for revolution. As he waited for and looked forward to the revolutionary moment for militant action, he was not easy to get along with.

Reed, whom some friends faulted for his sombre mood and critics found harsh and bitter, even arrogant, would have preferred to write poetry but drove himself to grapple with revolutionary tactics. Some saw in both Reed and Bryant at this time people intent on figuring out the correct next revolutionary steps, very much like Lenin brooding in 1901 over his pamphlet, *What Is To Be Done?* But Bryant was hard at work putting her book together.

There must have been occasional social evenings for them, however, when Reed was not speaking in Chicago or Detroit or elsewhere. William Carlos Williams, known to the Village more as a poet than pediatrician, which profession he practiced in Paterson, New Jersey, in writing of parties around Fourteenth Street, remembered

> one night when Reed showed up. A plump, good-natured guy who had taken the bit in his teeth and was heading out. He played with the poem but was not primarily interested in writing. The story went around that he was a sick man, had already had one kidney resected, but it didn't seem to put much of a crimp in his style. He looked at us as if he couldn't quite make out what we were up to, half-amused, half-puzzled. Louise Bryant, his wife, who was with him that night, had on a heavy, very heavy, white silk skirt so woven that it hung over the curve of her buttocks like the strands of a glistening waterfall. There could have been nothing under it, for it followed the very crease between the buttocks in its fall. No fault there. She too looked to be outward bound along with John of Portland, Oregon. Wise man he to get started early.[6]

Reed was confident that revolution was imminent. To Roger Baldwin, who was facing trial as a conscientious objector (and would be sentenced to a year in jail October 30), Reed was encouraging, assuring him that the workers would set him free long before his sentence ended.[7] To Louis Waldman, soon to be elected to the State Assembly on a Socialist ticket, he gave equally confident advice. A cutter in his youth, active in the International Ladies' Garment Workers Union, Waldman put himself through college and became an engineer; at the time he was studying law at New York University. He describes how Reed, putting his arm affectionately about Waldman's shoulder one night at the Civic Club, said:

> "Louis, stop wasting your time running for the Assembly and stupid things like that. And above all, don't bother studying law. By the time you finish your course there'll be no more lawyers. Do you know what we did to your high and mighty members of the Bar in Russia? We set them cleaning cesspools for the proletariat!" Reed laughed uproariously and went on: "Louis, my boy, stick to engineering. The American Soviets will be able to use engineers, even if they're political reformists."[8]

"Jack was an attractive, romantic person," Waldman said more recently. "He returned from Russia convinced the proletariat here was about to rise. Jack was in, up to his neck—a propagandist. And Louise was with him all the way. She always championed everything Jack said."[9]

Not everyone found Reed so bumptious, however. Sherwood Anderson met him one night on Fifth Avenue and Ninth Street and they stopped to talk. Anderson wondered aloud whether poets should lie low and try to get an understanding, or give themselves to the fight. Reed did not know about others, but for himself, his choice was made, one of political action over poetry.[10] It could not have been an easy choice. Nor did he ever cease to believe that he would get back to poetry.

In the summer of 1918 Reed spoke at Cambridge in the Harvard Union, the poet Conrad Aiken recalled. Aiken was sitting in the front row and when Reed left the platform he went at once to Aiken and greeted him warmly. "We were very close," said Aiken. They did not talk of poetry—although Aiken admired him as a "damned good poet." At opposite poles on the Bolshevik Revolution, that is what they spoke of for ten or fifteen minutes, remaining friendly and affectionate. "I told him, 'Jack, you're going to regret it.' And he said, 'No, I'm not.'

"He looked very much the same. Still with that young look; a vigorous, vital, gay person. He sparkled. Loved life, always. That was Jack. It was the last time I saw him."[11]

Bryant also spoke in Boston, addressing "an exciting meeting" in the Tremont Temple on her Russian experiences. A ninety-year-old Marxist, S. D. Levine, remembered hearing her and enjoying it.[12]

Scott Nearing heard both Reed and Bryant speak. Judging them only as speakers, in a period that abounded with great labor platform artists, he had scant regard for either of them. But, he admitted, they had a subject![13]

Bryant and Bessie Beatty were invited to speak at one of the Heterodoxy's fortnightly luncheons.[14] This fascinating group of women, whose speakers always were women, was described by Mabel Dodge Luhan as "fine, daring, rather joyous and independent women."[15] The members were all suffragists or feminists—two groups far from synonymous. All were women who had achieved high status in their chosen fields of work and were picked solely on the basis of their own contributions, without consideration of who their fathers, husbands, brothers, or lovers were. Reporters were barred.

Bryant and Reed since their Russian experience were fired with a sense of urgency to spread understanding of the Bolsheviks and to arouse a protest against intervention. They were more closely bound now. Neither doubted that the social revolution would spread worldwide, breaking down the system until the tyrants fell and the wretched inherited the earth. This gave a new dimension to their marriage, but it did not mean that all ran smoothly or that when Reed was beset by doubts and discouragement Bryant was not affected.

If Reed when in the same city with her felt "distressingly lonely" much of the time,[16] it is not surprising that she felt shut out and became resentful. Added to all this was the fact that Reed now seemed to be out of town more often than when he traveled on a *Metropolitan* expense account, whether it was to make speeches, which provided some income as well as furthering enlightenment, or to cover stories for the *Liberator*—without pay but allowed a modest expense budget.

In those months in Russia each had become more serious, more focused. Upton Sinclair only betrayed his naiveté in calling Reed at this time "the playboy of the social revolution."[17] Also unjust was the pronouncement of one young woman, Isobel Walker, just emerged from Columbia College as a starry-eyed revolutionary, that Louise Bryant was "frivolous" because she came home in a Russian fur coat and hat. For that she was taken to task by Mary Heaton Vorse. "Exactly," said the older woman, "and Louise is fighting for the revolution. That's what it's for—so everyone can have a fur coat." "It was my first lesson in revolution," said Isobel Walker Soule.[18]

Just the same, neither Bryant nor Reed was born anew in the crucible of the Revolution. They emerged larger but remained them-

selves, many frailties intact: two extraordinary but very human be-
ings.

One friend and loyal admirer of Louise Bryant, Hazel Hunkins, in
whose Washington apartment she stayed on various occasions, was
convinced that Bryant would have preferred a monogamous relationship. On the basis of an unhappy experience she had with Reed, she
felt that such a relationship with him could only be hypothetical.

At a party in her flat, "and on very short acquaintance, John Reed
started to make love to me. Much as I admired the things he stood for,
I disliked him for his promiscuity—and with a wife like Louise! He
was a handsome, big, muscular man, *very* sexy. For him to make love
to me was, I thought, pretty stinky, when he knew I was in love with a
man equally dedicated, and he knew Louise and I were friends." It
was her belief that any relationships Louise had with other men were
only "a reaction to Reed's behavior and naturally foreign to Louise."[19]

But Bryant's feeling for Dasburg was not a "reaction," it had a
reality independent of Reed. Unquestionably she felt neglected and
alone in the summer of 1918, with Reed away for weeks at a time. She
had heard Dasburg was back from New Mexico and in Woodstock. At
some point in that summer she turned to him for solace.

In the war-heated summer there could have been no refuge more
ideal than Woodstock, worlds away from the cacophony of the slogan-
makers. *Give till it hurts. Don't be a slacker. Do your bit! Down with
the Hun! Make the world safe for democracy.* It was an escape from
New York. Not that the smallest crossroads settlement was entirely
isolated. If it had a church, from a nearby town would come a leading
banker, educator, or editor to make a pitch every Sunday during the
drive to sell Liberty Bonds; then in a cloud of dust he'd drive away
headed for the next village.

Bryant would not stay long. Page proofs to correct for her book
would be waiting for her, and an article to complete for *McCall's*
magazine, now edited by Bessie Beatty. Bryant also was busy apart-
ment-hunting in Reed's absence, meanwhile living in Reed's old
apartment at 21 West Eighth Street. But it was delicious getting away
for the weekend. It would be good to talk to Andrew—a good listener.

In Woodstock there was still a dialogue between the aesthetes and
the politicals. In the Village the gap had widened between them. Or if
any dialogue took place it was because most of the Villagers, once
counted on the side of the social revolution, were beginning their own
metamorphoses into aesthetes.[20]

Dasburg met the stage, which connected with the train at West Hurley, and as they walked up the winding road from Woodstock to the house on Overlook Mountain she impressed Andrew as light-hearted.

When they reached the familiar house of brownstained shingles some five hundred feet up the mountain,[21] Dasburg deposited her overnight bag, then watched her as she went from one window to another, looking out. It all looked good to her. She admired his flower bed in front, and he promised to show her the pine trees in back and she would see how they'd grown. He told her she did not seem much changed for all her adventures. Oh, but I am changed, she challenged him smilingly. You'll see—but just now I want to be happy and carefree.

If either had wondered whether it would be difficult to pick up a relationship again after such a long absence, such doubts were soon dispelled.

"Our relationship was so perfectly normal," Dasburg said quietly and rather wonderingly in later years. "There was no secrecy about it. None that we felt. Of course, one doesn't invite the public in at such a time."

Louise had a surprise for him—a very beautiful old Russian ikon. He was touched, and she savored his appreciation of its artistry. It was, she told him, one of several she had bought in the markets of Petrograd. But he could read about them in her book when it came out.[22]

Of course Bryant and Dasburg could not pretend forever that the world was not just outside the window, a world bleeding from the slaughter that still continued. When they did speak of it, it seemed to bring them closer. "We all hated the war," Dasburg said.

That weekend they dropped in to see the artist Henry Lee McFee and his wife, Aileen—and probably Judson Smith, as well as Konrad Cramer and his wife, Florence. (Bryant may have met Cramer in 1916 in Provincetown; he was a friend of Reed's.) To Andrew and his artist intimates Bryant spoke a little of what she had witnessed in faraway revolutionary Russia, mentioning the Russian-American Bolsheviks and the anarchist Bill Shatov and their contributions.[23] As she talked it was evident to Dasburg that an idea had seized her and that to it alone she was giving the best that was in her.

One evening when they were alone she spoke of how lonely she had been in Paris in the spring of 1917 and asked him what it was like when he was there in 1909. Oh, he replied, it was not lonely but intoxicating. "We knew we were living in a wonderful era—in art, a revolutionary period that presaged other changes. Why, Picasso singlehandedly had changed the world of art!"

Bryant thrilled to his words. He was "visiting with her," and she asked, "And what was it like to come home?"

Dasburg said that there was a real breakthrough in America, too, beginning with 1905 and continuing until the war—a conscious smashing of the straitjacket of puritanism, and along with it all sorts of old forms were crumbling. "It was the birth of a new world!"

Then, said Louise rapturously, he could understand how she felt. But Andrew had understood all along.

When the time came for him to walk her to the stage, they spoke little in their descent down the mountain of a mile or so. It was another farewell without tears, without regrets, and without reproaches.

"Louise and I never let things of the world come between us. We just belonged together, you know. Not that either of us tried to change the circumstances of our lives, for that would have altered others' lives," Dasburg said in later years. "Used to saying goodby, we never let it tear us up." He was silent a minute, then added: "We loved each other very much, and our lives were dictated by circumstances."[24]

Bryant was on hand when the second trial of *Masses* editors, the beloved cartoonist Art Young and Merrill Rogers, the business manager, opened at the end of September in the Federal Court of Judge Martin Manton. (Another artist, H. J. Glintenkamp, named in the indictment, was in Mexico, "slacking.")

Reed's offense as cited in the indictment was that he wrote a headline over an item culled from the New York *Tribune* on the prevalence of mental disease among soldiers, "Knit a Strait-Jacket for Your Soldier Boy." Bryant heard him being grilled by the court on his purpose in writing the headline. After reciting some of the horrors he had witnessed in Europe, Reed said it was "to call attention to the fact that war was not what we thought it was."

When the prosecutor asked whether he was interested in the "war of the people against capitalism," Reed said frankly, "To tell the truth that is the only war I am interested in."[25]

Bryant was a witness briefly on the same day, October 3, and identified what parts of the story on France under their joint by-line she had written."[26]

The courtroom was jammed. The jury again failed to agree. Reed, writing the *Liberator*'s story of the trial, called Max Eastman's three-hour summation "the one great factor in our victory."[27]

The minute the judge left the bench, the defendants were surrounded by well-wishers. Apparently Bryant was not there at the time. At least she does not figure in an intriguing description of a celebration of the outcome by Floyd Dell, Edna St. Vincent Millay, and Jack Reed. Millay, whom Dell had renounced as faithless, had appeared at the first recess, much to Dell's delight, and when the jury disagreed, Dell introduced her to Reed and saw her blue-green eyes shining in approval. The three set out to see the New York harbor and skyline.

It was not the ferryboat ride that Millay apotheosizes in verse, and for Dell, not all that merry, but interesting. At the time, Dell was thirty-one and looked younger; Joseph Freeman speaks of a "thin, translucent, sensitive face, with its large eyes and 1890 sideburns."[28] He was more handsome than Reed (whose face Eastman likened to a potato) but it mattered not at all. Jack Reed was the underground hero, the counterculture's warrior returned from the barricades. Riding back and forth half the night on the Staten Island ferry in a dense fog, Reed, wrote Dell, "was telling her his most thrilling adventures as a war correspondent and Communist conspirator, and she said, like Desdemona, 'I love you for the dangers you have passed.' "[29]

But, as he told it later, there was more to the story than that. "For a time Millay was quite mad about Reed." He saw the beginning of it on the ferry as Reed told of perilous feats of derring-do in the world-shaking days of Russia. "I kept away from her after that," Dell said stoutly. "For quite a while, that is."

Nor, claimed Dell, did this new infatuation for Vincent, as he called her, end with the ride on the ferry. One day when "Louise had gone off somewhere to make an important speech on Russia," Reed and Vincent met in the Reed cottage in Croton. It was on a hill, and a rear entrance opened directly into the basement. Reed left her on the floor above and had gone to the basement to get wood for the fireplace. As he stood, arms loaded with logs to carry up, an apparition met his eyes on the stairway. "It was Vincent, descending with a lighted candle in one hand. She was in the nude."

But before the descent was completed, and as an admiring Reed gazed up at the vision, the basement door opened and a shriek was heard. "Louise had returned—then rushed out the doorway, straight into the arms of Sally Robinson, close by on Mt. Airy Road. Louise wept and screamed and swore Sally to secrecy." Dell learned of the incident many years later—from his wife, B. Marie, who had heard it from Robinson.

Dell was convinced that Reed's erotic adventures with the poet did not end with that.[30] But as he failed to supply any details of subsequent trysts, it is possible that his certainty was but an extension of his self-laceration over Millay. Dell wrote Edmund Wilson that eventually he "had got over being in love with her in every other way" except for a "terrible feeling of responsibility for her."[31]

It has been suspected, though, by someone who knew both Millay and Dell, that the mocking blithe spirit of the youthful Vincent continued to haunt him through all the bleak years when "he buried himself in the bureaucracy of Washington."[32]

Reed and Bryant moved into the upstairs flat at 1 Patchin Place that fall. Reed's papers had finally been returned from Washington, and Boni and Liveright advanced enough to allow him to work solely on his manuscript of *Ten Days That Shook the World*. He gave up trying to write at 1 Patchin Place and took a room in the attic above Paula Holladay's Greenwich Inn off Sheridan Square, telling only Bryant. According to one account, he had tried Croton, and when there were too many interruptions, walked up the road a little way and asked the owner of a farmhouse with a giant tree if he might build a tree house there. He did build it and repaired to it with pad and pencil.[33]

Before the end of October Reed was hard at work on the book. But by October 19 Bryant's *Six Red Months in Russia* was released by George H. Doran in an illustrated edition, and Bryant became preoccupied in reading reviews. They were largely favorable.

The *Dial* noted that Bryant was a pleader for the Bolsheviki but at the same time the reviewer was disarmed by her frankness, and found that her "partisanship, fortunately, does not mitigate her reporter's gift for accurate observation." The "straight record of fact" presented was "exceedingly valuable." The *Nation*'s reviewer after a rather patronizing beginning conceded that the book was interesting and that it "contains a wealth of information."

Frank Harris's *Pearson's Weekly* praised her fearlessness in putting down what she saw "without prejudice and without any preconceived theory." The reviewer went on: "Indeed she seems to have no theories and because of that the impact of her sincerity is overpowering and her reading of events singularly convincing."[34]

Floyd Dell's review in the *Liberator*, in the form of a letter to the author, agrees that she is no theorist but speaks of her "persuasive clarity."

"Fortunate you," he writes, ". . . you were there and saw the very birth of the Future. . . . And you have made us see it with your eyes . . . the panorama of those six tremendous months passes like living reality before us." He especially applauds her compassion and fairness in depicting the various revolutionary women whatever their relation to the Bolshevik Revolution:

> . . . you were in the midst of the events that gave the time its color and meaning. You knew "the old Breshkovsky," as she signs herself in the photograph which is the frontispiece of your book, and Kollontai, and Spiridonova, and the "women soldiers" (of whom you give a different and vastly more human account than any we have heard before!).[35]

12.
A New Voice

SEVERAL THOUSAND PERSONS packed Poli's Theater in Washington on Sunday afternoon, February 2, 1919, to hear Albert Rhys Williams and Louise Bryant speak on "The Truth About Russia." The meeting went well. But in the wake of the lurid story in the *Washington Post* on the speeches, and amid wild charges on the Senate floor, a resolution authorizing an investigation of Bolshevik propaganda was unanimously passed.[1] Thus Senator Lee S. Overman (Democrat, North Carolina) and his subcommittee of the Senate Judiciary Committee, originally set up to investigate possible connections between brewery and liquor interests and German propaganda, got a new lease on life. It would go down in history as the grandfather of the House Un-American Activities Committee and a score of congressional witchhunt groups.

Bryant, Reed, and Williams had wired Senator Overman asking to be called as witnesses but received no replies. So Bryant hung around Washington listening to a string of friendly witnesses, one of whom testified about a Russian decree "nationalizing women."[2] Finally she confronted the chairman in a recess and demanded to be heard, wringing from him a promise to tell her the following day when she could testify; she wrote Reed jubilantly. She told him other news: she was staying with Hazel Hunkins[3] and her old friend from Oregon, Clara Wold, and could remain in their big apartment as long as she liked. The National Woman's Party had paid her expenses up to then and would pay her fare home. She knew this would be welcome news to Reed, as they were existing on very little income these days. What's more, she wrote, Millie Morris stayed in the Hunkins-Wold apartment much of the time, and had promised to help her get plays taken for movies.[4] Louise was at work on one now. Senator Hiram Johnson had sent word to her in jail (Reed knew she was to picket the White House with the suffragists) and she was to see him. She also wrote that Senator LaFollette asked about Reed affectionately; she urged that when he came to Washington he should not mail, but bring copies of *Die Fackel (The Torch)* that he and Williams had worked on for the Bolsheviks. She ended:

> I tremble when I think of my Honey in the clutches of so many sex-hungry ladies and I don't blame them for it either. . . .
> I have a sneaking notion that the hunger strike did me good. . . . My legs are a little shaky but that is my only remembrance of the horrors . . . of prison. I have a peach of a story. . . .[5]

On February 20 Bryant appeared before the Overman subcommittee as the first unfriendly witness. The senators seemed unwilling to let her go. She was on the witness stand all day and again on the following day. It was late in the day before they called Reed, and then Williams. Her interrogation began this way:

> Senator OVERMAN. Miss Bryant, do you believe in God and in the sanctity of an oath?
> Miss BRYANT. Certainly I believe in the sanctity of an oath.
> Senator KING. Do you believe there is a God?
> Miss BRYANT. I suppose there is a God. . . .
> Senator NELSON. Do you believe in the Christian religion?
> Miss BRYANT. . . . I believe all people should have whatever religion they wish. . . .
> Senator NELSON. You are not a Christian, then?
> Miss BRYANT. I was christened in the Catholic church.
> Senator NELSON. What are you now, a Christian? . . . Do you believe in Christ?
> Miss BRYANT. I believe in the teachings of Christ, Senator Nelson.
> Senator OVERMAN. Do you believe in God?
> Miss BRYANT. Yes, I will concede that I believe in God, Senator Overman. . . .
> Senator WOLCOTT. Do you believe in a punishment hereafter and a reward for duty?
> Miss BRYANT. It seems to me as if I were being tried for witchcraft. . . . Very well; I will concede—I will concede that there is a hell.

Senator King asked where she had stayed in Washington. For a time, she said, at the Woman's Party headquarters. Senator Nelson asked if she belonged "to the picket squad."

Miss BRYANT. I do not know what that has to do with the truth about Russia, but I did. I believe in equality . . . even in my own country.

Under Nelson's questioning she readily admitted she had taken part in the burning of the President in effigy, adding that she had gone on a hunger strike in jail. One member wanted to know what a hunger strike was, and she told them.

Senator King, after going into her first and second marriages, asked whether she hadn't participated in Bolsheviki meetings. She took down notes as other reporters did, she replied. She was asked about her husband's employment for the Bolsheviks. Yes, she said proudly, he worked getting out propaganda for a revolution in Germany. "My husband in Russia did a great deal toward bringing about the German revolution." She tried to show them copies of *Die Fackel*.[6]

Senator Nelson said he wanted facts, Bryant said the papers she held in her hand were the facts, Nelson told her not to be so impertinent, and the record noted both applause and hisses. The chairman threatened to clear the room if the noise was repeated. It was, and he did. After an hour, the crowd was allowed to return, with warnings against any more "cheering."

Senator Overman asked her the purpose of the meeting in Poli's theater, and she replied: "The purpose was to protest against intervention in Russia. I, as an American, believing in self-determination, cannot believe in intervention. I do not see how we can fight for democracy in France and against it in Siberia. . . . I believe we ought to take our troops out of Russia . . . it would be better for both nations to have have friendly relations."

It was the first time she had been allowed to make a statement at such length. Senator Nelson set about trying to shake the witness's calm. Was she "anxious" for the Bolsheviks to remain in power? "I am anxious—" she began.

Senator NELSON. Answer my question. Are you anxious to have the Bolshevik government there as a permanent thing?
Miss BRYANT. I think the Russians ought to settle that.

He put the question again, and she replied: "I answered you. I said I believed in self-determination."

Senator NELSON. Self-determination at the point of a gun?
Miss BRYANT. All governments have had to be self-determined at the point of a gun. There never has been a government established except after a war.

Nelson demanded she answer whether the Bolsheviks believed in securing socialism by evolution. "They do if they can; but they could not do it in Russia," she said.

> Senator NELSON. But if they can not, it is by revolution?
> Miss BRYANT. Yes.
> Senator NELSON. By blood and sword, rapine, murder and fire. Do you believe in that?

Senator Wolcott drove on, despite her saying she did not. He wanted reassurance, since it was "commonly understood" that she advocated the Russian program for the United States. Bryant explained that she really had not advocated the violent overthrow of the U.S. government as the *Washington Post* story said. She added that she did not know "whether I am a female Trotzky or not, but I know the other accusations are not true." Senator Wolcott asked if she had not praised, in speeches and her writings, "the soviet government as a good thing for the Russians." Yes, she said, she believed it was the government desired by the majority, and that "it fits Russia."

"It has your personal indorsement for Russia?" he demanded to know.

"Yes," replied Bryant; "but I would not fight for it or against it. I would not ask for intervention to keep it in Russia. I think the Russians ought to settle their internal troubles, and I think it is a shame to have American boys killed determining what form of government there should be in Russia. . . ."

"Would it be a good thing for America? That is a plain question," Senator Wolcott shot back.

"I do not think it would fit America at the present time," she said.

Later Wolcott returned to this. Did she mean the Soviet form of government would not be a good thing here? "That is what I said," Bryant replied. "You see, it is very difficult to tell you, for you will not let me talk in order to explain." He agreed to let her if she kept to the point.

"You see," she said, "all socialists believe in government ownership. But whether it would ever be worked out in this country as it is worked out in Russia I am not able to say, and that is why I said I doubted very much it would work out exactly as it did in Russia. Russia is more of an agricultural country. I have not been advocating it one way or the other in the United States. I have simply been telling how it worked in Russia. . . ."

After the hearing opened the next day, Bryant asked the chairman if

she might be permitted "to speak a whole sentence before this
committee without being interrupted." He agreed. She then complained of the character of the hearings: all the Russian refugees and
other people with picayune grievances had talked as long as they
liked, and she, the first witness to declare against intervention, was
asked questions and not allowed to answer fully. She had been, she
charged, treated like "a traitor."

> Senator OVERMAN. . . . You seem to want to make a martyr of
> yourself, when you have not been treated unfairly that I can see. You
> are a woman and you do not know anything about the conduct of an
> examination such as we have in hand here. We are going to treat you
> fairly and treat you as a lady.
> Miss BRYANT. I do not want to be treated as a lady, but I want to
> be treated as a human being.

She complained that Senator King of Utah had put her through "a sort
of third degree." At which the Southern banker in the chair declared
that Senator King as a judge on the bench (in Utah's last territorial
years) frequently had before him witnesses who were charged with
having no faith in the Christian religion. Bryant asked, "How would
he have treated me if I had been a Jew?'"

Senator Sterling said her testimony put her "in the position of a
partisan and friend and defender of the Bolsheviki," and she replied,
"Surely. Why not?" She complained, too, that she had been "given
lectures."

> Senator STERLING. You were not given lectures. You were cross-
> examined. . . .
> Miss BRYANT. Even my morals have been suggested by Senator
> Nelson. He has given me regular lectures as to what I ought to think,
> and how I might, somehow, come out of this terrible slump that I
> have gotten into.

She asked if she could go on with her testimony, and took up the
matter of the "nationalization of women." Bryant explained that what
had been read into the record by Major E. Lowry Humes of Military
Intelligence as a decree that was printed in *Izvestia* contained only
four paragraphs from the original "decree," and that that was passed
not by the government but by an anarchist club in Vladimir. After
numerous diversions and interruptions she was allowed to go on. "The
rest were added as a satire by a comic paper, the Moocka [*The
Fly*]. . . . It was published in the late spring of 1918 in Moscow, and it
was considered nothing but a great joke in Russia."[7]

Reed followed Bryant as a witness. Apparently the committee had no desire to tangle with him. He was crisp and clear—and allowed to depart shortly.[8]

A check for seventy-five dollars from *McCall's* had come for Bryant, and Reed hoped it would let them have a week in the country loafing.[9] But first they must go to Philadelphia for his trial. Here Reed's optimism failed him: he as well as Bryant expected a conviction on the "inciting to riot" charge, which carried a maximum penalty of two years and a five hundred dollar fine. There were other charges; one for seditious utterances was dropped earlier, but there was still an assault and battery charge. Bryant had protested when a socialist local wanted two hundred and fifty dollars for its attorney to represent Reed.[10] Luckily, a lawyer engaged largely in corporation law asked to defend him without a fee; David Wallerstein also urged the two to be his guests while awaiting trial. Already, they learned, Wallerstein had obtained a dismissal of the assault and battery charge. He told them he intended to argue solely on the free speech issue. On February 24 he put Reed on the witness stand in his own defense. Bryant could not believe it when the jury came in with an acquittal on the first vote. Now Reed faced only one other indictment, that growing out of his Hunt's Point Palace speech.[11]

They were in a holiday mood, gladdened by the promised early appearance of *Ten Days*. They set out for Croton feeling each had earned a rest. But Reed was at once plunged into activities of the recently organized Left Wing of the Socialist Party of Greater New York. Bryant dashed off two pieces on her experience with the Senators for *Pearson's* and the *Liberator*.[12]

Bryant was making notes and working on a sample speech for a speaking tour on "The Truth About Russia," and Anna Louise Strong, on the staff of the daily *Seattle Union Record*, was organizing it. Strong wanted Reed, but he was too involved in political work for the Left Wing.

Margaret Reed had written her son that "they are arresting Bolsheviks out here." Her letters were unrelenting in citing her fears.[13] Louise was more worried over whether she could keep up the unflagging pace that Anna Louise would expect. Having just taken part in the Seattle general strike, the first in America, Strong was brimming over with more energy and ideas than ever. She "drove herself and others with a sort of neurotic energy coupled with a quick and hot temper that made even her best friends uneasy in her presence."[14] Anna Louise Strong, born in 1885 (as was Bryant), never could understand it when people she liked did not always do exactly what she ordered them to do. In her social worker phase in St. Louis she was engaged to Roger Baldwin. The day came when she told him he would have to quit smoking cigarettes. "And you will have to forego those cocktails you drink, you know, too." Baldwin replied that he would smoke and drink cocktails when he liked. The engagement lasted three months: that was enough for both of them.[15]

Strong assured Bryant that she would keep in mind her fatigue, and her hope for time to visit her mother. "I may try to spread the engagements a little," she conceded.[16] But the human dynamo, finding that Bryant was being eagerly bid for up and down the Coast, in Butte and Minneapolis, and by proper matrons as well as laboring masses, did not find it in her heart to spare Louise. Conflicts were inevitable—Bryant was far from meek—but there were triumphs, too; the tour was wildly successful. The miracle was that these two women became friends for life.[17]

From Detroit, where she made her first speech, she sent word to Reed. "This town is solidly *against* intervention." Later, resting at Hull House in Chicago, she wrote more fully:

> They gave me a grand reception in Detroit. The papers carried *big* stories . . . leave here for Minneapolis at 1:15 tonight. . . . The most tiring thing not even excluding the sleeping on cars is the everlasting talk *between* times. Everyone gets a "group" together and that just exhausts me. I don't know *what* to do about it!
>
> I have decided to cut out Butte because I have to be in Spokane on Sunday. . . . Then I have Yakima, Seattle, Takoma, Portland. Some days *two* meetings. I'm wiring Anna Louise I can't do that. She has San Francisco . . . [and] Los Angeles [in] April. . . .
>
> Anna Louise only plans $50 a week above expenses. Whew! I'll have it out with her there. It's not much. She is also negotiating with Salt Lake City and God knows where else. . . .
>
> There's more feeling about Debs here—Everyone is incensed and excited.
>
> Old Darl, how I'd love to be there in the country. I don't want to *think* at all.[18]

From Minneapolis she wrote that more people were turned away than could get inside the hall, and "Sinclair Lewis is here . . . he brought over a flock of newspapermen and with the Socialist bunch— I've been having a busy time. . . ."

Her throat was a little sore, but her voice was all right, and after that night's meeting in St. Paul, "I can rest on the train."[19]

The next day she wrote Reed from the train that both meetings had cleared a thousand dollars. Her books were sold at each, and the stores swept clean of them. At St. Paul, "people sat on the aisles and on the stage, and I had room only to speak and not to promenade . . . very hard on me . . . At one meeting more than a thousand were turned away."

To her surprise, press coverage was generally sympathetic. She was pleased that she was to address a real working class audience in Spokane, and farmers in the Yakima armory. She urged him to be "awfully careful, please"—which could mean "no more arrests or indictments" or "stay away from women" or both—and to get lots of rest, warning that when she got home she would let him do all the work and she would rest.

The train was cold, the landscape snowbound, like everyone on the train she was sneezing, and a large cold sore blossomed on her face. But there were many newly returned soldiers and sailors, and she had to sound them out: "not one believed in intervention." Businessmen joined in, "and they do not agree with the soldiers on a single point! I'm not over-optimistic, but a little more hopeful. Businessmen have war in their heads and the fighting men have peace."[20]

It was not strange that Bryant, largely inexperienced as a speaker, was besieged by audiences, that halls were filled to overflowing with listeners loath to let her go, keeping her speaking and answering questions for more than two hours. There was an inordinate hunger for knowledge of the Russian Revolution. In the United States, as in other Allied nations, most of the reading public was misinformed as to its background; few correspondents witnessed its momentous events and "even fewer understood enough of what was happening to appreciate their significance," Phillip Knightley demonstrates.[21] Readers in America had been told even less about the massive Allied intervention which was under way with the idea of overthrowing the Bolsheviks. It was almost a hush-hush operation until a few Senators began speaking out.

Although 1919 was a year which has gone into the annals of this country as unspeakably repressive and barbaric,[22] with members of the I.W.W. or those assumed to be members suffering outrageous attacks and the foreign-born jailed awaiting deportation, there were evidences of growing dissent. Strikes were increasing; the great steel strike was yet to be quelled; a few of the many Socialist and radical papers closed down by the government in the war had begun printing again. A few pro-war Socialists such as the writer Upton Sinclair were now concerned about intervention.

Some who were not radicals were voicing hope for the future of the "Russian experiment." Elmer Rice, calling available news about Russia "scarce, contradictory and unreliable," heard Raymond Robins at the Foreign Policy Association, and Lincoln Steffens at a public meeting, back from Russia by way of the Versailles conference; he felt that their accounts of Russia "fostered the hope that from the shambles of war there might arise a society based upon the principles of justice and humanitarianism."

It was hardly the prevailing attitude, Rice said, citing the New York Legislature's expulsion of five of its members duly elected on the Socialist ticket; the establishment of its infamous Lusk Committee; and a revitalized Klu Klux Klan on a binge "to shield 'the sanctity of the home and the chastity of American womanhood.' "

Max Eastman, raising money for the *Liberator* by lecturing on the Bolsheviks a fortnight or so before Bryant, said that at many meetings, as he looked around at the police lining the hall, he felt "more like an invading army than a man on a lecture tour."[24]

Louise Bryant was not unaware of the dangers implicit in taking the stand for Lenin and Trotsky. But, according to Andrew Dasburg, to anticipate danger made the whole venture more alluring to her. When in 1920 he put her on a ship to begin a long, mysterious trip by way of the underground to Russia during the blockade, she was far from nervous. "No, she looked forward to it—there were peril and risk involved, you see."[25] This was a trait she would not willingly have conceded. She was far too busy upbraiding Reed for taking chances, and, with each new hazardous undertaking of his, sulking and fuming.

In Spokane, Bryant was bedridden; the throat infection had turned into influenza, again rampant through the country and almost as virulent as in 1918. When she arrived in Seattle she still felt shaky. Anna Louise Strong agreed that she should rest for two days before the five speeches scheduled for the area. (There had to be five because the only halls open to her were labor halls with limited seating capacity.)

Seattle labor was still euphoric over its well-organized general strike. Strong had written Bryant a lively letter about the strike,[26] and no doubt expected eager questions about it from her. Instead, Bryant, speaking of the Bolsheviks, told her: "You mustn't think they are pacifists over there because they withdrew from the war. They believe in armed uprising." Strong records this, and continues: "I answered, 'Of course'; but I felt a vague discomfort. It seemed we had forgotten something in Seattle. Where were our arms?"

She comforted herself, however. "If our theory was vague, our emotional loyalty was authentic. Seattle longshoremen led the strike against supplying arms to Kolchak, and it spread up and down the coast."[27] (Certainly their rousing response to Louise Bryant's speech in the Longshoremen's Hall had a fitting sequel in their September 1919 refusal to load arms to go to Kolchak.)

"Anna Louise is belligerently entertaining me," Louise wrote Jack on her second day of "rest." Strong, Louise wrote, insisted on parties, house parties, "and god knows what." At the moment she was across the Sound "at a country place I was dragged to last night . . . what a crowd! Everybody sits right near my elbow, 'so they won't miss anything *interesting!*'" From her affluent audience she escaped once into the garden, but it only made her homesick: "I want to dig in my *own* garden!" He should do anything he liked in the garden while she was away. "But *please,* promise not to plan to run away on a tour as soon as I come home. *I do so much want to visit you!* And it would be wonderful to work together, *even a week,* in the garden."

She told him of her bitter disappointment that no mail was waiting for her in Seattle. A postscript announced she would be speaking in the Auditorium in Portland—its largest hall. She hoped his mother would not mind.[28]

Her next letter to Reed repeated her old plea that he remain faithful to her, and in an effort to make it appear less heavy-handed she introduced "poetic" touches that only make it sound artificial:

> How hard it is to be away from you in the Spring! Last Spring you were in Norway and the year before the wine of the first warm breezes carried my honey away and wounded us both deeply. I refer to this, dear, not as a warning but to tell you that it [is] as difficult for me as it is for you. . . . I toss about restlessly all night and fall asleep only to wake from little troubled dreams of desire. Oh, my dear honey—try to wait for me! I am a prisoner bound. Without you I have no outlet.

For all its stilted quality, it is her first letter that tells him what he never quite believed: that women also have sexual needs. It probably required courage to write it. Like Reed, she found it difficult to speak with any directness about sex. In this letter she is at home only in speaking of the first Seattle meeting, and how a "silly Anarchist woman" got the floor. "I am so sick of the Anarchists!"[29]

She was rushing to get a train for Tacoma, where Todd Shipyard was laying off men and streets swarmed with the unemployed. She spoke under the auspices of the Soldiers', Sailors' and Workmen's Council. (Such councils, inspired by the Soviets, were springing up in some Western cities and in a few in the East.) As the weekly *Tacoma Labor Advocate* (the official organ of the State Federation of Labor and the Tacoma Labor Council) reported, 3,200 Tacomans jammed Tahoma Hall to hear her.

Her "ready wit and instant answers" were praised, and she was described as "this girlish and pretty young woman, with her hair banged in Russian fashion." A collection that filled four hats was taken up by the council, and after she departed a resolution was passed unanimously demanding that American troops be withdrawn from Russia.

Intervention, Bryant charged, was a betrayal of American soldiers as well as of Russia. "We did not betray them but our politicians did. The American soldier boys did not want to do this work. But the politicians at Washington are running things. I have two brothers in the service. They enlisted to fight Germany, not Russia. [She could not know then that the younger, Bill Bryant, would return home blinded, shattered.] Those are Michigan boys on the Archangel front. The people of Michigan have sent great petitions, with thousands of names of mothers and fathers, asking the Washington authorities to bring their boys home out of Russia. . . .

"There was no military reason for the invasion of Siberia. The general staff of the United States Army advised against it. But the politicians sent the troops in. It's a national disgrace, it's a national scandal. . . ."

The lies in the metropolitan press about the Soviets she compared to the accounts in the press picturing the Seattle general strike as a Bolsheviki uprising. "The reason they lie about it is that Soviet Russia is one great general strike against the governments of the whole world." Bryant upbraided Congress for failing to enact any reconstruction program on behalf of veterans. Each soldier and sailor should be given six months' pay on his discharge, she cried—to loud applause.

She spoke of legislation passed by the Soviets, spearheaded by Kollontai, that gave any working woman two months' paid vacation both before and after confinement. The law, she stressed, applied to unmarried women as well as those in wedlock, for "in Russia they don't believe that the sins of the fathers should be visited on the heads of innocent children."

Before ending her speech Bryant told her packed audience: "They accuse me of being favorable to the Russian Revolution. After what I've seen, I wouldn't have a drop of red blood in my heart if I was not touched by the greatest thing in the world—the Russian Revolution."

The questions reported by the *Tacoma Labor Advocate,* whose story began on page one and filled two inside pages with a running account of her speech, were many and intelligent. Bryant had not been in Russia for more than a year, and one question on how "this workmen's control of industry" actually worked she answered simplistically. She spoke with authority when in answer to another query she said that Lenin was ready to extend concessions to Americans who wished to do business with Russia—and especially to trade unions that could send over union-made materials; and that engineers or workers with experience would be welcome to help restore and improve Russian industry. [30]

The next day Bryant received two letters from Reed. The second, written after he received her telegrams about her illness, pleads with her not to tempt fate after the flu, and to stop speaking and return home. He warns of the danger in speaking if there is a throat infection, reminding her it was fatal to Inez Milholland. [31] If it was serious, he *must* come, at any cost. He is in the process of "making some money for us to take it easy on, thank God, and if you aren't dangerously sick, although it just wrings my guts, I think [I'd] better not break the contract." If she did go to Portland, she should "smooth mother down," as she "is accusing me bitterly of wanting to make her a charity dependent on the Proletarian State." Again, he said, "Nothing matters except that you come back here quick." It made him "helpless and blue" when she was sick. In the end his buoyant spirits come to the surface:

> It is perfectly heavenly in the country, and I am doing great work. The first articles are already in.
> My book is out tomorrow. Let people know it, will you? I happened to go into the Lib today . . . found that they'd sold more than three hundred of your books, already, and orders coming in for more all the time.

Reed's final note tells her a bit cavalierly, "Here's some mail, most of which I opened to see if I could do anything about it." [32]

In the earlier letter he explained the proposed debate with Henry Slobodin—a turncoat Socialist. It would pay fifteen cents a word on publication and provide "a little money so that we can have some leisure." But he looked on it as "a terrible job." He had spoken in Cleveland, "where I kicked up a hell of a row but managed to get off without being pinched." If she could fit it in, he could "get you a whopping big meeting in Cleveland, where they are crazy to hear you."

He asked her rather touchily not to "send any money to me any more, as I will soon be flush," and told her that "if you want any cash, just wire your Big." He was proud of the reception his "honey" was getting, and a trifle patronizing as he continued: "Why shouldn't she? She is a good Small. I am, as you know, always unreservedly happy at my honey's successes."[33]

Bryant wrote him happily that she had had two letters. She told him of the Tacoma meeting, "the best yet." The hall could seat 1,500, but it was decided to remove the seats so twice that number could be accommodated! "So from 7 until 10 they *stood*, packed like sardines."

She was tired: speeches three days running, and another in a short while. She would rest the next day, then go to Everett, Washington, to speak. She had cut out her Canadian dates. But without those speaking dates, "I will come home with practically nothing in my pocket. Anyway, I don't care. Maybe Millie will sell my movie scenarios. And you say you will be rich!

"I don't believe it. I think we will always be dead broke—from now on. Well if I'm with my honey, and we are well I'm sure I don't care."

She planned to stop at the Multnomah Hotel in Portland, and, possibly recalling meeting him in Sara Bard Field's room there, asked, "Isn't it funny?" She would do "the best I can with your mother but it gives me cold shivers to think of even *being* in Portland."

> Honey, I'm sick of *talking!* I could weep. What a poor and yet a good propagandist I am in spite of myself. I *believe* with my whole heart that it is wrong to have troops in Russia. I want to write it *once*, say it *once*—but I *have* to do *both* a *million times*. And all this in spite of Spring and my desire to be home.

With the self-centeredness not unknown to writers, she complained that there were never enough of her books in shops in the West—they sold out so quickly—before she thought to comment on his book. It was her turn to be a bit patronizing. "I'm so glad yours is out. I'll see that it is mentioned *at every single meeting!*" In a postscript she noted sourly: "You don't need to *open* my mail, dear, it will always wait."[34]

That night Bryant addressed another exciting meeting. Anna Louise Strong wrote: "I remember Louise Bryant returned from the revolution in Russia to dazzle the smoke-laden air of the close-packed Longshoremen's hall with her gorgeous amber beads and the glamor of the forbidden border."[35]

Too aroused to go to sleep, Bryant wrote Reed before she went to bed: "What a meeting! I have just come from it—the big one in the Longshoremen's Hall." It was in a vast barnlike building close to the docks, its acoustics abominable, and "the roughest, finest most wonderful audience!" She had read the news about the revolution in Hungary, and "can hear the feet of that great army across the world."[36]

On March 28, as her stay in Seattle drew to an end, she again heard from Reed. Still worried over her illness, he implored her to "hurry back to your darling." He asked if she remembered Ludwig C. A. K. Martens, a friend of Ludwig Lore and Louis G. Fraina. He'd been made a representative of the Soviet Government for the United States, and promptly announced he would spend 200 million dollars *in gold* for U.S. products. The businessmen were flocking to see him, and "probably that $200,000,000 will do more than anything else to get recognition for Russia." He then added drily: "And did you see that President Wilson has sent Lincoln Steffens, Bill Bullitt and two or three of that sort to Russia on a destroyer to investigate the Soviets?"[37]

Bryant, with two more speeches to go, one in nearby Ballard, a dock-workers' and shipyard workers' district, was worried over the looming challenge Portland represented. By now she knew Anna Louise Strong had managed a tentative agreement to permit her to speak in the Civic Auditorium on condition that she submit a speech in advance. She wrote: "Well, I will because *no radical* has been able to open his mouth in any big hall there. I'm breaking down the opposition and they beg me to do it—and the 'Oregonian' is pleading my cause!"[38]

A brief note as she was departing from Washington: she was "off for Portland *very* tired and *very* bedraggled." She was "so *very* lonesome for you. And it will be wonderful to get home. *Don't forget about me!* I feel as if I have been away years."[39]

At the Multnomah Hotel, as soon as she called Reed's mother, Louise looked up recent newspapers. She was relieved to see that Portland's conservative A. F. of L. spokesmen in a restrained but stubborn way had gone to bat for her against the City Council and won her right to speak. One of the delegates presented her petition, which was at first denied, City Commissioner Bigelow reminding the labor

men that under the state criminal syndicalist act, city officials were
held responsible for what speakers in the Auditorium said. Harry
Anderson, president of the Central Labor Council, observed that in
his view "the city has sufficient police power to control meetings in
the Auditorium." Otto Hartwig, president of the State Federation of
Labor, favored letting her talk and, to ease nervous councilmen who
he felt were still uncertain, agreed to preside over the meeting.
"Everyone knew I was no Wobbly," he explained. [40]

Four thousand people filled the Auditorium to hear her. The labor
press was enthusiastic, the *Oregonian* fair. She told Reed his mother
and brother heard her and seemed impressed. (She probably did not
know it, but Paul Trullinger was there also, applauding.) [41] Her own
mother would be with her at San Francisco's St. Francis Hotel next
day. [42]

More vivid than news accounts are the reactions of three who heard
her speak at the Auditorium. Horton W. C. Nicholas, eighty-three, of
San Jose, wrote: "I didn't know Louise personally at the University. . . . I heard her speak in Portland when she first returned from
Russia, and she was wonderful. I could hardly believe it was our
Louise; Louise Bryant who had led such a carefree butterfly life at the
University (like we all did). I am not a Communist or a Marxist, but
that night my vote would certainly have gone to Louise Bryant . . .
[who had] dedicated her life to the cause of the Russian revolution." [43]

Ethel Bernard Myers, class of 1910, *summa cum laude*: "I can see
her as she faced that tremendous crowd and spoke without even
looking at a note. At the end, when the applause broke, she flicked
open a cloak lined in red. A red flag was not permitted in those days.
But Louise had her red lining in lieu of a flag, and it was dramatic, that
twirl she gave to it as she left the platform." [44]

Mabel K. Strong of Portland: "She wore a cape and used it in what
some people said was a very ostentatious way. I felt it wasn't that at
all. The cape was lined with red and she threw it back so that the
lining showed before she left the platform, I suppose to show her
sympathy for the Communist cause. She spoke very well. And she was
beautiful, wasn't she?" [45]

In Berkeley a new hurdle appeared when Mayor Samuel Irving said
he would in no way allow Bryant to speak in the Burbank School or
anywhere else, as he regarded any Bolshevik as "an emissary of the
Germans." She promptly called a press conference, with the result,
she wrote Reed, that "every paper carries a big story." She had been
tipped off "that they were 'framing me' to break a city ordinance just

as they did you in Philadelphia." Charles Erskine Scott Wood, poet and lawyer she knew in Portland, had called and left a note for her. [46]

After the first of two meetings she wrote joyously to Reed at one-thirty in the morning, after she tucked her mother in bed: "It was a marvellous meeting! About 5000—Sarah and C.E.S. and Mrs. Mooney weeping on the front seats. [47] I never *saw* such enthusiasm— and they sent me roses and violets, and carnations and tulips and roses to the platform. I'm just home now. My mother is absolutely *bewildered*. She isn't sure whether I am a Bolshivik or a patriot or what it is all about." She would be home in ten days. [48]

At the first of two meetings Bryant addressed in Los Angeles on April 15, she reported to Reed, she began by saying, "Today Eugene Debs is on his way to prison," and that her entire audience burst into tears. Two more meetings on her way home, and they would be together. [40] He had written her from Croton that her letters "full of enthusiasm and emotion over the meetings" were "simply wonderful." [50]

What is unquestioned is that in a volatile, highly charged time, Louise Bryant's voice was heard across America. Misrepresented, castigated, reported objectively, even reluctantly admired by the press at times, in the labor halls it sounded clear as a bell, with or without the amber beads, the first woman to go among the huskings to defend Lenin and Trotsky. Her message was simple: "Hands off Russia!" "Bring the boys home!"

13.
Another Farewell

APPREHENSIVENESS ABOUT REED had become virtually built into Louise's personality. On her return to New York late in April 1919, she was met at the station not by Jack but, by chance, Max Eastman, and saw he had a black eye. "Max," she cried, "if you have got that, what has happened to Jack?"

Max assured her, drily, "Nothing's happened to Jack. I got this in an automobile accident." Relieved, but still surprised—a black eye on the Adonis of the left wing seemed so "unconnected with his personality"—Louise took a taxi to 1 Patchin Place. All was in order, and empty. She walked to a Childs restaurant, had some coffee, came out on the street—and there was Jack. He had been writing all night in his room on the top floor of Paula Holladay's Greenwich Village Inn (where he had written *Ten Days*). They had more coffee at Childs, and then returned to Patchin Place. There, sticking under the door, was her telegram. "Separations," Jack told her, "are the cruelest things in the world."[1]

Soon after their reunion they went to Croton, and the work of gardening, laying flagstones, and setting out a few fruit trees was in full force when Reed fell ill with influenza. The epidemic that had laid Louise low was still raging, she could not get a nurse, and for a doctor to make a house call was out of the question. Louise telephoned a doctor in New York to ask what to do and was told what the patient required: "aspirin and eggnog with plenty of brandy."[2]

It was scarcely more than two years since she had written Reed from Paris offering to do the cooking if he could get to work on his novel; they would shut out the world and work hard writing. Now she had to carry out her part in the idyll, whatever else was missing. She nursed him, waited on him, kept friends and comrades at bay, and concentrated on his recovery.

Except for the very sick man she was alone in the house, about a half-mile from the village of Croton. It was still very cold. She moved a bed to face the fireplace, chopped kindling, brought in armloads of logs, and soon had a fire roaring in the big fireplace. She gave him a daily alcohol rub, "starting with his toes and working all over his body." It was a vicious type of influenza that took many lives in 1919, and "for some days he seemed not to understand anything." Jack was a big man, and it was hard to turn him over. But there were then no antibiotics to treat bedsores if they occurred, and Louise realized the importance of frequent shifts of position for her patient. The danger of contagion was such that Louise did not ask for help from neighbors. When she had freshly made up Reed's bed and turned him and replenished the fire, she would go down the hill to the village to get supplies and toil up Mt. Airy Road carrying them as fast as she could.

At last he was well enough to sit on a sofa by a window. By then the snow was melting and spring was slowly coming on, with the inevitable lifting of spirits. Bryant left him long enough to don the "extremely nice dress" she had had made for her lecture tour. She had worn it before she went away (and almost every time she spoke) and was wearing it when she got off the train on her return. He had never commented on it, but now, when she appeared in it, "he said to me in a rather surprised way, 'That's a very nice dress you're wearing.' " And she in turn was surprised, for "Jack never paid any attention to my clothes."[3]

She had ordered some trees, and on their delivery promised Reed he could decide where they should go. Mike Robinson was to help her do the planting. She went out meanwhile to inspect the hedge. It was a matter of special pride with Reed, who when they had moved in had planted the first sprigs of the box hedge, watering them daily. Most of them sprouted, others were added, "but if one died, immediately he discovered it" and would halt whatever he was doing to plant another. She found the hedge grown perceptibly and healthy.

Robinson stood outside with Bryant (apparently still afraid of contagion) while Jack gave directions through the closed window as to where they should plant a small hawthorn tree, tapping and pointing through the glass with his finger. They found the spot he wanted and planted it.[4] In later years she wrote a poem, "Spring in Croton," about the red hawthorn tree.

> All the fruit trees were in bloom
> They were little girls
> Going to communion
> But the hawthorn broke my heart
> It was the little son
> I dreamed about and never had.[5]

And now began a battle of words. Bryant wanted Reed to give his body a chance to build and put on weight. She also selfishly wanted to have some time with him. She reminded him that he had promised to "visit" with her a little while when she returned before he rushed off again. They had a house in Truro, and had not been near it for almost three years. Had he forgotten how much he liked it, how he thought Truro ever so preferable to Provincetown?

Reed on the other hand, as a principal sparkplug of the movement that hoped to capture the Socialist Party in the fall convention and convert it to a communist party, must attend the National Left Wing Conference in New York City convening June 21. He was geared to see this thing through. It was to be no silk strikers' pageant, no one-night stand. There were articles to be written for the now combined *Revolutionary Age* and *Communist*. Louise had refrained from any urging until his recovery from the flu, but she was determined that they would get away for a holiday. Reed seemed unshakable. Louise saw the stubborn set of his jaw; Mabel Dodge had called it "the real poet's jawbone."[6]

Louise also could be stubborn. She knew it would be useless to argue that it would be to his own good to go to the Cape. It developed that their old friends Carl and Helen Walters from Portland, now in the East, could go with them as their guests. Reed had an assignment to cover the A.F. of L. convention at Atlantic City for the *Liberator*— and it now paid at least something for articles. He would have a chance to swim at Atlantic City before the Left Wing Conference opened. Possibly Reed secretly wanted to go to Truro or Louise would not have won. She had maneuvered and had temper tantrums in the past without changing him. Now she pleaded her own health. She had been away, after all, on a demanding lecture tour, had been ill herself for a week with the flu, and returned feeling "absolutely broken."[7] Reed capitulated. Not long after the National Left Wing Conference ended, they packed their bags for Truro. What bliss!

Before they left Croton, however, Jack had resumed his routine: he not only wrote at night but walked at night, at times "walking miles and miles over the hills of Sleepy Hollow." One night he came home from one of these tramps with a little trailing woodbine he had uprooted with care. It had been growing around a stone. He worried aloud that one of its delicate roots was broken, but planted it by his studio, a small retreat set far back from the cottage. Before they set out for the station—at that time there was a railway to the Cape—they examined the woodbine: it seemed rather feeble.[8]

Together they swam and lay on the white sands at Truro, or walked over to Provincetown to see friends, had picnic suppers with the Walterses, and watched the evening sky reflected in the water. Louise savored each day. She saw that Reed really could relax here too. Without a telephone, with only occasional mail and papers, they could momentarily forget the class struggle: it was like checking luggage in the station, with the knowledge that one would have to return for it.

In a letter from Truro July 19, Bryant wrote: "I came down here on the Cape with Jack. He is not well at all and has no idea how to take a vacation near New York. Here he cannot even hear the rumblings of battle." Addressed to an editor of *Soviet Russia*, the letter notes she is returning his check for fifteen dollars, payment for an article she had written, stating in a rather lofty vein:

> I have never taken a cent for any work I have ever done to help Soviet Russia and to prevent my country from continuing in its criminal efforts to destroy the Russian revolution. I have a feeling that if I ever did take money it would seem too much like a job.

To spurn the token payment of the struggling periodical was folly when Reed had been suspended from the Harvard Club for owing thirty-four dollars; they were so broke that to make the trip to Truro Reed had had to travel again, as he had in 1918, to the pawnbroker with his prized gold repeater Swiss watch, the case engraved with the initials J. G. (for John Green, his grandfather's brother and partner in Oregon's first gasworks). Perhaps playing the grand lady who did not write for money made Bryant feel less poor.

In a distinct *non sequitur* she went on to tell the editor that she had not held herself "within the limits of any organization—not even the Socialist Party" because she felt it was the only way "to be honest with my own conscience."[9] There is no reason to doubt her statement. Nor does it necessarily contradict her unhesitating declarations volunteered to the investigating Senate subcommittee earlier in the year that she was a socialist; she was a socialist by conviction. But how different in tone this niggardly statement!

The truth is that Bryant was in a resentful and apprehensive mood as the time drew near when Reed would leave her, first for Chicago and then, she feared, for Russia. Whatever organization evolved in September in Chicago, she knew with a sickening certainty that Reed would be sent as an international delegate to plead its cause with the Communist International.

Her uneasiness about Jack's prominent role in the coming battle in Chicago was not unrelated to what was going on in America at the time. Reaction was growing apace, employers were widely using the Bolshevik scare as a weapon in combatting strikes. Her inner turmoil did not allow her to trust her own thinking. Was the revolutionary blossoming in America doomed, premature? Or was she simply scared, terrified for Jack?

She told herself that she did not want Jack to be less committed. At the same time she was aware that however involved he was, the political spectrum did not constitute the whole of life for him, no more than it had for certain Bolsheviks beloved by both of them, such as Lunacharsky. But while Lunacharsky was, as she would write, the only man in Russia capable of holding together "the temperamental army composed of the artists of Russia," still, he had "left off composing sonnets."[10] There was the rub, and she was not averse to reminding Reed of the sonnets yet unwritten.

Actually Jack worried about those sonnets himself. One evening Susan Glaspell and Jig Cook walked from their Provincetown house to the Reed place in Truro. As they rested beneath the big tree in the yard, Reed told them: "I wish I could stay here. Maybe it will surprise you, but what I really want is to write poetry." No, they weren't surprised—but then, why didn't he? Susan asked. Hearing her query, Jack shook his head, troubled, "saying he had 'promised too many people.' "[11]

There were days now when the magic of the water, the wheeling gulls, the graceful shoreline of the bay side of the Cape, the dry mild air itself made it impossible to brood, even to think, and it was enough to be alive and sensate. After long delightful days, inevitably for Louise the pearly twilight, the water luminous and serene, brought on a sadness, always known since early childhood in her innermost being but now intensified. Only later in the night, in Reed's arms, her passion swelling and breaking like a great wave and followed by ever lesser waves, she forgot her sadness and felt at home; for the moment, Jack was her harbor.

Even when her anxiety over his coming departure surfaced annoyingly like an itching scab she must compulsively scratch, even when she thought up things to hurl at him (which might include the Millay candle scene she had interrupted—how long ago?) and he shouted, and they were both unmannerly, angry, the two were locked despite everything in deep-lying trust. It was a fierce bonding whose reality made itself felt no matter what the hurt. On Louise's part she was not at all sure she wanted such love, and at this crucial time she rebelled wildly against this concern for Reed which was enveloping her and threatening her identity. She fought against it, but the bonds which always brought them together no matter how they quarreled were enduring.

As if invoking the spirit of Kollontai, she set about planning a program of work for herself. Just making notes for plots and ideas provided a change of focus. Occasionally, though, she could not resist little jibes at some of the tactics the Left Wing pursued. Reed was imperturbable, nonetheless. He was certain the radical Left had shaken up the once comfortable Socialist Party and that it would never be the same again.

However they disagreed on tactics, she and Jack agreed deeply on the future, amorphous as the form they envisioned for it might be. [12]

News which Reed received about the action of some comrades in the Left Wing shattered their near idyll at Truro. [13] Before their planned stay reached its end they set out for home, Reed muttering imprecations against the perfidy of the betrayers. As for Louise, her misery at actually departing a month before the Chicago deadline of August 30 was so acute that it left her curiously calm. Back at 1 Patchin Place, Reed was plunged into deep discussions with their neighbor Jim Larkin, Benjamin Gitlow, and others such as Eadmonn MacAlpine over the new situation. For they were in effect now no longer the majority wing of the New Left. Often they met at Larkin's. Bryant took little part in these talks, [14] and spent as much time at Croton as possible.

Somewhat grimly she began to work on scripts which she hoped, with or without the help of Millie Morris, to sell to the movies, and on short stories for which she had at least the kernel of a theme. Let Jack, Jim, Ben Legere, and the rest thrash out their next moves; she was locked in an important battle of her own. To save herself she must become immune to Jack's fortunes, must free herself from this obsessive worry over him, stop this terrible emotional involvement, and get to work. She would need money, and even more to the point, she had to find herself again, her old self-confidence.

All-absorbing strategy sessions on the new political situation so

occupied Reed day and night now as to make him almost unaware of
Louise's departure when she was away, and certainly unmindful of
what went on in her head.

Occasionally Bryant, in the city for the day and night, would break
away from her writing and join Reed and Legere and Larkin in the
latter's house on Milligan Place. Larkin, a teetotaler who drank tea
endlessly, would brew her a fresh cup. If she expected to find them in
a gloomy mood, she was wrong. At times they spoke of the "One Big
Union"; Ben had seen it in motion in Canada and Reed was enthusiastic about it and would remain so. Or they spoke of how Socialist ranks
from Oregon and Washington to the Bronx were in ferment. All three
were working to build the militancy of the dissenters. Reed, already
sniffing the smoke of the approaching historic battle, appeared in fine
fettle. At times, though, Larkin would belittle a too bookish phrase
from the Manifesto which the majority they represented had issued in
June, for Larkin always spoke in language workers understood. [15] He
reduced Marxism to its fundamentals. Like Big Bill Haywood he was a
poet. Reed adored him, and between Larkin and Louise there was a
special bond.

In view of the mushrooming repression, how had the leftward shift
in the Socialist ranks come about? There were factors that had not
existed in 1909, when a split had occurred and the emergent left was
smashed and demoralized, nor yet in 1912, when again the left was
crushed, after which the National Executive Committee succeeded in
obtaining the recall by referendum (in January 1913) of the great
fighter Haywood. Now in 1919 the example of the October Revolution
irresistibly fed the hopes of the wretched of the earth—and fostered
belief in the achievements of revolution. In the ferment, even the old-
guard Socialists were loud in their support of the Soviets. (Victor
Berger on the first anniversary of the October Revolution had written
that the Russian people "are the Soviets. Here is a government of the
people and for the people in actual fact.")[16]

An event that took place within the walls of the Kremlin in the first
week of March 1919 had an impact on Socialists in various lands, and
in the United States—even in such unlikely places as Kansas, which
along with California would fall in behind John Reed in Chicago the
following September.

In a hall which had served as an imperial court of justice, Lenin had
opened a conference to consider the formation of a Third International. Fifty-odd delegates attended, thirty-five with voting rights, in
response to a January 24 call. Although many came from weak groups,

embryonic parties hastily organized or even merely pacifist circles, and although the delegate from a real Communist Party formed in Germany in December 1918 came with a mandate to oppose an International on the basis that, save for the Russians, the others were too weak, a Third International was formed. Before they adjourned, a second congress of the Communist International was scheduled for 1920. What had emerged, not by design but by accident, was the predominance of the Russians over other nationalities.[17]

To Socialists everywhere, the existence of a Third International signaled a breach of sorts in the blockade that surrounded Russia since the war's end. Delegates from other lands, just by rubbing shoulders with these Bolsheviks whose survival was something of a miracle, felt their own power magnify. So they gladly promised to press their governments by all available means, including revolutionary measures if need be, to halt intervention, and agreed to work for recognition of the Soviets once they were home.

The Manifesto of the Reed group declared that the revolutionary upsurge in the Socialist Party was not due solely to European conditions, but to the "experience of the American movement." The Left Wing, it proclaimed, had been merely "invigorated by the experience of the revolutions in Europe."

Both statements were not mere rhetoric but manifestly true. Bryant in March had heard, with news of the Hungarian revolution, "the feet of that great army across the world"—clearly envisioning worldwide revolution. But marching this year of 1919 was very real, and included the tramp of American workers on picket lines. No longer bound by no-strike pledges extracted during the war, longshoremen, stockyard workers, telephone operators, shoe factory and shipyard and subway workers, railway brotherhoods—in all a record total of some 4,000,000—were striking in America by year's end, with the great open-shop bastion of steel the most significant.

The triumph in Hungary lasted but briefly, and the next Soviet regime, in Munich, fell to German armed forces in only a few weeks, but Bryant, like Reed, was confident that world revolution would triumph. Louise was less outspoken on the platform, but there was no division between them. It was still, in Eugene Debs's words, "the springtime of revolution."[18]

For that matter, if Bryant and Reed did not tack and trim their sails as revolutions abroad collapsed and repression at home escalated, it must be remembered that they were not tacticians. (Louis Fraina was considered one of the astute theoreticians of the Left; the group he had lined up with was now branding Reed's "the Centrists," but there were no major differences in their positions.) Bryant and Reed and countless others can be forgiven for thinking all was possible. The contagion of victory hung in the air; it seemed to have spread from Russia to America; soon all Europe would be aflame with revolt, no doubt about it. [19]

Reed, however, had overhauled his position on the timing of the revolution. He no longer believed, as he had in 1918, that the United States was in a revolutionary situation. As the old Left Wing majority said in its Manifesto, it was "not the moment of revolution" but "the moment of revolutionary struggle."

Bryant's position had remained consistent with her statement to the Senate inquisitors when they had demanded to know whether she thought the Soviet system fitted America, that she thought not "at the present time." At the moment she was not involved, and she was determined not to become so in the struggle to win more delegates for Reed's insurgents. She was not indifferent to the message of the Comintern; she just wished that someone other than Reed would be sent to seek the Comintern's blessing.

Because she felt she was being subjective, she made efforts to be not only considerate but housewifely with Reed, even if it conflicted with her writing. On one occasion when she was working at 1 Patchin Place, she wrote him at Croton, begging him to rest but suggesting that, if he had the energy for it, he should give the dog a bath (she had presented him with a dog, an advance birthday gift). With a show of pride, she asked if the house did not look nice—and were not the flowers wonderful? "I wanted everything to be that way when you arrived." She also asked his forgiveness for her not being there in the country with him, and went on: "I am sitting in our room savagely writing and rewriting this fiction story. I am not going to leave this place until it is finished." [20]

Reed's book was having a brisk sale, but they had used up a considerable advance payment. He had been added, however, at a small salary, to the staff of the new *Communist*, as contributing editor. He would not be covering the convention for the *Liberator:* Max Eastman would do that, along with Art Young; and there was not money enough for Bryant to go with Reed to Chicago, nor did she want to. Her main concern was to support the Soviets in her own way, to work at her new craft, to make herself fit to earn some money. As to the Soviets, she would soon let the Soviet representative in New York hear from her on that. [21] Meanwhile Reed departed, anticipating with zest his confrontation with the old guard of the Socialist Party. Bryant, somewhat sour about the goings-on in Chicago, was left to confront her own inadequacies as a writer of fiction.

Her writing was going fitfully. She did not want to think about Chicago and worry about Jack's getting into trouble. She moved all her writing materials into Patchin Place; she would use Jack's big typewriter while he was gone. It would be comforting to be near Larkin, who also had stayed away from Chicago. She felt that he would be informed should some serious crisis occur. In any event, she would feel better having him just steps away.

Late one night she knocked at Jim's door. A wire had just come from Jack: "Wonderful convention. Everything going fine."[22]

As Louise expected, Reed was thrown into feverish activity almost from the moment of his return from Chicago. He was intensely occupied, in addition to meetings, with *Voice of Labor,* to which he had been named editor by the labor committee of the Left Wing before the Chicago convention. He was enlisting contributions from others and writing and making up pages, using a vacant loft for this work in a deserted building on Twelfth Street, a hideout which he had been invited to share by Carlo Tresca, long the lover of Reed's good friend Elizabeth Gurley Flynn. Tresca was editing an Italian language newspaper there.

Louise's apprehensions about Reed's safety were scarcely mollified by his activities in this period, accompanied as they were by constant surveillance. New York Police Department detectives, federal agents, investigators for the New York State Lusk Committee trailed him. In the three weeks after his return from Chicago until he sailed, she had frequent occasion to note with asperity what an unconvincing conspirator Reed was. She was not the only one to think so. The writer Don Marquis, atop a Fifth Avenue double-decker bus, saw him waiting at a bus stop and, having seen him infrequently of late, climbed down to greet him. Where had he been? What was he up to? Reed laughed and said he was in hiding. What a hell of a place to pick to hide in, said Marquis in mild consternation. "None better," Reed replied, "and besides, the Red-hunters never catch anybody."

Bryant was not of this opinion. Reed's light-hearted approach made her furious and deepened her anxiety. One visitor to 1 Patchin Place at this time recalled it as a period when both the Communist Labor Party and the Communist Party could supposedly operate in a sort of twilight zone of semi-legality but that "for all practical purposes we were underground." After the notorious Palmer Raids, rehearsed in

1919 but full fledged in January 1920, the deep-freeze would set in in earnest. The visitor was James H. Dolsen, one of California's six-man delegation, all of whom had walked out of the emergency Socialist Party convention and into the Communist Labor Party meeting in the I.W.W. hall on Throop Street. Named chairman of the C.L.P. constitution committee, Jim Dolsen had come to New York to see Reed and others on some policy issues which had been left ambiguous at the convention. It was nighttime when he approached the little alleyway lined on either side by two-story buildings. Cautiously he kept glancing back to see if he was being followed, and, wondering nervously whether it would open, knocked on the door of Number 1. Louise came to the door, decided the tall young man with the innocent blue eyes bore no resemblance to a "gumshoe," and led him up to their second floor flat. He introduced himself and was taken aback when Reed, having just emerged from his outsize bathtub, walked in nude, still dripping, a towel in hand; he slapped the visitor on the back, welcomed him jovially, and introduced him to Louise. Such casualness was unsettling to Dolsen. "Everyone was hiding, or running—it was a terrible time—and Reed seemed oblivious. I was rather shocked," he recalled more than fifty years later.[23]

Reed would have preferred to go to Russia at another time, according to Hicks, but "the decision was taken out of his hands; he was doing his revolutionary duty."[24] The idea now was to get there if possible before Louis Fraina, who would be Moscow-bound in behalf of the Communist Party to plead for recognition by the Comintern's executive committee, which functioned between congresses.[25] With the blockade in effect, Reed's eleventh crossing would not be made in ease. He was going as a stoker on a Scandinavian vessel, carrying a seaman's identification card, its owner Jim Gormley having jumped ship. It was nine years since Reed set out, fresh out of Harvard, to work his way over on the cattleboat *Bostonian*. Physically he was a much reduced man now. He had not been a carouser, drank little, in fact (according to Dasburg) never had. But since the loss of his kidney he had not been well, and he had driven himself mercilessly. Bryant had every right to be very worried about him.

However altered in his capacity to endure, Reed was not so changed in other ways since that first trip overseas. Gregarious as ever, he had invited a few friends to see him off.[26] This was toward the end of September. Surrounded by an appreciative audience, relishing the drama of the scene to the full, there was a boyishness about this "Jim Gormley" in his worn working gear that dragged at Louise's heart, just the same. He was gay and lively through the short farewells, and when, his sea pack on his back, he stooped to kiss Louise, she managed her flashing grin and tried to withhold any reproach from her eyes.

She turned and quickly made her way alone from the dock, before Larkin or anyone could catch up with her. She walked rapidly, almost blindly, overcome with a sudden sense of complete aloneness. She felt abandoned, that was it—more abandoned than she had ever felt since . . . she could not remember, but it was an overwhelming feeling. (Perhaps subconsciously it was a reminder of the time when as a very young child she mourned for the father who had abandoned her—a pain not to be borne, so that even as she recorded it she must remake it into the more acceptable grief for a dead father. And the father was like Jack, or Jack like the father, quite able to make a good living as a journalist if he so chose.)

Hating herself for this sense of abandonment and resentment, such as any clinging bourgeois wife might have, she hurried along.

Reed had promised that he would be gone this time only three months, but she did not believe it. Opening the door at 1 Patchin Place, she stood irresolute. How could she stay here? But then, where should she go? In Croton, she would feel less alone. She would go; and then realized she had no idea about late trains. It seemed too great an effort to phone to inquire. Wearily she undressed.

No, Jack would not be back in three months, of that she was sure. In her fright she felt the shadows closing in on her. Was this what was left of Louise Bryant, who had held thousands in the hollow of her hand as she told them of the great upheaval in Russia and stirred their hope for change? What was she now, a cringing creature who thought only in melodramatic terms like abandonment? Oh, if Andrew were only here now, she fumed.

Dully at first, then sharply, in this unwonted mood of conscious vulnerability, it occurred to her that Andrew, dear thoughtful Andrew, who had never once raised his voice to her, had also never attempted to stop her, to keep her with him when, on those weekend trysts, she said farewell. In her unreasonable mood she forgot that he was still bound, and she more than he. She was bound by more than unbroken marriage ties. As much as Louise ever would be bound. Reed had described her in that ecstatic and slightly ungrammatical letter to Sally Robinson as one who "refuses to be bound, or to bound." Flinging herself on her pillow, Louise was sure that even Andrew had abandoned her.

Louise could not forgive Jack for having said, "Separations are the cruelest things," and then leaving her once more. She forgot that she had first loved him because "there isn't another soul anywhere so free." Compulsively she continued to expect him to change: to be far less free than her first idolatrous letter defined him. However much he missed Louise when they were apart, however wonderful their reunions, the high adventure he lived for was not love, with one woman or another, but his work. He could do without her. The same was true of Dasburg, a titan for work. Although many women would figure in his life, he was—and remained until shortly before his death—a tremendous worker, true to his art alone, refusing to allow love or sex or any of those pleasant pursuits to keep him long from his easel.[27] Yet here was Bryant, feeling impoverished by Reed's departure, and in her rising hysteria picturing herself as being abandoned by both men. But she could only think, unreasonably, of fleeing to Dasburg. Within days or weeks Louise found that he was indeed still in Woodstock. She would be most welcome.

Remnants of her woebegone mood remained when she arrived. It was in late October or early November, as Dasburg recalled. The familiar sight of the big uncluttered living room, the bare or almost leafless trees visible through the large windows, was pleasant. Just the sound of Andrew's unhurried speech always soothed her. He took her face in his hands, brushed back the soft dark hair, noticed the shadows under her eyes which deepened their violet hue, and the sadness of her eyes, and murmured, "I know, I know, you will tell me about it," or words to that effect. Gradually she let them out—her frustrations, her fears about Jack, her resentments, even this creepy feeling of being abandoned.

Only when dinner was on the table did Dasburg begin, slowly and gently, to poke fun. He asked what he was to make of this new Louise Bryant who, instead of flitting from continent to continent, now yearned only to stay home and keep Jack by her side. Supposing she could make Jack over, what about herself? How would she respond the next time a call came to speak somewhere on Russia? Would she reply she was unavailable, her place was in the home? At last he got her to laugh at herself—a bit ruefully.

Actually, he understood far more than he let her see at the time. To be able to live with Reed without living for him must be a strain. He thought that one reason for Louise's hating each time that Reed left her was her anxiety about his susceptibility to women. Certainly Andrew was aware that her fears were not without reason. He had never forgotten Reed's treatment of Frieda (Freddie) Lee, the artist and wife of Dasburg's close friend, the sculptor Arthur Lee.

Reed was in Paris during the summer of 1914, supposedly covering the war. Hearing that Freddie was ill with diphtheria, he generously urged the Lees to move in with him in the flat left him by Mabel Dodge when she sailed for home. Dasburg, also in Paris, was called in to mediate after Reed nursed Freddie so tenderly that Arthur Lee, threatening to shoot Reed, moved out. When the lovers moved to a chateau Reed took Dasburg along as chaperon. Lee finally agreed to a divorce. Dasburg sailed for home after Freddie set off to break the news to her family in Germany. Reed gave her the name of the boat he would be on; it was agreed that she would meet him at an Italian port at a certain time, go with him to another part of the war zone, and then return home.

Only when Reed eventually returned to America did Dasburg learn the sequel. Reed asked him to lunch at the Harvard Club and said he had changed his mind about Freddie; he never got off the boat. Dasburg called him a damned brute, they quarreled, and later patched it up. The Lees got back together. But Dasburg had lost a friend: Arthur Lee never spoke to him again.

He had never told Louise about the Freddie imbroglio, but remembering it, he made her feel that night that she was cherished and loved. By morning she was again Andrew's "cheerful Louise." As had happened before, however, the outside world intruded on the haven of Woodstock this time and claimed Louise. What the particular news was that sent her flying back home the next day Dasburg could not recall, only that it was of an ominous nature. Possibly it was the first Palmer Raid of November 7, anniversary of the Bolshevik Revolution, or it may have been some other horror.

Before going Louise clung to Andrew silently for a moment. Both were aware that it was a dark period for America; moreover, whatever came about, Louise inevitably was out in front, as visible as a red flag. She was calm and matter-of-fact. All those wretched self-centered fears, the cocoon of abandonment she had crept into, were forgotten. She let Andrew know she would be back—some day.[28]

14.
The Terror

IN THE FIRST LETTER to reach Bryant from Reed on his journey across forbidden boundaries, written in Christiania, he spoke of men of various nationalities who had, in terrible adventures, performed prodigies of heroism before reaching that port, while others were shot most brutally. "The White Terror blows out of the East, and its breath is like ice."

But for about a fortnight the terror, American brand, seemed to be all around her. The terrible year of 1919 was destined, it appeared, to go out with a bang, not a whimper. Timed to coincide with the second anniversary of the Bolshevik Revolution, the "experimental" Palmer Raid had taken place the night of November 7, concerted raids striking in New York, Philadelphia, Newark, Detroit, Jackson (Michigan), Ansonia (Connecticut), and other cities. Attorney General A. Mitchell Palmer was running for President—the first, but hardly the last, to run on the premise that the U.S.A. faced a terrible Red menace.

A new "Radical Division" in the Justice Department's Bureau of Investigation headed by young J. Edgar Hoover, aided by slews of new agents, succeeded so well in routing out foreign-born, herding them into detention centers and threatening deportation, that the Palmer Raids of 1920 were ever bolder and bigger. Newspapers of November 8 reported that a number of persons in the Russian People's House on East Fifteenth Street were badly beaten by federal agents and police from the New York City Police Department. In other cities, too, the target was often the Union of Russian Workers, which, according to Robert Dunn, had been so imprudent as to vote at its 1919 convention an endorsement of the steel strike.[1]

Another raid that followed the Palmer Raid of November 7 within twenty-four hours and carried a personal impact for Louise Bryant involved investigators for the New York State Legislative Committee Investigating Bolshevism, headed by Clayton R. Lusk, who swooped down on Communist Party and Communist Labor Party offices in New York City. Of the thirty-five people arrested for questioning three were held—Jim Larkin, Ben Gitlow, and Harry Winitsky—and charged with "criminal anarchy." Literature and all the correspondence that the gumshoes could seize were carted out, among them the letters that would reveal John Reed's departure for Moscow.

For Bryant, Larkin embodied the cause of Irish freedom she identified with her father. After he was indicted on the criminal anarchy charge along with ex-Assemblyman Gitlow and Winitsky, Bryant worked with Gurley Flynn and her Workers' Defense Union and others in their defense. As an example of the nervousness of the times, even donors of bail money feared to use their names and gave it in the name of counsel Walter Nelles of the Civil Liberties Union who for the time being was their attorney.

The language of Reed's letter, sent by courier, was pithy and breathed his response to the White Terror: as usual, the very smell of danger increased Reed's adrenalin flow and heightened his senses—as well as his hunger for Louise. He had thought about her so much "that I am really half crazy . . . from now on we must never be separated." In Norway the Party was "entirely won to Bolshevism." The *Voice of Labor* was greatly admired there ("I am the big cheese in these parts") and he had met two Norwegian intellectuals who praised her *Six Red Months*. He was telling everybody "how my honey broke the Overman blockade." He would cross the Swedish frontier the next night on foot. She should write him very seldom.[2]

Bryant was confident that worse tidings were in store on this side of the Atlantic. It did not make her resigned to his facing dangers there, but in one way it was just as well that he was gone. She had not long to wait: on the night of January 2, 1920, the Palmer Raids went into high gear, federal agents swarming into Communist Labor and Communist parties and Socialist Party meeting places throughout the country.[3] As soon as the raids took place agents were primed to telegraph Hoover, who had established a system of card index data on 200,000 "individual agitators" and on organizations, societies, publications, and special localities, as well as all writers, editors, and publishers connected in any way with radical movements. [4]

The January 2 raids in seventy or more cities by G-men netted 10,000 arrests of men and women. Agents were handily assisted by strikebreakers and vigilantes, and arrests were made in such a fashion as to move Federal Judge George W. Anderson to say: ". . . a mob is a mob, whether made up of government officials acting under instructions from the Department of Justice, or of criminals and the vicious classes."[5]

Three weeks later John Reed and thirty-seven other members of the Communist Labor Party and eighty-nine members of the Communist Party of America were indicted in Chicago by a special grand jury on charges of conspiracy to overthrow the government by force. Reed, according to *The New York Times* page 1 story of January 22, had left the United States some time ago, shipping out as a coal passer to Denmark and was then in Russia.

Bryant fervently hoped he was, and that she could persuade him to remain there. Perhaps it was even then that the thought formed in her mind that became almost an obsession as the violence against Reds or anyone who could be accused of being sympathetic to the Bolsheviks escalated: she must get to Russia and somehow keep him there.

On November 13 raids against the I.W.W. throughout the Northwest were launched by local authorities following the Wesley Everest lynching in Centralia.[6] Seizure of the *Seattle Union Record* was credited to Palmer after the paper advocated calm and fair trials for the Wobblies. In Chicago also the I.W.W. headquarters were raided, as well as an I.W.W. hotel where visiting Wobblies stayed; sleepers were turned out into the street and arrested in the middle of the night. Dorothy Day, then working in Chicago, had gone to the rescue of a woman acquaintance who was ill and occupying a room the I.W.W. had given her. Both were arrested and charged as prostitutes!—a chilling experience Dorothy Day never forgot.[7]

The massive steel strike and a widespread coal miners' strike were still in progress, however, and the strike fever spread until even Samuel Gompers struck and walked out of the President's labor-capital peace conference in the autumn of 1919.

Then on December 21, six weeks after being arrested in the November 7 Palmer Raid and incarcerated under cruel conditions on Ellis Island and far worse conditions on Deer Island just outside Boston, some 249 foreign-born men and women were loaded onto the transport *Buford* for deportation to Russia—including Emma Goldman and Alexander Berkman. Among the many leaving wives and children in the States, very few were "anarchists." But all were called anarchists because the Deportation Act of 1918 provided for the deportation of aliens who were anarchists or who believed in or advocated, or were members of organizations that advocated, overthrow of the government by force.

In the end the steel strike was broken, the Red scare a factor. Now the National Association of Manufacturers, benefiting greatly from the Palmer Raids, pursued its open-shop drive with the same weapon. Actually the Red scare had a long history in the United States: in the mid-nineteenth century it was used against the Abolitionists, in the 1870s against the Molly Maguires in the Pennsylvania coal fields, in 1877 against railway strikers, and ten years later it was an element in the hanging of advocates of the eight-hour day. [8]

With two miniscule Communist parties on the scene, the orgiastic onslaught against the foreign-born and radicals became in 1920 the great hope of the open-shoppers. Certain labor organizations and small publications fought back, however, Among the latter was the *Voice of Labor,* and since Reed's departure Bryant had aided Gitlow, the business manager, in providing editorial copy. With Gitlow under indictment, her efforts increased. Her first contribution was a poem in the November 1, 1919, issue, "Out of the Sunset (Dedicated to British Diplomacy)," which read in part:

> We are the Russian children
> Murdered by British guns!
>
> British tanks have been our ruin,
> British gas has sucked our breath,
> British brains contrived against us,
> British schemes have caused our death.
>
> We shall raise a phantom army,
> We shall march on silent feet
> Into every British household,
> Into every British street. . . .
>
> Into every sun-filled morning,
> Into every star-filled night,
> Till the blossoms wither blackly
> And your blood is cold with fright. . . .
>
> We are the Russian children,
> Murdered by British guns. [9]

Bryant, familiar with the stories of how the Wobblies filled the jails until they won the free-speech fights in Spokane, San Diego, and elsewhere up and down the West Coast, wrote an editorial carried on page 1 in the next issue of *Voice of Labor* saying in part:

"The jails are filling up. JAILS FULL OF POLITICAL PRISONERS ARE THE MOST FAITHFUL INDICATORS OF HOW NEAR A COUNTRY IS TO REVOLUTION."[10]

She seemed to be enjoying speaking to workers, and with her new writing, finding renewed confidence in revolution at home. The despair she had felt after Reed's departure, the personal hurt, the sense of abandonment, had been burned away in her anger at what was happening in America. Her response to the arrests and deportations, the beatings and midnight raids, the frame-ups and the savage treatment of I.W.W. members, and the indictment of Reed and others in the two new parties brought about a transcendence in Bryant.

A second letter from Reed said he had been in Helsingfors (now Helsinki) for ten days but until then was unable to write a letter. Now he had a chance to get word to her by the underground. He had expected to be "in headquarters" by now, but still hoped to get home by Christmas. There had been "terrible police raids at Viborg" resulting in the breaking up of the organization; people he had counted on were under arrest. Trying to put it in a better light, he writes:

"If I had gone there when I expected I should now be in the jug, instead of in the comfortable house where I now fret and fume at my delay, and spend the time thinking about my honey and wanting her."

But her heart sank at the last sentence in his closing: "I do nothing but long for my honey. Other people don't at all matter. All my love. Don't try to come this way. It would be ghastly for you just now."[11]

That meant that there were still serious dangers ahead for him. And it made her prospects for getting there dubious. She had had no new passport since 1917 and would be dependent on his making arrangements with the underground. She could do one thing in the meantime: pound away on Reed's old typewriter with the big tin top. For the December 15 issue of the *Voice of Labor* she again wrote the lead article.

Beneath a page 1 cartoon of an impudent-looking newborn babe held aloft by a rapscallion crew of unlikely fathers, labeled Militarist, Lyncher, Interventionist, and so on, Bryant declares it is they who "are creating the American Revolution," and by violence.

"Now the American Revolution, when it arrives, will be *some baby!*' she continues. The "Rising Generation" also is represented in the cartoon, and she predicts that these young people "will undoubtedly show you that [they] can take care of the revolution more wisely and scientifically than you could ever imagine."[12]

Earlier Bryant had written the first of what was intended as a series of "Fables for Proletarian Children." It appeared in *The Revolutionary Age* of January 25, 1919, under the subhead, "How the Revolution Began in America." (The magazine was short-lived, Bryant was occupied with a speaking tour, and no other fable appeared.)

In a dream she hears Scott Nearing's grandson telling Russian children how all the deposed royalty of Europe and the cast-off rulers of other states gone Bolshevik—Italy, Ireland, India, China, Japan—flocked to the U.S.A. Eventually they were seized by the itch to rule and, unable to agree on who gets which of the forty-eight states, go to Washington to lobby their claim. Congress already has had to levy vast tax increases, called Royalty Loans, and enact wage controls while food prices soar. "It was while Congress was debating the most workable plan for the separation of the states into kingdoms," Nearing told the children, "that our revolution began."

Bryant never had believed that Reed would be back by Christmas. Christmas came and went, and she looked at his picture on the wall and tried to remember his face when he told her goodby at the pier, but it was blurred. She had one aim now: to get to Russia and keep him there. Whatever conflict she may have experienced in loving two men was now resolved in this cold agony of fear she felt for Reed. Both he and Dasburg as living personalities seemed equally far away.

Since his second letter she had heard nothing from Reed. She was frightened but would have been far more so had she known the circumstances in which he had arrived at Helsingfors. His hostess there in later years wrote, "He was carried up to my house one winternight with one foot frozen and scarcely able to speak for utter weariness after a 12-hours motor journey in a heavy snow storm."[14]

However lonely and haunted, it was a creative period for Bryant. She wrote "Russian Memories" and the *Dial*, most prestigious of journals at the time, accepted it. In five stanzas, it nowhere mentions to whom it was written. The last stanzas are:

> Three ikons
> And your photograph
> Hang on the wall.
>
> You've been there so long, dear,
> With the same expression

On your face
That you've become an ikon
With the rest.

Ikon, ikon,
I can think of only one prayer.
One more time before I die
I want to see you.[15]

On March 17 newspapers carried a story that a man believed to be John Reed was arrested in Abo, Finland. Subsequent press accounts told of his being held on a technical charge of smuggling: he was carrying diamonds worth more than $14,000 and about $1,500 in several currencies, letters from deportees deposited in Russia by the *Buford* to relatives at home, inscribed photographs of Lenin and Trotsky, and what was termed "propaganda."

No longer could Bryant tell herself that it was better that he was in Russia rather than facing trial on the Chicago indictment. To be imprisoned in Finland, of all places, where the Whites were supreme, could mean torture.

Up to now it was an impersonal angst Bryant felt: America was bleeding at the pores and she wanted to be spared none of it. Reed's fate had become blended into that of thousands. Then one day all her fury over the obscene violations of due process, of rights guaranteed by the Constitution, of human decency, peaked and exploded within her. On April 9 newspapers carried a story that John Reed had been executed in Finland.

The next day *The New York Times* reported in a page 10 item that the news of his execution was erroneous. Finally on April 15 Washington authorities announced they had investigated and learned that Reed was indeed alive.

Bryant had shown on other occasions—when Reed was held in Christiania, when she set out on her speaking trip to the West, and at several difficult junctures on the trip—that in a crisis she kept a cool head. She did so now, working with others to urge important people to send wires to Secretary of State Bainbridge Colby.[16] If Jack was not dead, it was possible he would be—unless the State Department stirred itself to intervene. That was her thinking, and after waiting until more influential voices spoke, she herself wired.[17]

The Secretary of State received messages from many persons of note, among them Jane Addams, Fred Howe, Assistant Secretary of Labor Louis Post, Arthur Garfield Hays,[18] Oregon Republican Senator Charles L. McNary, George Kirchwey, Bourcke Cockran, Carl

Hovey, H. J. Whigham, Scripps newspaper executive Gilson Gardner, who wrote in response to Bryant's appeal,[19] and even Reed's maternal uncle, General Edward Burr. William Hard, Raymond Robins's biographer, saw Bernard Baruch as he was about to take a train back to New York, and described Reed's plight. On inquiring who Reed was and being assured that no one was more radical, he nevertheless went at once to the State Department to have his say, and took a later train.

The true story of Reed's "execution" came out later. He had been to Russia, had presented the case of the Communist Labor Party to the Comintern executive, and was making his second attempt to return to this country to make himself available for trial. He hid in the bunker of a Finnish ship bound for Sweden, when he was arrested at Abo (Turku).

"At first the Finns were not sure who he was and he was held in an ordinary jail. Eventually he was identified and was then subjected to rigorous cross-examination. Despite severe beatings and threats of torture and death he refused to talk and was thrown in a dungeon and held incommunicado," wrote Eadmonn MacAlpine. His letters to American diplomatic officials went unanswered. When he failed to hear from Bryant he was convinced the State Department was maintaining silence on his whereabouts. He figured out one way to make American officials take some action, at least to publicize his whereabouts. He persuaded a Finnish liberal, Mme. Aino Malmberg, who had visited him in jail, to take a story he had written and get it to a news agency. Thus the first definite news of Reed's whereabouts, MacAlpine wrote, "was the announcement of his death—written by himself."[20,21]

With her heart in her mouth Bryant covered Jim Larkin's trial during these anxious days. Picking of the jury began early in April and the trial lasted three weeks. Day after day Bryant sat huddled over her pad and pencil at the long table reserved for the press. Serenely unmindful of risking a contempt of court citation, she wrote that Larkin, acting as his own lawyer, "struggled to find Justice—Justice which has, at least temporarily, departed from these United States."

During legal arguments Bryant's mind wandered, she acknowledged. Once she looked at her sheaf of notes and saw that she had idly written, from Victor Hugo's *Ninety-three*,[22] "There is Mt. Himalaya, and there is the Convention." Beneath it she had written: *"There is but one Irish freedom and it is precisely that deep and all embracing freedom conceived in the heart and brain of Jim Larkin."* As she wrote in the *Liberator* story of the trial:

> Nevertheless, they railroaded Jim Larkin to prison as they will railroad every leader they can reach until the tide turns. Men like Weeks and Rorke and Palmer . . . would close the singing mouths of all the poets in America, if they could comprehend their songs. They would shut up Lola Ridge and Carl Sandburg and Arturo Giovannitti, as well as John Reed.

Larkin, like Harry Winitsky and Ben Gitlow before him, was found guilty of "criminal anarchy." He was sentenced to from five to ten years in prison. Gitlow was defended by Clarence Darrow, who told Bryant that "from the very first" he realized that the case was "hopeless."[23]

Reed was allowed to communicate with her finally, and sent Louise the cable, "Nothing yet decided. Have everything necessary. Are you all right?" In his first letter from the Abo jail he told her he had received no word from her since leaving New York. He'd seen Emma Goldman and others from the *Buford* in the Astoria Hotel on his way out of Russia, so he knew that she was still alive. He had been "fearfully worried—about your health, about whether you had anything to do, enough to eat, etc." He worried especially that she might not know where he was. "I thought perhaps it would be as it was in 1918."

Up to then no charge was placed against him other than smuggling. "This case has been tried, the diamonds all confiscated, and I have been fined five thousand marks (about $250–$300). I have appealed. But this is not what keeps me in prison. It is the question of whether I have committed treason towards the Finnish state." He asked her to please not try to influence the American government to help him.

He was, he insisted, "almost all the time cheerful enough. But the thought of you drags at me sometimes until my imagination plays tricks, and I almost go crazy."

He had sent another letter to Croton, and two cables; would she send his mother one of them? "I hate to ask you—but will you try to save my watch." This was the first of many mentions of the watch—the gold repeater heirloom watch which he had pawned frequently in recent years.[24] He ended, "Spring is coming here, and I long for Croton. Your loving Jack."[25]

As he had received none of her letters, he doubtless learned that she was living at 72 Washington Square South from the cable she had sent regarding a lawyer, through the State Department. Beside the address, he had written: "Aren't you at Patchin any more?" Dasburg, who had an apartment at the Washington Square address that he was not using, was asked if he recalled offering it to her rent-free so that she could sublet the Patchin Place flat, but he had no clear recollection of it. It was possible, he said; he was in Woodstock at the time. [26]

Reed wrote again in ten days, sending the letter to a friend, assuring her that he was quite all right and "able to stand it indefinitely." She was to tell Horace [Liveright] that "the big chief thinks my book the best," a reference to Lenin, adding: "Many compliments for yours." He had received "your dear letter of April 23" that day. He had heard that she was planning to come there. If it was to help him, "I beg you not to do so. But if it is because you want to come abroad, and possibly to be with me in case I am delayed—and of course, if you can find the money—do it by all means. But wait for a cable from me before you actually sail." He would send her some money, too.

Two days later Reed wrote, jubilant over getting a second letter from her, written on April 28; at that date she had heard nothing from him. He had cabled three times and this was his fifth letter; he had sent about three hundred dollars two days earlier. The efforts of friends in America, which she had described, were "a great surprise." But he was *informed by the Finns that I am kept in prison at the request of the United States Government!* Still, the disciplined, self-confident tone of his first letters was sustained. He was far from despairing even when he said:

> Now my darling, this is the tenth week of my imprisonment, and as far as I can learn, there is not the slightest chance of my getting free. . . .
> If I fail in all other ways to get a decision from the Finnish authorities, I shall probably try a hunger-strike.

The Finns, he wrote, were asking the U.S. consul to issue a passport to him. He considered it unlikely that it would be issued. If refused, he would be ordered to leave the country in twenty-four or forty-eight hours. If he went to Sweden he would be "hustled to America . . . more or less deported, in fact. So I have demanded, if I am to be told to leave . . . to go to Esthonia." He was seeking a permit from the Esthonian government, and in that event, would return to Russia "for a short time."

After he openly threatened a hunger strike, the Finnish government promised his release. Within a week, he wrote, he should be out of there, "and perhaps able once more to undress at night. . . . Also to walk around, to hope to see my honey soon."

But the expected release appeared to be stalemated, and no reply came to his request for passage through Reval (in Esthonia) to Russia; to add to all the tension, Louise's letters stopped coming after the first two, and Reed was depressed. A deprivation almost worse than the wretched diet (which he never mentioned) was the lack of writing paper. He had hoarded a few sheets and made a start on a novel of New York politics and an autobiographical novel. But now that he had the few sheets of paper, he wrote Louise, he was "almost crazy that I cannot write." Notes he made for the autobiographical novel are little more than lists of names and places from his past. They end with the words "Peace and Bolshevism."

A letter begun on May 30 asks her why her letters have stopped. He assured her he was exercising, had kept very well in prison; he had been to a dentist and had all his teeth fixed. These heartbreaking efforts to alleviate her worries only strengthened Bryant's determination to get to Russia to care for him. He reminded her of the dates when interest on the Croton and the Truro houses would be due, and urged her again, "Don't forget my watch!" A bleak postscript, "Still no word from Esthonia," told her that the enormous optimism Reed possessed was finally flagging. Another postscript added on June 1 was agonizing for Louise to read: "Still no word. . . . My mind is getting dull. Honey, the house ought to be rented."

On June 2 Reed wrote: "Still not a whisper. It is dreadful to wait so, day after day—and after three months, too. I have nothing to read, nothing to do. I can only sleep about 5 hrs. and so am awake, penned in a little cage, for 19 hrs. a day." Then came a jubilant paragraph:

> 8 P.M.—Just this minute *word came!* I am to go to Reval on Saturday's boat from Helsingfors—or maybe I must wait until Tuesday. Anyway, *I'm going!* This is the last letter to my honey from this place. Wait for news from me, dearest.
>
> > Your loving
> > Big

This letter also told her that if she could come abroad, to go to Stockholm, and whom to see there. They would give her messages from him. In the margin he wrote: "Get ready, but don't start until later word from me!" From Reval June 7 he wired her, "Passport home refused. Temporarily returning headquarters. Come if possible."[27]

Reed's departure from Abo was the signal for an exchange of cables between the U.S. consul at Helsingfors and the State Department, and one from the Acting Secretary of State to the American Embassy at London. Moreover, the Department notified Louise Bryant June 8 that "Mr. Reed had been released and left that day for Reval."[28]

For Bryant, a great weight lifted. Reed was safe for the time being on his way to Moscow. Now she must find a way to make some money and be prepared to make her way to his side when he sent for her. She still was not sure he would not again try to return to the United States to face trial on the Chicago charges. She hoped to prevent that.

Unknown to Bryant at the time was the exact way Reed was enabled to get out of Finland. In MacAlpine's account written for Bryant "as told me by Jack in Moscow," it happened this way:

> Once the Russians knew where he was they got busy. At this time they had several notable White Finns in jail in Russia and eventually an exchange was effected—three Finnish professors for Jack Reed.
>
> Jack returned to Russia and Lenin told him in my presence that the Finns had made a bad bargain as he would have exchanged a whole jail-full of Finns—not merely three professors—for Jack.[29]

15.
Perilous Journey

WITH REED SAFE IN MOSCOW again, Bryant settled down to wait for word that he had made arrangements for her underground journey. It was a relatively tranquil time for her. She again went through the procedure of seeking a passport, figuring it would be unavailing, as it was. In Washington she stayed with Helen Hunkins in her big flat on Fourteenth Street, but was silent as to her plans. Remembering how vivacious she had been when a guest there in 1919, her hostess thought her strangely subdued and withdrawn.

"It was not until long afterward that we learned the reason for her secretiveness and seeming aloofness. She had gone to Sweden, traveling under another name, to get into Russia."[1]

Without being too specific as to the time and details of her departure, Bryant renewed contacts made with Hearst executives when her series on the Bolshevik uprising ran in, among many newspapers, the *New York American* in 1918, and made arrangements to write for International News Service if she reached Russia this time.[2] She wrote Reed's mother, Margaret Reed, in June, as she had done when Reed was released from the Finnish jail earlier. Mrs. Reed wrote that on the day when she received her June letter she also had one from Jack:

"It was such a happiness to hear from him—& more of one to know that he is back in Russia. He says he hopes to come home this summer—which is something to hope for—and live for."[3]

For Bryant this news was dismaying. It showed all too plainly that Reed, stubborn man, was still determined to return to turn himself in to answer the Illinois indictment charging violation of the State Criminal Syndicalism Act. A short note to Louise by courier, without being entirely reassuring, did promise they would be together "before the summer is over." He enclosed one hundred dollars and urged: "In the meanwhile *please do not leave* until a friend comes with a note from me telling you what to do. Trust me and try to hang on." He would have to stay there until after the International Congress (Comintern), which would open July 15.[4]

A week later he wrote her again—this message also marked to go by courier—saying that she would get more money soon. He must remain there until the end of July, and by then all should be arranged.

"We shall not be separated another winter. It is beautiful here now, and everything is going so well. Great events are expected. I can say no more now, except that I love you and want you all the time."[5]

Now that he was in the midst of exciting events Reed said not a word about his health, and the omission was worrisome to his wife. In addition, she felt frustrated over the vagueness of his plans for her— and over the lack of money. She wrote to his publisher in the hope that royalties were due him, but with totally disappointing results.[6]

Then came a brief note from Reed headed "Do not mail! Please *hand* to *Louise Bryant*" with the address, 72 Washington Square, New York, beneath.[7] He asked if she had received the one hundred dollars, again assured her more would be coming soon, and added the cryptic message: "If you haven't arranged to leave America, don't do so. You will soon know why."[8] Was he becoming fearful of her chances to get through at this particular time? Still, he had asked her to trust him, to hang on, and she must do that, and assume that the "you will soon know why" alluded to the forthcoming plan for her journey.

Bryant went to Croton to make sure all Reed's papers and books were put away in good order. The garden, even in its neglect, had a poignant derelict beauty. She could have cried. She must remember to tell him how the fruit trees he planted the previous year had grown. In a life as mercurial as theirs, it struck her as an amazing thing that they ever had managed to achieve and retain this beloved home. She turned the key in the door and wondered when if ever she would be back to unlock it.

She was to spend the last weekend of her stay on this side of the Atlantic visiting Andrew Dasburg at Woodstock. She would return on Sunday as on other visits, and he would come down to the city on Thursday and take her to the pier early Friday. He saw her blithe smile as she descended from the stage. It was a day in late July. As they trudged up Overlook Mountain she chattered away like a chipmunk, making a great to-do over the wildflowers. She was sure they'd all have blossomed and faded, but look at the daisies and wild asters. On seeing some Indian paintbrush, she had to stop and pick a few. She asked him about his summer classes and if he'd take her to his studio to see what he was working on now.

Once within the familiar walls she fell silent. Dasburg took her in his arms. She needn't try so hard, he said quietly. I guess not if I'm all that obvious, she said, and laughed. As she watched him stir a pot of stew she announced she'd made a discovery: now that she was here she really didn't feel dolorous. Andrew suppressed a remark he wanted to make: that he knew she really was delighted at the journey as it would mean danger and peril. He knew well this trait in her, but it was one he would not dare to remind her of, for she would never admit to it.

Instead, he observed in his low-key fashion that, after all, whenever she had been in Woodstock neither knew when she would return. "I'm hungry," she said, dismissing the subject. Watching her attack the stew, he noted there was nothing wrong with her appetite. Why then did she look so thin? I don't like my cooking as well as yours, she teased. Then she confessed she'd been forgetting to eat. She had not wanted to go to familiar haunts such as Three Steps Down; it wasn't a time when she wished to confront acquaintances and their queries. Then, too, there had been so much to do.

She had found Reed's moving piece written when she was in France and he was nearing his thirtieth birthday. It was almost the finest thing he'd ever written, and it told much about him. It made her quite wild to think it remained unpublished. [9]

At dinner the next night Louise said she hated to go away without seeing his son. (Alfred had had his ninth birthday in May.) Andrew replied that once more she had just missed him. "I'm going to write him about Sappho, and that she will be his while he's here," he said, alluding to the turtle Louise brought him on her last visit. "He'll be with me again soon and stay until school starts. And I'll hint that he'll probably be getting some Russian stamps before long." [10] Besides, he began, there will be other—

No, don't say it, Louise interrupted. Then, quite calmly, she said that there could be other times perhaps, perhaps not. Suddenly in a rush she said she wanted him to know that she was going to Jack not only because she felt she must; she wanted to. Over there I'll be working, busy. Jack will be writing, he can go on with his second book on the history of the Russian Revolution.[11] It seemed that at last the tide had turned there, that the Bolsheviks were winning, while here at home it will continue to be awful for quite a while longer, and I'll worry about *you*.

So, promise me you'll never feel—. She hesitated, hunting for a way to finish. She had her own ideas about loyalty, learned when very young from her Grandpa Say. You never turned your back on someone who needed you. You were true to yourself, you held your head high, and if hurt, no tears or regrets. She had not felt guilty about loving Andrew, and she was aware that, however deep the bond between him and Johnson, he had no sense of guilt about his relationship with Louise.

"Promise me you'll never regret my going," Dasburg remembered her saying. Perhaps that was as near as she could come to saying that in her eyes it would constitute a disloyalty to her, Louise Bryant, if he ever "felt sorry" for her. That would be quite intolerable. Or perhaps she did not know why she was saying it.

Before she had to think of starting back, she took out of her valise a small snapshot of herself. It was for him, she said, so that he wouldn't forget what she looked like. He held it to the light, and declared that if he had to depend on that to remember her it would be out of sight, out of mind. Her hat was too big, he could see little but her chin, he complained, and nothing of the eyes he loved.[12]

She told him the few details she knew about the first part of her journey. She was to sail on a Swedish tramp steamer as the wife of a Swedish businessman. Do you think I'll pass muster as a proper bourgeois wife? She asked with a grimace. That brought a laugh, but then Andrew turned serious. He came over to her, took her face in his hands, and looked into her eyes, outlining her eyebrows with a finger. Louise, he began, you know that—

"Don't say it," she interrupted, and took his hands away, but kept them in her hands and examined them as if for the first time. She spread out the fingers and remarked that they were too practical for an artist's. She thought he must have some good peasant blood despite that long line of aristocratic Dasburgs, the remnants of whose castle overlooked the lovely Our river that flows into the Moselle. It's the German discipline in you that I envy, she said, and she was no longer teasing when she said that.

They would have to start down the mountain in half an hour, he told her, and motioned to her to sit down as he got out the tea-cups. Then he said impulsively that he couldn't bear to think of her on that final stretch she would tackle on her way to Russia. The preliminaries were of no concern to him, but she must know that it was all the bunk that the Allied governments had withdrawn the blockade; it was still in effect to the extent that she would be taking fearful risks. "Are you determined to go?" he asked.

Bryant gave him a disapproving look; it was like the glance of an ersatz schoolmarm. Then the haughtiness dissolved and she rambled. She had to save Jack for all of them. She must; he was too valuable to lose. She knew Larkin would manage, but Larkin had been in many jails.

Dasburg laughed. He would remind her, he noted, that Jack for years had taken joy in flouting police and getting into jail. He himself had been held prisoner overnight with him in France.[13]

"Oh, stop," Louise said crossly, "you sound like Walter Lippmann."[14] Angrier than he'd even seen her, her blue eyes blazing, she said that he forgot that Jack had grown up and that the world was no longer bland—if it ever had been—and Jack no longer had to create confrontations; he was not play-acting now, he was a revolutionary. This was for real, and they were all out to get him. Andrew, upset himself, knew full well this was different. At last he told her so, and put his hand on hers.

Yes, she said, still sputtering with anger, and so was that Finnish dungeon different. Then, her temper defusing, she put her other hand on his and said, never mind, but what would he, Andrew, do once she was gone? He must promise to work very hard (it was a way of telling herself that she must), he must believe in a day to come when the world would not be torn asunder. Disjointed words followed. You have to . . . help me believe . . . not always easy . . . you love Jack too, you once said so . . . we're in it all together.

On Friday morning, July 30, Andrew loaded Louise's light luggage into a cab at 1 Patchin Place. During the short distance to a Hudson River pier they held hands wordlessly. He carried her luggage to her cabin, and they clung together a moment. Louise kissed him passionately and murmured he was not to worry, she would write lots of letters.

Dasburg left the steamer in a daze of emotions. It was obvious that no trace of nervousness was felt by Louise, but he was nervous as a cat. He was proud of her grit—but annoyed, too. She seemed actually to be in a transport of joy over this whole venture: at last she had found something dangerous enough to suit her. He strode along, seeing her dazzling smile as he turned to go. He hoped that the arrangements Reed had made for her worked. Reed . . . yes it was true that he loved Jack as he had told her early in their association. He both loved him and could not forgive certain things—such as the braggadocio with which he'd say, as they sat in a Paris café, "See that pretty girl in blue? I'm going to conquer her." Who else but Jack, though, would have opened for Louise a whole new world?[15]

It was a hot, breathless night. As it happened, the boat left the pier five hours late. Once the ship moved out to sea she noted the motionless water. Her first letter to Dasburg was headed "Fifth Day at Sea" and, without salutation, began: "Already the north winds begin to fan our faces. . . . Most of the time I've been lying on the upper deck where the officers go to smoke and the passengers seldom come," she wrote. "The sun and the sea have worked on me—so that I feel more at peace now. Everything was so difficult at the end. I felt very cruel leaving you—and that feeling made me incoherent and aloof. Now I am still worried. Will I really get through? At night I dream that everyone is clawing at me and shouting: 'Who are you?'

"I think now how nice it is now in Woodstock. How peaceful. My dearest Andrew, please, please be happy. Work hard and do great things. I, myself, must work. The whole journey must just be one tremendous task so that I will not again have to find myself stranded and ill as I did last winter. And I must keep J. from coming home. Will you let me know how the Chicago case comes out?[16] It will surely be in the papers. I will send you an address as soon as I have ground beneath my feet and a roof over my head. If J. comes he will only go to prison and that will he horrible. Always to know he is there—more dependent than ever—it would destroy us—you can see that. It would destroy all three.

"I am traveling with good natured Swedes. Not an American on the ship. Everynight they dance and all day long they eat and play cards. I read and darn my stockings. . . .

"I keep remembering things that I should have attended to. The taxes and interest on the Truro house worry me most. I hope Esther gets notices.[17] . . . Please go and see her when you are in town. She is so nice.

"There is no more to tell. I will write news and send you many letters if I land. Best love to you, dear. Be courageous. Nothing can happen to me.—and I will come back again when I can rest and be happy. L.[18]

The mood of the letter seems distracted, except for that description of Reed, "more dependent than ever." (It was a thought Dasburg never had associated with her feeling about Reed.)[19] Those words make sense only if she was feeling a bit sorry for herself. If so, it may have been like whistling in the dark to tell Dasburg to be "courageous," when of course it was she who would be jumping borders without a passport of her own, always near the edge of catastrophe and having to lean on strangers who would be running serious risks in aiding her. "Work hard and do great things. I, myself, must work. The whole journey must just be one tremendous task. . . . " She did not stop to consider that it was precisely this subjugation of all else to duty that so riled (and intrigued) her in Reed as he took headlong risks, had exceedingly narrow escapes.

Something had gone awry on her arrival in Sweden, necessitating a complete change of route and another twelve days before she could reach Petrograd. In spite of this Bryant appeared cheerful, otherwise she would not even speak of returning—for she meant to keep Reed out of the United States so long as the hysteria gripped it. It was never the effects of a short prison term for Reed at which she quailed, but she reasoned that if Larkin drew a sentence from five to ten years, Reed might get twenty. Now she wrote to Dasburg with a light heart:

"I will go all the way to Murmansk—across Norway first and then up and around the coast by devious and difficult routes. I feel as if I shall eventually arrive at the moon instead of Moscow." She was writing this "from the smelly middle of a third compartment—the only thing I could get." She was thinking how much he would love Sweden, as "the architecture is so terribly interesting."

Whatever else was true, the die was cast: Bryant was on her way to Reed—without knowing too much about where she stood with him after this long separation. Nor did she now define, if she ever had, what her love for Reed was, what its color or contour or depth. She only knew that it called for action now. She was at home in concepts of action, not in self-probing. When much of the Village turned from Socialism to Freudianism, she was unaffected. In some interior way that she did not want to recognize, she needed Reed. He provided some spark that up to now she found essential in order to create effectively. This was so no matter how fragmented their relationship. She could tell herself that the excitement of living with Jack was not worth the cost, she could rebel against the role of perpetual audience, resolve not to let herself be vulnerable, keep aware of the danger of being engulfed by him. Whatever it was, life apart from Reed lacked a certain bite.

After twelve days on the ocean Bryant arrived at Gothenburg at nine on the night of August 10, and the next evening set out on an overnight journey across Sweden for Stockholm. It was a short trip over the ocean compared to the trip made with Reed three years earlier, but in her solitude it seemed endless. She had stopped for a cheap fur coat in Gothenburg. But, she wrote Dasburg, "it nearly broke me—so Hearst or the devil will somehow have to bring me back."

Apparently worried as to what would be gossiped about regarding her departure, she instructed Dasburg:

> When the Woodstock & Washington Square sleuths find that I am gone—it is best to say I ran away *without* a p + port and say I worked my way over. They will try to prove some other *act* against me and I see no reason for that. Say I went as a boy if you wish. It will at least set them off on the wrong track.
>
> Can't believe that there is at least one sea between us. I send you my love.

Although this letter had a salutation (My dear, nice Andrew:), it was not even signed with an "L," but a sort of unshapely cross. Bryant left Stockholm bound for Narvik, a port in northern Norway, on her way to Vardö. In 1920 no Norwegian railway ran to Narvik, and even today none goes as far as Vardö. At Narvik she wrote on a postcard: "Dear Andrew: How many years it seems since I set sail! These scenes are now familiar. I am north of the Arctic circle, and it is hard to think that it is still summer in New York—here all is white again."[20]

Narvik was then an important port on Ofoten Fjord opposite the Lofoten Islands. At Narvik, Norway is extremely narrow: from the Swedish border it is only 10.8 miles across to the harbor. As it was bound to be well guarded, since it served with its ice-free harbor as the Atlantic port for the Kiruna iron mines in Sweden, Bryant could hardly have left the Swedish train and entered Norwegian territory without a passport of some sort.

The only way to get from Narvik to Vardö is by ship. Her way led past the immensely intricate, jagged coast of Norway with its deep fjords and little fjords, its rocks rising abruptly from the Barents Sea— cliffs inhospitable to all but vast numbers of birds at home in their crevices. This was Finnmark County, named for the Lapps (called Finns by Norwegians) and its reindeer herds were still the special province of the Lapps. Fishing was the other chief occupation of this largest and least populous of Norway's counties.[21]

In the few words Bryant ever wrote for publication about this journey to Russia she speaks of sailing for days in the Arctic Ocean in order to skirt Finland on "my illegal journey across the world."[22]

In a letter headed only "Vardö," without salutation or signature (other than a cross), Louise wrote to Dasburg:

> I have been waiting here two days for a storm to wear itself out so that I can proceed. It is the most dangerous part of the trip—entirely an underground one. I have been hiding two days in a little room with three others (all men) of different nationalities. At midnight when it is calm we will set out on a 24 hour journey, in a small boat on the open sea. We will land in Soviet territory.
>
> I am deeply depressed, mostly because I am terribly tired—there is no bed here and we have only one meal a day. It is a great experience—this one—and will make a fine tale but just now I cannot write it because it is a secret and because I do not have the energy.
>
> What are you doing I wonder. I am so close to the North Pole that summer does not seem to be part of the world. Yet I know that flowers bloom in Woodstock. . . .
>
> . . . I'll write more when I have crossed the line.[23]

An information officer at the Norwegian Embassy, Inger fel 'Dotto, surmised that once Bryant reached Vardö, it should not have been too difficult to find a fisherman familiar with the route to Murmansk, even a fisherman who had made the trip there with a load of fish to market. After all, Russia and Norway had an active trade for many years. Russia found Norway's ice-free ports most attractive, for until the Murmansk port was established in 1915, Russia had no year-round ice-free harbors in the north.

Ms. Fel 'Dotto turned the pages of a book to point to a photo of a one-masted boat used by Lapp fishermen in 1910, with its sturdy prow and stern modified only slightly from the Viking original. These were plentiful in that region in 1920, she said, and mused on how likely it was that a fisherman would take his boat, four passengers, and another Lapp to help him, onto the open sea. "It is possible; after all, they did cross the Atlantic in boats not so different," she smiled. However much a fisherman was paid, she said, he would be reluctant to consume fuel all the way. But skiffs with one-masted sails and an auxiliary motor were common among fishermen, Ms. Fel 'Dotto stated.[24]

Traveling under sail at five or six knots an hour, Bryant could have reached Murmansk in from one and one-half to two days. Her route had been changed once after landing in Sweden; if she did indeed enter Soviet Russia at Murmansk, the hazards of this scariest part of her journey were not necessarily at an end. Murmansk was then in Allied hands.[25]

16.
The Death of John Reed

JUST WHEN OR HOW Louise reached Petrograd from Murmansk, if she did as she expected and entered Russia at that port, is unrecorded. But when she did arrive in Petrograd, Reed, through no fault of his, was not there to meet her. A letter written from Moscow August 26 awaited her. "Dearest little honey—," it began, "I am so disappointed not to be able to meet you when you enter Russia. I had made all arrangements to go to Petrograd, and if possible farther on the road north, in order to come back here with you. But yesterday I was informed that I must go to Baku in the Caucasus, with the rest of the Executive Committee, to attend the Oriental Congress."[1] He was setting out that night for the Congress.

> To this I thought my honey would love to go. I asked for permission to stay and come later with you. But they refused. Then I asked that you be sent after me. That also cannot be done, because there is civil war going on down South, and we are going in an armored train, which is the only one to go.

He had left word that as soon as she entered Russia he be wired, "so that I may hurry back at the first possible moment." (If Bryant had left Vardö on August 19 as she planned, she may have been in Russia when he wrote the letter, but she may have encountered difficulties at Murmansk.) His trip would take no more than ten days—less, he hoped.

He had received all her recent notes saying that she was on her way, and had been "eagerly awaiting." But he had worried when "last night I got your note saying you were going from Stockholm over

Murmansk, because there have been many people arrested there lately."

The letter was filled with suggestions of people she should see when she came to Moscow—unless she would be more comfortable staying in Petrograd until he returned. In Moscow she should go to the Dielovoy Dvor Hotel and see the commandant, who had instructions about a room for her. Kollontai was living at the National Hotel. Balabanova if she was in Moscow was in the National—or perhaps the Dielovoy Dvor.[2] "Balabanova is in love with you," he wrote, perhaps surprisingly, as Bryant knew her only through one interview in Stockholm. And, Reed wrote, Vorovsky "also is in love with you."[3] She could find Vorovsky's room: he now lived in the Kremlin.

If she chose to stay in Petrograd until he could meet her in Moscow, Jacques Sadoul "will be very nice to you."[4] In Petrograd too she would find Petrovsky (Nelson) living at the Astoria. "He's all right, but don't believe the stories he tells you about the condition of things here in Russia.[5]

"I am longing to see my honey more than I can tell. It seems years. . . .

"But I am worrying about only one thing. I must soon go home, and it is awfully difficult to get out of here, especially for a woman. That is why I tried to get word to you to wait for me outside. But as soon as I found out that you were coming, I was so glad that I was to see my honey sooner." Scrawled in longhand were the words:

"I love my honey with all my heart and am happy to be able to see her again   Your Big"[6]

Possibly the thought of seeing her always interesting old comrade Aleksandra Kollontai made Bryant hurry along to Moscow. If she did see Kollontai she doubtless learned much about the Second Congress of the Communist International then recently concluded, and about how extraordinarily well Reed had been received when the cause of the Negro in the United States was, as Carr wrote, "eloquently pleaded by the American, John Reed."[7] Kollontai would also have let Bryant know that he had fought a stiff fight and lost overwhelmingly in opposing the Congress resolutions on trade union policy.* Yet he had

---

*Events at the Second Congress of the Comintern figured importantly in Max Eastman's attack on Granville Hicks, charging he was withholding the truth in his book *John Reed* in 1936. Eastman was not present at the Congress, and used undocumented conversations he said he had on two widely separate occasions with Louise Bryant many years after Reed's death. Theodore Draper, in an analysis of Eastman's and others' claims that they quoted Bryant, points out that her writings suggest nothing of the kind. Draper fails to rule out disillusionment altogether on Reed's part despite the contradictions among the many tales. See Appendix: A Note on Historical Questions.

been awarded the Comintern's highest honor: a place on the executive committee (E.C.C.I.).

Of course Reed's saying that he must return home soon, although it was to be expected, pierced her. And she was not about to throw in the sponge!

On the morning of September 15 Reed ran shouting into Bryant's room in the Dielovoy Dvor.[8] Each had so much to tell! As he held her close she could feel the slenderness of the once big body. They clung together, adrift in a mounting wave of relief and happiness. She asked silently: why did he have to wear clothes that were little better than rags; why had he not regained more of the weight lost in that Finnish prison cell? The questions could wait. But her gorge rose at the shame of it. As she touched his face, with its feel of gauntness, he seemed "older and sadder and grown strangely gentle."

It was a time of rediscovery for each of the other, and as she wrote soon after, "we were terribly happy to find each other." He told her of his experiences in the Finnish jail, of his dark, cold, wet cell, his miserable diet, his three months of solitary confinement. He spoke of nights of delirium when he imagined her dead. At times he'd expected to die there. He made up a little verse, and on the little scraps of paper rationed him or on books brought by Mme. Malmberg, compulsively wrote over and over:

> Thinking and dreaming
> Day and night and day
> Yet cannot think one bitter thought away—
> That we have lost each other
> You and I. . . .

They should not be separated again, each said; and, as they walked in a park beneath white and silver birch trees and talked through brief happy nights, "death and separation seemed very far away."[9]

Louise implored him never again even to think of that fragment of a poem that haunted him in the Finnish jail, "Yet cannot think one bitter thought away—/That we have lost each other/You and I." She may have thought of the poem, "Letter to Louise," he had written during another long separation, when he was in Christiania—a poem which she thought of frequently in the last lonely year. It would be nice to hear it again; she could remember if he forgot lines. Her copy of it, with its mark "Norway 1918" and its title "Letter to Louise," reads:

> Rainy rush of bird song
> Apple blossom smoke

Thin bells water-falling sound
Wind-rust on the silver pond
Furry staring willow-wand
Wan new grasses waking round
Blue-bird in the oak—
Woven in my word-song.

White and slim my lover
Birch tree in the shade
Mountain pools her fearless eyes
Innocent, all-answering
Were I blinded to the Spring
Happy thrill would in me rise
Smiling, half-afraid
At the nearness of her.

All my weak endeavor
Lay I at her feet,
Like a moth from oversea
Let my longing lightly rest
On her flower-petaled breast
Till the red dawn set me free
To be with my sweet
Ever and forever. . .[10]

For three weeks she had longed for him.[11] They had the red dawn now, what were they waiting for? Certain it is that Reed joyously showed her that her nearness inspired no lingering half-fear.

He took her to meet Lenin and she sensed the quick warmth between the two. No debates on tactics had made their affection less.[12]

It was useless to question Reed about why, after returning from Finland in a depleted state and seriously malnourished, he had not managed to obtain good food and rest to rebuild himself. "He was so impressed with the suffering around him that he would take nothing for himself. I felt shocked . . . unable to reach the pinnacle of fervor he had attained," she wrote.[13]

Obviously Victor Serge's sour criticism of foreign delegates at the Second Congress did not apply to Reed: "The only city the foreign delegates never got to know (and their incuriosity in this respect disturbed me) was the real, living Moscow, with its starvation-rations. . . . Sumptuously fed amidst universal misery . . . shep-herded from museum to model nurseries, the representatives of international Socialism seemed to react like holiday-makers or tourists within our poor Republic, flayed and bleeding with the siege."[14]

Louise began to connect Reed's ebullient spirits, his wish to relax, to see the opera and ballet and take her visiting, with an ever-present mood among the Bolsheviks she met. All seemed to feel that the Second Congress was a great success. The war-weary Red Army, having defeated Denikin, Kolchak, and Yudenich, after seizing Archangel when Allied forces had to contend with mutinies, now by a supreme effort pushed back the invading Pilsudski forces beyond the border and began a mighty sweep into Poland. [15] At the time these victories lent an aura of unimpeachable success to the Congress, and the feeling of imminent revolution in the West grew among the delegates while the Bolsheviks themselves felt new hope in the destiny of the Russian Socialist Federal Soviet Republic. [16]

Reed told Bryant that while Trotsky had put in only a fleeting appearance at the Congress because of the pursuit of Polish armies, he would be available to them one day, he had learned. To her pleasure, he took her to see Trotsky. He also introduced her to Bela Kun, who had come out of jail at Budapest to take power when Hungary became a Soviet Republic March 22, 1919. On his way to Russia that year Reed had written her, "In Hungary, thanks to the American Food Controller, who smashed the Hungarian Soviet government, there is at present the most terrible white terror."[17] He and Bela Kun talked at length about the Oriental Congress they had attended, and the future of the East.

As they talked it had to be obvious to Bryant that however much he hated for her to arrive after her difficult journey and have to wait for him in Moscow, he wouldn't have missed that congress for the world. Turks, Persians and Parsees, Chinese, Kurds, Arabs, Armenians, Georgians and Caucasian and central Asian peoples—former subjects of the tsarist empire and now a part of the Russian Socialist Federal Soviet Republic—were assembled. [18]

The Oriental Congress was by far the largest international group sponsored by the Comintern up to that time, and for Reed, the spectacle of a large hall full of Eastern peoples breaking into shouts, brandishing scimitars and yataghans in the air, and crying in many tongues "Death to Imperialism!" was an unmitigated joy. He was one of the speakers, and in vivid descriptions of what had been accomplished in the Philippines, in Central America, in Cuba, Haiti, and Santo Domingo by the United States, warned them not to put their trust in any sugared words of that country. His final words: "Follow the red star of the Communist International!"

On the return trip, when the train was attacked by bandits and soldiers unlimbered machine guns and placed them on carts preparatory to pursuing them, Reed pleaded to go along and the soldiers let him. [19]

He told her more about his Baku experience, which she later used as background for a chapter in *Mirrors of Moscow*. He took her to see the notorious Enver Pasha, a most unlikely figure on the Russian scene: a one-time Turkish minister of war under the Sultan's alliance with Germany, after the successful nationalist revolution led by Kemal Pasha he fled to Berlin and later, by a ruse, to Moscow. For some reason Zinoviev had supposed he might be useful at Baku. The opposite proved true. Not only did all 235 Turks present shun him as a renegade, all 157 Armenians there, who knew him as one of the originators of the Armenian massacres, felt even more strongly about Enver. It was decided to keep him out of sight. [20]

In addition to all their visits about town and walks alone in parks, Reed had conferences and meetings with the Comintern executive committee. Bryant also had work to do. She was beginning to file some stories for Hearst's International News Service. On one of their last strolls through a little park, seated close together on a bench, smoking cigarettes and holding hands, Reed let her know there had been a Russian woman[21]—but Louise for once stopped him and had no word of reproach. With all the privations he had suffered being very much on her mind, she refused to let him berate himself. But if she was gentle now, as he was, it does not follow that she told him about Dasburg, nor is there anything to indicate she did.

One short week after Reed returned from Baku he became ill. He complained of dizziness and headaches and went to bed. Almost at once Louise was able to get a doctor—who made a wrong diagnosis. He said Reed had influenza. Louise nursed him, feeling how tired and ill he was, how near a breakdown. Early in his sickness she asked him "to promise me that he would rest before going home since it only meant going to prison." She had learned that those with whom he was indicted under the Illinois state syndicalist law faced a maximum of five years (sentences generally were for less) but still felt that in Reed's case other charges now would be added.

But he only looked at her and said, "My dear little Honey, I would do anything I could for you, but don't ask me to be a coward."[22]

Ill as he was, with fever, he began worrying again as he had in the Finnish jail over his gold repeater watch; Louise brought him up to date and he insisted on writing the pawnbroker the letter that would eventually place it in the hands of Esther Andrews to hold for him. [23]

When after five days his symptoms were worse and he became delirious, Bryant asked for a consultation and other doctors arrived; they diagnosed typhus and ordered him to the Mariinski Hospital. [24]

Bryant was aware that because of the blockade Moscow hospitals were desperately short of medications. (Nor was she alone in pointing to their scarcity and connecting it with his plight.)[25]

With murder in her heart for American imperialism, not to speak of the more guilty British and French variety, Bryant quietly asked if she might be allowed to accompany him. She was given the privilege of staying with him, and in all the days that followed "he held me tightly by the hand."[26]

John Reed died on October 17, 1920. He would have been thirty-three years old on October 22.[27]

Louise Bryant, in her letter to Max Eastman for the *Liberator* staff, said in part: "Of the illness I can scarcely write—there was so much pain. I only want you all to know how he fought for his life. He would have died days before but for the fight he made. The old peasant nurses used to slip out to the Chapel and pray for him and burn a candle for his life. Even they were touched and they see men die in agony every hour.

"He was never delirious in the hideous way most typhus patients are. He always knew me and his mind was full of poems and stories and beautiful thoughts. He would say, 'You know how it is when you go to Venice. You ask people—Is this Venice?—just for the pleasure of hearing the reply.' He would tell me that the water he drank was full of little songs. And he related, like a child, wonderful experiences we had together in which we were very brave. . . .

"Five days before he died, his right side was paralyzed. After that he could not speak. And so we watched through days and nights and days hoping against all hope. Even when he died I did not believe it. . . ."[28]

Earlier, on October 20, Louise wrote to Margaret Reed, a letter to go by courier, beginning "Dearest Little Mother." In addition to telling her the facts related later to the *Liberator* staff, she spoke of how on his return from Baku, "for one brief, happy week we walked about the city and talked and lived through a second honeymoon. . . ." When he was taken to the hospital, "I got permission to stay with him although it is by no means customary to allow any one but doctors and nurses to remain with a patient." She stayed from then on, she said. "The last five days I did not even take off my shoes at night but stayed by his bed. . . . He fought so hard for his life— never giving in—trying and trying to smile and to breathe." He was not able to speak after the stroke "but he held me tightly by the hand through the hardest hours. . . .

"Dear little Muz, how sorry I am for you! And—for myself—my life is nothing now. . . . Do you know that as I sat there all those days by that bed . . . I have grown quite grey. . . . I have no silly red cheeks now. . . .

"I just want to do one thing—and that is to come home and get his papers in order. . . . The only plan I have in the world now is to do as well as I can this last service for Jack." She wanted to bring copies of all his papers and works to Russia and to get his unpublished works in print in America.

She confided, "I never had any children because our life was so troubled. . . . But when I met him here this time he told me he thought we ought to have one child anyway no matter what the circumstances might be and I agreed and we were very happy thinking of all this. . . . I feel very far away but the Russians have been very kind to me. They have spared no effort to make things easier for me. And they loved Jack greatly and they give him every honor in their power."

As she wrote his mother, he was then lying in state in the Labor Temple, guarded by fourteen soldiers. "He will be buried in the most honored spot in Russia beside all the great heroes in the Kremlin." And she told "darling Muz" she must know how honored he was there, and how all foreigners will visit his grave for all time. [29]

The day of the funeral was cold, with a lowering sky. Rain mixed with sleet began to fall as the procession set out from the Labor Temple. The great tin wreaths, traditional ornament of burials for the poor, which Louise first saw at the Red Funeral in 1917, were carried from the hall. She walked alone behind the hearse at the head of the cortege, wishing to follow another Russian custom. A military band played the Funeral March, which Reed in *Ten Days* describes as "that slow, melancholy and yet triumphant chant, so Russian and so moving,"[30] and whenever that dirge was struck up, people uncovered their heads.

In Red Square, Louise tried to stand facing the speakers. Speeches were in English, French, German, and Russian and took a long time. A mixture of snow and rain now fell. As a backdrop above the grave was a large red banner nailed upon the Kremlin wall with gilt letters in Russian spelling out the legend, "The leaders die, but the cause lives on."

To the remaining Bolsheviks, death was an old story. Russian-Americans who befriended and guided Reed and Bryant, Albert Rhys Williams, and Bessie Beatty in 1917 were gone except for a few, buried on battlegrounds where they fell: the best of the young Bolsheviks, sent by Lenin as political commissars when the civil war battles were fiercest, took their places at the head of the front lines. [31]

Of those who spoke, Kollontai knew him best, and she poured forth a passionate tribute to the fine manhood and generous soul of Jack Reed. Of Kollontai, Alexander Berkman wrote: "With painful sincerity she questions herself—did not John Reed succumb to the neglect of true comradeship." Kollontai, outspoken, impulsive, may well have questioned others by implication in upbraiding herself. Bukharin, Radek, Reinstein, all were formal, correct and cold in comparison to her. At the same time they represented the top leadership of the Comintern, and, in Reinstein, a tie with the past, as Reed and Williams had worked under him in 1917 in the propaganda office. Alfred Rosner, a French syndicalist, and J. T. Murphy of Britain, who worked with Reed at the Second Congress, also spoke.

It was a great throng of people standing at the graveside. An American face stands out sharply among many of Eastern cast (who came probably to pay honor to the young American who spoke at Baku) in photographs of the day: Big Bill Haywood, long an admirer of Reed's.

Louise Bryant heard little of the speeches, remembering only that when the broken notes of their voices ceased and the first shovel of earth sounded as it rolled down on the coffin, she fainted. She awoke in her hotel room. Beside her were two physicians, a Red Army officer, and Emma Goldman and Berkman, whom she presumed to be old friends.

17.
Alone Again

THE BLOCKADE WAS STILL in effect when Bryant went to Lenin and told him she would like to travel in the Middle East. When she had put the same request to the Foreign Office it was flatly rejected, but Lenin's reaction was otherwise. "He simply looked up from his work and smiled.

" 'I am glad to see there is someone in Russia,' he said, 'with enough energy to go exploring. You might get killed down there, but you will have the most remarkable experience of your life; it is worth taking chances for.' "[1]

Lenin's ready acceptance of her request may have been simply another instance of his kindness after the death of John Reed. But he was intensely interested himself in that Eastern region. Moreover, as she had interviewed him, he knew her work. In all likelihood she obtained permission for the interview when Reed took her to meet Lenin. On what date the interview was held is not indicated on the pages whereon his words in Russian and English, in typescript and longhand, appear in connection with the interview.[2]

In the *Washington Times,* a Hearst afternoon newspaper, her by-line story of the interview appeared on page one, October 14, 1920, under the headline, "Russia Europe's Only Solvent Nation, Says Lenin, Soviet Chief." It was datelined "MOSCOW, by wireless to Berlin, Oct. 13 (night)," and was copyrighted by International News Service. Bryant has described her initial problems with Chicherin, head of the Foreign Service, who had to approve every word sent out of Russia;[3] it can be assumed that he took his time on this story, and that after it won his approval there might have been a further delay if he submitted it to Lenin. It appears, however, that Bryant's vigil by Reed's bedside was interrupted for the interview—possibly four or five days or even a week before his death.

I.N.S. considered it important enough to preface it with a statement that it was the only interview ever given by Lenin to any American newspaper or press association. (Bryant, writing of it later, said it was the first he had granted since the blockade began.) Her story, using the first name given him incorrectly in the West, began:

> Nicolai Lenin today gave an exclusive interview to the International News Service. He received the correspondent in a large, plain office, in the former Law Courts building, now the headquarters of the council of people's commissars.
>
> There was an absence of all guards and all ceremony. Lenin was dressed like a conventional man of affairs.
>
> He was extremely cordial and his conversation was animated. He was curious, asking innumerable shrewd questions which showed an extraordinary knowledge of American politics.
>
> On Lenin's desk was a copy of an American newspaper describing the Farmer-Labor Party convention.
>
> "This is a most important and interesting development," said Lenin, glancing at the newspaper. "I suppose the reactionaries call these fellows Bolsheviks."
>
> Lenin laughed and added: "What are these forty-eighters? Aren't they American Fabians?"[4]

The heart of the interview was American policy toward Russia. Lenin recalled that in the early days of the Bolshevik takeover he had told Colonel Raymond Robins of the American Red Cross that it was in the interest of the United States to be friendly with Soviet Russia. Even then concessions were offered to American capital. "American business men now arriving in Moscow agree with us." American capitalists, he added,

> know perfectly well what they want. They see coming a struggle with the Japanese for domination of the Pacific. They realize that America must soon challenge England for supremacy in the world's markets.
>
> Whether they like it or not, Soviet Russia is a great power.
>
> After three years of blockade and countless revolutions, military intervention and the Polish war, Soviet Russia is stronger than ever.
>
> America will gain nothing for herself by President Wilson's virtuous refusal to deal with us because our government does not suit his tastes.

He pictured the immense unexploited reservoir of raw materials offered by Soviet Russia, saying candidly that Russia needed American manufactured goods. He added that the new revolutionary state could pay for them. Then, supremely confident, he continued:

" 'After the great war Soviet Russia remains the only solvent European country. . . .' "

Two days after Lenin agreed to Louise Bryant's plans for travel in the Middle East, she was on her way, accompanied by two soldiers and bearing a letter from Lenin insuring her passage on any train and her occupancy of a room in any government hotel.[5]

The trip was taken by Bryant not out of sentiment but a news sense that told her the developing relationships of the Soviet government with regimes in the East were a turning-point of importance. But her awareness of events at the Baku conference—the revolutionary government's first substantial look toward the East, with even China in Lenin's mind—had been gained from Jack Reed. She had thus been prepared for this journey, and it was linked indissolubly with Reed's last glowing adventure in Baku.

Her timing was perfect. As she would write in a 1921 series of stories for Hearst newspapers, she "spent a month wandering through the middle east to see for myself" how Russia's new friendship with Turkey, Afghanistan, and the old emirate of Bokhara, a former state in Central Asia, was developing.[6] In February 1921 the agreements between Moscow and Persia, and Moscow and Afghanistan, became realities, and then in March another treaty was signed with Turkey.

In the short space of time since the Second Congress of the Comintern the direction of foreign policy had altered. The Congress had blazoned forth world revolution as its goal, and faith in its imminence was high among delegates both from abroad and Russia. The appeal of the Baku Congress of Peoples of the East lay in the assumption that Eastern colonial peoples would be the next to be ignited once revolution swept Western industrial centers. All would be swept along the road to socialism, oppressed peoples and proletariat marching together.

But the revolution in the West remained stillborn, so this idea while not abandoned was considerably dimmed. What remained of the Baku congress was a recognition of the importance of Asia both as a reservoir of potential revolution and as a useful ally of the Moscow government in its stance against hostile capitalist powers of the West. As the Western proletariat still failed to deliver a revolution, the Eastern peoples were for the moment more important.

Before setting out on her journey to the Middle East, Bryant wrote

Andrew Dasburg, saying in part: "Two very old letters came through from you one day last week. I am quite another person, Andrew. I wonder if you would know me or find it happy to. Jack's illness and his death brought me closer to him than all our life together did. And when he had gone I found myself alone in a strange world and everything smashed to hell."

Despite pessimistic reports on her health from doctors, she wrote, she felt herself stronger and would leave the following week for the Crimea, and perhaps later go to Persia. Moscow would be her permanent address, but when she was able she would return to America. It is a letter of farewell—except for a slight suggestion at the end:

"What shall you do, Andrew? I will be back by early Spring and then you will tell me."[7]

Perhaps the discipline of a wire service, the impersonality of writing in cable jargon, helped Bryant to face life day in and day out. On her way to the Middle East she traveled through the famine area. A second successive year of drought brought widespread hunger and devastation. But whether witnessing the endurance of ordinary people in the food crisis, or riding in a train without lights and watching the stars from her berth, there were times when the past rushed back.

Two poems written to Reed in this period and published in 1921 are testimony to this. The first, "In Memory," evokes the cottage and garden in Croton, and begins:

> Now you are gone—and past our garden hedge
> Walk strangers . . . little knowing
> How brave and fine a soul
> Has loved these clapboard walls,
> That scraggling lilac, yonder spreading elm.

An unpretentious and strangely moving poem, it ends:

> What matter if I wake in tears at cock-crow?
> I'll have the dreams again at night . . .
> And after many dreams, the long dream
> From which I'll wake not
> And no spell of stars be broken.[8]

The second poem to Reed, "Aftermath," appeared in the *Liberator* and was reprinted the following year by *Current Opinion*. Two of its five stanzas are given here.

I cannot cry any more,
Too burning deep is my grief. . . .
I dance through my spendthrift days
Like a fallen leaf.

If only the dance would finish
Like a flash in the sky . . . oh, soon,
If only a storm would come shouting—
Hurl me past stars and moon![9]

Although Lenin's letter allowed Bryant to get on board any train, military or otherwise, that came along,[10] entries in her diary as she made the trip over the Kirghiz Steppes in February 1921 indicate the slowness of such travel. At night the train was stopped by snowdrifts.

"At 2:30 this afternoon our train still stands. It is terribly cold. At this station there is no hot water [for passengers to make their tea] because that part of the station where the water was boiled was shot away during the fighting. We have had no tea all day but nobody seems to care. In Russia one must learn to be philosophical.

"An old peasant woman came on board to sell cutlets. They were far from clean, but still I bargained. I haven't had any meat for over a week. She did not want rubles but gave me the two cutlets for a piece of bread. She promised to bring me milk. I suppose it will be like drinking poison because it will be unboiled but I am too thirsty to wait any longer.

"The peasant woman is curious because I am an American.

" 'Why, you look just like we do.' she said, 'just like a Russian. I expected Americans to look quite different. May God give you a good future.'

"I have to smile. I don't think an American would recognize me as a fellow countrywoman. I haven't washed in two days. I wear an old fur hat and a shuba, a ragged dress and Tartar boots. . . .

"At 7 o'clock [about two days late] the train moved again. We all wonder how long it will be before we run into another drift."[11]

In Tashkent, Bryant found Jacob Peters, who in 1917 had befriended American reporters and such English reporters as M. Philips Price of the *Manchester Guardian* and Arthur Ransome of the *Daily News;* he was now acting as virtual governor of Turkestan. A Lettish-Englishman who returned from exile in London after the February Revolution, he had been entrusted by Lenin with many responsible posts on far-flung fronts considered difficult. Earlier he had been chief deputy to Dzerzhinsky, head of the Cheka. Here in historic Turkestan, geographically and historically a bridge between East and West through which many of the famed conquerors and migrating peoples had passed, Peters was in another sensitive spot.

Preceding Peters, some Soviet official had made the mistake of closing down all the little bazaars in Tashkent. As Jake Peters told Bryant, the Muslims long had conducted trade in this fashion, and knew no other way of life. "You could hardly call them counterrevolutionaries just for living." So Peters opened the bazaars—and until it was understood that they were to remain open, he sent his men to protect them.

Bryant found Peters and his second wife, a red-haired Russian schoolteacher now working on adult education under Krupskaya, living in one small room. "Do you really have to live in such a small room?" she asked. Housing conditions in Tashkent, he replied, were terrible, so why should they expect more? "There are some Soviet officials who try to be privileged characters," he observed, "but no one respects them and they do not last long. My idea is that if you ask others to undergo privations you have to set the example."

In her story on Peters, Bryant admitted that she had wanted to ask him exactly how many death warrants he had signed "in those hysterical days which followed the assassination of Mirbach and the attempted assassination of Lenin." There were various estimates, she wrote, including that of the Soviets as 3,000. "I wanted to ask him . . . but I could never do it."[12] After all, Peters had been a good friend. For once her objectivity failed her. There were too many memories.

To see how the Soviets' new treaties with Middle Eastern nations— they extended "clear down to the very edge of India"—were working, wrote Bryant, she "traveled a hard but intensely interesting journey over the Kirghiz Steppes, the Desert of Kizil Kum, through Turkestan, Bokhara, and to the edge of Persia and Afghanistan. I am the only reporter who has been there in six years. Vast changes have come to pass in that time."

In the early days of the October Revolution a declaration was addressed to all Muslims within the old Russian empire, Bryant wrote, declaring their religion and customs free and inviolate. "The present fine crop of treaties is the legitimate outcome of that early planting," she added.[13]

Traveling into the region, Bryant had cause to wonder at the temerity of the many invaders and the migrating peoples who crossed Turkestan, so many were the natural geographic difficulties.[14] There were various things she wanted to know, and so she persisted, and whenever possible, interviewed people—including the 24 year-old president of Bokhara, who gave her the departed emir's Arabian horse to ride but little information.

"I wanted to know, for example, whether the Russians were trying to make Communists out of the Mohammedans first or whether they were more concerned with freeing them from Western domination and then using the strength of that new power as a threat against England and other aggressive powers." Her conclusion was that Moscow was "leaving them a pretty free hand to develop in their own way."[15] Many leaders in the Middle East found no insurmountable differences in dealing with the Soviets, she reported.

The Soviets had made political concessions to the Eastern nations to gain favor with the Muslims. Further, it was those concessions she described as "extraordinarily sentimental" that were precisely those "the value of which can scarcely be overestimated in Mohammedan countries." Most dramatic of these was Moscow's return of "the sacred Koran of the Calif Osman [founder of the Ottoman dynasty under whom the canonical text was established by Arabic scholars] which was meant to be kept forever in the holy city of Samarkand." Instead, "the Russian Imperialists had carried [it] away to the library in Petrograd and thereby outraged the whole Mussulman world."

However inconsistent with "the free ideas regarding religion, or lack of religion, by Communist leaders," Bryant found their policy regarding the religion of the Mohammedans a sensitive one. "The policy of Czarist Russia was to divide the Eastern nations and so keep them weak. Soviet Russia aims to unite them and combine her strength with theirs. What is the menace in that? To us—nothing.

"But when Turkey and Afghanistan and Persia, Egypt and India grow close to each other, what will prevent them from throwing off the yoke of European domination?" she speculates. "And anyone that knows anything about English politics knows that the British Empire would be shaken to its foundation by a successful revolt in India.

"Nevertheless, there is a sort of divine irony in the whole situation when the Emir of Afghanistan, who is one of the last of the feudal kings, declares publicly of Lenin, 'He is the defender of civilization, may Allah bless him.' "[16]

On her travels southward Bryant met Christian G. Rakovsky, before the October Revolution a successful writer and now the most powerful figure in the Ukraine. He was married, she wrote, to a princess who still used a lorgnette, preferred to speak French rather than Russian, and was a member of the Communist Party. Rakovsky at first impressed Bryant as more like a suave old-world diplomat than a revolutionary. She soon saw, however, that he had "Lenin's quality of facing squarely difficult situations and discussing them with brutal frankness."

So frank was he on conditions in the Ukraine that Chicherin suppressed her cable account of the interview. Once back in New York, she wrote it for the newspaper series on her journeys of that time. Here is Rakovsky discussing with candor the ubiquity of both bandits and pogroms in the Ukraine with Bryant:

"The discouraging thing about pogroms is that we used to believe they were only possible because they were instituted by the Czar's government, but now that the government is entirely opposed to them, they go on just the same. They don't occur in Great Russia because the Soviets are so well organized, but in the Ukraine we have never had a chance to really work things out because we have been fighting all the time."

Pogroms were more frequent, of course, he said, where the White generals' forces were concentrated. Rakovsky went on:

> Usually it is a matter of looting. But there are many instances where Jews have been killed simply because they were Jews. That is the result of years of superstition and deliberate poisoning of the minds of simple peasants.

As for the problem of bandits, the central government of the Ukraine meant to cut off their supplies of ammunition and already they were running low on cartridges. Throughout Russian history, he explained, the Ukraine periodically was terrorized by bandits, so it should not seem strange that "we are always carrying on guerrilla warfare." That their numbers were so large at the time was due to so many years of war and civil war. He added drily:

> The revolution has initiated a differentiation of classes even among the bandits. Before the revolution they were just plain thieves, but now they give themselves airs—some are monarchists in a vague romantic way, while Machno [Makhno, N.], for example, has an anarchist leaning. He was operating on the right bank of the Dneiper.
>
> Now on the left bank of the same river the bandits were of a national character and were, therefore, even more dangerous to the state because of their tendencies toward Petlura and Skoropodsky. Other bands were also formed in Bessarabia and Poland.

To make matters worse, some of the rich peasants had hired bands to fight for them "as if they were still living in the Middle Ages." Rakovsky saw "the proper stimulus" for order coming only with the resumption of trade and the reconstruction of the Ukraine. [17]

18.
Bryant Writes Unsparingly
of Revolution's "Gray Days"

WITH LOUISE BRYANT'S ARRIVAL in Riga, Latvia, in late April, 1921, and her request for a passport, cablegrams flew between Riga and Washington and continued until finally on July 11 she was permitted to sail—without a passport.

The concern over Bryant was shown some two weeks before she arrived in Riga. At that time the Secretary of State, Charles Evans Hughes, was informed by authorities in London that Louise Bryant was about to leave Russia for a time, to be replaced "by person named Day." It was suggested in the cable that this was "of possible interest" to J. Edgar Hoover and the Military Intelligence.[1] (Dorothy Day confirmed that her brother Donald Day was engaged by the Hearst press to go to Russia but on arrival at Riga was denied a visa by the Russians and, she said, fired by Hearst.[2])

On April 30 the consul at Riga telegraphed the Secretary of State that Bryant wanted to go to the United States by way of Berlin and to spend a month in Germany recuperating from a recent illness. Was he authorized to obtain an emergency passport? "Am obtaining much information which will follow."[3] His query was followed by orders from Washington, the orders were then countermanded—the consul misunderstood but was not enlightened.

A memo from W. L. Hurley in the Under Secretary of State's office suggested Bryant should make a statement showing "how she left this country the last time." The memo continues, "There is no record of her ever having applied for a passport," despite the large amount of correspondence and data in the Bryant file of the State Department, compiled in 1920 when top editors and lawyers for International News Service intervened.

But on May 17 the Secretary of State received a letter from attorney Arthur Garfield Hays regarding a cable from Louise Bryant Reed to the effect that she had been waiting in Riga some time for a passport. As she had not indicated the reason the passport was refused or delayed, he would appreciate further information, "as I know she is in poor health."

On May 25 a message signed by Hughes and sent in cipher to Gray, the consul at Riga, instructed him: "Obtain emergency Louise Bryant Reed immediate return United States. Before delivery obtain from her full affidavit showing document she used in leaving United States."

A day after Consul Gray informed the Secretary that Bryant objected to making any affidavit and contended that she was entitled to admission to the United States as an American citizen, a Division of Passport Control memorandum urging that "this woman" be denied a passport "until she furnishes the information demanded by the Department" made its rounds and brought an objection in the cramped writing of a P. Adams. "A refusal at this time will raise a hornets' nest," he wrote. Lest he be misunderstood he added: "P.S. It will undoubtedly be alleged by the radicals that we are persecuting a widow on account of her husband's opinions. It would be well to go slow in this matter I believe."

Below that, in an even smaller script, a J.N.J. wrote: "I don't believe we can refuse to issue a passport because the affidavit is not forthcoming. I suggest instructing the Consul to tell Mrs. Reed that she does not need a passport to enter the U.S. If, however, she insists on having a passport then let the Consul give her the 'emergency' which is coming from Warsaw in spite of her refusal to give the affidavit."

Secretary Hughes on June 21 sent a ciphered cable to Gray, having apparently accepted these suggestions from Adams and "J.N.J.," instructing him to point out to Louise Bryant that passports were not now required to enter the United States and ending: "You should not insist on securing affidavit. Hughes." To this the bewildered consul at Riga replied that she had been "informed previously"—he did not say whether by Attorney Hays or U.S. officials—that American citizens may enter without passports, and continued that she had up to then insisted on having one: "She is now apparently inclined to proceed on direct from Libau without passport which I understand I am not to deliver until after execution affidavit."[4]

On July 13 Gray informed Secretary Hughes: "Louise Bryant Reed sailed direct to United States Steamship LATVIA from Libau July 11th. Having declined to execute required affidavit she sailed without passport." As with other messages from Riga this was countersigned for distribution within the Department by Hurley, and on this one, P. Adams wrote in his minute script: "Informed Mr. Hoover 7-20-21. He said he would let me know if anything was done in the matter."

Actually, repeated denials of a passport to Louise Bryant seemed to have been determined for all time in April 1920. It was then, at the time of Reed's imprisonment in Finland and Bryant's concerted efforts to obtain a passport to fulfill her contract with International News Service, that J. Edgar Hoover wrote to W. L. Hurley at State that "it is respectfully requested that the issuing of a passport to Louise Bryant be deferred until such time when the Bureau of Investigation will have completed its investigation of Louise Bryant."[5]

The Hoover letter opened with his saying he was advised that Bryant "will in all probability endeavor to secure a passport in the very near future." Obviously the Bureau never completed its investigation. And Hoover's request prevailed over the eminently reasonable requests of Hearst editors and lawyers who felt that an accredited correspondent for I.N.S. had a right to a passport.[6]

Bryant's new series, sixteen articles in all, were featured in the *New York American*, "the pride and joy" of William Randolph Hearst, Sr.[7] The first story ran August 16 in New York and August 17 in San Francisco. In her first story she stated that all the average American reader expects of a reporter "is to be a sort of phonograph with a moving picture attachment." She would write from her own experience, she declared, adding:

"It is not necessary to exaggerate about Russia to be interesting. The days are too swift and the life too stark and terrible to be dull. Personally, I feel as if I had lived ten years in one.

"In Moscow and Petrograd I met and interviewed every Soviet official of importance. Lenin I knew best and liked most. Many of my friends were not communists and some were even monarchists."

But 1921 was a year of famine and

> one of the richest experiences of my life was to watch Helena Soohachova through a superb performance of . . . Shakespeare and afterward go with her to her cold little flat, where she cooked kasha

on a tin stove for a dozen hungry actors, every one of them famous.

Beyond all this I know what it is to be hungry and lost in an alien land and what it is to have a great sorrow. In short, I know Russian life as it is today.[8]

Bryant was still in Russia when Lenin proposed what was later known as the New Economic Plan (N.E.P.) to the tenth Party congress that opened March 8, and in her second story explains how he was able to hold power despite the first sharp reaction against the new policy by many in his own party. It was a return to a limited form of capitalism, she explains, embodying the restoration of the freedom to trade, and while new decrees made it possible to own private property—even stores or factories—the principal beneficiaries were the peasants.

After the defeat of Wrangel, which marked the virtual end of civil war, there was widespread peasant unrest with, as Lenin admitted, "tens and hundreds of thousands of disbanded soldiers" taking part in banditry.[9]

Describing the initial opposition that greeted the unfolding of Lenin's proposal to introduce a little capitalism to save the revolution, Bryant told how one Communist arose and called Lenin a traitor and said that he ought to be shot. "Lenine replied very coolly that he had come there to be shot and continued the discussion."*

As Bryant put it, Lenin declared, "We must fight a victorious peasantry or we must compromise." Faced with famine and the demands of the peasants, Lenin had elected compromise. His way, said Bryant, was to walk around it when he encountered a stone in the path he could not step over.

Bryant suggested candidly that "it is a good thing to keep in mind that no matter how far the communists have to retreat in Russia— even if they have to go all the way back to capitalism, which, as far as recent decrees and new laws are concerned, they have done, Lenine will be master of the retreat and it will be carried on in good order and without relinquishing the political power."

Naturally, the reader wonders how Lenine is able to overcome the opposition of leaders in his own party. For example, our papers are always full of the differences of opinion between Lenine and Trotsky.

---

*Even by 1921 newspapers in this country had not uniformly adopted the correct spelling of the name Lenin. In Bryant's first story, *The San Francisco Examiner* used "Lenin" but made his wife "Madame Lenine." In the second, he was again "Lenine." Neither was the *New York American* consistent. I have followed copy, even when in the same story "Lenin" may lapse into "Lenine" at times.—*Author's note*.

As a matter of fact, Trotsky never seriously opposes Lenine, but there are other members of the communist party who do. Madame Kollontai is one.

Madame Kollontai has tremendous courage, but no political following. All the strong leaders are with Lenine. . . . Lenine stands head and shoulders above them all. And he is a terrific fighter. He has the tenacity of a bulldog. He never lets go in a congress or a party conference until he has his way.[10]

Since her return to New York, Bryant wrote, she often was asked if the new decrees would not defeat communism. In reply she explains that communism has never existed in Russia. "There has been a dictatorship which was established in order to work out a communistic state. When the state was established the dictatorship would automatically cease. But communists never believed that a single communist state could exist in a capitalist world, therefore, they aimed at world revolution."

And there was a time when Hungary went Soviet and Germany's fate was in the balance and Italy was shaky, that the dream did not seem so impossible of realization. But these movements practically collapsed. The blockade continued. Fighting went on on half a dozen fronts. Reconstruction was impossible and trade with the outside world was cut off. The communists held on.

Outside the famine areas the peasants were better off than they ever had been, she wrote, but they demanded more.

"Lenine is the only man in Russia with the strength to hold it together. If he were overthrown only chaos would exist. . . . It is true he will not abandon his hope for a world revolution and only the future will tell, if through another great war at some other great human upheaval, his dream will again be near realization."[11]

If the tone of Bryant's 1921 newspaper series on Bolshevik men and women and Russian life in general is sober and at times unsparing, in contrast to her often rapturous reporting in her 1918 stories, it is in keeping with the candid comments of many she interviewed. Aleksandra Kollontai, then active in the Workers' Opposition and in organizing a women's movement, told her:

"Remember these are the gray days of the revolution. Everything has settled down into the monotonous, undramatic task of reconstruction. If you look for that high elation you saw here in 1917 you will be disappointed."[12]

Much was changed since then and some of the changes were surprising. Her first glimpse of soldiers in 1917 was of men who had done away with saluting officers, who had ripped off any insignia from their uniforms that suggested the tsar—men who were rigorously egalitarian. Now Trotsky, the War Minister, had restored the strictest discipline within the Red Army. No longer were officers elected by men in the ranks, Bryant wrote.

"The Red Army has become a great machine, and everything sentimental has been eliminated from it. There is only one order the Red Army or any part of it would not obey. And that would be an order from Trotsky to arrest Lenin. . . . And Trotsky would never issue such an order. He has a great affection for Lenin in spite of their political differences."

In her first interview with Trotsky after her return to Russia, she asked him if he liked being War Minister. He replied frankly, "I was never so happy in my life as when I began to turn the Red Army into a Labor army. That was before the Polish invasion. I made a mistake. I will never do it again. Soviet Russia must have a big fighting force always on hand to meet unexpected attacks."

"An organizer is not apt to be popular," Bryant wrote. "He has to step on too many people and interfere with their lives and pleasures. Last year Trotsky started putting the railroads in order. He began by ruthlessly disciplining the trainmen, insisting on order and cleanliness. He arrested and dismissed, and cleaned house generally. But the railway men made such a protest that Lenin had to pacify them. So Trotsky resigned."[13]

Despite the vilification of Trotsky in the American press, Bryant wrote, "He runs his War Office in a smooth, efficient manner that would delight any American business man, and Russians will agree that he is the one great organizer produced by the revolution."

Only in the Red Army, however, was he allowed to organize without interference, and "that is why it is one of the marvels of modern times. It was built out of the ruins of an old army that would not fight, it was fed, clothed, inspired and recreated by Trotsky. . . ."

At a reception at the General Staff School in Moscow to which she was invited, Bryant was introduced to a number of professors who taught there long before the Revolution. She described youthful officers strolling about, smart in a variety of uniforms. Many were peasants but there was "a generous sprinkling of the old bourgeoisie."

"A countess and a princess who sat near me during an exceptionally good musical entertainment which followed the reception seemed to be quite at home," she wrote. "The officer who accompanied me was the son of a rich Swedish banker. He was a Communist and at the age of twenty-six held the rank of lieutenant-colonel."

"Trotsky insisted he had not become a militarist," Bryant reported.

He would like nothing better than to spend his energies on reconstruction. "We want to live in peace with our neighbors, we want to build up our country and we want trade. But the rest of the world does not want Soviet Russia to exist. They force us to have a great army. Personally, I would let my soldiers go back on their farms tomorrow if I could."[14]

Of Louise Bryant's sixteen stories in the 1921 series, all but one is professionally crafted. Only in writing of Emma Goldman does she abandon her coolly objective reportorial style in her sympathy for the aging anarchist rebel whom she had known so long.[15] It has been pointed out elsewhere that both Goldman and Alexander Berkman had naively envisioned a libertarian utopia in which, as leading U.S. radicals, they would be given positions of importance.[16] But Bryant was careful to say nothing that might belittle her friend in any way and simply wrote from the heart—although, as will be seen, in later years she was not so treated by Goldman.

Goldman told her she would like to go somewhere and write. Somewhere out of Russia? To which Goldman replied: "Yes, life is too difficult here. I am too distracted to write."

She and Berkman had been given a special train and for a year had traveled through Siberia and then the South Caucasus collecting material for the Revolutionary Museum in the old Winter Palace. On her return Goldman had gone to be with her lifetime friend Prince Kropotkin and his family, remaining until some time after his death, and now would work on collecting materials for the Kropotkin Museum, which had been established in Moscow.

"But any woman who has had the leadership of a group of radicals in America with all the excitement and publicity which goes with it," Bryant wrote, "can hardly be satisfied to spend the rest of her days as an obscure collector."

She ended her lengthy story:

"Life in these days of war and revolution is full of tragedies but the tragedy of Emma Goldman, deported from America, overlooked and forgotten by the Russian revolution, which has been her ideal, is a theme that is unsurpassed."[17]

Louise Bryant had been unable to foresee that as soon as her old friends crossed the Soviet border[18] their "one great mission now became the unmasking of the Bolsheviki, and their attacks were more virulent and hysterical than those of the most extreme reactionaries," the books they would write on Russia "charged with fanatic hatred."[19]

It was in 1921 that Vincent Sheean, a cub reporter on the *Daily News*, met Bryant. Sheean, twenty-one, tall, broad-shouldered, handsome, an intellectual with the deceptive appearance of an athlete, had a room in one of the buildings that lined Patchin Place, as did his friend Walter Franzen. Bryant had kept her lease on 1 Patchin Place and was staying there. Franzen, described by Willard Trask as "simply one of the most brilliant minds and attractive personalities that I have ever encountered,"[20] took Sheean to see her.

On the wall Sheean saw the framed original of the Boardman Robinson cartoon showing her before the Overman committee of the Senate, which stayed in Sheean's mind as

> a hum-dinger, Louise looking small, shy and frightened (which of course she wasn't), seated on the edge of a chair while a long-haired senatorial giant looms over her with a menacing finger pointed. The caption: "Be you a Soviet, Miss Bryant?"

After that, Sheean and Franzen often dropped in to see her. Bryant at the time was thirty-six, but Sheean said she seemed just about his age, and described her as "slim, lissom I think is the word, blue-eyed, black-haired and vivacious, with ready laughter and just as ready tears."[21]

Sheean, who was a freshman at the University of Chicago at the time of the Bolshevik seizure of power, wrote in *Personal History* about his year on the *Daily News* and his thirst to learn something of all the events that had occurred while he was a student. "To talk with people who had actually been present at the Russian Revolution (Louise Bryant, Albert Williams) or at the making of the Versailles Treaty, these events, once as remote to me as if they had taken place five hundred years before and on another planet, came to have a meaning at least as immediate as that of my latest interviews with the newest divorcee or murderess. They were soon to acquire more— much more."[22]

It was also at this time that the black poet Claude McKay, an early figure in what came to be known as the Harlem Renaissance, met Bryant for the first time. She had come back after John Reed's death and was turning out "a brilliant set of articles about Russia for a Hearst newspaper." McKay was then a co-editor of the *Liberator*. He first saw her, he thought,

> at Romany Marie's in Greenwich Village and she was encircled by a group of nice young men, collegiate-like. At that time she was a pretty woman with unforgettably beautiful eyebrows. She had sent

The Liberator a pathetic poem about her sorrow, and we had published it. I told her that the poem had moved me more than anything that was written about John Reed's death.[23]

When McKay next saw Bryant—at Max Eastman's, he believed—they talked about John Reed, and McKay told her that when he was in London in 1920 and Reed in Moscow, he heard from Reed, who invited him to come to Moscow where the Comintern was meeting.[24]

"We talked about writing. I was interested in her opinion of so-called 'bourgeois' and so-called 'proletarian' literature and art. Externally her tastes were bourgeois enough. She liked luxurious surroundings and elegant and expensive clothes and looked splendid in them. But her fine tastes had not softened her rebel spirit."

He found that she thought, as he did, "that there was no bourgeois writing or proletarian writing as such: there was only good writing and bad writing." This encouraged him to tell her on one occasion that he and Eastman were engaged in an ongoing dispute. He wanted to write stories of his people in Harlem, "straight and unpolished." Max discouraged him, saying he should stick to verse and write his stories in that medium. But his thinking in poetry was "so lyric-emotional" that it didn't go with the stories he had in mind.

Bryant encouraged him. Max was too romantic about poetry, she told him. She felt McKay should write in prose, and told him that John Reed had written some early stories about ordinary people "with no radical propaganda in them . . . and suggested that I should do the same about my Negro studies—just write plain tales."[25]

Louise Bryant was the main speaker at a memorial meeting for John Reed on October 17, 1921, in the Central Opera House in New York. As the *New York Call* noted the next day, the audience of 2,000 who filled the hall stood in tribute to Reed as his widow stepped upon the stage following the singing of the revolutionary funeral song honoring the martyrs of the 1905 revolution and the "Internationale." Louise said in part:

"The splendid stand of Russia caught the imagination and great heart of John Reed and sent him to Russia to fulfill the mission of the most humane government the world has ever seen. For a year he worked and starved and suffered in Moscow; now for twelve months he has been lying in a grave in the Red Square."

Nor, she said, was John Reed the only one willing to die for his ideal. "Eighty per cent of the October revolutionists are dead today. In every front line of every battle, carrying the standards, march the members of the Communist party. In Crimea the soldiers literally advanced over the bodies of the fallen Communist youths."[26]

Bryant said that 25 million were starving within Russia's borders. "Things are not well with Russia," she warned. Correspondents who live in Moscow hotels cannot know Russia; to know Russia "you must starve there, as I starved when I lost John Reed. Do you think Lenin wanted to change back to capitalism? Russia has need of her friends. What she needs is not charity but trade. She needs help, but . . . intelligent help. Thus can John Reed be honored."[27]

One of Hoover's Bureau of Investigation's boasts when, in February 1921, it woke up to the fact that Louise Bryant had left the United States without a passport, was that she "would be apprehended on her arrival for having violated the passport regulation." She wasn't, but she was terribly anxious to get a passport and return to Russia and her job. So this time she made an affidavit, after waiting a reasonable time and hearing nothing from her application, and submitted it to the authorities, declaring she "is not opposed to organized government, nor is she a member of any radical organization or society" and that her "sole purpose of now desiring to proceed abroad is to make a livelihood by means of writing articles for the King Feature Service."

She also stated that she went abroad in 1920 to be with her ill husband and that the reason she stayed abroad after his death was that she herself "was ill the greater part of the time." The affidavit was dated May 24, 1922.

But Hurley of the Under Secretary of State office was already at work, having learned of her application. "I am having an investigation made in New York of the 'Newspaper Feature Service,' " he wrote May 22, 1922. As usual he could call on J. Edgar Hoover for his ready stock of misinformation. At times the most far-fetched concoctions seem to be inspired by Hurley, only to appear later in Hoover's file as fact. Hurley in April 1920 decided that Bryant's "recently concluded" lecture tour—of the spring of 1919— was "in the interest of the Communist Labor Party" and financed by same, although it was not organized until September 1919. This appears in her dossier as "*October, 1921:* Subject is a member of the Communist Parties or America Unified, and of the Friends of Soviet Russia."

19.

"Famous Correspondent"

ON JUNE 4, 1922, the first of four stories on Lenin and the men around him appeared under the title "Mirrors of Moscow" in the Hearst press. Copyrighted by King Features Syndicate, each carries under the byline of Louise Bryant the designation "Famous American Newspaper Correspondent—Author of 'Six Red Months in Russia.' "

Lenin had had his first stroke on May 25, 1922, losing for a time the ability to speak and being partly paralyzed.[1] In the text of the four long articles, Lenin's illness is mentioned only in passing, as when Bryant pays tribute to his chief secretary, Lydia A. Fotieva, for knowing so well how to manage things that "she is almost an assistant premier. On days when Lenin is ill or in the country, she actually is in charge." Although there is definite evidence Louise Bryant spent part of 1922 in Russia, it is uncertain when she arrived.

It is a more human Lenin than she has heretofore presented that emerges in her first article. She reveals he had favored allowing political enemies to leave Russia, disagreeing with the Cheka on this point. She pictures him as far from faultless. As to his approach regarding mistakes, she had this to say:

> He made all manner of blunders, but that he was able to admit his mistakes emphasizes his quality of mind: it is a scientific mind. A mind so well disciplined that he is able to face every fact, failure as well as success.

Regarding his stance toward "political enemies," she maintains that it "shows an unexpected softness in his make-up which only those who know him well comprehend."

She explained his differences with the Cheka in this way: "Lenin has by no means a forbidding personality; revenge never occupies his mind. He will flay an opponent in a debate and walk out of the hall arm-in-arm with him."[2]

In her second article of the series she declares that Lenin's plans, no matter how carefully thought out, "could not have been materialized without the solid base of Trotsky's bayonets."

"No man will overshadow his eminence in the history of the revolution except Lenin," she writes of Trotsky. "They will remain the two most distinguished personalities and they are complementary figures."

When in 1918 Lenin was shot and "terribly wounded by an assassin," an emotional speech Trotsky made on the nation's grief and rage

> lighted the torch of Red Terror as a backfire against White Terror, already so far under way that the very life of the revolution was at stake.

But here she adds an important assessment of Trotsky when she states,

> it is well for Trotsky and for the Revolution that Trotsky did not direct that terror: he is too passionate and too thorough a soul to have been entrusted with such a conflagration.[3]

In her final story of the series, in which Bryant goes out on a limb and declares that "Krassin is the logical successor to Lenin," events, of course, proved her wrong. But she should be forgiven. She didn't even know Stalin![4]

Krassin, then representing the Soviets in parleys in England, she described as inspiring less panic among the British than had Litvinov because "Krassin came from the same class that Lord Curzon did . . . [he] is as polished and as coldly polite and as well dressed as if he were in the House of Lords. He is tall, middle aged, fine featured and has great personal charm."[5]

Louise Bryant's movements throughout 1922 are somewhat difficult to trace, especially as to timing. The four long articles in this series, like those in her 1921 series, did not carry a Moscow dateline and may have been written in part in New York while she was making efforts to obtain a passport. Records obtained through the Freedom of Information Act reveal that her efforts met with no more success than earlier ones. But she had traveled from continent to continent without a passport since her return from Russia in early 1918.

Once more, the Bureau of Investigation, as it was then called, supplied information to the State Department said to be based on reports of agents and informants to the Navy and State Departments, and her testimony in 1919 before a Senate subcommittee. An earlier report on her testimony by the Bureau incorrectly quoted her as saying that Colonel Raymond Robins was "in sympathy with the revolutionists." This was now further bowdlerized on May 24, 1922, to read: "Worked with Col. Raymond Robins, because he was a bolshevist, in Russia."

Meanwhile the State Department had instructed its Chief Special Agent R. C. Bannerman to investigate Bryant's employers in connection with her passport case. Bannerman sent Special Agent Higgins to ferret out the facts. Higgins's report of May 23, 1922, related that "upon the most authentic source of information" I.N.S., King Features Syndicate, and Universal Service belonged to the William Randolph Hearst cluster of agencies, all operating from 241 West 58 Street.

At the head of the bureaus "are two old and well-known American journalists, both said to enjoy excellent reputations, but curiously enough, having Russian names." They were, he said, M. Konigsberg (at one time managing editor of the *Chicago Evening American*— Moses Koenigsberg, actually, although Mr. Higgins did not say that) "and a party named Gortatowski."[6]

"Louise Bryant," he reported, "works for the combined outfit and is well known in newspaperdom to have been for a long time exclusively employed by Hearst."[7]

Whatever the date on which she returned to Russia without a passport, the only radical in the class of 1908 at the University of Oregon, Floyd Ramp, was in his hotel room in Moscow in 1922—he believes it was in June—when someone knocked on his door, and he recognized his visitor as Louise Bryant. Having learned of his presence in Moscow, she came to greet him. Ramp did not recall what they talked about, possibly the state of the world and conditions in Soviet Russia.[8]

"Of course when I . . . went to Russia in 1922," Ramp has been quoted as saying, "it was perhaps the worst year that they had. 1921 was the famine year and the situation that was developing at that time was a very desperate one. Had it not been for the ingenuity of the Brain Nikolai Lenin, I don't believe the revolution would have lived."[9]

A letter to Louise Bryant from the radical lawyer Frank P. Walsh[10] written in September 1922 on his return from a stay in Russia, makes it clear that he spent time with her in Moscow earlier in the year and became her confidant. The letter was addressed to her in care of the International News Service in London, but she may have been scheduled to go elsewhere as it was marked "Please Forward." He says in addition that he hopes she is enjoying her holiday in Paris. [11]

Bryant is next heard from in large headlines at the time of her confrontation with Mussolini in Rome. Her employers had wanted an exclusive byline story by Mussolini, and she obtained it—an over-blown, self-serving document, filled with bombast. [12] But in the month or so she spent hanging around to get it she did a thorough job of research on the Fascist program; when she finally had her own interview with Mussolini, she was able to put questions that yielded a far more informative story than the usual laudatory account of him appearing in the press of the day.

As an example of the usually flattering tone adopted by the press following the Fascisti's march on Rome on October 22, even so careful a reporter as Lincoln Steffens had summed up his impression of Mussolini with these words:

"He knows . . . he is the hero of a living romance of modern Italy in which all Italians are taking a part. . . .

"He will go some distance, but whether he will go right or left—nobody seems to know; everybody guesses."[13]

Louise Bryant in her story was under no illusion as to which way Mussolini would go. He had imposed no new taxes on the upper class, whether manufacturers or the aristocracy that lived off rents, she pointed out. Workers, on the other hand, already were sacrificing greatly.

"All reforms that it has taken many years to bring about, like trade union restrictions in regard to shop rules and the eight-hour day," she wrote, "have no place in the extreme nationalist programs of Mussolini.

"Under Mussolini's plan for a revitalized Italy laborers must work longer hours without additional pay and accept a tax of from 4 to 6 per cent upon their weekly salary. The middle class is just as hard hit as the workers." The dictator, she added, was cutting expenses by disbanding the Royal Guards, numbering 40,000, who were now added to the rolls of the unemployed; trained for nothing but fighting, they were now idle and disgruntled.

For a time she got on well with Mussolini, suspecting it was because he could see that she questioned him from a knowledge of his aims and program. "Whatever slight advantage I gained in his imagination

. . . was lost by a casual reference I made to the political rights of
women. He demanded a pencil of the secretary and wrote painstak-
ingly in English the following sentence and signed it."

> I am not a feminist because I believe woman must think only of
> beauty and the home, and should not concern herself with politics.

"This is Mussolini," Bryant continued. "His best quality is that he
never beclouds the issue. . . . There is no mistaking Mussolini's
attitude." She proceeded to make her own attitude just as clear:

> I believe he would ruthlessly destroy any attempt by women to
> bring enfranchisement before the people of Italy. He believes in less
> suffrage even for men. One of his first utterances as Premier was:
> "We are moving away from democracy."

In all her roaming through government offices, she noted, she had
never encountered a woman secretary, a woman clerk, or any woman
at all. Not even Madame Mussolini ever entered those masculine
portals. "She has never been to Rome. She has not seen her husband
since he rose to the Premiership," she declared.

A month before her confrontation with Mussolini, Bryant was in
Milan, bent on seeing the Premier's family.[14] "I went to the office of *Il
Populo*, Mussolini's newspaper, now edited by his brother. The staff
informed me that they were forbidden to give the address of the wife
and three children. Mme. Mussolini had strict orders not to give any
of them out."

Nevertheless Bryant found the modest house in the workingclass
district of Milan—with two guards outside—where the family resided.
"The little concierge got red in the face with embarrassment when I
sought to enter." Bryant asked her if reporters often came.

"No, you are the first. Madame Mussolini cannot receive her old-
time friends because they are all Socialists." Then the woman added
with a flash of anger: "If she were here now she would talk to you
anyway. Benito Mussolini could say whatever he wanted to."

That night Bryant found the wife of the country's Premier in the
market with a basket over her arm.

The son of a blacksmith, Mussolini, according to Bryant, "is as
rough and as heavy-boned as a day laborer" and at times "tactless,
coarse and repellent." He had raised himself from bitter poverty—
poverty "which the masses of Italy know only too well." Now ruler of
Italy and head of the Fascisti—the King a seemingly forgotten figure—Mussolini, said Bryant, finds himself "fighting all that he once

believed in, the religion of his father, who was a real figure in the annals of Italian Socialism, against all that he himself suffered imprisonment for."

Bryant quoted Mussolini as calling Lenin's method of making a clear sweep "a leap in the dark," while declaring that "Rome's method is to go forward with ordered ranks."

But among the many she interviewed about Mussolini, an Italian nobleman told Bryant: "It sounds very well, but how are we to know in the end his ordered ranks will not march round to state socialism?"

In Milan, interviewing "one of the greatest financiers in Europe, with an immense factory," she asked why Mussolini did not tax all classes, and received the reply: ". . . An astute politician never defies all the elements of the population. He keeps solid support somewhere. . . .

"If Mussolini can restore Italy's productivity . . . (Italy has no coal, oil or timber, her wealth being in the bodies of the Italian people) . . . he can attack us later. . . . That is our fear."

But when Bryant asked the financier if that meant that "the upper classes remain aloof," her informant responded: "No . . . it is better to be taxed later and have our factories . . . than lose daily now through sheer inefficiency, delays . . . and sabotage." He urged her to point out that no man in France "has had the courage to attempt to balance the budget. Mussolini has dared to do so."

Bryant described Italy as a land where peasants were "scarcely able to keep alive" and living conditions for the poor within the cities "are appalling" and saw Mussolini as the symbol of efficiency. But, she wrote, "efficiency cannot be introduced in a day. Also, in order to get it, he has had to create hordes of dangerous enemies."

"Premier Mussolini," she asserted, "thrust up out of a foaming, boiling mass of anarchy, indecision and despair, much as a mountain might rise out of the turbulent sea, is like a mountain. He is firm and relentless, but lonely."

Her last vision of the dictator was in "the great white and gold foyer of the Grand Hotel under a huge crystal candelabra slouching wearily into a graceful Louis XV, ivory and enameled chair." It was just that once in the entire time she was there that he entered the foyer. His strong body bulged over the edges of the seat, she noted, and his legs were spread wide over the pale rose-colored velvet carpet. An absurdly delicate cup of black coffee rested near his heavy hand. The foyer was filled with Italian nobility, ignored by the Premier as they swept by with cold hauteur.[15]

Reviews of Bryant's second book on Russia, *Mirrors of Moscow*, began to appear shortly after it was released by Thomas Seltzer on February 15, 1923. A full page in *The New York Times Book Review* quotes extensively from the book and reproduces all five of the superb portrait-caricatures by Césare that illustrate it, including Aleksandra Kollontai, befurred and bewitching, and Trotsky, his military uniform gleaming, seated on a prancing steed. The reviewer was anonymous, a general practice at the time in newspapers. Wearied from too solemn writings about Russia, he welcomed Bryant's approach. She and Clare Sheridan,[16] he suggests, "deserve the thanks of the non-Russian world for having introduced a note of insouciance and devil-may-careness into what other writers were rapidly converting into a morass of metaphysics, mathematics and melancholy." Miss Bryant, he asserts,

> is strongly pro-Bolshevist in her sympathies, yet she manages some-how not to let this bias interfere too much with the objectivity of her observations. Nor does she let it cast too rosy a hue over the Bolshevist leaders whom she portrays. After all, it is in the personal touches that she excels, and in these she "lets herself go" completely, without relying for her effects on any admiration which she may feel for the personage with whom she deals.[17]

The World declared that *Mirrors of Moscow* "is of interest and value. Its author has the golden gift of terseness and a pretty taste in similes."[18]

The *Freeman* found that "Louise Bryant's book will cause the reader at least, to pause and reconsider and herein is its great value. The style is attractive; the movement never lags, and one can get much pleasure from reading it, even one who disagrees entirely with its conclusions. Césare's illustrations are as usual incomparable."[19]

K. S. Angell in *The Nation* says in part: "Miss Bryant's book, without being deeply significant, is very useful because it gives an authentic picture of Soviet Russia and visualizes and humanizes for us the men whom most Americans now see as either monsters of cruelty and lust or as gods of enlightenment and prophets of a new Paradise. The book is journalism at its best and something more."[20]

Not all reviewers agreed. *The Times* of London in a long review concluded sourly: "It is clear that the only mirror in which she has seen her Bolshevik heroes and heroines is that of her own enthusiasm; but enthusiasm without a historical background or the ability to form an independent judgement . . . is not likely to present accurate reflections."[21]

And the *Bookman* complained: "One would be willing to take a Bible oath that every word in [the sketches] is rigidly truthful; for this very reason, they are not as interesting as they might be."[22]

A new periodical that made its bow on March 3, *Time,* declared *Mirrors of Moscow* to be "something more than a collection of character sketches. It is also an outline of conditions in Russia under the Soviet Government. To be sure the Bolshevik oligarchs are shown in a most favorable light." But it featured numerous colorful excerpts, truncating the sentences to conform to its staccato "*Time*style." It is not a review but a feature story in *Time,* and sets forth that the author is "a beautiful girl in her twenties, with large brown eyes, chestnut hair and an impudent air of self-assurance that disarms diplomats, statesmen, detectives and editors."[23]

The *Time* reviewer was correct in noting that *Mirrors* does not give solutions. But while Bryant eschews the didactic she does give hints. An important one in the chapter on Kollontai may be found in her statement, "Rightly speaking there never was a woman's movement in Russia until after the revolution. Equal suffrage came first and political education afterwards."[24] Despite all the errors Kollontai made, resulting in her removal from office as the only woman member of Lenin's cabinet, the story might have been otherwise had there been a movement of socialist-minded women prior to the seizure of power, a movement that specifically fought for women's rights and agreed on what those rights were.

20.
Palace on the Bosporus

SINCE JOHN REED'S DEATH, Louise Bryant alone, without him to encourage her and lacking the haven that Woodstock and Dasburg represented to her more than once, found that insofar as her career went, she could do very well indeed. In effect she had followed Kollontai's teachings to women, "not to put all their hearts and souls into the love of a man, but into the essential thing—creative work."[1]

By dint of much hard work and a refusal to become emotionally involved again, she had mastered her profession and by 1923 had a lucrative, satisfying position with the Hearst organization and was "clearly a top Hearst writer of her time."[2] With the publication of her second book a fortnight away, she sailed from Paris for the United States on February 1, [3] but not for long.

She had met William Christian Bullitt in Paris by autumn 1922, possibly as early as 1921.[4] His first marriage, to the beautiful Ernesta Drinker, had failed. Member of a prominent Philadelphia Main Line family, prematurely bald but attractive, a man of reputed charm, Bullitt was fascinated by Louise Bryant. An exhilarating and vital woman in her own right, she was all the more alluring in his eyes because she was the widow of John Reed. Strangely, for all Bullitt's flair for elegant dress and worldly trappings, he was emotionally caught up in a posthumous idealization of John Reed, in reality the least elegant of men.

Because Bryant never wrote of Bullitt save for a brief mention in her book, *Mirrors of Moscow*, it is a matter for surmise just why at this time, at the peak of her writing abilities, she was drawn to Bullitt as a lover. Although she would soon return to her work in the Constantinople bureau of International News Service, she would live secretly with Bullitt in a palace on the Bosporus and eventually marry him.

To her former associates, her marriage to the fastidiously turned out, dapper Bill Bullitt, surrounded by servants and servility, would seem improbable when they learned of it. To his Social Register friends and family, his marriage to the dashing journalist, widow of John Reed, may have seemed equally inappropriate.

But for that matter, in Kollontai's fiction her heroines often failed to maintain the desired stance of invulnerability, thus inviting a variety of woes, for the reforms in man-woman relationships that she preached remained only an hypothesis. When Kollontai herself insisted on marrying Dybenko, her teen-age son reproached her for having "put down the flag of freedom."[5] If Bryant had not put hers down—she may not have intended to attach herself to her lovesick lover for long—she at least had allowed it to dip somewhat. They talked about Russia and he appeared to be serious about it. Bullitt also was interested in Turkey and the exiles who had been among its leading figures. He loved to hear about John Reed, too. It may even have been true that she was in love with him—or simply lonely.

Numerous factors in Bryant's life may have conspired to lead her to gravitate toward Bullitt when she met him. A delayed sense of her personal loss may have set in after the death of John Reed, once its drama and the impact of a heroic personality fighting to survive were less immediate. The lack of food and daily deprivations entailed in living in Russia in the time of famine, days and nights of riding on trains fit for the junk-heap, had taken their toll. She was now in her thirty-eighth year (to which she did not admit) and may have suddenly been aware that she had no personal ties. Before she returned to Moscow in 1922 she had seen Dasburg briefly and learned from him that he and his son, Alfred, had gone to live with Ida Rauh and her son, Danny Eastman, in Santa Fe (the boys were just two years apart in age). At the time she saw him, Ida and Danny were to move to Woodstock soon to set up housekeeping in the house Louise knew so well.[6]

Mirrors itself indicates that her ardor for the October Revolution still burned, although considerably subdued with the introduction of the New Economic Plan. Rationally she accepted N.E.P. as a necessary concession to the peasants; she even defended it, listlessly. But

America in 1923, when accommodation was the watchword and the prosperity opening up with hoopla signaled the jazz age, bootleg whiskey, and complacency, was not a scene likely to invite her.

"It has been terrible to come back," she had written Reed's friend Anne Dennis Bursch before sailing for Russia. "More terrible than I ever dreamed. I want to finish all these things I have to do so I can go away and not come back."[7]

After again failing to obtain a passport she had returned to Russia in 1922—how is not a matter of record—but was a stranger in her beloved Russia now in the throes of modified capitalism under N.E.P. Now in 1923, tasting "normalcy" under President Harding, with the Teapot Dome scandal seeming to typify the normalcy, she again was a stranger. A revolutionary without a revolution is lost without sustenance from others, the elixir of debate.

Bullitt was a charmer. He has been described by the historian Kenneth S. Davis as: "Ardent, charming, brilliant, highly emotional, a romantic idealist of conspiratorial temper for whom everything was purest white or deepest black (from first to last he had an excessively vivid sense of plot and counterplot going on all around him), he had several characteristics of the spoiled rich boy who won't play if he can't make the rules.

"He was proud and willful—and, though he had a rare ability to generate authentic and frequently creative excitements (centered on himself), he was also inclined to over-commit himself to people and then be bitterly disillusioned when they failed to act according to his preconceptions."[8]

Bryant initially may have thought that if cohabiting with Bullitt did not work out she had her work and could depart. If that was her thinking, she did not know the strength of his tenacity when kindled by a new enthusiasm (and would know only later how quickly it could turn to bitter disillusionment).

A gifted man, with a quick eye for the complexity of developing international events, Bullitt often managed to be near the center of them. His first spectacular experience of the kind was during the peace conference at Versailles. Bullitt was twenty-eight years old then and his actual role with the American Commission at the peace parley was a minor one—an information attaché. A Yale man and former *Public Ledger* correspondent in Washington, from the start he was at the center of informal American-British conferences; his boundless belief in himself apparently fueled acceptance by others.

The idea of a secret mission to determine whether the Lenin

regime was viable enough to even consider some accommodation was first suggested by Lord Northcliffe, the newspaper publisher, and the English were heavily involved in the scheme—but not officially. Nor was Wilson's approval a matter of record. All the Allied governments had sent invading forces into Russia to prop up the White generals in their attempts to overcome the Bolsheviks. But from a realistic point of view they could not send additional forces because of the prevailing sentiment against intervention and the general labor unrest at home. [9] In January, Wilson remarked that some mission of inquiry had been in his thinking, too; Bullitt, and Steffens likewise, proposed a mission to Colonel House, Wilson's adviser.

All the visiting heads of delegations had departed for urgent business at home. Moderates such as House and Philip Kerr, first secretary to Lloyd George, were anxious to get a mission under way before efforts by the French for greater intervention escalated. But the slippery Lloyd George, whose efforts to appease the Tories could assume an inscrutable character, before his own departure for London had named to act in his place at Versailles none other than Winston Churchill, his war minister. Churchhill, aware of the political danger of sending in more troops, proposed that the Allies send in more money, arms, and equipment to help the Whites and encourage volunteers from the citizenry instead of troops. His proposals were narrowly defeated February 17.

On February 19 Secretary of State Lansing signed an order directing Bullitt to "proceed to Russia for the purpose of studying conditions, political and economic, therein, for the benefit of the American Commissioners."[10] If the few who were privy to the plan (no other American commissioners were let in on the secret) had no idea that the mission would do more than assay the durability of the Soviets, the inventive character and unconditional self-assurance of young Bullitt were underestimated.

In four days the group set out for London: Bullitt and Steffens, a military intelligence man who spoke Russian fluently, and a naval aide as secretary. Steffens has explained that "House, knowing I was regarded as a friend of Russia, wanted me to go unofficially as a friend of Bullitt, capable of official repudiation." The British provided, gratis, trains and boats, and their consuls speeded the group through Scandinavian countries. The problem was Finland. "Bullitt managed the Finns . . . and when at the Russ-Finn border an arrogant Finnish officer drew up to stop and search us, Bullitt outdid him in arrogance—'Hands off, you. Telephone for orders. We pass.' The man wilted, and the cordon of troops opened. We sleighed across the line to the special two-car train that was to take us to Petrograd."[11]

In a week of parleys with Lenin, Chicherin, and Litvinov, Bullitt won important concessions. Territorial concessions were vast, greater than the Brest-Litovsk peace had demanded. A year later Lenin explained:

> When we proposed a treaty to Bullitt . . . a treaty which left tremendous amounts of territory to Denikin and Kolchak, we proposed this treaty with the knowledge that if peace were signed, those governments could never hold out.[12]

Bullitt telegraphed the full text of the Soviet proposals to House. He returned to Versailles to report at length to Colonel House on March 25, 1919. President Wilson had returned from Washington four days before his telegram was received; House telephoned the President, but he would not see Bullitt. Whether or not he had read the wire, he had changed his mind. He never did see Bullitt.

When Lloyd George was asked in Commons about the peace proposals Bullitt had brought back from Russia, he replied that he had only heard reports "that a young American had come back from Russia with a communication . . . if the President of the United States had attached any value to it he would have brought it before the Conference, and he certainly did not."[13]

Bullitt wrote formally to Lansing resigning from the State Department May 17, and on the same day wrote a letter to the President and presumably leaked it to the press, naming seven areas including Russia where, he claimed, Wilson in signing the Versailles Treaty violated principle and prudence. If Wilson had fought in the open, not behind closed doors, he would have had public opinion with him. It ended, "I am sorry you did not fight our fight to the finish."[14]

Thereafter Bullitt's allegiances would undergo many transformations. He came away from Versailles what he had not been when he went there, a Soviet sympathizer. From that date he allied himself with the cause of urging U.S. recognition of the Soviets.

It will be remembered that earlier, when Bryant was on the West Coast speaking against intervention, Reed wrote her with unconcealed scorn: "And did you see that President Wilson has sent Lincoln Steffens, Bill Bullitt and two or three of that sort to Russia on a destroyer to investigate the Soviets?"

Not everyone on the left in America agreed with Reed's refusal to take seriously the concept of the investigation of Russia plotted—and then abandoned—by Wilson. But in recent years a revisionist historian has concluded that "Bullitt was no *sympathisant* or fellow-traveler. He had a reformer's instincts."[15] Moreover, Arno J. Mayer explains, the conclusions Bullitt brought back on conditions in Russia (gathered by Steffens) make it evident that Bullitt's object in seeking a truce was distinctly different from Lenin's. Lenin needed a truce in order for the Revolution to survive. Bullitt sought to provide "an effective instrument for containment."[16]

Given the complexities of Bullitt's personality, his fierce pride, and a streak of vengefulness, even vindictiveness if "wronged," it was predictable that from then on he would reserve for Wilson a relentless animosity that extended beyond the grave. That summer, when called to testify before the Senate Foreign Relations Committee, he divulged confidences involving Lansing and in general revealed secret deals made by the great powers at Versailles. His career temporarily at a dead end, he had been "angry at everyone, angry at the world," according to George Biddle, and for thirteen years remained aloof from politics—but all the while harboring a burning ambition to be a diplomat.[17] It was in this period that he met Louise Bryant.

For their unofficial honeymoon Bullitt had rented the storied house on the Bosporus built by Kyöprülü Hüsseïn Pasha, noted as a friend of the arts. The famed golden room where ambassadors used to be taken by sultans was in a kiosk in Hüsseïn Pasha's garden, but in modern times a house was added to it. A book on Constantinople's famous houses describes the ceiling of the room as "the most precious thing of its kind in all Constantinople, if not in all the world."

> On the water side an unbroken succession of windows . . . look north and west and south, and bring the Bosphorus like a great sparkling frieze into the pavilion. They also make the water light, by reflection, the upper part of the room. . . . And above all hangs a golden ceiling, domed over the fountain, over each bay hollowed into an oblong recess, lovely with . . . Moorish traceries of interlaced stars, and strange border loops of a blue that echoes the jars below or the sea outside, and touches of a deep green, and exquisite little flowers, all shimmering in a light of restless water.[18]

Bullitt describes something of the life they lived in this seventeenth century palace in a letter to a close associate and confidant:

> Meanwhile you may picture me as lord of the old estate of the great Kyoprulu Hussein Pasha, with the Bosphorus under my windows and a golden room with a marble fountain in the centre, filled with goldfish—and all the Judas trees and wistaria and purple flags and

roses in full bloom. I have a flock of goats and sheep, three dogs, five boats, herdsmen, gardeners and other slaves.

Presumably Bullitt was discreet enough to refrain from showing this letter to Bryant, who would not have appreciated his debonair allusion to slaves any more than an old friend of hers did who also knew Bullitt, to whom this excerpt was sent for an opinion. He found it not funny but deeply characteristic, and maddening. [19]

If the letter seems to suggest a life of idleness, that was far from the reality. Not only was Bryant still working and subject to assignments in Turkey and in Italy, she was also gathering material for a book. Bullitt also was working diligently, writing a novel, *It's Not Done,* calculated to outrage many first citizens of Philadelphia. Dedicated to Louise Bryant and published in 1926 by Harcourt, Brace, it was a novel he had long been trying to start. Like his hero, who finds he can write fiction when involved in a successful sexual adventure with a sculptor, Bullitt with Bryant at his side was able to move ahead with his novel. It was, with little disguise, an autobiographical novel. His heroine the sculptor was "a sort of counterpart of Louise Bryant." [20]

Orville Bullitt has written that *It's Not Done* created a furor in Philadelphia, that it "castigated the social life and satirized the aims and ideals of the rich" and went into twenty-four printings. "The book also dealt with sex, which in those days was usually treated as almost nonexistent." [21]

It is a novel of recurring impotence, which the newspaper editor hero blames on the frigidity of his wife until near the end, when he discovers with a shock that he has not understood her sexuality. Although he had found sex and life exciting with the sculptor, he has married a true Rittenhouse Square product approved by his mother.

As in real life everything was "purest white or deepest black" for Bullitt, so it is with the lineaments of his characters in the novel. But many traits of the hero bear a verisimilitude to the author's, not least the importance he attributed to fatherhood.

In the novel the hero feels an upsurge of pride, delight, and concern when he sees his illegitimate son, a duplicate of the young John Reed, and it is easy to imagine Bullitt in the summer of 1923 feeling some such transports when Louise Bryant became pregnant with his child in the flower-laden atmosphere of the palace on the Bosporus. That the coming of this child became a happy obsession with Bullitt is borne out elsewhere. [22] Symbol or reality, it was for him a consummation for which he felt only gratitude. Now if not earlier he was determined to make it all legal. Already restored by his lover, so warm, attractive and understanding, he now had this badge of security, this living pledge freeing him from past humiliation. The woman who was so important to John Reed and the mother-to-be of the Bullitt heir was one and the same.

This was all very well, but what of Louise Bryant? No known record exists of her reactions at this time, or whether she feared the permanence presaged in tying herself to a man so different in his values from others in her experience, or whether doubts mixed with her eagerness. The prospect of tranquility and security in a life that had scarcely known either with Jack Reed could have been tempting. If she felt a pang over the baby she and Reed had planned in that happy week together before typhus struck, she could think with wry resentment that this child she carried would at any rate be provided with all the material things of life—more than any child Reed could have fathered.

One thing is known with certainty, however: once the child came, Bryant loved her for herself, thought of her as "a person," as she would write Bullitt, and continued to love her for the rest of her life.

On December 10, 1923, four days after she mailed her story on the latest assignment she had received, [23] Louise Bryant and William C. Bullitt were married in Paris. [24] Ernesta Drinker Bullitt had been given a divorce earlier in Philadelphia. The secret marriage to Bullitt took place two days after Bryant's birthday; she was then 38 years old. Bullitt believed her to be 29. He was 32.

Meeting her a year later, Bullitt's confidant who stipulated anonymity, thought her "a beautiful woman." She was in his eyes "vivacious, utterly charming—and *very* sexy." "Louise and Bill were absolutely in love."

Actually a period of turbulence was not distant—and it would be unlike any she had known in the stormy years with Reed. In those days, the greater the risk, the possible danger, the more she had been exhilarated. [25] The risks she now faced revolved around whether she could fit her life to that of a spouse who found much in life to interest him but, if he was the double of his fictional counterpart, nothing quite so interesting as himself. In his own mind he already possessed the unborn baby, it would seem. But if it ever came to the point of trying to possess the mother, he would run into a hornet's nest.

21.
From Paris to Vienna

BULLITT LIKED TO TALK about his forebears, especially those who "opposed oppression." He felt a kinship with William Christian of the Isle of Man, hanged as a rebel, and with Fletcher Christian of mutiny on the *Bounty* fame. He counted Pocahontas, Patrick Henry, and Thomas Walker, guardian of Thomas Jefferson, as relations. His grandfather, John C. Bullitt, drafted the first city charter for Philadelphia, introduced in the legislature by his son, William C., Bullitt's father.

His father abandoned politics and the law and founded the family's fortune by supplying anthracite coal, which he named after Pocahontas, to the Navy and transatlantic steamship lines.[1]

If Louise Bryant had known that her father, Hugh J. Mohan, worked as a boy in the anthracite mines of Pennsylvania that supplied the Bullitt family with its wealth, her husband could have boasted that his wife too sprang from the oppressed, and rather more directly than he.

Orville Bullitt, the banker brother of William Christian, in the volume on William's correspondence with Franklin D. Roosevelt that he edited, reports that his brother married "Anne Moën Reed, the widow of John Reed and daughter of Hugh Moën and Anne Fiennes Moën of San Francisco."[2]

"Bill was a controversial person," wrote Orville Bullitt, but however he was described by others, he saw him as "in effect conservative, with a deep feeling for the rights of man and an intense dislike for the rigidity of the ruling classes and of the status quo."[3]

However much he disliked them, Bullitt was at the same time a prisoner of the rigidities—and affectations—of the Main Line families. "Moën" may have sounded more distinguished to his ear than "Mohan." When Louise married John Reed she listed her mother's maiden name as "Say." Perhaps "Fiennes" sounded more aristocratic. At any rate, as explained by Bullitt's anonymous confidant, on the supposition that more descendants of Lord Say living in England used the surname Fiennes than that of Say, with the Bryant-Bullitt nuptials Louise's mother posthumously acquired the name Fiennes. Louise's "Grandfather Say," it will be remembered, was in fact her step-grandfather, loved by her not for who he was but what he was.

Among the early visitors at the Bullitt ménage in Paris were Padraic Colum and his wife Mary, co-authors of *Our Friend James Joyce,* in Paris then at Joyce's suggestion. It was at a time when "everyone in Paris was talking about Russia," and they looked forward to meeting Bullitt. "But although Bullitt seemed interested in Russia, what he said was not very significant, and he seemed keener about communicating all sorts of things about his family and their connections in Philadelphia. Louise sat listening and holding a cat. My wife and I thought it a wasted afternoon."

To illustrate the way literary circles in Paris were seething over the Bolsheviks at the time, Colum said that he had been taken to hear Lincoln Steffens on Russia by Ezra Pound, "a man who didn't know a thing about the Russian Revolution. It was a good lecture, all favorable to the Revolution, and Pound liked it. He was without money at the time and conceived of the Revolution as a way of running society without money, as a good idea."[4]

Not everyone agreed with Colum. George Biddle, painter and sculptor and Bullitt's friend since childhood, had a studio in Paris then and saw the Bullitts frequently, and pronounced both "very serious about Russia."

"Bill had a passionate love affair with Louise in Turkey. I saw them soon after the year they lived together in Constantinople and they were still terribly in love. But Jack Reed was the real love of Louise's life, and she talked a lot about Jack. Instead of minding it, Bill seemed to make Reed *his* love mystique, too."

Far from uncritical about his old friend—"Bill had an overriding ego and conceit"—Biddle found this "their happy period." He was unsparing toward Louise, too, finding her "a prima donna, and like La Pasionaria—not my type exactly." But now each was absorbed in the coming of the child, a first for each, and "as content as two such people, each liking to be the center of attention, could be. Louise was at her peak—captivating, and an able journalist, and Bill seemed loving. At least there was not the competitiveness between them that there had been with Ernesta and Bill. Louise did not compete with him."[5]

Their first establishment in Paris was a house near the Parc des Princes, which Elinor Glyn had redone when she occupied it. Vincent Sheean, calling on them at a time when "Louise was very pregnant," described it: "There was a ceiling of mirrors—right in the bedroom! And the bed had a canopy like one of the eighteenth century, suggesting Marie Antoinette or the Marquise de Pompadour. The bedroom was all in mauve and violet. Louise thought it very funny, and Bill was amused by the ceiling."[6]

That Bullitt felt a certain pride in the house he rented seems evident in a passage from a letter: it was "perfect for its type, Louis XV—Elsie de Wolfe, soft gray curtains, mauve taffeta curtains, green walls, curtained glass doors."[7]

In these first months in Paris the Bullitts were visited by a number of old friends of Reed's other than Colum.

Steffens came, bringing along the attractive young Englishwoman Ella Winter. To his sister Steffens wrote, "Louise kept writing that I must come; she couldn't have the baby without me, and Billy wanted me there too."[8] Ella Winter, writing in 1971, explained that Louise "wanted Steffens to come over from London and talk about Jack! The main thing I remember about Louise is her lying on sofas in these exquisite Paris gowns. She always seemed alive, though. Billy didn't want Louise to read *Ulysses* aloud lest it influence the baby!"[9]

The painter Charmion von Wiegand, taken to the Bullitt home by her mother, Inez, remembered Louise in "a beautiful red velvet tea gown, a Poiret original." She felt that their arrival interrupted a quarrel: raised voices subsided with the ringing of the bell. More interested in a secret door that led to a passageway than the polite talk of her elders, she was struck nevertheless by one remark of Bryant's: "I live a useless life." Inez, who had met Bullitt through her husband Karl, thought him "most handsome."[10]

Kay Ehrgott at seventeen visited the Bullitts with her mother Sara Bard Field, and Charles Erskine Scott Wood, and recalled that Bullitt was "fastidiously dressed and a pleasant host."[11]

Sara Bard Field Wood had very clear memories of their host. "After Jack Reed, to go to something so superficial, very rich and very society—I couldn't believe it of Louise."[12]

After the birth of the baby, Anne, Bryant was in a happy, tender mood, according to Hazel Hunkins-Hallinan, who received a letter from her "on the ecstasy of motherhood," a letter "filled with emotion and love and exhilaration. She knew I also had a baby daughter. Her letter made me feel I had a glimpse of the real Louise shorn of worldly desires for fame or even for the emergence of the world she had hoped for; it breathed contentment."[13]

George Biddle, who with Clive Weed the cartoonist had called on the Bullitts the evening before the birth, found "both Bill and Louise very nervous, so we stayed fully half the night." The birth took place in the home, and Biddle was rewarded for his patient vigil by being named her godfather; his duties as such he took seriously, then and later.

For a time he felt pleased at the seeming stability of the marriage. But before the first year of their stay in Paris was up, he noted signs of restlessness in Bullitt. He had finished his novel, and Biddle suggested he write another. " 'Why should I?' Bill replied. It was typical, this answer. He had shown he could do it. Nothing was big enough for Bill. I did not think it was a very good novel, but that was not Bill's idea."

Bullitt was worried enough about his health to consult a physician and reported to the painter that the doctor had urged travel and a complete change of scene: roughing it with a man friend in the mountains would be ideal. He had talked it over with Louise, and they both thought of his oldest friend.

First Bullitt came to see him, and then Louise came to Biddle's studio to plead with him to go on an extended journey with her ailing husband. "For some reason—there was some psychological thing involved—they thought Bill needed this. Bill exerted all his charm, which was considerable, and offered to pay all expenses. He wanted to travel through the mountains of Spain. Louise too was charming—by this time she knew I liked her—saying, 'Go, it will do you good, and it might help Bill.' "

Her attitude toward her husband had changed subtly: she was now very maternal with him. "It was evident to me that it was all for his welfare that she came on this mission. Both Bill and Louise wanted rather desperately for me to go away with him." But he was cutting a head in mahogany and not of a mind to interrupt his work. He did not go to Spain. (According to a later statement of Bullitt's, Louise did go to Spain with him in October 1924.)[14]

One evening on visiting the Bullitts, Biddle heard his old friend describe some recent experiences that made the ailing man feel he should be psychoanalyzed. Bullitt's manner as he related them was his usual one of self-confidence, and each story was invested with the drama which in his eyes surrounded his every act. One had to do with his crossing a street: he saw a big truck bearing down on him but, for a moment, just stood there; finally, in the nick of time, jumping back. In another he was out riding, when one of his feet slipped and he almost fell off his horse. He added: "George, can you even *imagine* my ever falling off my horse?"[15]

When Biddle, bored by horsemanship, remained glum, Bullitt went on imperviously: "Then it dawned on me: I had *wanted* to fall off my horse. Frightening. Fortunately I've read a great deal about psychoanalysis. I know all the theories. And I knew, George, that there was only one man for me to see: Freud. Why not go to Vienna? I love Vienna."

George Biddle was not an unkind man, nor was he unsympathetic with Bullitt's problems, whatever they were ("Bill's phobias were many and powerful"). He was irritated by his playacting, though. "Bill's friends always discounted much of what he said; at most, fifty percent of it could be taken seriously. Frankly, I didn't believe a word of the suicide-complex business."

Apparently Freud was less suspicious. In Vienna, Bullitt called on the great doctor, was told by a man who opened the door that he was not well and was seeing no one. Bullitt replied that he just happened to be in Vienna and thought he would look up Dr. Freud, adding: "Just give him my card and tell him Mr. Bullitt called."

George Biddle continued: "Freud must have been waiting at the top of the stairs. Down he came, *running* down the stairs, saying, 'You're not Mr. *William C*. Bullitt, are you? Mr. Bullitt of Philadelphia? Oh, I have been so interested in your work, I have wanted to know you.' He was not taking new patients, but he would take Bill— on one condition only. 'I'll give you my word that I'll not see anyone else in this period, but you must give me yours that you won't desert me!' "

It was with real sadness then that Biddle continued (for whatever Bullitt's pretensions and foibles, Biddle's creed was never to renounce a friend whatever he did short of going off with one's wife): "When Bill began his psychoanalysis with Freud, both Bill and Louise were still trying to be very much in love."[16]

In 1925, when Biddle married for a second time and left France for Croton with his bride, Jane Belo, the Bullitts were not in Paris.

Vincent Sheean had missed the birth of the Bullitts' child, Anne; he was in Spain covering events for the *Chicago Tribune*. He had received a letter telling of her arrival and sent off a telegram to her mother that helped get him in trouble with Primo de Rivera's regime. It was thought to be in code, and he was charged with "providing tendentious information with the design of bringing down the exchange value of the peseta."[17] Eventually the American Embassy succeeded in having the charge quashed, and, back in Paris, Sheean found the Bullitts had moved from the Elinor Glyn house and were in the neighborhood of the Faubourg Saint-Germain on the Left Bank, at 10 rue Desbordes-Valmore, where Anne was born.

"I was, we used to say, the baby's *un*-godfather, although in absentia." He found Bullitt still "romantically dazzled by Louise—perhaps that was his way of being in love. . . .

"Louise never stopped talking about Jack, it is true, and Bill was fascinated by the whole *idea* of Jack, besides having a particular personal feeling about Russia."[18]

Of three luxurious domiciles Bullitt rented in the 1924–25 period, the one where Anne was born was the most elegant, said Sheean. In the second and grandest of the three, "Bill employed along with other servants a Turkish butler, Philippe."

Sheean, who often dropped around to see them when he returned from an out-of-town reporting job, recalled the time when Philippe "brought in cocktails all ready-made in a shaker with glasses on a big silver tray, and I said to Bill: 'Don't you make your own cocktails?' He answered in his loftiest, fake-aristocrat manner, 'Certainly not. I'd as soon think of cooking my own dinner.' "[19]

Louise may have appeared to "live a useless life," and may have jested about it to callers out of fear that her marriage to Bullitt could turn into just that. But she was working on a book on Kemal Pasha and mailed a number of chapters to her editors within days of the birth of her child. Three long stories on the new Turkey under Kemal appeared in the *New York American* over its copyright, datelined Constantinople, February 15.

Once banished by the Sultan, Kemal rose steadily in revolutionary ranks with his maneuvers against the Allies in the war. He organized a rival government in Angora (Ankara), then a dreary little town rich in history. It had thrived under Augustus, the first Roman emperor, grandson of Julius Caesar's sister, and it was here that Tamerlane in 1402 defeated and captured Sultan Bajazet. But when Kemal was elected head of the nation and the army by the Grand National Assembly in 1920, it had none of Constantinople's magnificence.

When Anatolia was invaded by the Greek army, encouraged and financed by the British, Kemal and his forces drove the invaders into the sea.

The Lausanne conference, representing the Allied governments but not America, Bryant wrote, offered Kemal world recognition. "Kemal's opportunity to apply his ideas had at last arrived. All Turkey was at his feet. He had the firm allegiance of the two hundred million Moslems throughout the East. . . . All Islam looked to him for a divine plan to lead them out of their difficulties. . . .

"What Kemal gave and what he was expected to give is a vast tragedy of broken ideals and a promise of new wars instead of peace." Even within his Popular Party, men who asserted themselves were sent to distant posts. One of its founders, Rauf Bey, enormously popular, fell from favor.

"Kemal, ruling his party with an iron grip . . . recently declared Turkey to be a 'republic' with himself as President as well as head of the Assembly. Since there is not a government in Europe so completely controlled by one man the label of 'republic' is an absurdity."

Bryant predicted what by the time the stories were printed had become fact: the expulsion of the caliph and his family. Kemal's humiliating treatment of the caliph, she wrote, was dividing all Islam.

Her most scathing denunciation of Kemal is reserved for his suppression of Turkey's beginning movement for women's emancipation just as he was being wrongly praised in the Western press for freeing women. In Angora she was "given the impression" that he believed in equal suffrage. Back in Constantinople, she attended a suffrage meeting which voted to ask Angora to make it possible for women to take part in elections two years hence.

The day after the meeting was reported in the press, a sharp rebuke came from Angora. "The suffragists were forbidden by Kemal to use the innocuous name of 'Woman's Committee' or to hold future meetings or commit 'political acts.' They were told they could serve the state by looking after their own and the orphan children." An appeal to Madame Kemal went unanswered.

"In the provinces," Bryant wrote, "women are as backward as they were five hundred years ago." In Constantinople, "women wearing raised veils are but a handful," a few hundred at most.[20]

In August 1925 Kemal divorced his wife, and Louise Bryant wrote "A Turkish Divorce," which *The Nation* published in its issue of August 26. It began:

"The Pasha has divorced his wife. Kemal has sent Latife Hanoum[21] back to her father's house in Smyrna, from which he plucked her abruptly four years ago when his victorious army drove the last of the Greeks into the sea. Thus ends a romance which promised once to alter the history of the Near East, killed presumably by the slow poison which has been fatal to so many romances—childlessness.

"In the Western world rivers of ink have been spilled describing the beauty, talents, courage, intelligence, progressivism, and charm of Latife. Few such rivers have run in Turkey. For Latife is not the bravest, most beautiful, most intelligent, and most charming of Turkish women. She is the richest." Ambitious, dictatorial, jealous, she at once caused the disappearance from Angora of the famed woman warrior Halide Edib Hanoum, "who had fought through the war at Kemal's side," Bryant wrote.

After the advent of Latife, there were no more wild evenings for Kemal such as he occasionally enjoyed in his soldiering. "The two lived in the closest domesticity in Angora," Louise wrote. "A six-room house was their home—a small space in which to confine two temperaments so wilful. Too small a space, evidently."

Latife's dismissal meant little to the women of Turkey. Outstanding leader of the women's movement was Nezieh Hanoum of Constantinople, "and Halide Edib Hanoum is its brightest star." But, according to Bryant, in the old houses of Stamboul and on the banks of the Bosporus were "hundreds of magnificent women, like Madame Ferouk Bey, who are as completely women of the world as any to be found in London or Paris or New York—brilliant women, superbly educated, tolerant and progressive. They hope to achieve woman suffrage before many years, but the greater part of their time and all their money are at present being utilized in caring for the hundreds of thousands of orphans and refugees who are starving in Turkey today. They have had a lonely fight to save the lives of the sufferers."

> The Near East Relief rushed to rescue the Greeks who had left Turkey under the exchange of populations, but no one helped the Turks. The Near East unhappily collects its funds by propaganda urging Christians to save fellow Christians from the horrible Turks, and its expenditures for the aid of the Turks have been negligible.

As for Kemal, still President of the Turkish Republic, Bryant wrote, "He will always remain the savior of Turkey in her darkest hour, but he is no longer the half-god which he was three years ago. The possibility that he might now assume the Sultanate seems infinitely remote. His star has passed its zenith. To found a dynasty one must have a family, and he suspects, perhaps, that his lack of an heir was not altogether Latife's fault."[22]

So concerned about keeping intact all of Reed's writings and letters after his death, Louise Bryant was exceedingly careless about her own. Neither in her late letters nor her fragmentary memoir was there any mention of this compelling piece. One person who had not forgotten it was Padraic Colum; he remembered it as "brilliant."[24] Obviously life with Bullitt, concern over his problems that made him seek psychoanalysis, or her own fears of what she termed "a useless life," did nothing to blunt her acuteness as a reporter.

22.

Louise and Claude McKay

AT THE TIME HE was ambassador to France William C. Bullitt denied that he had ever been psychoanalyzed and claimed that he had merely "studied with" Dr. Sigmund Freud.[1] In later years word went around that not Bullitt but Louise Bryant had been Freud's patient.[2] One of Steffens's published letters was so interpreted. Sent to his wife Ella Winter but written to their son Pete, not as old as the Bullitt child, it read in part:

> I saw a dandy Irish girl for you today. Ann Bullitt is her name. She is almost two years old now, talks a lot in two languages and says jolly things; "My mama is my friend," she said one day, and when someone asked if her papa wasn't also her friend, she answered, "Oh, no; he is God." Her mama repeated that to Freud one day, and he was delighted. "That child is articulate," he said. "I have a theory that many children think that. Yours is the first to actually say it."[3]

When Vincent Sheean was told of the Steffens letter he instantly replied: ". . . it was Bill, not Louise, who went to Vienna for treatment with Dr. Freud. He had a very long analysis, with occasional brief returns to Paris; Louise went to Vienna a couple of times to talk to Dr. Freud as part of the analysis—that is, to *help* that great man deal with Bill's intricate muddle of complexities and silliness. . . . Freud never treated Louise at all, separately or with Bill. . . ."[4, 5]

In 1926, however, when the analysis was under way, Bullitt spoke of it readily to acquaintances. It was at this time that Mura Tsiperovitch met him through her fiancé, the American painter Adolph Dehn. A dancer and choreographer, she was then living with her mother in Vienna, to which Dehn traveled frequently from Paris. Before she met Louise she and Dehn went out with Bullitt more than once, and her mother had him to dinner with Adolph, she said.

When he told them of the problems which, he said, led him to Dr. Freud, he spoke with fluency and ease, according to Mura Dehn. Unlike George Biddle, she did not interpret them as suicidal, but "more complex." Nor did she find his recitals of his difficulties fanciful. To her they were "unnervingly convincing."

"He had this feeling—a desire, a fear—that whatever course he set for himself he would carry out exactly according to his prearranged plan; he would let nothing whatsoever swerve him from it."

If he set out for a walk, he related as an example, and told himself he would continue at a certain pace in a straight line, he would do so no matter what the obstacle, even if it led to a chasm, or to the edge of a precipice. He would not be stopped by prudence or any ordinary fear, and he recognized this quality in himself as a thing to be concerned about, according to Dehn.

"In effect he was afraid of his lack of fear. I think it was true that he was afraid of nothing; he was audacious. This was why he was with Freud, he told Adolph and me. He assured us he was quite sane in actual life, but he had these desires. As he talked I could well imagine his carrying out this compulsiveness on several levels of his life, even though it threatened disaster."

(That could serve as a description of Bullitt's plunge into what George Kennan called his "passionate indiscretion"[6] once President Wilson refused to see him at Versailles on his return from interviewing Lenin. Certainly he pursued his plan of striking back to the end. Two weeks after Bullitt's Senate testimony wildly breaking confidences, Wilson collapsed in Colorado and had to abandon his speaking tour on behalf of the League of Nations. But publication of the book on Wilson offered as the joint work of Bullitt and Freud only days before the former's death, was evidence of his refusal to give up any cherished hatreds, even after death had claimed the object.[7])

The first time Bullitt was a dinner guest in her home, Mura Dehn said, her mother had placed paper napkins—then new to Vienna, and of a flimsy quality—at each place; in a receptacle were spare napkins. Bullitt talked in a lighthearted, casual way, telling funny stories, laughing, all the while taking one napkin after another and absently wadding them up. Her mother was amused; the daughter felt that he had no knowledge of what he was doing. At the same time, incongruously, he seemed "completely at ease, in control."

To Adolph Dehn and his fiancée Bullitt also talked of Louise Bryant even before they met her. Mura Dehn, who is Russian, romantic, dramatic, felt that "he longed for Louise."

On one of Bryant's few visits to Vienna at the time, Mrs. Tsiperovitch invited the Bullitts and Adolph Dehn to dinner. This time Bullitt seemed calmer. "And Louise was very elegant, casual. That negligence with which she wore her clothes!" Mura Dehn remarked. "She looked as if she were born to elegance."

That night they talked of the Russian Revolution, and Adolph later commented that the Bullitts seemed to think of it from a mutual point of view. Mura herself as a youngster had been enchanted with the Red Army men who came to her father's factory, and she and her brother and mother were "all for the revolution." But they became refugees nonetheless—"but *never* White refugees—they were the enemy."

Another evening Bullitt was the host at dinner; Bryant wore a little jacket of ocelot or jaguar. Mura Dehn continued: "I quite fell in love with her, she was so free, so lighthearted, so beautiful. Unforgettable. Nor have I ever forgotten her. To me she seemed half bird, half tiger. There was a glamor about them both—he so very good-looking, she with that shining quality. It seemed to me then that she had a power, a tranquilizing effect on Bullitt. All he had to do was to look at her to feel that everything was all right."

But on another visit Bryant made to Vienna it became clear that all was not well, and that whatever demon Bullitt had been coping with under Freud's guidance had surfaced, according to Dehn. "They had seemed very much in love. But now I saw Louise alone. Something had happened that left her shaken. Bullitt had locked himself in his hotel room and would not let her in. She was alarmed.

"She returned with friends, and he finally let her in. But after summoning her, to refuse to see her—it was a situation that left her saddened. Still, when I saw them together on this same visit, she was gay, lovely. She had been frightened, though—and not only for him, but on her own account, too. I thought of this later in Paris."[8]

Vincent Sheean described the same incident in more brutal detail. "I have remembered various things about Bill's analysis, or the period in which it took place, even though I don't really recall the precise dates. On one occasion when [Louise] went to Vienna to see him he had barricaded the door of his room at the Imperial Hotel with all its furniture so that she could not get in. An embarrassing scene, among many."[9]

Sheean thought that Louise never took "Bill's" analysis too seriously—nor believed much in analysis, influenced probably by Marxist dogmatists of the kind he had heard proclaim in the twenties that "there is no neurosis in the Soviet Union." She "told anecdotes of the sillinesses, chiefly, in Bill's analysis." The one he recalled is of interest as the first documented reference to her drinking:

"I know she once said the doctor told Bill his second wife took to the bottle because his first had been named Drinker—or something of that kind: something about the influence of names, etc., which Louise thought very funny and which often is, although there's also a lot in it. (Whatever Freud did say, she certainly had an ultra-simplified version of it.)"[10]

Kitty Cannell, an early-arriving expatriate, renewed her acquaintance with Bryant and met Bullitt when they were in the Elinor Glyn house. It was when Bullitt was in Vienna that she became Bryant's confidante. "She clung to me through the time that Bill was being analyzed by Freud. Almost every night I had dinner at the Bullitt home, and later she and I would go dancing in Montmartre with whatever attractive American was around. Most often it was with Jimmy Sheean.[11] He was fun, and a very good dancer, as was Louise. And I was a link with Louise's past. Although I had only known John Reed during those days we played in Louise's *The Game*, it was a bond."

In the beginning of Bullitt's analysis she saw Louise as little affected by it; certainly she enjoyed those dancing excursions with Sheean. But as time went on, lighthearted moods alternated with dark ones. "I remember once when we were with Jimmy, sitting at a table in the Dôme, or it may have been the Select, suddenly Louise leaned her head on his shoulder. 'Now, Louise,' he said, and pushed her off. I think he knew she was depressed, and was really very fond of her. He was a very charming young man."

Often when Bullitt came in from Vienna unexpectedly, Cannell joined them and Bullitt took the two women out, at which times he was universally agreeable and unfailingly generous. But Kitty Cannell remained completely Louise Bryant's partisan until the end of her days.

Kitty said: "The truth is that Bill Bullitt had had problems with impotence. Anyone who read his novel would know that—the burden of it is that his first wife made him impotent. When he found Louise, she was still beautiful. It was a new and different experience, and he thought he was all over that, and could therefore write about it. But now it had returned. The honeymoon was over. And he was with Freud, seeking a cure. He would return home, hopeful that the cure was working. It never did."

Louise continued trying to cheer him up when he got depressed, but it became harder to get him to respond. Increasingly, Cannell said, Louise thought of all that she had given up: her career with Hearst, her independent income, her self-image as the widow of John Reed who had shown that she could advance in her writing quite independently of him. Cannell thought Bryant had given up her writing; but although her last published work appeared in 1925, later letters show that she did attempt to write.

"Another thing," said Cannell. "Louise was always the feminist. I never was. I think Bill's impotence began to take on a symbolic meaning for her: the marriage itself began to seem hollow to her. I began to feel that she thought of it as a threat to her identity. Perhaps that was why she fantasized Jack even more obsessively."[12]

In 1926 the encouragement Bryant had given Claude McKay when he confided that he wanted to write fiction took more practical shape and absorbed her interest. As McKay has written, she heard from Clive Weed that he was ill and sent a doctor to see him. When McKay had begun to recover, and

> she was sending me off to southern France for my health, Louise Bryant warned me: "Remember our conversation in New York, and don't try to force your stories with propaganda. If you write a good story, that will be the biggest propaganda." She gave me a check big enough to keep me living simply and working steadily for three months.[13]

Bryant wrote McKay that she had just returned from Vienna and found his manuscripts and letter. She had sent Max Eastman, who with his Russian wife was in Paris, a *pneumatique* and would try to get McKay's message to him. His manuscripts "must have been here almost two weeks. I'm very sorry." She hoped he was feeling better, and would write in a day or two. "Of course I'll send your mans. to the stenographer as soon as they are ready," she added in a postscript.[14]

Almost two months later, after a lapse of time that doubtless seemed endless to the proud and sensitive black writer, she wrote that she had had to forego the trip to America "on account of Bill's health" and would remain in Paris at least until September. She was going over his stories, but it would be another week before she was done editing them, and then they would have to be retyped. That was why

she had not had a carbon copy made for him when she had originally
had them typed.

"You are splendid when your characters talk to one another. When
the author talks the trouble commences. Too much repetition, trite
expressions—" Bullitt and Bob McAlmon, early expatriate and publisher and writer, had read the stories and were enthusiastic. When
they were all finished "Bill" would write Mr. Harcourt; his book had
just been published by Harcourt, Brace "and it's a tremendous
success." Possibly he could get a five hundred dollar advance. "Shall
we try that?"[15]

On June 11 in a letter to McKay Bryant first mentioned her own
illness. Whether or not this was the first sign of a serious illness, long
undiagnosed but not for lack of consulting various doctors in different
countries,[16] is unknown. She wrote that she was "so sorry—but I have
been ill—and in bed—and didn't finish the stories." She would get
them off to him in a few days. Bullitt was returning home again July
17, "so no time has really been lost."[17] But on June 20 she wrote that
she was still ill.

"Bill is home and he is going over your stories. You will *positively*
have them by the end of the week. He writes and edits as carefully as
if he were sending a diplomatic message and you are in luck to have
him do this." He had already written Mr. Harcourt and suggested that
if he found the stories interesting the publisher offer him an advance
of five hundred on a novel, whether or not the firm would publish the
stories.[18]

To McKay, who had been living from hand to mouth, working as a
general servant for two hundred francs a month in Menton, quitting
after a month to work on a construction job, leaving that because he
had no time to think, the delay was unbearable. His long handwritten
letter from Marseilles reminded her that when she told him she would
take his stories to America in May he had been happy, although he did
his best writing *after* seeing his work in type. Because of his desperate
straits he had had no choice but to agree.

> You are an artist and you can imagine how I felt about my stuff being
> read by editors without knowing what form they were in!
> I know I must not, I have no right to complain, when you have
> taken upon yourself the burden of looking after the stories—gener-
> ously giving of your time and money when I have not the slightest
> claim on you. I know it is your love for literature and . . . for seeing
> obscure talent recognized, that makes you do it. Besides you have
> been ill—you have duties—other things to do.

But, he told her, it had been four months since he sent the stories, and all that time he had been hoping, waiting, existing, trying to write, in the midst of flies and bugs and filth, and by now he was utterly despondent, absolutely despairing. Before he left Nice, she had promised the stories in a week. She had told him he was "impatient." It was not impatience, it was sheer misery. If she could not finish them, he would do so on the lines she indicated. Before he had to leave Marseilles for "God knows where" he wanted to work on those stories, to feel the joy of having completed something. He wanted them at once, no matter how they appeared now.[19] The letter in an eloquent cry of anguish.

Writing McKay next, Bryant said she was enclosing a thousand francs so he could go on with his novel. She was returning the stories in three envelopes—all except "Home to Harlem," which needed no correction. "Bill read them all but the comments are mine. Whenever you send them to me I will send them to Harcourt.

"They are really fine—and you will be writing very smoothly soon. I am very interested in the novel. Good luck to you."[20]

In her next letter to McKay she told him she had written a play she hoped to place when she and Bullitt reached New York; they would sail September 1. She would try to manage a few more francs before she left and, in America, find someone who would take a typewriter to him. She asked: "Where are the manuscripts?" Would any part of the novel be ready to show a publisher? She hoped he was well and in a working mood.[21]

The stories arrived the day the Bullitts left Paris for America.[22]

The *New York American* interviewed Bryant September 11, 1926, the day the Bullitts and their infant daughter arrived in New York on the French liner *Paris*. Under the headline "Dictatorship Child of War/Democracy Lost in Europe" appeared comments that suggest she did not view with special warmth the successors to Lenin:

"Looking at the map you will see that the net results of the war seem to be dictatorship, not the democracy for which so much treasure in blood and money was spent.

"To the south there are Spain, Italy, Turkey, with dictators. Looking eastward toward Russia, the supreme example of dictatorship, there are Hungary and Poland. And to the north is Belgium, whose king has been give a dictator's powers." She saw little difference between "Zinoviev and his crowd" and "the Stalin group" that replaced them. She added prophetically:

"I look to see Russia become one of the conservative nations of the world, and I believe all signs point toward this and most certainly against any possibility of the much-planned realization of the slogan, 'Workers of the World, Unite.' "

She saw only futility in the accomplishments of the League of Nations, and as an example cited Italy's taking of the island of Corfu in the Mediterranean. "You will remember that the League as a unit and its members as individual powers continued inactive while the Italian navy put in force against Greece the imperialistic proclamations of Dictator Mussolini." The League, she stated, was dominated by Britain for the sole advancement of her interests.

She predicted the fall of the Poincaré government soon before a more representative coalition, and said reports of anti-Americanism in France were exaggerated. What minor demonstrations there were, she said, were caused by bombastic and bumptious Americans who advertised their "hundred per cent Americanism" unwisely.

Bryant was described as wearing tailored blue suit and green felt hat and looking "the typical brisk athletic young American business woman." It was recalled that "Mrs. Bullitt as early as 1920 made a solitary tour of Russia, unmolested, because of the confidence the Russians placed in her for her fearlessness, courage and honesty in treating Russian problems."[23]

Two weeks later Bryant wrote McKay from the Plaza Hotel that she had just received his letter and was sorry he had been having such a rotten time. "And I'm sorry I didn't know before I left France." She was enclosing what money she had in her purse, adding, "This will help for the moment."[24]

In the same letter she told McKay that Alfred Harcourt had returned and that he now had the stories. If he got the advance, she advised him to come home—she had found New York "very stimulating." Had he lost his passport? He needn't worry in any case. "You know I didn't have one at all when I went on that last sad journey to Russia to see Jack . . .

"All I can say to cheer you at the moment is that your experience now will make wonderful material later." As if sensing that this would mean small comfort to the distraught black writer, she added:

"And I'm sure your stories and your book will go. I'll help you any way I can with it. . . . And I'll give you Jack's typewriter. I'm sure he would like you to have it."[25]

Five additional letters to Claude McKay were written by Bryant while she was on this side of the Atlantic in this period, all but the last one recounting the ups and downs of her dealings with publishers regarding his work. All were written with care that he not lose hope. When she reported that Harcourt had rejected the stories (he had published McKay's poems but complained that they did not make money and that short stories rarely did), Bryant counseled: "Don't let this discourage you. Bill's book was turned down by Horace Liveright last year. He said to Bill, 'It will not sell three hundred copies.' The book now is in its eighth large printing—having sold more than 25,000. . . . So one never knows."

She took McKay's work to Viking, found editors there immensely interested in Negro stories, and expected to have an answer in two days; if accepted there would be an advance. She lunched with Albert Boni and there was talk of a contest; entering it would be a sure win for him as there were fewer entries than expected, and that would mean one thousand dollars at once.

But she also set about finding him an agent. Bullitt had rented an apartment at 12 East Eighty-second Street, and Bryant had a long talk there one afternoon with William Aspenwall Bradley, the foremost literary agent in Paris and, as she told McKay, Ford Madox Ford's agent. The Bonis had turned down the stories, but Harper's told Bradley that they were "splendid." It was interested, as were the Boni brothers, in a novel around a black doughboy and his return to Harlem, with the title of his best story, "Home to Harlem." But despite the Bonis' competition for black writers, she told McKay she felt Harper's would do more than the Boni brothers about the novel.

Bradley, she said, would leave New York January 5 and go directly to Antibes, where McKay was staying with Max Eastman. She urged him to remain there until then, and hoped he would accept Bradley as his agent. "I'm terribly pleased and feel you will be really launched on a successful career within another year. I think I know, too," and she told him how she "used to beg people to read Gene O'Neill's manuscripts" and had placed his first story for publication. "It is all going to turn out wonderfully."

After settling with Bradley, she advised in one letter, he could go to Paris, take "a small and *warm* room," and work on the novel. If the contract provided fifteen or twenty dollars a week while he completed the novel, "you'll find yourself free of this whole damned burden of poverty. . . . Here's $10 for a Christmas present." A postscript said that Ford had promised her he'd write an introduction if the short stories were published. "Write me any other instructions you have. Some of the stories are not as good as the others and may be left out— so send the new ones."

In another letter she wrote that Harper's had agreed to give him an advance on the part of the novel completed if it suited them. She confidently predicted that it would be enough for him to continue writing in comfort. She even went so far as to say, "My feeling is that if you can only get them to be interested in the novel you will never have any more financial trouble." And she warned, "Don't frighten them off with any talk of politics now and I think we can all get you safely back here." She concluded: "Anyway, Claude, be cheerful and work and I'm sure everything is going to turn out well for you now."[26]

What McKay couldn't know was that when she wrote "Claude, be cheerful" she often was depressed herself—unless her approach toward her marriage had undergone a radical change from that of the days in Paris described by Kitty Cannell, and there is no reason to believe it had.

Bullitt later stated that Bryant was drinking heavily on this visit to New York, but this was not reflected in the reminiscences of those who saw them. George Biddle and Jane Belo, who were married in Paris in 1925, were having a housewarming in the Croton house bought from Gloria Swanson by Belo, a wealthy Texan.

"Everyone was there," recounted Frances (Francie) Elwyn of Croton. "Peggy Bacon and her husband, Alexander Brook, the artists; Louise and Bill Bullitt and just everyone, many from New York. Oh, it was a noisy party, they sang all the songs and all the bawdy verses of the songs. It was some party!" The Bullitts had something to drink but no more than anyone had. "Everyone had quite a little. A drunken orgy, I suppose it could be called," she said cheerfully.

Mrs. Elwyn remembered "how pretty Louise was, with dark hair and blue eyes." Everyone was dancing, "and Louise was, too. But when Bullitt danced with another woman—and he and his partner were really swinging!—Louise grabbed a pair of shears and went for her. Oh, she didn't hit her, but she did say, 'Lay off my husband!' There seemed to be quite a little animus in it, too," she pronounced happily.[27]

George Biddle remembered the housewarming. He did not recall the incident of Louise and the shears, but commented, "Francie is completely sane. I'm sure it occurred." He remembered that "Bill was mad at me because I had so many overnight guests that I had gotten a room in some farmhouse nearby for Bill and Louise. He said he'd never been so insulted by a host, and reminded me that he was a Bullitt from Philadelphia. He was so furious that we wrestled. He prided himself on all the manly arts, and I wasn't so bad at wrestling in those days, either. So we were both giving it to the other, rolling on the floor, when some pretty woman, I forget who, came over and said, 'This is for the vanquor,' and kissed us both. That broke it up. I guess it was a draw."[28]

The Floyd Dells were at the party and were "shocked"—not at the drinking but because "Louise talked nonstop about Jack Reed and almost ignored Bill. It wasn't as if Bill Bullitt didn't think a lot of Jack. He did. He knew and admired him." Dell added: "Bullitt was terrribly serious about Russia then. As was Louise."[29]

Andrew Dasburg was a guest of the Bullitts at dinner one night. A resident of New Mexico by then, he still spent part of each year in the East.

He was the only guest at the Bullitts' that night. "Louise seemed perfectly at ease. But there was something artificial about the whole thing—the three of us together. Bullitt turned on the charm—but with a knowing smile, which didn't help." Dasburg had the unmistakable impression that Bullitt knew that he and Louise had been lovers. "I also felt that he wanted me to know that he knew."

Asked if there was evidence that Bryant was drinking heavily, he said, "None at all. I never had seen her drink, nor did I then. We never drank, and even Jack was only a social drinker. I never saw him tight."

As he recalled it, there was no discussion of what the years had held for him. It was possible, of course, that, when he had seen her alone in advance of the dinner, she inquired about Ida Rauh and he confirmed that she and he still were together, making a home for their boys, Alfred Dasburg and Dan Eastman.[30]

But neither was there any revelation that evening that would help explain what Dasburg regarded as a strange marriage for Louise Bryant to have made. To see her in the midst of all that affluence, the elegant but cold decor, presiding over a dinner served with all the formality Bullitt demanded, jarred Dasburg.

"I couldn't escape the feeling," he said in a reflective mood, "that as well as I had known her, the wife of William C. Bullitt was a complete mystery to me. It was not only that the scene itself, the three of us together and she so calm, as if it were the most natural thing in the world, was unreal, but that all that had happened was—somehow beyond reason, as though all of us were pawns in a game of chess. As if what had happened was beyond her wishes, if she had any, and beyond mine—as if control had left us somewhere along the way."

It was the last time he saw Louise Bryant.[31]

Some years later, he did not recall how many, Dasburg received a letter from her that was angry in tone. He destroyed it but its troubling quality remained in his mind. Some unfriendly person must have told her something about him that was untrue, he said. He felt sad about it still. [32]

In addition to the essential mystery that attaches to the Bullitt-Bryant marriage, other happenings, one probably associated with this 1926–27 visit of the Bullitts to New York, remain mysterious and seemingly insoluble. The night Willard Trask met them "could well have been in 1926," he said, but he was not certain of the year. It was at 1 Patchin Place, the Reeds' old apartment that Bryant retained, where Trask assumed the Bullitts were living. Trask had been taken to meet them by Coburn ("Colby") Gilman, writer and editor, " a great epigramist and a good friend of Bullitt's."

"All that I remember about that evening," said the translator, "was that they were in the process of adopting, or had just adopted, a Turkish boy, and there was some difficulty about it. Louise Bullitt was very animated. Bullitt was more quiet—and very intelligent, I thought."[34]

Bryant wrote one more letter to Claude McKay before her return with Bullitt and their baby daughter to Paris. The letter was on the letterhead of the Chateau Frontenac of Quebec.

"I was touched by your letter," she began. "Of course, I don't think that I ever did a thing for you worth thinking about. I *will* like, more than I can tell you, to have you inscribe 'Home to Harlem' to me. I am so sure that it will have a great success. And you—also—less worries ever after."

She was glad he had sent her the Bradley letter. She felt confident that she could "get them to give you more," adding: "And, anyway, my play seems to be going on soon. If it does I can help you myself.

"Best luck always and my most sincere and humble thanks for the dedication. Louise."

A postscript asked that he write her at the New York address (the return address on the envelope was 12 East Eighty-second Street) and explained: "I came up here for a short rest. It is a small Canadian French village. Only the hotel stationery looks so grand."[35]

23.
The Desperate Years

LOUISE BRYANT AND BULLITT returned to France in the late fall of 1927. Bullitt again went to Vienna,[1] and Bryant fitfully tried to cope with the still undiagnosed illness she would have for the rest of her days. At times she felt alcohol only made her sicker and resolved not to drink again; at others she drank to excess.

She saw Kitty Cannell occasionally, but there was no longer anyone to go dancing with when Bullitt was in Vienna. Sheean had gone to China and in Hankow became immersed in the Chinese revolution— before the collapse of the revolutionary government in the face of Chiang Kai-shek's counterrevolution.[2] He returned to Paris at intervals in 1928, and may or may not have seen Bryant.[3]

"Louise was drinking," Cannell said. "All the expatriate crowd drank a lot." She spoke of having just read a review of a book of memoirs of that period under the headline, "We Had Such Good Times."[4] "Frankly, I don't think of that period as all that much fun. I have the feeling we were all rather desperate, and that's why we were drinking ourselves to death."[5]

In December 1927 Bryant again began writing Claude McKay. William Aspenwall Bradley, his agent, had just been to see her, apparently with a part of McKay's new novel, *Banjo*, and told her of Claude's need of money. It just happened, she wrote, that she had helped six people that month, so was rather broke. She knew them only as "Italians who get driven out now and hide about in terror, having committed no other crime than being able to still believe in humanity against all the reasons they ought not to. I am sure Harper's will help you soon and I enclose this bit for the moment."

She then turned critic, taking up *Banjo* and urging: "Write to me, Claude. We must 'fix up' this last novel. It is a lovely idea but you simply haven't written it. If you were in Paris I could show you where each line goes off. But it would take days to write all I mean."

She had assured Bradley that he knew how to accept criticism and then rewrite, adding:

> Claude, Jack Reed often wrote a short story as many as seventeen times! But in order to do that one must not be rushed. Lose sense of time! I am sure after your novel comes out you will, at least, achieve a certain economic ease. Just now I know it is difficult. But, anyway, write and tell me the exact situation. And good luck to you always—6

Two weeks later she wrote McKay again, enclosing her Christmas present to him. "Do, please, change the dedication," she wrote, alluding to the novel *Home to Harlem*. "And don't ever, ever be *grateful* to me! What I would like you to inscribe would be: 'To my friend Louise Bryant.' " She advised him not to bother writing articles now: "I have a feeling that you do not realize how good 'Home to Harlem' really is. I think it stands a fine chance of getting the annual Harper $10,000 prize. Wouldn't that be lovely?" She urged him to send her what he wrote. "I, with a new eye on it, can show you a word or a sentence that is out of harmony and send it back to you without any delay. A happy Christmas to you—and the best of luck!"7

In these letters she had not spoken of her illness, and the two that followed also are silent on it. Doubtless it was the best "medicine" Bryant could have, to feel this obligation to buoy up the black poet's hope. In making the effort, her own may have revived momentarily. In the next letter he was told not to worry: "Work and be tranquil." She said she would write to Eugene Saxton at Harper's, "a deeply understanding person." She would see Bradley again, too. In the meantime if he needed anything Claude should let her know.

"Saxton wrote me a few days ago," she continued, "about a book he wants me to do and asked me to help boom yours. I am writing Carl Van Vechten and two men on the New Yorker—all old friends of mine. So go ahead, Claude, work and try to be happy."8

"I'm so sorry!" her next letter to McKay began. "Bradley wrote me a week ago saying that he had arranged everything for you and you were to get monthly payments again for some months. So I thought you were in clover. I am enclosing 200 frs. and I am seeing him this afternoon. I will write you again after I talk to him."

Her next paragraph suggests that his last letter probably had shaken her badly, but she handles it unemotionally and puts a question to him to which she provides an answer that McKay, a scrupulously honest man, could not deny. "Don't be silly, Claude, about giving up writing. Everyone gets to that point when the struggle is bitter. But if you did—what then? How defeated you would feel!"[9]

In March Bryant wrote him the first letter about herself, but even so it begins and ends with her usual theme: McKay's work. Considering the contents of the one paragraph about her illness, it is a model of restraint—a restraint she faithfully maintained in relation to her illness. McKay was apparently one of the few friends to whom she ever spoke of it. Her first words were for the novel, *Home to Harlem*.[10]

> The book is lovely and Bradley tells me that you are doing very good work on the new one now.
>
> I have been quite ill again and I went to London to see some specialists. They looked me over solemnly and then told me I had something called Dercum's disease and that it was incurable! So the trip was not much of a success. All the happiness I got out of it was flying. I went both ways in a little plane and that was exciting. I am really pretty depressed because I have been almost continuously ill for about five years. Too ill to work. I am trying to do a novel now and I sit here hour after hour at that. I can tell you all this because I know how ill you have been yourself.
>
> I wrote about twenty critics while I was ill in bed in London about your book. I feel sure you will have a quick success and also that it will not spoil you. I asked for it in Brentano's here and when they had no copies I told them it was going to go very well and they immediately cabled for fifty copies. Just keep at it Claude and I am sure everything will be right with you.
>
> And thanks again for the book!
>
> Louise.[11]

At the time of the diagnosis Bullitt telephoned his brother from abroad and asked him to see Dr. Francis X. Dercum of Philadelphia and ask what could be done, Bullitt's confidant remembered hearing. The answer came back: nothing. It was indeed incurable (and still is). The confidant was under the impression Louise Bryant had contracted the disease in 1927; Louise's letters suggest she had bouts of illness of some sort earlier. He attributed her last tragic years to the disease, aggravated by drinking.[12]

(In 1892 Dr. Dercum described a strange malady found in three patients in the wards of Blockley Hospital in Philadelphia which he called "adiposis dolorosa," a syndrome to which his name became attached. Medical literature calls it a rare disease, or at least, rarely diagnosed. Only a small fraction of the cases described is made up of men, and in those cases the symptoms are usually milder. It is largely a disease of menopausal women between the ages of 35 and 50.

(In 1928 Louise Bryant was 43 years old. The syndrome is without a known etiology. In general the woman victim of adiposis dolorosa was described as "markedly obese at the time of onset, though weight loss and asthenia appear as the disease progresses, and severe emotional involvement is common." It is a disease ushered in by "noninflammatory, painful, subcutaneous tumors, which may appear at any site except the face and head."[13] Other features are more variable. "Frequent association with rheumatic heart disease," weakness, and irritability are noted in the medical literature, and in some cases, loss of hair. Attacks of shortness of breath are common.[14] A number of patients were described as frequently weeping, which may have inspired Dr. Dercum's apt name for the syndrome.)

Claude McKay for long appeared to be the only friend who even knew of Louise Bryant's illness*—except for George Biddle, who learned of it not from Louise, but from Bullitt. Biddle spoke of it often, but could not recall its name.[15] Mura Dehn and Kitty Cannell were unaware that she had any illness. Among the people who cared most deeply for her, none knew she had Dercum's disease.

In April she wrote Claude from Baden-Baden, where she had been for two weeks. The regimen at the sanitarium was "pretty severe." She had lost more than a pound a day. "I am so thin that my clothes look absurd. But I'm feeling better." She would be leaving for Paris in a week, to sail for home May 5. She urged Claude to type the information he had sent Bradley pertinent to getting a passport and send it to her at 44 avenue Victor Hugo.

"Mr. Bullitt knows a man on the League of Nations—the British representative—and I imagine he could help you get a passport." She was enclosing a letter received that day from Carl Van Vechten, saying that if he wished to write him he might send her the letter, which she would give to Van Vechten, "a very nice human being."

In the same mail she had had a letter from Eugene Saxton, who handled McKay's work for Harper's, "saying that your book is going splendidly. It had already sold between 6,000 and 7,000 copies. That is really good. He said, 'The book has had a splendid press and is

*The John Storrs Papers, Archives of American Art, temper that assumption: see chapter 24.

undoubtedly headed for considerable success.' First novels rarely go so well. I am so glad for you."[16]

These letters to McKay since her return from America seem to have been written by someone poised, selfless in her concern for his progress as artist and human being, generous, yet retaining her critic's eye—and in addition, someone who took the devastating news of her illness courageously and was untroubled by any personal problem other than that.

But Mura Dehn in an accidental meeting with Louise Bryant, probably early in 1928, discovered for the first time how bitterly Louise felt about her marriage. Mura and Adolph Dehn since their marriage were living in Paris but visits with the Bullitts were infrequent. She ran into Louise one day at the Montparnasse *gare* (station). "She told me she had made her decision: she meant to leave Bill because he was so difficult. She even used the word 'insanity.' "

In Mura Dehn's opinion Bryant was "in perfect condition." Far from appearing unhappy, she appeared radiant. "She felt liberated, she said. She was going back to work, to journalism." Dehn insisted that this chance meeting was unforgettable. "This was Louise as I like best to remember her, as she stood talking to me of her plans. She looked beautiful; she sparkled as she talked. She would be on her own from that time on. She gave me the feeling of a bird in flight. And even let me think that I could go flying to new heights in my own orbit. 'You can do it, too,' she said. A friend, Desirée Liven,[17] passed by and waved, and later told me, 'You two looked as if you had the world in your pockets!' "

It was Dehn's first recognition that the relationship between the Bullitts had changed. Before long, as the Bullitts' troubles surfaced sensationally in the expatriates' colony, Dehn felt that it had deteriorated disastrously.[18]

But for all her brave words to Dehn, Bryant did not go back to work. In reality she was far too ill. She sailed for home as planned, with Bullitt and the child. The Dells remembered seeing them at a time when Louise was showing the effects of the disease, mistakenly described by them as elephantiasis. They did not remember the date, but the occasion was a ball at the old Waldorf-Astoria Hotel, much like the balls the *Masses* had put on to raise money; this also was a fund-raising affair, for a forgotten cause, and also patronized by writers and artists.

Louise dressed skillfully to disguise her disfigurement: she wore a lace mantilla which fell over her swollen arms. "Bill seemed very attentive and devoted." They believed she eventually recovered—a mistaken belief. [19]

It is not known how long Bryant suffered from Dercum's disease before she was diagnosed. If she had been sick for five years as she told McKay, the onset could have coincided roughly with her first months in the palace on the Bosporus. A photograph of her taken at Gabriele D'Annunzio's place that appeared with her 1923 story on the Italian poet and playwright, shows a heavier, more matronly figure and fuller face than her 1921 photos. An internist who had seen Dercum's disease cases said: "It is not fatal, though incurable, but the person who has it is simply miserable. To take to drink or almost anything that promised momentary relief is understandable." [20]

From the Bullitt place in Conway, Massachusets, Bryant wrote McKay a subdued letter. She would sail for France on September 17 and go straight to Baden-Baden, returning to Paris November 1 when the sanitarium closed for a few weeks, then going back to Baden-Baden. "I mean to get well this time. I had a dreadful summer, full of collapses. . . . I got thinner and thinner but I weigh 104 so I'm still visible." A poignant sentence followed on the progress of her novel. "I didn't work much on paper—mostly in my head but I could finish the novel in two months if I felt like anything." She had not abandoned her support for McKay. "Your book still seems to be going strong. You must be doubly sure of the next book. They all fly at the second book to see if it is worse or better. You *must* make it better. I'm anxious to see it."

They would be returning to 44 avenue Victor Hugo the coming winter, but she urged him to write her in care of Dengler's Sanitarium, Baden-Baden. "It's a lovely place. I walk hours in the Black Forest. It is right in the heart of it, you know."

She hoped to see him before the year was up. She had learned to drive a car that summer. "I have a Chrysler. I might get a sport car over there and tour around. I get so damned restless because I have been too feeble to carry out anything but I find it's not tiring at all to dash around in a car if I'm driving. I hope the book is getting on beautifully. Do let me know how you are." [21]

*　　*　　*

Except for servants he had brought along when they sailed for America in 1929, Bullitt was the only witness at the preliminary hearing of his divorce suit against Louise in December 1929. To withhold from the press the testimony in uncontested divorces is customary in Philadelphia, not as a matter of law but of policy; the record was made available to the author in this case.

He described at length her drinking, stating that it was in excess in 1926–27 and continued and grew worse. Before he finished he also charged that she had a lesbian relationship with Gwendolyn Le Gallienne, a daughter of the English writer Richard Le Gallienne, then living in Paris.

The lesbian aspect of Bryant's association with Le Gallienne was proved to Bullitt, he said, when in 1929 he found letters in her purse to and from Le Gallienne as Louise, intoxicated, lay sleeping. Bullitt failed to read from the letters in part or in entirety and they were not introduced into evidence. Bullitt's testimony in his action against Louise Bryant was given before a Master as is the practice in uncontested divorces in Philadelphia—in this case the Master was an old family friend, Francis Biddle, brother of George Biddle and later attorney general of the United States.

The lesbian interest figured in events of 1928 Bullitt described from the witness stand. It was in about January 1928, he told the Master, that "a Mr. McAlmon" (the writer and publisher and early expatriate Robert McAlmon, unidentified by Bullitt but mentioned in correspondence with Claude McKay by Louise as one who, with Bullitt, was reading his stories) asked the Bullitts to go with him to a reception at the home of an unnamed French author. There Louise, he said, introduced him to two women who stood near the door, Gwen Le Gallienne and "Miss Ledoux." When he realized that the people in the room were divided into couples, "men talking to men and women talking to women," he took his wife aside and told her it was obviously "a party of homosexuals" and that "I would like her to go home with me at once." She wanted to stay, Bullitt continued, telling him she was "amused by the antics of the people there."

"She said, 'Look at Le Gallienne, she is wild with jealousy because another woman is talking to Ledoux. Gwen and Ledoux have been lovers for three years and Gwen is now frantic because she is getting tired of her.' " As Louise refused to go with him, he said, he went home (to 44 avenue Victor Hugo) and to bed. At five o'clock, he continued, Louise came in "with the Le Gallienne girl, the Ledoux girl and Mr. McAlmon. They were all quite drunk. They had got some champagne from the cellar and I had really a very unpleasant half hour, because their conversation was pretty disgusting in every possible way."

(In the light of what Vincent Sheean said about the elegance of the first three houses of the Bullitts and, in addition, how Lincoln Steffens was awed by the grandeur of their home in 1926,[22] it is reasonable to assume that 44 avenue Victor Hugo was no flimsy-walled dwelling of cramped design. Perhaps Bullitt was able to overhear the conversation from his bed—he did not mention leaving it—by means of an intercom, considering his well-known paranoia about being spied on and his fascination with the gadgets of spying.)

Also in January 1928, Bullitt testified in the preliminary hearing before Master Biddle, Louise "left home one day and did not come back—did not turn up. I searched all over Paris for her and finally found her in the apartment of Mrs. Marquis." He persuaded her to return; her drinking continued.[23]

The particular summer in Conway (1928) when Bryant wrote Claude McKay she was dashing about in her Chrysler she'd learned to drive was recalled by Bullitt in another way in testifying against his wife. He observed that she "invariably began drinking before breakfast, in the morning, and hid liquor to drink at all hours of the day."

At the end of June, Bullitt testified, they went down to the Yale-Harvard boat race, having been invited by the chairman of the Regatta Committee to go on the committee boat, "which follows the crews down the lane of yachts." Just as the varsity race began, he said, Louise staggered on deck and started to fall overboard, she had been drinking so much down below. He caught her and held her and kept her from going overboard, but she protested that she had a right to fall overboard if she wanted to. "This was on the Committee boat," he emphasized again, "an exhibition for thousands and thousands of people, many of whom we knew quite well." He helped her to the dock and the automobile and the hotel where they were staying: "She took her clothes off and rushed through the hotel stark naked. I ran after her and picked her up in my arms and took her back."

"What part of the hotel had she gone into?" questioned his attorney, Thomas Raeburn White, Philadelphia's most prominent, and widely known nationally.

The answer: "Just into the corridor—the main corridor on the first floor—not the ground floor but the first floor."

On their return to Paris from the United States in the fall (1927), "I had to manage the household entirely, managing the servants, arranging the meals, etc." Bullitt's testimony reads.

At one point in his testimony Bullitt indicated that almost three years from the time he fixed as the onset of Bryant's excessive drinking, they still moved in exalted circles. On January 4, 1929, he said, "we were dining with the Duke and Duchess DeRichelieu, and Louise . . . was very insulting to the Duchess and kept pawing the Duke and letting him paw her in a way which was almost intolerable for me to witness."

Departing, he didn't wait until they were home to speak his mind, but there on the pavement below "told her it had been really shocking." She in turn "said I was just a horrible petty bourgeois who was trying to turn her into a respectable bourgeois wife, which she did not intend to be. . . . She would not come in the house with me again; and she in fact did not return to the home for several days."

He declared that his wife had gone away with Le Gallienne at one time when he received a letter from her; he read it into the record:

Dear Duck:

I want to say to you only one thing—I have lived too long with unconventional people to be suddenly made into a Bourgeoise. This thought of mine will sound drunk—crazy—anything, but it is what people call "straight from the shoulder" in that country I happen to be born in—America. I want to *work*! And I *can* work. Anne is not a mediocre, she is a *"person."* She will not mind if I do something during this little "passage" we call life which somehow matters to people. I have no neurosis. I am an artist who has gone back to work after a too long vacation. I will see you after some days, I am tired now—full of flu. Forgive any hurts I do to you.

Louise

Louise's letter is specific about how much her writing meant to her. In contrast to this, Bullitt, when asked what his wife's occupation was, made a curious reply early in the proceedings: "She is an artist, sculptor, writes." Later on a similar lapse of memory seemed to occur. He was relating that on a certain day Louise had lunch with him and the baby; she said, he testified, that she wanted to take the baby to the "studio" as she wished "to do some sculpture."[24]

At the start of the hearing Bullitt was asked the whereabouts of his wife Anne Louise Moën Bullitt. He replied that he did not know precisely where she was. "The last I heard she was in Algiers and then returned to Paris. I believe she is in Paris at this moment." As to where Louise was when he filed the suit on December 4, he said, "She was either in New York—I am not exactly certain where she was—the Brevoort Hotel in New York, I think."

A copy of the passport application of Louise Bryant Bullitt, sworn to November 16, 1929, and stamped "Passport Issued Nov. 18, 1929," was obtained through the Freedom of Information Act, and in it she declared that she intended to leave the United States from the Port of New York on board the *Paris* November 29, 1929.

What this suggests is shocking indeed—did Bullitt, in order to make charges that would assure his obtaining full custody of the child, whom Louise considered "a person" and not a possession, arrange it so that Louise Bryant would be out of the country before he gave his damaging testimony or even filed suit? No less an authority than his brother Orville states in the book he edited on the FDR-Bullitt correspondence: "Bill and Louise continued to live in Paris. . . . The marriage ended in divorce in 1930, and Bill was awarded custody of their daughter Anne."[25]

Bullitt failed to say in his testimony that his wife had an incurable disease. He did testify, in telling how he discovered the Bryant–Le Gallienne letters that to him constituted proof of a lesbian relationship, that he called Dr. Lorber, who advised a sanitarium. An attempt was made to call a neurologist, Dr. Wechsler, Bullitt told the Master, "when Louise came into the room stark naked. [Dr.] Lorber wrapped her in a blanket, started to talk to her."[26] It was agreed, he said, that she go visit her brothers in California.[27]

Bullitt was informed, he said, his wife had attempted suicide or at least had taken an overdose of a sleeping drug. He went to New York and found her at the Neurological Institute, where she had been taken by Dr. Lorber and Dr. Wechsler, Bullitt said.[28] That was in October.

Bullitt was granted the divorce March 24, 1930, in Common Pleas Court Number 5, after the Master's report by Francis Biddle was stamped approved on March 13.

In Bullitt's novel *It's Not Done*, his hero, John Corsey, on learning that his wife had a lover, urged divorce. His brother-in-law Wayne was the governor, and his Uncle Drayton a lawyer, and he told his wife confidently, "Between Wayne . . . and Uncle Drayton we can certainly arrange private hearings and a decree without any publicity."[29] Once Louise Bryant had been hustled out of the way and was on board that ship bound for Algiers, it had all been just as easy as the fictional hero John Corsey promised it would be.

* * *

In describing Louise's "time of desperation before the divorce," Kitty Cannell saw it this way: "She was becoming a victim in a tragic farce. That she was the victim I never doubted. Bill had been in love with her, and needed her, but that was true only so long as he felt she had restored him. Then he tolerated her, waiting for the miracle Freud would help him achieve. It didn't happen that way. So he saw his goddess with feet of clay."[30]

With Bullitt, as has been described by others,[31] once the process of disenchantment set in, once he could no longer view his idealized figure as other than flawed, the onset might be prolonged but inevitably he came to view that person as morally bad, one to deserve his hatred. Always, as was the case with Woodrow Wilson and as it would be with Franklin Delano Roosevelt, his hatred became all-consuming.[32] This personality trait, highlighted unmistakably in historical events that show him turning against a famous figure he first hero-worshipped, ran true to form in his relations with Louise.

His brother Orville in *For the President* attempts to put this trait in the most favorable light: "He formed rapid and strong attachments and was bitterly disappointed when such acquaintances did not live up to the high standards which he expected of them. When this happened he would break the friendship with little compunction."[33]

Bullitt's term as the first U.S. ambassador to the U.S.S.R. began in December 1933 on a wave of euphoria and ended, typically, in bitter hatred of the U.S.S.R. Resigning in 1936, he was named ambassador to France, and threw himself into efforts to bring about a Franco-Nazi rapproachment. Experienced correspondents have pointed out some wildly inaccurate reporting to F.D.R. by Bullitt, which his brother Orville does not ignore.[34]

As for the second historic instance of Bullitt's turning on a leader who failed him, there is no way in which his brother can resurrect any high moral principle that guided him. One who served under him in Moscow as third secretary of the embassy, later becoming the U.S. ambassador there, Charles E. Bohlen, liked much about Bullitt, his quality of exuberance, his "effervescent charm" and the brilliance of his writing, but said, "There were no neutral colors in Bill—he was a vindictive man." After he broke with F.D.R. "he was *savage* about Roosevelt." He broke with everyone associated with Roosevelt, and as Bohlen acted as Roosevelt's interpreter at wartime conferences with Stalin, he had no further contact with Bullitt.[35]

It is to Orville Bullitt's credit that he includes the memorandum Bullitt dictated on his return from the Oval Office (he was virtually ordered out) after his confrontation with Roosevelt on April 23, 1941. The Bullitt memo helps delineate the complicated personality of its author and thus, despite the fact that in 1941 Bryant was long dead, is relevant in assessing the final years of the doomed Bullitt-Bryant marriage. Bullitt had tried, in his interview with F.D.R., to get him to fire Under Secretary of State Sumner Welles for alleged homosexual acts. In the memo Bullitt speaks of Welles's "crimes." In 1943 when Roosevelt heard that Bullitt was spreading stories of Welles's "crimes" and that a Washington columnist was about to break the Welles case into the open, he asked for Welles's resignation and sent for Bullitt. [36] (Dean Acheson in *Present at the Creation* alludes to Under Secretary of State Sumner Welles's "malign enemy, William Christian Bullitt, a singularly ironic middle name.")[37]

In the story told by George Biddle, who heard it from his brother Francis, then attorney general, F.D.R. told Bullitt: "Bill, you'll get to heaven and Welles will be coming up behind you and you'll take St. Peter aside and say, 'You don't want that fellow here—look at those ugly rumors!' And Peter will beckon to Welles and say, 'Come on in, we don't care anything here about gossip,' and to you he'll say, 'Now you're to spend ten thousand years in purgatory and then go direct to hell.' "[38]

It is possible that Bullitt's homophobia, which made him see something suspect in any example of the European commonplace of men embracing—his correspondence with Roosevelt is sprinkled with such recitals and the inferences he draws—found a parallel in his reaction to women who did not fulfill his traditional concept of the model feminine role.

His woebegone testimony that eventually he had to manage the household and the servants and arrange for meals is more comic than otherwise, inasmuch as Louise had never done it—never when married to John Reed and certainly not since she and Bullitt first cohabited—since they always had flunkeys and servants about them. Moreover, Bullitt excelled in it. Ten years later, as ambassador to France, it was chronicled, "He had no housekeeper, has a finger in all the menus. . . . For a big dinner party of thirty or more, he doubled the staff of Embassy footmen so food may be served the only way he likes it—hot and punctually. He's been known to cut a guest dead who arrived for dinner half an hour late."[39]

24.
Final Days

ON THE SHIP CARRYING her back across the Atlantic, Louise Bryant was aware of being spied on by a man and a woman. Apparently she went from Algiers to Vienna and made her way to visit Freud. The detectives had seen him first, "told him who I knew and was with in Vienna so that he was able to tell me as soon as I arrived."[1] This may have been the first time that she was shadowed and attributed it to Bullitt but it was not the last time. His well-known obsession about being spied on, noted by his first wife on their honeymoon,[2] now had its corollary, with Bryant the victim.

Not long after Bullitt was awarded the divorce decree in Philadelphia, Bryant wrote to Claude McKay from Les Rosaires, Brittany. Penciled in even lines, the letters formed with care, the language spare, the letter is devoid of self-pity, is instead self-critical, and is eloquent testimony that she is making an effort to come to terms with herself. To McKay she can talk about her illness—and share with him her considerable triumph: she has finished a short story.

> I have your notes. I very much wish I could try Spain but I am afraid that I will have to go back to America for a brief time. I have been very ill again and I came down here to be by the sea and live with simple peasants.
>
> So many sad things happened to me this year. I tried to forget it by drinking too much and that only makes me ill.
>
> I hope you are well and working and happy. I am sitting in bed writing this and I have just finished a short story. The first one I have written in years.
>
> Do let me hear from you soon again. My best address is always: 84 rue D'Assas, Paris.[3]

She soon returned to Paris with the hope of writing a book on John Reed's life. An impossible dream, for she was in no shape to get out a book—but it remained for years her guiding principle. At times she did attain clarity and wrote letters to Reed's friends asking for recollections. At other times she drank, lived a life of chaos, tried again to get hold of herself.

For long McKay was the only friend Bryant was known to have told about her illness, but among the twenty letters or notes she wrote to the American sculptor living in France, John Storrs and his wife,[4] the last sad letter to them did make mention of her illness without revealing what it was. That summer she wrote:

> Dearest Marguerite and John:
> I have not written you because I have been so ill. My whole life has fallen to pieces. My half-brother, gassed in the war, has now lost his eyes and his legs have had to be cut off at the knees.[5] I send him any money I have. Bill is sending me all Jack's belongings but does not say on what boat or when. I have to stay here in my studio to wait for what is sent. I never have news of Anne. It is difficult for me to work.
> Please, please forgive me if I have not answered your dear notes very soon. Let me know when you will be in Paris. Louise[6]

McKay has related that he found Louise Bryant in Paris and told of the traumatic effect on him. "It was our first meeting since she took my manuscript to New York in the summer of 1926. The meeting was a nerve-tearing ordeal." If he was correct that it was about two years since she had written him of "a strange disease," it would have been in 1930, the year in which she wrote him from Brittany. "She had undergone radical treatment. The last time I had seen her she was plump and buxom. Now she was shrunken and thin and fragile like a dried up reed.[7] Her pretty face had fallen like a mummy's and nothing was left of her startling attractiveness but her eyebrows."

As for Louise, he continues: "She embarrassed me by continually saying: 'Claude, you won't even look at me.' Her conversation was pitched in a nervous hysterical key and the burden was 'male conceit.' I told her that the female was largely responsible for 'male conceit.' "[8]

The poet-novelist, himself considered "profoundly ambivalent regarding his sexual preferences,"[9] goes on to describe Bryant's companion. "Often when I had seen [Louise] before she had been encircled by a following of admirably created young admirers of the collegiate type. Now she was always with an ugly-mugged woman. This woman was like an apparition of a male impersonator . . . simulating a hard-boiled accent. A witty Frenchman pronounced her a *Sapphomanqué*.

The phrase sounded like a desecration of the great glamorous name of Sappho. I wondered why (there being so many attractive women in the world) Louise Bryant should have chosen such a companion. And I thought that it was probably because of the overflow of pity pouring out of her impulsive Irish heart."

Remembering "the beautiful poem which she sent us for publication in *The Liberator* after John Reed died," he quoted "Aftermath" in its entirety, and concluded his reverie over meeting the woman whose expressed belief in his talent had been unfailing, with this sad, wryly accurate tribute:

"And I thought if I could not look frankly with admiration at Louise Bryant's face, I could always turn to the permanently lovely poem which she had created."

He saw her twice again in Paris. He, his companion Carmina, and Bryant spent an evening together. When Claude, trying to find something to praise in Louise's appearance, complimented her on her hair, "neatly shingled . . . gleaming black," and "Louise smiled her appreciation," Carmina said in a loud whisper, "Can't you see it's dyed!" "A blighting frost descended on the party," he wrote.

McKay wrote of the other meeting: "One night I was drunk and maudlin in Montparnasse and Louise Bryant shrieked at me in high intoxicated accents, shaking her forefinger at me, 'Go away and write another book. Go home to Harlem or back to Africa, but leave Paris. Get a grip on yourself. She looked like the picture of an old emaciated witch, and her forefinger was like a broomstick. Perhaps it was her better unconscious self warning me, for she also could not get a grip on herself and get away from Paris.

"I heeded the warning."[10]

Obviously Bryant had changed her plan of going to America, for she wrote Margaret Reed urging her to join her in Paris to work on the book, it can be gathered from the warm reply she received. She wanted to come, was "all excited about your doing the book," and she felt Louise needed "mothering." But on one hundred dollars a month could she pay her share? She would start at once "to get all Jack's things—sort them out and have them ready."

"I dare not write down my sense of outrage about the way Bill is behaving," Mrs. Reed wrote. "It all seems so impossible—and as if no person with any sanity at all could do these things." She was glad Louise was to "take back Jack's name." (Actually she was known as Louise Bryant through all three marriages.) "You are my dear daughter and you belong in the family."[11]

In her next letter she spoke of Louise's letters, but she failed to understand many things. "And about Anne—does it mean that they have taken her away from you? . . . That was a dastardly thing for Bill to do. Could you not have cabled to someone to stop them?"[12]

What Bryant said to her may only be surmised. But it is possible that when she was hustled off on a ship bound for Algiers before the divorce preliminaries, she had no idea that the result would be the loss of Anne. The fact is that Bullitt did keep the child—obsessively—until she was grown.[13]

Some idea of the vagueness of Louise's letters may be gained from Mrs. Reed's replies. She would be glad to write the attorney Frank Walsh, she wrote, but "from your letter I can't find out what you want me to write him about." In Bryant's confusion she may have been daydreaming—thinking that all was not over and that Walsh could get Anne for her. Had he represented her at the 1929 hearing, true, all might be different now. (As it was, her attorney of record was Samuel Scoville; whether he was present at the hearing was not clear in the record.)

The bewildered Mrs. Reed asked again if she could maintain herself in Paris on her small income. She had clipped and dated all Reed's articles from magazines. "I have cried so much over them—and over his letters to me and his father that I am ill and worn out." She was ready to send everything but how could she if Louise did not return to this country?

"*Where* is Bill—and how do they conceal that he is off his head?" she asked in a postscript.[14]

"I used to ask myself," said Mura Dehn, "how this man, so charming, even courtly, as I first knew him, could be so merciless with Louise. Then I remembered what she told me that day at the Montparnasse *gare,* using the word 'insanity,' and I feel that he was frightened. Perhaps he feared what she would charge, and a case with lots of publicity. He did not want this life he had built up so carefully to collapse. He may have thought, it's better she than I.

"It is the only explanation I can make, as he had not seemed to be an unkind man. Of course, at a later date, they both went around saying that the other was crazy. But by then he had the divorce—and the child.[15]

Mother Reed wrote Bryant again, in September, "I still do not understand how they could take Anne away from you."[16]

On October 6 she wrote her that the box had gone off that day. It is a tender letter, and she assured her that the two things she had kept, her favorite photo of Jack and an illuminated book of his verse "which he did for me in Paris," would be sent her at once if she wanted them. "If I could only be with you—I could tell you so much. . . . He had always such a sunny, happy nature—like his father. I can't remember Jack ever being sullen or bad tempered."[17]

But before April 1931 Louise Bryant had returned to New York, still intent, at least intermittently, on doing the book on Reed. Her behavior at times was erratic, even bizarre, according to friends or acquaintances.

Although uninvited, she put in an appearance briefly at the great stone house George Biddle had completed in Croton when, to celebrate, he had "not exactly a housewarming—about a dozen couples were invited to see it." The date is uncertain, but the house was finished in late 1930 and the party was held some time before he married Helène Sardeau, the sculptor, in April 1931.

Louise made a scene, Biddle said mournfully: "Emotionally she had gone to pieces because of this disease she had. She became irresponsible, would get very angry. It was this disease that destroyed her. It was very sad that night. A lot of her old friends were here. She had many devoted friends, and they felt terribly about it. Henry Poor, from across the river, was there, and the moment Louise came in she began quarreling with him. She acted very badly."

Was it the party the Dells had described, at which she insisted on dancing with his black butler? George Biddle replied crossly: "He wasn't a butler, he was a caterer. Yes, the Dells were here." Apparently it was painful to him to discuss Louise Bryant's behavior that night. He felt, he said, that some day science would find that that disease changed the victim's personality. "She would say to the caterer, do this, do that. It made everyone miserable. Then she ran out and down Mt. Airy Road.

"Everyone was worried about her. It was very upsetting. She came back about four in the morning. It was the last time I saw her. A tragic woman."

Memories differ. Biddle thought that Bryant had "put on a lot of weight."[18] B. Marie Dell, though, thought that she had been cured of what she mistakenly called "her elephantiasis." "I can see her now as she looked that night, dressed in a long-sleeved white satin shirt with fancy studs and a man-tailored dress coat of black velvet. A handsome outfit. She looked very nice; but her behavior was wild, as if she were all doped up."

The caterer was rescued by the arrival of his cab. Shortly afterward

"Louise turned to George and said, meaning it for all of us, 'I guess I've had about enough of you, and you've probably had enough of me,' and she was gone." Dell said everyone was uneasy about her "until someone suggested that she probably would go over to Max's." It was B. Marie Dell's belief that before the disease was diagnosed "Bill took her to every big medical center in Europe, and at some point drugs were prescribed and that's the way she became addicted."[19]

Joe Pass, who in 1919 when he was twenty had met Bryant in Seattle and heard her speak, saw her again in New York in the John Reed Club one evening in 1932. They talked about Jack Reed, and the book that should be written about his life. He felt that she had reached some realizaiton that she would never bring it off; she even said at one point she planned to turn over all the material she had to Alexander Trachtenberg, head of International Publishers. But, she added, she was definitely opposed to Mike Gold's writing it. It seemed to upset her that he had been suggested.

"I made a date with her for luncheon the next day. I wanted to talk to her about Mike, for I thought to myself that there could be two books on Reed—one factual, not Mike's—and the other could be a song. That would be Mike's.

"We had that lunch," Pass said unhappily. "There was no point in raising the subject of Mike. Louise was incoherent. Not herself. She didn't even look like the same person I had known."

They had only one drink. Reluctantly, he was more explicit. "I did not *see* her take any drug. But I did think she might be under the influence—still, I think I was influenced by what Steff told me."

He had seen Steffens in the fall of 1930; he was reading proofs of his *Autobiography*. Pass was then with the International Labor Defense, and Steffens had come to the I.L.D. wanting a picture of Jack Reed. The one he wanted "we didn't have—but we got to talking. It was then that Steff told me what shape Louise was in when he last saw her in Paris. He told me she was on drugs."[20]

But Steffens had left Paris to return home in 1927, arriving in New York harbor with Ella Winter and their baby in March. Whatever he was volunteering about Bryant in the fall of 1930 had nothing to do with Bryant as he last saw her.

There was talk of drugs in 1930 during her stay in New York. Martin Kamin, a book dealer and man of letters, told of being taken to see Bryant by Justin Sheffield the lawyer; "it was 1930 or around then." She was then staying in what Kamin described as "a fleabag hotel"— the Maryland, on Forty-seventh Street between Broadway and Sixth

Avenue. Sheffield introduced Kamin, and Bryant introduced them to two young actors who were interested in doing a film on *Ten Days That Shook the World,* whose copyright she owned. The actors were Noel Coward and another British actor, Archie Leach—later known as Cary Grant.

"Louise was high and we did not stay long," said Kamin. "Not long afterward I heard that she was on drugs."[21]

In 1931 the Depression was in full force, banks were closing, and in December Margaret Reed wrote Bryant that her bank had closed, leaving her with twenty-five cents in her purse. She would answer her questions fully later, but could not "put my mind on anything just now." Bus she did put it on one thing: she "would rather not have my name appear in the book. . . . Also I think you had better let me see proofs, as you seem mixed about lots of things." She wished her a merry Christmas and signed, "Love, Muz."[22]

Another letter from her a few months after the entire family had moved to the Los Angeles area was sharply critical, even exasperated in tone. Louise's letters were delayed as she addressed them to an old Portland address. All the letters Margaret Reed had sent Louise were returned—from the only address she had for her. Almost as if she felt Louise was hallucinating she continued: ". . . the idea of my going to Russia is impossible. I don't know that I would want to go—even if I could. Don't understand about the Russian Ambassador. We have no diplomatic relations with Russia—so how can there be an ambassador?"[23]

This passage in Mrs. Reed's letter suggests how well Louise Bryant's mind worked in this period when she was "falling apart": however wild her scheme of going to Russia (and with Margaret Reed to back her she may have dreamed of confronting Bullitt and demanding to see Anne), she was not as irrational as she sounded to "Muz." She still retained shrewd insights and prescience about politics. Mrs. Reed's letter was dated May 27; the historic 1932 Democratic convention was but days away. With soup lines and hunger marches to Washington, Hoover had to be on his way out.

It took no prophet to know that Franklin D. Roosevelt would be nominated at Chicago. But Bryant doubtless reasoned, too, that not for nothing had Bullitt kept in touch with Colonel House ever since Versailles. Could she forget, even in her cloudy condition (punctuated at times by sharp and witty observations), that luncheon Bullitt gave for House, the Turkish ambassador, and Kemal Pasha in the palace on the Bosporus, even though she absented herself from home that day?

Bullitt had long been writing scintillating letters on the world situation to House. Orville Bullitt reports: "As early as December 1931 Colonel House wrote to Bill that he wanted to show a letter of Bill's to Mr. Roosevelt. . . . House wanted Roosevelt to know how valuable Bill would be to him on foreign affairs, if he should become President."[24]

Nor would Bryant be slow to estimate, even in half-lucid intervals, that with a change in administration, the desperate plight of the country would indicate a move away from the right. Thus the long overdue recognition of the U.S.S.R. seemed to be politically fated. F.D.R.'s sense of the dramatic might make it of top priority, so that it would come soon after his inauguration. In any event, when it came, who more logical for the ambassadorship than "Bill," much as it doubtless galled her to think of that contingency?

Apparently the lucid intervals even now in 1932 enabled her to write competent letters asking for material for her book on Jack Reed, judging from the warm reply she received from Sherwood Anderson:

> Indeed I remember you very well and the breakfast I had with you and Jack. Also many other vivid memories of Jack himself. Your letter fired me to write about Jack and many impressions of the man. . . . I think with me, as regards Jack, it was a case of love at first sight. I have never met a man who awakened as much quick affection in me. Your letter awoke in me something that has been sleeping in me for a long time. I want to do, if I can, a rather comprehensive article about Jack, what he meant to me, what he gave me, etc. You know he was a giver.

Anderson's final sentences suggest that it was not to Mother Reed alone that Bryant was confiding her hopes of going to Moscow:

> I hope to be in Moscow in November and to spend the winter in Russia. Perhaps I will have the job done, as regards Jack, by the time I see you.
>
> All my love,
> Sherwood Anderson [25]

On October 11, 1932 Louise Bryant, who was prevented by J. Edgar Hoover from obtaining a passport for so many years, applied for a passport. Although she "desires to proceed to Russia," and this was questioned by one official, the passport was handed her on the day she made the application.[26] She gave her occupation as journalist and stated that she intended to sail from the Port of New York on the

Lafayette in October. Her photograph on a copy of her application shows a bloated face, all but unrecognizable as hers except for her eyes.

She did not go to Moscow but to Paris, where Hugo Gellert saw her not long after, on his way to Moscow. [27] He was seated alone at a table in the Dôme, having just said goodby to a Hungarian artist friend, when he heard a voice say, "Oh, Mr. Gellert was always so aloof!" It was Louise Bryant.

"Of course I wasn't aloof. But after greeting her I did not linger. I assumed she was still married to Bullitt. I have never understood that marriage to the very rich Mr. Bullitt."

Judging from that passport photo, Gellert, had he wished to, might have remarked on her appearance in crueler words than McKay used. But Gellert, a gentle person, would only say, "Louise seemed quite amiable."[28]

Bryant now had the large collection of Reed's papers she had saved and all that his mother had sent her and their own letters and those sent her by his friends. In fitful starts—terrified, as her letters showed, lest something happen to these materials—she tried to write about Reed and did manage a fragmentary memoir. But her recurring need for alcohol occasionally sent her to the old Montparnasse haunts.

Kitty Cannell was at the Delambre drinking—with Bob McAlmon, as she remembered it—when she had an experience that left her shaken. She was uncertain of the year, except that it was before 1934, for in that year Cannell quit drinking altogether, and forever.

"Louise came in. At first I didn't recognize her. She was wearing a black Russian hat, indistinguishable from her hair. She looked bloated, fat. But her eyes, her lovely blue eyes, were the same. Her escort just then made some derogatory remark to her, and I went over and bawled the hell out of him for it.

"Then she came over and sat down next to me and said, 'Oh, Kitty.' It made me very sad."

It was, Cannell said, one of the last times she saw her. "And I blame Bill Bullitt completely for her becoming a hopeless drunk." Learning of Louise's incurable disease did not alter her judgment. [29]

Mura Dehn saw Louise Bryant three or four times in those years "when she wasn't herself." The first was at the Dôme. "It was a terrible shock. For this was Louise Bryant, the most glorious of women, made for brightness and achievement. The transformation was unbelievable. . . . And her hands—they were small—were dirty."

Dehn at once went over to her. Louise seemed to bristle with the suspicion that Mura would try to patronize her. Anything like being *kind* was off bounds, she let Dehn know by a glance.

"I said she wasn't herself. But she proved to me that she was. She was still Louise Bryant and proud. However disheveled she appeared, nothing had touched her core."

Mura Dehn would come to America only later, but she had heard much about Bryant's bravery in a time of fierce repression in years gone by; even Bullitt had boasted of her courage before the two women met. "I am sure, however," she added slowly, "that no period in her life required the consummate courage that those last years demanded. And she had it."[30]

On December 8, 1933, the newly appointed ambassador to the Soviet Union and such key aides as the Russian-speaking George F. Kennan and Charles E. Bohlen passed through Paris on their way to Moscow. Before the train pulled out, a lone figure waiting on the platform caught Kennan's eye: it was, he was told, Louise Bryant.[31]

Recognition of the U.S.S.R. and the naming of the new ambassador had been announced jointly and proclaimed in headlines of November 19. Bryant doubtless hoped to get a glimpse of Anne. After this preliminary trip to Moscow, Bullitt returned to Washington to hand-pick his embassy and consular staffs, and it was later in 1934 that Anne departed for Moscow, with much attendant publicity. Interviewed aboard the S.S. *Harding*, she, all of 10 years old, said, "No, this is no experience to me. It's my nineteenth crossing." From then on photos of father and daughter appeared often in *Time* and *Life*, as she lived in the embassy in Moscow and then in Paris.

In June 1934 the eviction of Louise Bryant for nonpayment of rent hit the press, but in general, newspapers that took notice of it did so only in a paragraph accompanying a photograph. It showed a pleasant-looking woman, her face agreeable although a bit heavy, her hair becomingly fixed, her white suit and dark blouse neat, in contrast to the bleary appearance of the passport photo.[32]

But the *Sunday Mirror Magazine* of June 24 carried a tearjerker that, with photos of Bullitt, Reed, and Anne, an artist's drawing of Bryant "Found in Her Studio," and a backdrop of the Kremlin, ran for more than a page of the tabloid. The *Mirror* was not the *New York American*. The latter was William Randolph Hearst Sr.'s "highbrow" experiment; the *Mirror* fulfilled the Hearst legend of never letting facts stand in the way of a good yarn. The headline: "Behind a Studio Eviction—This Epic Romance of 1 Girl, 2 Men and 2 Nations."

Parts were authentic. Louise Bryant before a Senate committee had been "a defiant witness" and "left the field with flying colors." Reed in 1920 was "stricken down in the typhus epidemic, his wife at his side." When he died he was "an honored, powerful figure among the Communists." "It was in Russia that Louise Bryant attained the zenith of her career as an international correspondent and a writer."

All that was needed was to juggle some dates and add a number of *Mirror* touches, and the writer reached this conclusion: "It's a long journey from Rittenhouse Square to the Kremlin. Yet a man named William C. Bullitt, born and reared in millions of Pennsylvania coal dollars made that leap. And Louise Bryant had more to do with the fact that Bullitt today is the first United States envoy to Moscow—that the United States has recognized Russia at all—than is generally appreciated."

The trouble was that Bryant was not in Russia when Bullitt undertook his mission to Lenin and did not meet him until 1922, or at the earliest, 1921. For all its inaccuracies, the story was among the few to say without qualification that Bullitt "became a regular patient of Dr. Freud, of Vienna." It also stated that although the divorce was without notoriety, "Bullitt was given custody of the child."[33]

It was probably after the eviction that the Dells attended a social function in Washington and Mrs. Dell found herself next to Francis Biddle,[34] to whom she said that a friend had told her that Louise appeared to be in dire financial straits. Biddle replied that that was ridiculous: his law firm handled the "substantial sum" Bullitt settled on her, sending it by the week or month and paying her rent direct "so she wouldn't go through it all for drugs for herself and friends and then be stranded." In his opinion "Louise went back to Paris as drugs were easier to get there."[35]

In 1934 the Harvard Alumni John Reed Committee began negotiations with Louise Bryant to obtain her vast collection of Reed material. The artist Robert C. Hallowell, who was a close friend of John Reed's at Harvard and who knew Bryant, was delegated to approach her. When Harry Reed wrote Granville Hicks, who was to write a biography of Reed, that his mother had sent Bryant "everything of Jack's she had," Hicks wrote Hallowell: "That makes it all the more necessary to work as tactfully as possible on Louise Bryant. I must get that material if it's humanly possible."[36]

"As for Mr. Hicks," Bryant wrote in part in answer to Hallowell's first request, "however honest, straight, decent," he did not know about Jack's life and "may never have met him." (He hadn't.) She could not forget "that Bobby Rogers, Dave Carb, Bobby Jones etc. avoided him completely in his last days in America. Perhaps if Jack was alive he wouldn't feel [so] tender about Harvard.

"However it may go, Bob, I mean to stand by Jack in his death as I did in his life. It was only I saw his going . . . in a typhus hospital. . . . Whatever I have to reproach myself for, I am sure I did not fail Jack." He should tell Mr. Hicks "to work with me and not be in a great hurry about such a book. At least he could send me a list of questions—so he might get a few things straight." She closed, "With my sincere regards for the success of your book and the hope you will send me a questionnaire, I am always, Louise Bryant."[37]

It was her first but far from her last plea that Hicks, or, when he studiously ignored her, someone from the Reed Committee, send her a questionnaire. She never received one, but up to a month before she died she continued to ask for it; in its absence, she sent notes to secretary-treasurer Corliss Lamont to be sent to Hicks, as she remembered incidents of her life with Reed or events of his childhood which had been described to her.

In one of her letters to Hallowell, when she was still holding off on agreement to part with the Reed papers, she spoke—obliquely—of Reed's difficulties with Communist leaders. After listing various events in Reed's life that Hicks could not have known of, she adds: "How could he know . . . of his extraordinary difficulties with many Communist leaders and probably himself, not so 'left' as you think."[38]

Had Hicks deigned to ask her what she meant by this he might then have checked it out with persons likely to know. In that event he would have fared better when, on its publication, his book was attacked by Max Eastman, let alone the spate of biographers and commentators who followed, described by Alan Cheuse as those "who attempted to resurrect Reed in order to project their voices through the lips of his corpse."[39]

Bryant's statement to Hallowell was made in the mildly aggrieved tone in which she claimed, in the same letter, that Mr. Hicks could not possibly know "of what Jack was writing and doing" in the days after the *Masses* trial, "of what poetry, plays, stories are still unpublished. . . . Or of his later so intimate and influential work with Lenin, of their notes to each other at meetings."[40] Was this the letter of a woman whom Hicks or any of the sponsors of his biography had need to fear?

"To me intelligence is not a matter of sex and age is not a crime," she wrote in "Notes to Corliss Lamont, or John Stuart or Hicks." "Why doesn't the Committee keep in touch with me?"[41] "I will be most happy if I can help you with any information. And please do understand I am not a person who hugs an animosity," she wrote Hicks at one point.[42] She wanted "Jack's story to be *clearly* written."[43] But despite her pleas and her gifts to Lamont of letters and papers she had withheld or had recently come across, she was never encouraged in any way to contribute her own recollections.

Remaining remarkably good-natured toward the Committee and especially Lamont, she continued to offer her recollections. Except for his initial letter taken to Paris by John Stuart when he obtained the Reed collection, Hicks never made any response to her often poignant requests to be allowed to help in providing information.

When he was asked why, in 1977, he replied furiously: "Because she was always drunk!" He paused for a moment, then added in a muted voice, "At least so I was told."[44]

Why was it that the truth, or the approximate truth—whatever was known—about Louise Bryant's condition was never told? On Hicks's part was it a desire to protect Reed's image? Or was it out of misplaced chivalry? If the latter, was it any kinder to imply, as he did, that she had never been reliable or responsible than if he had stated candidly that she was ill, had become an alcoholic and possibly a drug user?

There is a sexist pattern here. Louise Bryant, once a beautiful woman, stricken with Dercum's disease or adiposis dolorosa, was no longer beautiful. Except for her eyes she was scarcely recognizable to those who had known her. In Claude McKay's honest description it is not difficult to see that even he could not forgive her for this. But McKay remembered her great Irish heart. For the pious, such as Hicks, because she drank she was now considered shameful, beneath reproach, so that one need not even bother to write to her.

Another letter to Hallowell Bryant began: "After I sent you the letter I felt a little sorry that we could not all get together on this John Reed affair. I'm quite sure I could arrange to take all the luggage to Boston if I had enough to take a boat direct there." Then came her real concern: "I tell you truly, sometimes I'm so afraid to suddenly die and lose all those things I have guarded so long. Any old stupid person might think the best things Jack ever wrote—(and unpublished) are just pieces of paper."[45]

But to the Harvard Alumni John Reed Committee, dreading nothing so much as that Bryant would arrive along with the precious materials, this meant only one thing: John Stuart must hie himself to Paris to obtain the priceless Reed material.

Granville Hicks may not have been aware of Bryant's rare and incurable disease. But he had heard of the drinking, and doubtless knew of reports of the drugs as so many among the Left did. What scandals she might cause if she returned to America! What an embarrassment to the Harvard men who longed to forget about her! A woman hasn't the right to have her life wind up in tragedy. What a pity Bullitt was unable to have her tucked away in the "nursing home" one writer said he had attempted to get her to enter. [46]

No one, whatever his or her politics, faced the implications of what Art Young revealed: "Poor Louise Bryant committed a slow suicide— went the sad road of narcotic escape." The members of the Harvard Alumni John Reed Committee admired the "courage, idealism and independent mind" of John Reed. No one in that period, however, was conditioned to understand the kind of victim Bryant had become. Certainly Mr. Hicks was not equipped to cope with the problem of drugs or of alcoholism—or of sexuality, for that matter.

After Stuart had come and gone, Bryant wrote to Lamont: "We have had a curious month—John Stuart and I—working in dirty weather and a *little* broke. That's nothing to *me*. I've always been too rich or too poor." [47] Other letters followed, some carefully written, a few almost illegible, written when she was obviously high on alcohol or drugs. Several letters marked to be sent on to Hicks recalled occurrences in Provincetown, or comments on Steffens, O'Neill, Fred Boyd, or Reed (many of which appear in part earlier in this volume).

Arthur Garfield Hays wrote to Corliss Lamont in 1935: "Enclosed is a letter that Louise sent to me and asked me to forward to you. Wherefor I do so. Her idea that she had been followed is not new." [48] Her letter to Hays complains of Stuart: "Of his promise to send me word of Anne, absolutely nothing. And it is now one year and a half since I have had news."

The fourteen-page handwritten letter goes into a long recital of her being followed and harassed. She said she had begun to be followed again "by the same detective Bill sent over on the same boat I left America on before the divorce. This man with his girl followed me to Algiers. There's no use for Bill to deny it. I know the man and have seen and met his girl, who is always with him. . . .

"Later—after the divorce, when Bill came to Baden-Baden to see me the same couple arrived and again the same story. The doctor who owns the sanatorium . . . threatened to go to the police but Bill went with me instead and told the Chief that he had nothing to do with the affair. . . ." About eight weeks ago, she wrote, they appeared again. "Only this time I think they were not working for Bill."

When she was staying in a little hotel at Rambouillet, she went on, detectives took a room next to hers, installed a dictaphone, and told the hotel owner that they represented the American government "and I was under investigation as a spy—for whom I don't know." Although ill, she returned to Paris—not to her studio but to a room in the hotel in which her studio was located.

Why, if she was afraid to return to her studio, she took a room with an inadequate lock on the door, she does not say. But if the following sounds as if she were fantasizing, there is no doubt that her fear was real. "They took a room next door," she says of two detectives, "shouted Heil Hitler . . . and insults to me." She mentions the faulty lock: ". . . two broke in the door. Each had a revolver. . . . They said they had come to kill me but they did not shoot. I was frightened not of dying, God knows that means only peace for me, but of what else they might do. I looked out the window. It was two stories from the ground. The shed of the kitchen below would break the fall. I took the chance and jumped." French police called a doctor. She was in a hospital for a month. Three bones in her left foot were dislocated.

To help meet the bill she cabled Lamont, who wired her one hundred dollars. The journalist and publisher Bill Bird, she told Hays, wrote Bullitt in Moscow, who sent two thousand francs—and she received her three hundred.[49] Consul Herbert D. Murphy called on her in the hospital and informed her that the two thousand francs still owing on her bill was paid through the consulate.

In a note to Lamont, Stuart, and Hicks she explains that she had written "my *last will and testament*" leaving all she had to the committee and sent it to Art Hays, "and as soon as I can I'll send you a last letter to Anne. (My daughter.) So if chances are not always in my favor some day she will know."A rather murky passage alluding to Stuart declares: "I *know* or have *found out why* the papers that he *told me* 'would not be out of his sight' were *held up for three days*. For the same reason that I am hobbling about Paris broke with a badly put-together foot. The same organization did it."

But with all her suspicions and new problems as well as old, she did not forget to end with the old refrain: "Why doesn't the Committee keep in touch with me?"[50]

Bryant's old dream of going to Ireland was fulfilled in 1935. On her return trip by boat, writing to Stuart, apparently continuing some talk they had had, she is in one of her sharply observant moods. "About Jim [Larkin] and Jack Carney, they had nothing to do with all that happened in Ireland. Jim was defeated in the elections and Jack is still going around in a dream.[51] Communism doesn't exist in Ireland. There are a few persons there who have had a free visit to Russia and they get together now and then. The Irish movement is entirely Irish and not Russian made. I doubt if it ever will be. And England is always hovering like a hawk over us."[52]

After the anniversary of Reed's death she wrote Lamont, sending him two of Reed's letters to her. "I spent a lonely 17th as you might expect. I had recieved a letter from Anna Louise Strong which I shall send on after I reply to it. There was a small procession in Moscow to lay wreaths on the grave. The best I could do was put some flowers before his photograph." She said of one of the Reed letters enclosed that it was "very personal but characteristic. Jack was a very faithful person either to a cause or a woman. We were more in love when he died than the first day we met."

Alluding to her will sent to Hays, she told of her possessions the Committee would have: first editions sent by authors and "all Jack's books and plays . . . original paintings and cartoons of the period. The Hartleys and other large paintings" could be sold.

"Anne will not need any money from me and all I wish is that she will one day know that I did not desert her but that she has been kept from even knowing my address in these last years. All this is a great sorrow to me. Stuart knows the story."

She had had a motherly letter from Mrs. Reed. "She really loves me," she told Lamont, "although she never forgave Jack for not making a rich marriage." She made her usual plea: "I always regret that you do not ask me questions in letters. It would put me on the trail in my thoughts of all sorts of events." A note for Stuart was enclosed: ". . . Boris was not such a what you called 'chizzler' . . . as you thought. When I came back from Ireland . . . I had a pathetic note, found him in a charity hospital dying of tuberculosis."[53]

Shortly before her death she wrote Dr. Lamont again—three days before her birthday. "So for my birthday I send you two gifts. One a little note from Lenin." She had just returned from Turkestan and "he wanted first hand information. I had it (in my head)." The note she translated incorrectly: instead of "I shall be waiting for you" it read "Food tax," but it was Lenin's hand and with his signature. The other enclosure was the cover of a French paperback novel bearing the signature of John Reed. "I thought they might be a nice souvenir to paste in a volume of 'One of Us'—" she wrote, "Even if I wish so many things written in it had not been as they are."[54] She added patiently:

"I think it wise we co-operate more closely in the future. You know I made a will leaving all I have to the Harvard Committee on the promise that one day they tell my little girl, Anne why—"[55]

Seeing Louise Bryant in her late unhappy years, one memoirist of those Paris years compared his impressions of her to those of his former idol, Emma Goldman, next to whom in the Select Café he often saw her seated. He found Goldman greatly changed: her "one purpose in life, it seemed, was to hate—to hate and forget." The younger woman's face, "despite the inroads that Montparnasse had made upon it, would have been remarked in any company. The eyes, particularly, those eyes that had witnessed the 'ten days that shook the world.' . . . At the time I knew Louise she was drifting from café to café and was famous for the daring studio parties that she gave in the early hours of the morning. She no longer seemed to care; yet, in contrast to Emma, she was invariably warm, friendly, altogether likable. . . ."[56]

Louise Bryant's last known communication written to anyone was a postcard to Art Young. To Young, she was "this lovely daughter of a Fenian," and her laugh contagious. To Bryant, Young was one friend who never turned his back on Jack Reed in troubling times. Young in his autobiography of 1939 quotes her greeting as follows:

> I suppose in the end life gets all of us. It nearly has got me now— getting myself and my friends out of jail—living under curious conditions—but never minding much. . . . Know always I send my love to you across the stars. If you get there before I do—or later— tell Jack Reed I love him.[57]

25.
The Death of Louise Bryant

COLLAPSING AS SHE climbed the stairs to her room in the old Hotel Liberia, Louise Bryant died of a cerebral hemorrhage later in the day, Monday, January 6, 1936, in the Laennec Hospital in Sèvres.[1] News of her death was withheld from the press until January 9 by the American Embassy, after notifying Bullitt, then in Washington, on the pretext of awaiting burial arrangements. But burial plans were never announced.

In the early resurgence of feminism in the years before the First World War, feminists differed. Some wanted the vote above all else and sought to mute discussion of such issues as birth control, sexual equality, or the peace movement. Others wanted equal suffrage and much else besides, and it was among these, with Portland's radical Clara Wold, that Louise Bryant stood. Among other things, they fought to create conditions in which women might love freely. That meant first of all a denial of that hypocritical romantic love in which woman was inferior, a property. To do away with inequality was the essence of free love, and it was only by asserting equality that women could affirm their sexuality.

As a speaker for equal suffrage in Oregon in 1912 (when it was placed before the voters and won); as a suffragist picket of the White House in 1919; as an "unfriendly witness" who told a Senate committee she did not wish to be treated as a lady but as a human being, Louise strove to weaken the bonds that have held women inferior.

In John Reed, Louise found someone who also was grappling with the concept of free love. However firmly they embraced the revolutionary road, each retained enough of the bourgeois to make discussion of sexual subjects difficult. But they persevered through confusions and trial and error, their strivings not so different from those of today when, despite improvements in the position of women, a workable man-woman relationship—in other words, love—remains a problem.

Aware of Kollontai's teachings, Louise often felt trapped. She rebelled against the entrapment, but it was the *conditions* of loving a man she rebelled against, not love itself.

Neither Reed nor Bryant set much store in marriage itself. It was only when Reed was to be hospitalized and possibly undergo surgery for his ailing kidney that he insisted on marriage. Scornful of property as he was, he was determined, such were the contradictions of the capitalist world, to leave Louise in the event of his death with some of the security she had abandoned when she joined him in New York. So he acquired two homes, both in her name.

To live with Reed and not live *for* him remained a goal imperfectly realized, but when Louise fled this marriage too, setting out for France as war corespondent in 1917, Reed's letters reveal a struggle on his part to face his shortcomings. He did not mention O'Neill to her but instead blamed himself for all his haphazard imbroglios with women. They were both miserable without the other, and she returned. Only when he met her at the dock did she learn they were shortly to set off for Russia to await what each believed imminent—the social revolution that would topple the Kerensky regime.

With Louise's commitment to the October Revolution also came a growth in her reporting skills and her first taste of economic independence. When Reed arrived home her newspaper series on the Revolution as she saw it was nearing an end, and her book *Six Red Months in Russia* was under way. For a time, while he waited for the government to release his papers seized on his arrival, her earnings from writing and the small sums each made in speaking on Russia enabled them to live.

More basic is what happened to her. As Andrew Dasburg put it, "Louise was serious about living. She continued living in the Russian Revolution."

Louise Bryant inspired loyalty among some, and, if not loyalty, the sort of fairness which marked the approach of Alice Bretherton Powell of Salem, Oregon, who knew Louise as an acquaintance at the

University at Eugene. "Louise lived a Bohemian life before she ever left Portland," she said drily. "But she was very smart. Look at her brilliance before a Senate committee!" For a time she read of her in the news of the day, then no word. "She was like a shooting star."[2]

The veteran writer George Seldes, though he remembered Gwen Le Gallienne or others bringing Louise into the Hotel Liberia "dead drunk" at times, also saw her there at other times when they talked and argued about Russia. He even suggested that if Gwen Le Gallienne were alive and accessible "she might have a story different from the ones which circulated in heterosexual quarters in Paris."

In several letters Seldes wrote that he and Louise "met as friends. I had known Jack Reed slightly in Greenwich Village in 1916 or 1917. However, when I defended the Social Revolutionaries, the followers of Kropotkin, or other dissenters in Russia, Louise and I quarreled, and ended what might have been a friendship. Louise, incidentally, did deny the reports of Angelica Balabanoff and others . . . that in his last months in Russia, Jack Reed had begun to waver in the faith—or had been prepared to repudiate it, as Angelica later told me. . . .

"In general I would say that Louise Bryant showed no disillusionment; she denied all my anti criticisms."[3]

Louise never faltered in her commitment to the Revolution. She was not happy with the New Economic Plan (N.E.P.) but it was not until 1926, two years after Lenin's death, that she indicated she was dubious about the course the Soviets were following. Interviewed by the *New York American* September 11, 1926, she spoke of Russia as "the supreme example of dictatorship," and prophesied that Russia would become "one of the conservative nations of the world."

That Bryant disagreed with Reed on his immersing himself in the politics of the two fledgling Communist parties in America, that she was utterly opposed to his going to Russia in 1919 to present his party's case to the Comintern executive committee when she knew so well his physical frailty with one kidney gone, made her commitment to the Revolution itself no less. In arguing that he would do more for the Revolution by writing (he planned to write two more books on it after *Ten Days*) than by being a politician, she was on unassailable ground. His *Ten Days* already had done more worldwide (and even in Russia) to deepen understanding of the October Revolution than all he might accomplish in the faction-ridden parties of that period.

Louise's return to Russia by the underground in 1920, a journey fraught with peril, she undertook with the idea of keeping Reed in Russia. Her consuming fear was that if he returned to answer his indictment he would be imprisoned for a long, long term. We know the sequel. She helped him in his valiant struggle for life in a typhus ward in Moscow and recognized for all time how strong their love was.

Louise Bryant was no sooner dead than she became fair game for slander. Some sought to make her posthumously responsible for converting John Reed into a turncoat,* and there were others aplenty. To begin with, and published only in recent years, there is the letter Emma Goldman wrote to Alexander Berkman on reading of her death. "The last time I saw her," Emma Goldman wrote, "was at the Select when two drunken Corsican soldiers carried her out of the café. What a horrible end. More and more I come to think it is criminal for young middle-class American or English girls to enter radical ranks. They go to pieces. And even when they do not reach the gutter, as Louise did, their lives are empty. . . . Of course, Lincoln Steffens was right when he said about Louise [that] she was never a communist, she only slept with a communist."[4,5]

In 1921 Louise Bryant had seen the tragedy of the aging Emma Goldman in Russia and wrote of her with marked sympathy. But Goldman could not see the tragedy of Louise Bryant at fifty, addicted (according to Goldman's friend Steffens), an alcoholic, ill with an incurable disease, her child taken from her. But her heart responded to other outcasts, impelling her to visit "Boris" (about whom she and John Stuart disagreed) as he lay dying of tuberculosis in a charity ward.

Mura Dehn was matter-of-fact about Bryant's companions. "Those were the friends on whom she spent money when she had it, going bail for them when they were arrested. And they took good care of her. They saw that she got home to climb her stairs again to her room rich in books but little else." Some of the soldiers Dehn had seen Bryant with were Moroccans, "and some quite beautiful." In the Paris of that day, however free it was considered, they were not accepted. They still aren't. "But to Louise they were friends. At the time, she could not have reached respectable people. Nor did she want to!"

It is possible, Dehn thought, that Louise was fighting in the only way she could—to keep from feeling destroyed by Bullitt. So she defied the world—and any chance pity an old acquaintance might dare to proffer. "Louise," said Dehn, "was in an extremity of need—for nothing other than a little humanity."[6]

---

*See Appendix: A Note on Historical Questions.

The special fidelity, unmistakable though not easily explained, that Louise Bryant could evoke is nowhere better illustrated than in the words of the author Diana Sheean, who never saw Louise but knew of her through her husband Vincent Sheean. "I don't know how precisely, but years ago, when I first met Jimmy and he spoke of Louise, this partisan feeling for her was awakened in me. I wish I knew just what it was he said that instantly made me feel so strongly for Louise and so subsequently outraged by misrepresentations of her." Louise, according to Diana Sheean, was a woman "who needs someone to fight for her. Let Shakespeare, as usual, come to the rescue and say what I mean. 'O God! Horatio, what a wounded name,/ Things standing thus unknown, shall live behind me.' "[7]

The death of Louise Bryant made it easier for William Christian Bullitt to proceed with his career unhampered by fear of embarrassing publicity. At the time of her death he was nearing the peak of his diplomatic conquests, his volatile temperament and dubious judgment not yet fully comprehended by F.D.R.[8]

In his embassy post Bullitt's high hopes[9] soon turned to intransigent embitterment. As Elbridge Durbrow, who was vice consul under Bullitt in Moscow, described it, not without a trace of admiration: "In three months Bullitt turned from pro to anti."[10] Chip Bohlen wrote that Bullitt "became so bitter an enemy of the Soviet Union that he favored a Franco-German rapprochement. It was not until the British-French sellout of Czechoslovakia to Hitler in Munich in 1938 that Bullitt concluded that constructive relations with Nazi Germany were impossible."[11]

Bullitt ardently desired to replace the ailing ambassador to France, Jesse I. Straus, whose imminent retirement was rumored; he returned home in June 1936 and in August was appointed to the coveted post, to begin his duties at the close of September. Tempting as the ambassadorship in Paris was, he might have hesitated were it not that Louise Bryant had died in January. After all, he loved publicity, but he wanted headlines about himself, not Louise. So Louise's death was even better, from his standpoint, than a "nursing home."

After Bullitt returned to Paris to assume the ambassadorship, it mystified Vincent Sheean that he "asked me to lunch *alone* with him in a private room at Drouant's." Since Bullitt was well aware that Sheean and Diana Forbes-Robertson, the British author, were by then married and living in Paris, Sheean assumed that he wished to talk about Louise's death out of a "sheer sense of guilt." Yet there was "no outpouring of confidences," and it seemed to Sheean "a strange episode. I don't see why he had to apologize to *me* for Louise's death even if he had been in some way responsible. (I, too, had heard stories, but nothing that surprised me much.) I simply told him I had not seen Louise for many years and knew nothing of the story and would really rather not know."[12]

In a column-long obituary on January 10, 1936, the *New York Herald Tribune* noted that Louise Bryant was once "a glamorous and exciting figure" in Greenwich Village where she "dominated a notable circle of young artists and writers.

"An unusually competent journalist, Miss Bryant sought to dispel many foolish legends concerning the Soviets that had gained widespread credence in the United States. Hatred and distrust of the 'bloody Bolsheviks' were still prevalent when she returned to the United States in 1918."[13]

The New York Times observed: "Like her first husband, John Reed, whose ashes are buried outside the wall of the Kremlin near the tomb of Lenin, Louise Bryant was a champion of the Bolsheviki. She was in Russia in the early days of the Revolution and wrote many articles about it for the Hearst newspapers."[14]

The New Masses in an editorial, "Louise Bryant Is Dead," called her an "indomitable fighter for women's rights," "a rebel woman of great charm and courage," and "one of the first-class journalists of her time." It spoke, as did the *Herald Tribune,* of her testifying before the Overman subcommittee of the Senate: "Her poise, clarity and wit under the fire of the pot-bellied congressmen gained many new friends for the slandered Soviets, and helped break the world blockade against them."

She shared with John Reed, said the editorial, a great zest for life, for adventure in every form, for poetry. She was deeply loyal, as he was, "to the cause of the oppressed."[15]

Whatever the conflicts in their turbulent years together and apart, John Reed's "friend and lover" shared a dream with him—of a world to come when all men and women would know equality and liberty. As her writing testifies, Louise remained faithful to the dream after his death. That stands above all else, so that inevitably she shares in the imperishable glow they achieved, the light of which lingers even in the dross and tragedy of her last years.

Pushkin once wrote:

> And long the people yet will honor me
> Because my lyre was tuned to loving-kindness
> And, in a cruel age, I sang of liberty
>   And mercy begged of justice in her blindness.

Appendix I: A Note on Historical Questions

Alone among those who heralded John Reed's "disillusionment" and used Louise Bryant as a source, Emma Goldman did so in Bryant's lifetime. Theodore Draper reveals that Goldman wrote three different versions; two refute each other and an earlier one denies both.

In Goldman's *My Further Disillusionment in Russia* (1924), it was Goldman who surprised Bryant by saying, "Caught in a trap, caught in a trap." Bryant was claimed to have said, startled, that those were the very words Jack kept muttering in his delirium. But Draper points out that seven years later, in 1931, Goldman published her autobiography, *Living My Life*, in which the same scene occurs, with some surprising changes in the dialogue:

> "I could not understand what he meant," Louise replied, "but he kept on repeating all the time: 'Caught in a trap, caught in a trap.' Just that." "Did Jack really use that term?" I cried in amazement. "Why do you ask?" Louise demanded, gripping my hand. "Because that is exactly how I have been feeling since I looked beneath the surface. Caught in a trap. Exactly that."
>
> Had Jack also come to see that all was not well with this idol, I wondered, or had it only been the approach of death that had for a moment illumined his mind?

In the second version it was not Emma who surprised Louise, but Louise who surprised Emma with those words. "In the first version, Emma Goldman was sure of Reed's disillusionment. In the second version, she merely raised the question." But, Draper continues, in *The Roots of American Communism*, "By the time she came to write both of these books, Emma Goldman had apparently forgotten that she had already taken a stand on the question of Reed's final attitude. In *My Disillusionment in Russia*, published in 1923, she had reported without qualification that Reed had died believing fervently in the Communist future."[1]

Whether Bryant took issue with Goldman regarding her 1924 book is not known. When the famed anarchist chose *The World* of New York to sell her bitter series on her experiences in Russia and they appeared in 1922, her credibility took a nose dive among the Left and many friends stopped writing her.[2] Bryant may have chosen to ignore her confused revelations.

It had been different in 1919: Bryant chose to challenge Goldman's interpretation. While she was in prison in Missouri, Goldman read Bryant's *Six Red Months in Russia* sent her by her niece, Stella Ballantine. Hearing from the latter of her aunt's displeasure at Bryant's treatment of anarchists, Bryant to "Dear Stella" wrote in part: "I find it almost impossible to argue and certainly . . . to be angry with Emma—even if she has grossly misunderstood me and certainly misquoted me. I have too much respect for people who go to prison for their beliefs; it actually awes me no matter how much I disagree with them. Emma is a brave woman and for that I love her." Bryant said she wrote with one idea in mind, to try to prevent intervention, and it was not important to her what the anarchists thought.

She reminded Stella that Jack Reed and she at dinner with Stella had explained the part played by many anarchists. "They deserted, even fought the Bolsheviki and went over to the bourgeoisie *at the most desperate moment of the revolution*. I don't say they *all* did so but many, many, many . . . I did not tell *that*. Emma asks me if I did not know that Shatov is an anarchist. I saw him daily and I knew him here. Yes, I knew that. The reason I 'praised him to the sky' was because he was magnificent in critical moments. I will not forget his white face addressing two of the greatest gatherings of Anarchists . . . in Russia. 'If this is Anarchism,' he cried to them, 'then I am *not* an Anarchist! If you are going to stab the revolution in the back—I am not with you. . . .' And he was almost mobbed. . . . Well, of course the majority finally came round to his way of thinking but the rest did serious damage.

"Bill did not start the Red Guards. Emma always makes statements of this sort just as if she were the last authority. . . . It was formed *before* Bill returned. He would be the last to claim the honor. . . .

"I am going to write the truth as I see it and I am not going to be attacked or dictated to by any Ism. . . .

"And as for you, Stella. . . . You have always hung openmouthed on every sentence of Emma's. I don't like servility. I think you would be a personality if you would stand on your own two feet. I wish to heaven you would. . . . You think she is above any criticism. . . . And she is human—and therefore full of faults— makes mistakes just like any of us. And remains a real, vital personality all the same.

"Please see that this reaches Emma."[3]

Max Eastman, who seems to have ignored Emma Goldman completely in his various versions about John Reed and Louise Bryant, originally asked Granville Hicks whether his 1936 biography of Reed contained "the fact" that Reed "resigned from the Executive Committee of the International on the day he went to his death bed?" But Eastman was forced to temper that claim.[4] A few years later, by 1942, Eastman centered his main attack on the "suave paragraph" by Hicks dealing with Reed's resignation. He quotes Hicks: "During one of the sessions of the executive committee, Reed peremptorily offered his resignation from the E.C.C.I. in protest against Zinoviev's decision on an organizational question."

Eastman objected: "The formula 'Zinoviev's decision on an organizational question' is sufficiently vague and noncommittal to suggest that facts are being withheld by those who know them, whoever they may be. The absence of all curiosity as to the details of this astounding incident is strange.

"Upon *what* organizational question did Zinoviev's decision push John Reed to this extreme and politically self-destructive act? Even assuming that he did apologize all around, hat in hand, and take it back, *why did he resign?*"[5]

Early on, Hicks agreed "that we do not know all the facts involved in Reed's resignation from the E.C.C.I."[6] But we now know that Hicks was curious enough about the facts to ask Louis Fraina, who had become Lewis Corey, a highly respected economist, for his recollections of this and other events. Preparing his book on Reed, Hicks submitted certain chapters to Corey, but because of a serious illness Corey's six-page letter of criticism was not sent until December 1935, late for all but limited alterations. Corey objected to Hicks's version of the resignation in the draft submitted to him, writing: "Not true. The ECCI had, after demanding that the two American parties must unite, made a decision in regard to the personnel of the new united party. Reed opposed the decision, with not a single member of the ECCI supporting him. After the ECCI's refusal to change the decision, Reed resigned. He was bitterly denounced by Zinoviev, Radek and Bukharin and several other members for false reasoning, for reprehensible factional and personal politics, for acting as a petty-bourgeois journalist."[7]

A second letter from Corey followed shortly, pointing out, "Your statement that Reed resigned because Zinoviev wouldn't recognize him is not only incorrect, but makes Reed appear rather childish; one simply doesn't resign from the ECCI on such an issue. If the statement were to protest against a decision in connection with the personnel (or organization, organizational policy) of the United Communist Party, it would be correct, and it would not make it necessary for you to tell the whole story."[8]

True, as Draper says, Corey didn't tell Hicks what it was all about. It could be, not that Draper says it, that Hicks, however good a biographer, was not a good reporter. The least that Hicks might have done, even without Eastman's warning he was going to challenge his book, was to write Corey and ask, "*What* whole story?" But in 1937 Hicks was writing of the resignation, ". . . the account I give is consonant with the facts we do have and his [Eastman's] is not."[9]

It remained for Draper to ferret out the whole story from an F.B.I. interview with Corey years later.[10] As unearthed by Draper, Corey told the F.B.I. that at the E.C.C.I. Reed argued that, while no one believed the old "spy" charges against Fraina (Corey), they had been widely circulated in the United States and thus it might be a good idea for Fraina to be inactive for several years on his return. "So hostile was the reaction that Reed was goaded into the defiant act of resigning, bringing on more recriminations and ending in his withdrawal of the resignation."[11]

For many there was an implausibility about claims by Goldman, Angelica Balabanov, Eastman, and above all, Benjamin Gitlow, regarding Reed's "disillusionment." But not until Theordore Draper, regarding them sympathetically, nevertheless examined all of them and checked them out in 1957 had anyone meticulously compared them. For Draper himself it was not easy to dismiss all the tales of disillusionment with Communism out of hand. When he learned that Fraina-Corey also wrote Hicks, "As one of the two or three Americans who saw him shortly before his death, I can affirm that Jack Reed kept all his loyalty to the Soviet Union and communism,"[12] instead of this bringing clarity, to Draper it served to "deepen the Reed mystery."

Although he had been deeply hurt, to say the least, by Reed's goof at his expense before the E.C.C.I., unpublished parts of the Corey letter show a deep appreciation of the whole man in John Reed. They also show Reed's efforts, helped along by Louise Bryant, to let Corey know how he was trusted—in fact, Reed depended solely on Fraina-Corey to make sense of the translations of his speeches.

"Could you not make more of Reed's illness?" Corey asks Hicks. "It was a dramatic thing and illustrated the finest of Reed's qualities. I saw the contrast between him and an English delegate who was not so ill and recovered [of typhus]. The Englishman was . . . interested in nothing but his chances of recovery. . . . Reed, on the contrary, was Reed to the end. He was brave, clear-headed, fighting every inch of the way against approaching death. Almost to the last he maintained his interest in the revolutionary movement."

Continuing, he corrects a detail in Hicks's manuscript: "I did not bring the stenographic rendering of his speeches (not reports) to him. But through Louise Bryant he asked me to revise them for publication, as the translations had made the speeches almost unintelligible, and it meant practically my rewriting them, which he felt I could truthfully do because I knew his ideas. He discussed the movement with me. This was five or six days before his death. There is drama in Jack's resistance to death and his clinging to life and ideas and the movement."

In another passage he said of Reed: "His real importance, which was momentous and which you do not, I think, stress sufficiently, was the elan given to the development of the left wing among the party masses by his direct contact with the Russian revolution and by his agitation in the press and on the platform (including, of course and most of all, the 'Ten Days'). Whether you agree or not with my other comments, this at least should be strengthened. It was a real contribution."[13]

Here Corey's letters in general bolster what Louise Bryant wrote after Reed's death and neither could have written as they did of Reed's desperate fight to live, and his sweetness as he fought, if disillusionment had been anything but a matter thought up sixteen years later by Max Eastman.

Not that Corey was without any criticism of Reed; he did not fail to fault Hicks for misinterpreting the trade union issue.[14]

In the last analysis Draper makes his own accommodation to the disillusionment theme. Having found that nothing Louise Bryant wrote bore out what she allegedly said; that Reed in what he wrote about the Second Congress reveals only his intrepidity, and that the witness he finds of first importance, Fraina-Corey, scoffed at the disillusionment aspersions, Draper concludes:

"If disillusionment means a final accounting with the Communist movement and its ideology, there is room for differences of opinion, with the burden of proof on those who claim a definitive break. But if disillusionment is understood intellectually and emotionally rather than organizationally, Reed was probably as disillusioned as it was possible to be and still remain in the movement."[15]

Rosenstone, Reed's latest biographer, understandably takes issue with that, declaring: "Having been driven to Bolshevism by world events and his own needs and goals, Reed had embraced a philosophy that allowed him to make sense of his experience, and he would not have abandoned it easily. . . . [I]t certainly would have taken much more than some disagreements with individuals like Zinoviev to turn him onto a different path."[16]

Although Hicks abstains from using more than a few words of Bryant's letter to Eastman on Reed's death, he indicates Reed said no to her urgings that he remain in Russia rather than return to answer the Chicago indictment. This allows Draper to point to one thing on which Hicks and Angelica Balabanov agreed. "In her moving letter to Eastman on Reed's last days, written only a month after his death, Louise Bryant stated: 'He was consumed with a desire to go home.'"[17]

Draper concludes: "Death took him prematurely, not only as a human being but as a political symbol. The mystery of John Reed is what he would have done in the last act of his life's drama. No one really knows, and everyone has written of it differently in his or her own image."[18]

Max Eastman replies, "My way of writing it would be to say that he would have come home to poetry and creative writing where he belonged. . . . His 'contempt and hatred' for Zinoviev and Radek hardly foretold a life of fanatical subordination to the organization they so arrogantly controlled."

Evasively, quite as if he had not initiated the years-long quest to distort the meaning of John Reed's life and death and, a more lasting effort, to shame his wife, Eastman says, in his last book published on his eighty-second birthday: "There are so many of these versions, and they differ so widely, that it is impossible to decide what did happen." He quotes Draper's passage, "Death took him prematurely. . . ." and, as if responding to a revelation, he recalls for the first time in all the years he has been writing of what Louise told him on two long-ago occasions, the letter Draper stressed, and declares blandly:

"I really think more light is cast on the mystery of the unlived chapters of John Reed's life by Louise Bryant's account of his death written to me from Moscow just after he died, than by any or all of those tales about his political feuds and arguments. He was consumed by a desire to go home,' she told me." He continues to quote from her letter:

> He was never delirious the way most typhus patients are. He always knew me and his mind was full of stories and poems and beautiful thoughts. He would say, "You know how it is when you go to Venice. You ask people—Is this Venice?—just for the pleasure of hearing the reply". . . . [19]

Vanished now from Eastman's pseudo-apologia is any reference to the fiction of Reed's being "shocked at the luxuries enjoyed by the delegates on the way to Baku and back—luxuries which necessitated pulling down the blinds as they passed through towns where men were all but starving."[20]

Of course this was relatively mild stuff compared to Ben Gitlow's creation, which represents the most barefaced exploitation of Bryant. She visited him at Sing Sing in 1921. Draper disposes of Gitlow by pointing out that in his first book, *I Confess* (1939), he did not even mention Reed's disillusionment. But in his second, *The Whole of Their Lives*, published in 1948, all of twenty-seven years after Louise Bryant's visit, "Gitlow was able to give three full pages of direct quotation of what she had told him."[21] Gitlow has Bryant saying that only when delirium set in was she allowed to be with Reed, and, out-doing Balabanov, has Bryant's final words: ". . . he died because he did not want to live."[22]

Gitlow, a widely discredited figure who spent his last years as a paid informer,[23] also in direct quotes claims Bryant revealed that Reed was shocked when "old Mohammedan women boarded the train followed by beautiful Caucasian girls. Some of them were barely fourteen years old. The old women disrobed the girls before the eyes of the delegates. The nude beauties stood before the gaping eyes of those who called themselves communists. . . . What followed turned out to be an orgy of drunken lasciviousness in which Radek was the central figure." This entire passage found its way into a 1967 biography of Reed, *The Lost Revolutionary*.[23]

In Barbara Gelb's *So Short a Time* (1973), this fabrication becomes: "But the style of the trip to Baku had shocked and sickened him. The armored train, passing through towns and villages whose inhabitants were starving, was supplied with an ostentatious display of rich foods and rare wines. When the train entered the Caucasus, it was boarded by beautiful young prostitutes, bought by the Bolshevik leaders for an unabashed orgy. Reed was appalled, not by the flagrant lust displayed by his traveling companions, but by their cynical and hypocritical employment of the capitalist system of barter."[24]

Balabanov also was at the Second Congress. Draper found her recollection, that Reed resigned before going to Baku because he was nominated to go, unreasonable, as he did go to Baku, and as Eastman put the date after Baku. Balabanov writing in 1937 is made a liar by Balabanov writing in 1921. The Souvenir Program of the John Reed Memorial meeting of October 17, 1921, in New York carries an extract from her story "John Reed, Poet and Revolutionist" in which Balabanov declares:

"John Reed willed and knew how to keep true to his course, and no deflection ever disturbed the harmony of his soul, of his mind, of his activity. He did not hesitate. As a fighter he entered conscious life, as a fighter he died. The last page of his rich, love-filled life is closed, sealed forever with the eternal seal of death. Now we may read that book and pronounce our judgment without fear that tomorrow or the day after something might be written to disturb the harmony of that already created. . . .

"It can be said without exaggeration that no other foreigner so well understood, loved and defended Soviet Russia as John Reed. His book on the revolution is a classic, it will sway a multitude of minds and hearts for generations. He loved the Russian peasants and workers and he realized the grandeur of their devotion to the cause of the liberation of the workers of all lands. . . ."[25]

By 1967, a decade after the imprimatur on *The Roots of American Communism*, John Reed's *Ten Days* again could be bought without the vituperative introduction by Bertram Wolfe.[26] It was a happy event when Granville Hicks again wrote an introduction to *Ten Days*, this in a Signet reprint (New American Library). Hicks had ended his affiliation with the Communist Party along with thousands of others after the Nazi-Soviet pact, and later named names before H.U.A.C., as he recounts in *Part of The Truth*. But in his new introduction he stuck by his guns. He quotes Draper and adds: "That Reed might have been disillusioned if he had lived seems to me quite likely. . . . That he was disillusioned at the time of his death I am not convinced."[27]

Also in 1967, the Soviet Union's fiftieth anniversary, a new anniversary edition of *Ten Days* with an eighteen-page introduction by the late John Howard Lawson, was issued by International Publishers,[28] whose own reprint of *Ten Days*, exhausted in 1938, was allowed to remain out of print for twenty-nine years. One of the saddest footnotes in the aftermath of the 1936 biography was to see how one of Reed's supposed champions, John Stuart, failed to take Reed's estimates of the October Revolution's leaders seriously. With all its virtues, Stuart wrote, *Ten Days* has "serious defects"—among them Reed's neglect of Stalin's role and Reed's "assigning to Trotsky a role that did not square with the facts." Appearing in 1950, the article was an abridgement of an introduction to a book of Reed's selected writings finally published in 1955,[29] presumably held on ice until after the death of Stalin, whose name appears only minimally in *Ten Days That Shook the World*.

Appendix II: Regarding William C. Bullitt

Efforts to learn who divorced whom in the first marriage of William C. Bullitt, to the beautiful Ernesta Drinker, and to learn how much money he provided for Louise Bryant when he divorced her in 1930, were unavailing. A letter dated March 28, 1977, from Thomas Raeburn White, Jr., of Philadelphia, attorney and son of the late noted lawyer who represented Bullitt in his divorce from Louise Bryant, declared: "I have found that all of our files concerning William C. Bullitt have unfortunately been destroyed and I have no personal knowledge of the questions which you raise."[1]

Others have pointed out that Bullitt's barely disguised autobiographical novel, *It's Not Done* (dedicated to Louise Bryant and published in 1926) targeted prominent Philadelphians, "easily recognized" in his brother's words.[2] As Justin Kaplan put it, Bullitt in his novel "settled a number of old scores."[3] Easily the cruelest—and least believable—portrait in the book is that of the hapless Mildred, wife of John Corsey, Bullitt's newspaperman alter ego, a character maligned beyond belief.

It is a depressing example of how, as his vindictive treatment of Louise Bryant illustrates, once he turned against a woman, Bullitt's antagonism was boundless. Perhaps it is a reflection of the Bullitt syndrome, a tendency to surround historic figures with all but hero-worship—and to break with them when they did not follow his advice. As his brother Orville wrote: "To Bill most decisions were either black or white; he had very little use for compromise in his character. . . . This characteristic led to his break with Woodrow Wilson and later with Roosevelt. . . . When they failed to accept his . . . strongly held convictions he left them. . . ."[4]

The fictional John Corsey has blamed his recurring impotence on the coldness of his wife Mildred. He discovers he has been wrong about her sexuality: she has a lover. He upbraids her: "Damn it, Mildred, what can you love in a guttersnipe like Milligan?" She replies: "Everything I've never found in you." She did not blame him but he was "too tender and gentle" and "too much of a gentleman." But, he asks, what did she want?

"Somebody terribly strong who'd take me without caresses, without gentleness, coarsely, brutally. . . ."

Corsey: "Rape as a steady diet! Why didn't you pick a nigger longshoreman?"

"I might have!" she shouted.

Describing another talk that evening between the "gentleman" Corsey and his wife Mildred, the author becomes personal and venomous. Corsey is laying down the law to her. "Her fingers reached out, imploring him to stop and her dressing-gown fell apart revealing the shriveled rinds of her breasts."[5]

Bullitt's brother Orville, who produced as honest and as charitable a depiction of William Christian Bullitt as possible, showed him turning against Wilson for idealistic impulses.[6] But he was unable to show any such factors in his turning against Roosevelt.

Various others have written about the Sumner Welles matter in connection with Bullitt. Like his father, a leading Southern liberal, Jonathan Daniels wrote that there were "certainly those who might have fabricated the story of homosexual acts between the austere, elegant Welles and menial blacks. The very ease of his relations with that other Groton-Harvard man, the President, inspired jealousy." This was an addition to his diary excerpts, as was the following:

"[Credit or shame for the original circulation of this story, however, definitely belonged to William C. Bullitt, another American of top-drawer Ivy League position. . . .]"[7]

George Biddle in interviews spoke more than once of the Welles matter and Roosevelt's dismissal of Bullitt when he was convinced that he had spread the rumors of Welles' alleged homosexual acts. Biddle declared that Bullitt never forgave FDR and never again entered the White House. "Bill might have been in some conflict himself as to homosexuality," the painter said speculatively. But primarily, as he saw it, Bullitt had acted from a simple motive. "Put very briefly, he wanted to be Secretary of State. And thought he saw his way to being such. As it was, it finished his diplomatic career."

The incident was a factor in Biddle's final judgment on his old friend: "Bill had enormous brilliance, but he lacked moral stature."[8]

In his review of *For the President Personal & Secret* the historian Kenneth Davis observed:

> Perhaps it is in the light of one's knowledge of the cause of this break [with Roosevelt] that one sees in Bullitt's correspondence a slightly excessive reference to physical contacts between men. In his report of the welcoming party given him in Moscow, he notes Stalin's "from time to time putting his arm around Piatakov's neck and squeezing him affectionately. At evening's end, Stalin took my head in his two hands and gave me a large kiss! I swallowed my astonishment, and, when he turned up his face for a return kiss, I delivered it."[9]

Actually there are many such references with all kinds of meanings implied, had FDR tended to take them seriously. For instance, from Paris, October 24, 1936, Bullitt wrote the President in part: " . . . I got away to a good start with [Leon] Blum. . . . He looks exactly like the caricatures of him, and has the sort of quicksilver intelligence and the little fluttery gestures of the hyper-intellectual queer ones. . .

"The aristocracy and upper bourgeoisie are just as dumb here as their opposite numbers in the United States. They show no sign of appreciating the fact that Blum is as conservative as anyone who can hold the situation together. If Blum were in for a four-year term . . . I have no doubt that he could do a highly constructive job and that the internal situation in France would right itself rapidly. But as he has to maneuver daily to maintain his position and as no one in the country has any fundamental respect for his character—since there is no one who does not know why he was fired from the École Normale—he is not exactly a Rock of Gibraltar. . . As it is, Blum is strong because of the weakness of his opponents."[10]

Earlier in a long letter to FDR on his arrival in Moscow, Bullitt took note that in Germany "the most fantastic thing which has happened" recently was "the christening of the new military academy 'Ernst Roehm Kadetten Erzieungs Anstalt.' In view of the revelations about Roehm, the English equivalent would be for the renaming of Sandhurst 'Oscar Wilde Institute.' " A footnote explains that the reference to Wilde "is because Roehm was also a homosexual."[11]

Bullitt's letters to the President also give evidence of various prejudices, biases and oddities in addition to his homophobia. His bias against the English was well known and remarked by his brother Orville. But the same letter from Paris on Blum suggests that to Bullitt all wives who were foreign were suspect. "I have at least discovered that every clerk in the Embassy *without exception* is married to a foreign wife! This includes all the confidential file clerks."[12]

Actually the Ambassador had revealed in no uncertain way his feeling about foreign wives in Moscow. When Elbridge Durbrow was asked if he had ever seen Bullitt lose his temper, he said, "God, yes. It was a real dagger dart he would send, too. Well, crack! He didn't want any married men around and we were all bachelors—with a few exceptions—and all the exceptions were married to foreigners. George Kennan's wife was from Sweden or Denmark; Lieut. Thomas D. White's wife was a foreigner, and I think one of the staff was married to a Russian. At dinner one night, Bullitt looked around the table and said: 'What do we have here? A regular tower of Babel, or a League of Nations—but not an American outfit, that is clear!' "[13]

In the book on Woodrow Wilson published shortly before Bullitt's death in 1967, which bears the joint by-line of Sigmund Freud and William C. Bullitt, women, foreign or not, seem to get short shrift. One reviewer noted the "emphatic insistence upon the virtues of masculinity *per se*" in "what is evidently Bullitt's contribution to the study he and Freud did of Wilson," and the portrayal of the feminine as "weak, timorous, deceitful." "Wilson is contemptible *because* his response to challenges is womanish."[14]

Erik H. Erikson, frankly dubious that Freud wrote anything but the Introduction, found that the chapters on Wilson's boyhood had some fascinating bits of description, but they were "strung together relentlessly on a thread of vindictiveness which does not let 'little Tommy' get away with anything, certainly not with the fact that 'he never had a fist fight in his life.' "[15] Erikson seems curiously unaware of Bullitt as a former patient of Freud's. He may not have known what Freud wrote to the German novelist Arnold Zweig in July 1930, as it was not published until 1970: "Indeed I would like to write nothing more, and yet I am once again writing an Introduction for something someone else is doing." A footnote identifies it: "Introduction to a study of Woodrow Wilson, by William C. Bullitt: *Thomas Woodrow Wilson, Twenty-eighth President of the United States: A Psychological Study*, first published in 1967."

When Bullitt ran for mayor of Philadelphia on the Democratic ticket his campaign was "disastrous," with religious groups digging up his novel and accusing him of being "both immoral and anti-Semitic," according to Beatrice Farnsworth in *William C. Bullitt and the Soviet Union*. Liberals cited his support for Vichy France and said he was pro-fascist. At the same time anti-Semites opposing him said his mother's maiden name was Hurwitz and that Bullitt was a Jew.[17] The mother's grandfather was an eminent Hebrew scholar who was converted to the Episcopal church.[18]

One of Bullitt's last messages from Moscow, to the Secretary of State, in April 1936, contains an anti-Semitic passage: "The Russians have always been and are bad bureaucrats. In consequence, extraordinary numbers of Jews are employed in all the Commissariats. Only one out of each sixty-one inhabitants of the Soviet

Union is a Jew; but twenty of the sixty-one Commissars and Vice-Commissars are Jews."[19] But he went much further in a letter to his confidant R. Walton Moore of the State Department, as revealed in a 1977 book by Daniel Yergin, alluding to "the influence of Mr. Umanski, the wretched little Kike . . . the Foreign Office, as you know, has been purged recently of all of its non-Jewish members, and it is perhaps only natural that we should find the members of that race more difficult to deal with than the Russians themselves."[20]

Kitty Cannell, in speaking of the period when Bullitt was being psychoanalyzed by Freud and returned on some weekends, said of Louise: "She found him awfully hard to take. She was a feminist and spoke up when she disagreed with him, you know. And at times he was very edgy, and she couldn't always be tactful."[21]

Notes

The Bibliography, pages 369-377, specifies the location and other information regarding the collections referred to below.

CHAPTER 1. THE VILLAGE

1. Louise Bryant memoir, Granville Hicks Collection.
2. Louise Bryant to John Reed, December 29, 1915. John Reed Collection.
3. John Reed to Sally Robinson, December 18, 1915. JR Coll.
4. LB memoir, Hicks Coll.
5. Granville Hicks, *John Reed*, 206.
6. Interview with Albert Boni, May 10, 1973.
7. Interview with Hugo Gellert in his home, Freehold, N.J., November 21, 1971.
8. Interview with Conrad Aiken in his home, Brewster, Mass., July 20, 1971. Aiken died in Savannah, Ga., August 17, 1973.
9. Interviews with Roger Baldwin: by telephone, December 15, 1971; in his office, New York Civil Liberties Union, January 4, 1972; and in his home, November 21, 1972.
10. Bercovici and Brooks quoted in Allen Churchill, *The Improper Bohemians*, 53.
11. Hutchins Hapgood, *A Victorian in the Modern World*, 353.
12. Claude McKay, *A Long Way from Home*, 29.
13. Vincent Sheean to author, September 8, 1971, from Leggiuno-Arolo, Italy. Sheean first went to New York in 1921; he based his statement on what friends said who lived, as he did, on Patchin Place and had known her in 1916.
14. Interview with Dorothy Day, February 1972.
15. Interview with Bertha Dorris Carpenter of San Francisco, who knew Louise Bryant at the University of Oregon.
16. Hapgood, *Victorian in the Modern World*, 383.
17. Referred to in letter, JR to LB, July 5, 1917, New York to Paris. JR Coll.
18. Mabel Dodge Luhan, *Movers and Shakers*, vol. 3 of *Intimate Memories*, 417–18.
19. Max Eastman, *Heroes I Have Known*, 213, 224–27.
20. LB memoir, Hicks Coll.
21. William Jennings Bryan had resigned as Secretary of State after Wilson's second note to Germany on the sinking of the *Lusitania*, but he was supporting the President in his reelection campaign. So was Reed, along with a number of

other intellectuals who thought he was sincere in his rhetoric about keeping America out of war.

22. JR to LB, February 1916. JR Coll.

23. JR to LB, July 5, 1917, New York to Paris. JR Coll.

24. "All of Andrew's lovers, in and out of wedlock," said his son, Alfred Van Cleve Dasburg, "were talented, strong, independent women." Interviews in New York, July 19, 1976, and in Santa Fe and Taos, N.M., July 19, 1978.

25. The account of Louise Bryant's call on him, and subsequent visits to Woodstock, where he then lived for part of each year, is Andrew Dasburg's. Interviews in Taos, N.M., March 22–23, 1972, and July 19, 1978.

26. Fortunately Grace Johnson came into an inheritance early in life and was always able to have a nurse for the child. Louise Bryant was alone in being poor among all Andrew Dasburg's lovers, said his son, Alfred.

27. When Louise Bryant was cross-examined as to her religion by members of a Senate subcommittee investigating Bolshevism on February 20 and 21, 1919, she offered this information as to her Catholic origins. U.S. Congress, Senate Subcommittee of the Committee on the Judiciary, *Bolshevik Propaganda: Hearings,* Bryant testimony, 465–561.

28. The so-called Molly Maguires constituted the militant core of the Workingmen's Benevolent Association of Schuylkill County, which took on the combined mine owners of the region after 179 men were brought up dead from the bowels of the earth in nearby Luzerne County in 1869. They organized a strike which was broken only when an Irish informer hired by the Pinkerton agency for Frank B. Gowen of the Reading Railroad Company infiltrated the largely Irish membership. The result was the trial in Pottsville in 1877 and the subsequent hanging of 20 men. See "The Killer King of the Reading" and "Hanged Heroes", in Richard O. Boyer and Herbert M. Morais, *Labor's Untold Story,* 43–56, 56–58.

29. "Hugh J. Mohan," *Pen Portraits,* compiled by R. R. Parkinson in Sacramento City during the 1877–78 legislative session (San Francisco: Alta, California, Printers, 1878), 96–97. This biographical sketch, which makes no mention of the Molly Maguires, was written when he was covering the legislature for a series of newspapers.

30. San Francisco city directories for 1879 and 1880.

31. District Court records, Reno.

32. All quotations direct or indirect on her childhood: LB memoir, Hicks Coll.

33. Obituaries of James R. Say in the Lovelock, Nev., *Tribune,* June 8, 1906, page 1, and the Fairview *Record,* a defunct newspaper in a ghost town, reveal that he was of English descent, came West in the early 1860s after going first to Virginia and New York state, and was active in mining from about 1861 to 1905. He was married three times; none of his wives bore him children. His second wife was called a "Mrs. Fleek", and a study of quitclaim records in Churchill County alone showed that in 1876 "James Say and Anna Say his wife" sold mining rights to one property for "$500 in gold coin." Louise's mother was the former Louisa Flick, whose widowed mother married Say.

34. See Orville Bullitt, ed., *For the President Personal and Secret, Correspondence Between Franklin D. Roosevelt and William C. Bullitt,* 15, on Bullitt's marriage to "Anne Moën Reed . . . daughter of Hugh Moën and Anne Fiennes Moën. . . . " Descendants of Lords Say generally took the name of Fiennes. Possibly Say after coming to the United States took the name "Say" as "Fiennes" was difficult to pronounce.

35. In 1886 Mohan was in Washington seeking a job in the field gathering statistics either in Nevada or California. In a letter to President Cleveland and another to Carroll D. Wright, Commissioner of Labor, Bureau of Labor Statistics, he gave as references such men of importance in California as Leland Stanford

and George Hearst (father of William Randolph Hearst). When he was given a temporary job in the District of Columbia at $100 a month, he quit in less than a month. (Information from Department of Labor archives.) In 1883 and 1884 he served as deputy commissioner of the Bureau of Labor Statistics, with offices in San Francisco.

36. Mrs. Marion Bryant, widow of Floyd Sherman Bryant, said that when they resided in Washington, at a time when Bryant was an assistant Secretary of Defense in the Eisenhower Administration, they were visited by a friend of a mutual friend, who told them he first met Louise Bryant "when she was the toast of Paris," and later saw her alone sitting in a café, sipping absinthe. He took her home to a bare, walk-up room. Bryant asked him if Louise still had the grand piano their mother had given her. No, said the visitor, the room appeared empty except for books all over.

37. Silas E. Ross was a former regent of the University of Nevada. He was remotely related by marriage to the Bryant family, which he described as an old Nevada family with a large farm between Wadsworth and Truckee when he knew them. Interviewed August 1970.

38. Interview with Millie Hunewill Hamblet, owner of a ranch at Wellington, Nev., February 25, 1971.

39. *Ibid.*

40. Letter from Lucia Wilkins Moore, artist and writer, of Eugene, Ore., to author, August 21, 1970, accompanied by a water-color sketch of Louise Bryant as she remembered her.

41. Interview with Lucia Wilkins Moore, April 25, 1970.

42. *Ibid.*

43. Interview with Bertha Dorris Carpenter at her home in San Francisco, July 27, 1970, by Evelyn Averbuck for the author. She was a reporter on the *Daily News* in New York for years, and for a time, on the *World* staff.

44. Interviews with Lela Goddard Fenton, Portland, by telephone, April 20 and 30, 1970.

45. Letters from Dr. Miriam Van Waters to author, July 11 and 24, 1970; interview in her home in Framingham, Mass., August 1970.

46. Taped interview with Floyd Ramp at age 88 in his home in Eugene, Ore., April 24, 1970, by Julia Ruuttila for the author.

47. Bertha Dorris Carpenter interview.

48. The letter from LB was to Ray Woodruff; interview with Ray Woodruff Jenkins in Milwaukie, Ore., July 17, 1970.

49. Bertha Dorris Carpenter interview. Hicks, *John Reed*, 205, says that Bryant after graduation taught on an island in Puget Sound.

50. The marriage was performed by the Rev. T. F. Bowen of St. Paul's Episcopal Church, in his home. She used the name Anna Louise Mohan, listed as parents Hugh J. Mohan and Mrs. S. D. Bryant, and her age as 21 (she was 24 in the next month). Trullinger was 29.

51. Interview with Jacob R. Proebstel, 79, artist, of San Francisco, formerly of Portland; June 9, 1970.

52. Interview with Marguerite Dosch Campbell of Portland, by telephone August 27, 1970.

53. Interview with Ruth Bradley of Portland, May 2, 1979.

54. Interview with Adele Trullinger and her daughter Lollah Cabanski in their San Francisco home, by Evelyn Averbuck for the author, June 1, 1970; Mrs. Trullinger died in 1971.

55. Interview with Ruth Trullinger, of Portland, widow of Paul Trullinger, October 30, 1970, and April 1, 1974.

56. Arthur Spencer of the Oregon Historical Society informed author of letter

from Brownell D. Frasier, May 4, 1976; confirmed in telephone interview on May 30, 1976, with Frasier, former head of the Department of Interior Architecture in the University's School of Architecture.

57. Interviews with Mrs. C. E. S. Wood in her Berkeley, Ca., home, March 26, June 26, and June 29, 1970. She died June 1974. In November 1912 the suffrage amendment won at the polls.

58. Dr. Trullinger's widow, Ruth Trullinger, had been told of the Emma Goldman visit by Trullinger.

59. Barbara Bartlett Hartwell in an address to the Portland Art Association, February 29, 1968, reproduced in the museum's *Jubilee Album* of April 1968.

60. Proebstel interview.

61. Interview with Marie Louise Feldenheimer, by telephone July 30, 1970.

62. Alfred Powers, author of *History of Oregon Literature*, interviewed by telephone November 11, 1970, said Louise Bryant "spoke often to her friends of 'the brilliant John Reed.'" He had heard, he said, that when she and Dr. Trullinger attended a party where Reed gave a talk, she told a friend, "I'm going to get him."

63. Taped interview with Floyd Ramp, April 24, 1970. LB memoir suggests a meeting earlier than 1915.

64. Interviews with Mrs. Wood.

65. Carl and Helen Walters had Reed and Bryant to dinner, but saw when they arrived they were already in love; Hicks, *John Reed*, 205–6. Brownell D. Frasier said that her mother, Jennie L. Frasier, poured tea at a friend's house in Portland on the occasion when Reed and Louise Bryant met; Frasier interview.

66. Marguerite Dosch Campbell interview. Others seeing Bryant off were Carl and Helen Walters; Roswell Dosch, sculptor, brother of Marguerite Dosch; and Clara and Jean Wold.

67. Interview with Adele Trullinger.

68. Interview with Mrs. Linley Crichton in Portland, April 19, 1970. Mrs. Crichton died on her eighty-sixth birthday in July 1971.

CHAPTER 2. PROVINCETOWN

1. Entire account of their arrival in Provincetown: Louise Bryant memoir, Granville Hicks Collection.

2. *Ibid.*

3. Max Eastman, *Enjoyment of Living*, 565–66.

4. Louise Bryant to John Reed, June 7, 1916. John Reed Collection.

5. LB to JR, June 8, 1916. JR Coll.

6. LB to JR, June 5, 1916, sent to Reed at Hotel LaSalle, Chicago, and then forwarded to the Hotel Sherman, Chicago. JR Coll.

7. LB to JR, Monday night, June 12, 1916. JR Coll.

8. JR to LB, June 11, 1916, from Chicago. JR Coll.

9. JR to LB, n.d., from Detroit. JR Coll.

10. LB to JR, n.d. JR Coll.

11. JR to LB, June 18, 1916, from Detroit. JR Coll.

12. Quoted by Mary Heaton Vorse, *Time and the Town;* 147.

13. Floyd Dell to LB at Provincetown, n.d. Theater Collection, Lamont Library, Harvard University. Under the title of "Six Poems" Bryant's poems appeared in *The Masses*, October 1916, 10.

14. Preceding quotations from "The Poets' Revolution," by Louise Bryant, *The Masses*, July 1916, 29.

15. Harry Kemp, "Out of Provincetown: A Memoir of Eugene O'Neill," *Theatre Magazine*, April 1930, 22–23, 66.

16. Susan Glaspell, *The Road to the Temple* (New York: Stokes, 1927), 253–54.

17. Granville Hicks, *John Reed*, 212–13. "Fog" was accepted by *Scribner's* in October 1916 but did not appear there until August 1919: *Ibid.*, 414.

18. Louis Sheaffer, *O'Neill: Son and Playwright*, 346.

19. Allen Churchill, *The Improper Bohemians*, 143, quotes John V. A. Weaver, classmate of O'Neill: "Women loved Gene. There was something apparently irresistible in his strange combination of cruelty (around the mouth), intelligence (in his eyes), and sympathy (in his voice). It made him seem hardboiled and whimsical, brutal and tender."

20. *Ibid.*, 143, re O'Neill and Bryant: "Mabel Dodge passed along rumors that the two were actually having a love affair. On the other hand, Max Eastman remembers them merely sitting for hours on the sands while Louise attempted to persuade O'Neill to curb his drinking."

21. Doris Alexander, *The Tempering of Eugene O'Neill*, 230–31. Reed submitted O'Neill's "Submarine" and "The Louse" on his behalf to Eastman, who rejected "The Louse." Reed read the poems after a talk with O'Neill in which they agreed on the war but not on everything. O'Neill "did not share Reed's belief that the workers would rise and create a new social order. Eugene thought the workers were 'cowards,' and their leaders 'asses,' who would never do anything but 'talk.' "

22. Arthur and Barbara Gelb, *O'Neill* (New York: Harper, 1962), 324.

23. Interviews with Dorothy Day, October 7, 1969; July 13, 1973; March 9, 1974; February 24, 1978.

24. Sheaffer, *O'Neill Playwright*, 348.

25. Louise Bryant, "Dark Eyes," *The Masses*, July 1917, 28.

26. This story was initiated by Agnes Boulton, O'Neill's second wife, in her undocumented *Part of a Long Story*, 114–15. The first to describe the "triangle" others seized on, she reveals in one sentence that it was in part fictionalized when she writes, "on and on this had gone; that summer; that winter; another summer—Louise sharing herself, never willing to give up one for the other . . . always the pivotal person, beautiful, passionate and strange." But Bryant was in Paris the next June and July, and as soon as she returned, sailed with Reed, destination Russia.

27. Vorse, *Time and Town*, 121–22.

28. Mabel Dodge Luhan, *Movers and Shakers*, 483–84, 483.

CHAPTER 3. REED WRITES A FARCE

1. Arthur and Barbara Gelb, *O'Neill*, 312.

2. Of Albert Rhys Williams's posthumously published *Journey Into Revolution: Petrograd, 1917–1918*, Robert A. Rosenstone, Reed's latest biographer, declares: "More than any other account it is important for understanding Reed." *Romantic Revolutionary*, 426.

3. See Hutchins Hapgood, *A Victorian in the Modern World*, 381.

4. See Granville Hicks, *John Reed*, 181.

5. Max Eastman, *Enjoyment of Living*, 566.

6. Mabel Dodge Luhan, *Movers and Shakers*, 283.

7. Louise Bryant to Corliss Lamont, November 4, 1935. One of many letters written by Bryant in the last year of her life in an effort to be of aid in the biography of Reed being written by Hicks. When she could get no answers from Hicks she took to writing Lamont, secretary-treasurer of the Harvard Alumni John Reed Committee, asking him to inform Hicks. Granville Hicks Collection.

8. Agnes Boulton, *Part of a Long Story*, 114 ff. Doris Alexander, *The Tempering of Eugene O'Neill*, 232–33, adds to Boulton's undocumented account, saying

that Reed "had been facing his own death" and that Bryant "had been helping him to face death. . . . She needed fulfillment to give her the strength to stand by Jack."

9. Louis Sheaffer, *O'Neill: Son and Playwright,* 350, points to O'Neill's "lack of aggressiveness, his basic feeling of unworthiness" and believes that without Bryant's taking the initiative it is doubtful that he "would have ventured a move toward Louise."

10. Doris Alexander, *The Tempering of Eugene O'Neill,* 242, quotes a letter O'Neill wrote to Barrett Clark in 1919 in which he speaks of "my feeling for the impelling, inscrutable forces behind life which it is my ambition to at least faintly shadow at their work in my plays." Alexander declares it a clear statement of his "mature artistic purpose."

11. Boulton, *Long Story,* 115.

12. From Emma Goldman, *Anarchism and Other Essays* (originally published by the Mother Earth Publishing Assn.) in Irving L. Horowitz, ed., *The Anarchists,* (New York: Dell, 1964), 282.

13. Luhan, *Movers and Shakers,* 71.

14. *Ibid.,* 259-61. Mrs. Luhan said it was the only letter of Reed's she did not burn.

15. The manuscript of the play is in the John Reed Collection. It is very possible that Shaw's *Man and Superman* gave Reed certain ideas. In 1916 it had its seventeenth printing in the United States. In his preface Shaw says that "the serious business of sex is left by men to women" while men "set up a feeble romantic convention that the initiative in sex business must always come from man." There are, he observes, "no limits to male hypocrisy in this matter."

16. From "Sex," by Elsie Clews Parsons, anthropologist, in Harold R. Stearns, ed., *Civilization in the United States,* 309–18. Parsons was a contributor to *The Masses.*

17. Marguerite Zorach's woodcut of the setting of *The Game* with idealized figures was used for some time on theater programs of the Provincetown Players, and for front covers of little paperback volumes of plays they put on after the first series, published by Frank Shay.

18. Helen Deutsch and Stella Hanau, *The Provincetown: A Story of the Theatre* (New York: Farrar and Rinehart, 1931), 15. Floyd Dell would not have agreed. In *Homecoming,* 265, he finds O'Neill's plays "obviously destined for popular success," but adds that his "romantic point of view did not interest me."

19. Interview with Heaton Vorse, newspaper editor, son of Mary Heaton Vorse, in his home in Provincetown, July 19, 1971.

20. Sheaffer, *O'Neill Playwright,* 351.

21. Max Eastman, *Heroes I Have Known,* 225–27.

22. Susan Glaspell, *The Road to the Temple,* (New York: Stokes, 1927), 259.

CHAPTER 4. THEY MARRY

1. Mary Heaton Vorse, *Time and the Town,* 126.

2. Robert A. Rosenstone, *Romantic Revolutionary,* 256. The title was *Tamburlaine,* a poem published in the *American Magazine* in January 1913. He included 26 poems, all but three of which had been written by the end of 1913.

3. Interviews with Kitty Cannell, dance critic for the *Christian Science Monitor,* Boston, October 26, 1971, and January 11, 1972, with telephone interviews subsequently up to time of her death. Kitty Cannell died May 19, 1974, at 82.

4. Carl Hovey to John Reed, October 11, 1916. John Reed Collection. The letter said in part: "I have read O'Neill's story . . . and agree with you that he can

write. The thing is genuine and makes a real man live before you. It would give a true thrill to the type of reader who is looking for good work. But my judgment is that it would not interest the majority. . . . There is a lack of either plot or a situation with suspense enough. . . . With all its fine sincerity and effectiveness, there is a kind of over-emphasis and sense of repetition which makes the story drag."

5. Louise Bryant memoir, Granville Hicks Collection, relates that she took it to Waldo Frank of *Seven Arts*.

6. Quoted by Leo Stoller in his biographical introduction to *"The Collected Verse of John Reed,"* Master's thesis, Columbia University, 1947. Used here with the permission of his widow, Constance Stoller, of Detroit.

7. See Robinson's letter to Granville Hicks, Hicks Collection.

8. Interview with Floyd Dell in his home, at Bethesda, Md., October 1968.

9. Cannell interviews.

10. Albert Parry, *Garrets and Pretenders*, 301.

11. Floyd Dell, *Homecoming*, 361, 368. Speaking of Cook's death in Greece in 1926, Dell wrote: "His death restored to my mind the gentle and prophetic dreamer that I knew back in Davenport. He saw, then, in the Russian Revolution of 1905 that failed, a Revolution that was to succeed. . . . I loved him, and I would have had his life and death other than they were. I would have had him die for Russia and the future, rather than for Greece and the past. And if I wrote a book about George, that is what I should wish him to do."

12. Dr. Trullinger had won a divorce from her in Portland July 7. Under its terms it was not to become final for six months.

13. Doris Alexander, *The Tempering of Eugene O'Neill*, 235.

14. LB memoir, Hicks Coll.

15. Louise Bryant to John Reed, headed "Sunday afternoon at 5 ..," but listed by librarians as written in November, 1916. John Reed Collection.

16. Aiken interview.

17. Actually *The Betrayal* was not produced. The Players had it for a time, then Colum took it away from them; Reed had suggested that he give them a play. Colum's tone was still peppery as he spoke of it, but tender as he spoke of Reed. Jim Larkin had introduced them. "I was impressed with him. There was something strong and powerful about Jack. His sincerity could not be doubted, unlike many in the revolutionary movement." Interview with Colum at his home, November 29, 1969; the poet was 88 years old in the following December. The title of the play was supplied by Colum.

18. JR to LB, headed "Johns Hopkins, November 13." JR Coll.

19. LB to JR. n.d. JR Coll. *Before Breakfast* opened in December.

20. JR to LB. n.d. JR Coll.

21. *Mother Earth* "blasted the proponents of preparedness in issue after issue," and Goldman excoriated the capitalist basis of the war before crowds of sympathizers. Charles A. Madison, *Critics and Crusaders*, 229.

22. The letter, from LB to JR, was headed only "Tuesday afternoon," but is listed as dated November 14. JR Coll.

23. Dr. Lorber is written of lovingly by many memoirists of the day, including Eastman, Hapgood, and Mabel Dodge Luhan.

24. LB to JR, "Sunday morning" (November 26, 1916). JR Coll.

25. LB to JR, headed "Saturday afternoon" (December 2, 1916). JR Coll.

26. The story of the brief incursion into Bohemia and the Provincetown Theater by the 17-year-old son of the famed actor Gibbs Mansfield received a gentle spoofing in the New York *Tribune* December 10 on p. 6. How he found the theater is pondered (a dig at the theater for not sending passes to drama critics):

"perhaps he had seen the magazine which pictured John Reed . . . in the fantastic garb he wore in one of the plays, and knew that such a creature would never appear north of Fourth Street."

27. Marcel Duchamp, whose "Portrait of a Nude Descending the Stairs" at the Armory show in New York in 1913 was widely publicized, was living in Greenwich Village by 1916.

28. LB to JR. n.d. JR Coll.

29. Alexander, *Tempering of Eugene O'Neill*, 234.

30. Agnes Boulton, *Part of a Long Story*, 114.

31. Louis Sheaffer, *O'Neill: Son and Artist*, 288–89.

32. LB to JR, headed "Croton, Monday night—9:30," probably December 4. JR Coll.

33. LB to JR, headed "Wednesday night," written December 6, 1916. JR Coll.

34. Boulton, *Long Story*, 45.

35. Louis Sheaffer, *O'Neill: Playwright*, 341.

36. Alexander, *Tempering of Eugene O'Neill*, 236.

37. Shaeffer, *O'Neill: Playwright*, 365–66.

38. JR to LB. n.d. JR Coll.

39. See *The Fallopian Tube: Structure, Function, Pathology and Management*, by J. Donald Woodruff, M.D., and Carl J. Pauerstein, M.D. (Baltimore: Williams and Wilkins, 1969), ch. 7, "Non-granulomatous Salpingitis," 117–30, esp. 126–27.

CHAPTER 5. REUNION AND FLIGHT

1. Louise Bryant to John Reed, December 12, 1916. John Reed Collection.

2. John Reed to Louise Bryant, telegram, December 12, 1916. J.R. Coll.

3. LB to JR, n.d., JR Coll. Headed "Tuesday," this letter is more like her customary letters to Reed—carelessly written, with words underlined and some scratched out. Her old warmth comes through in the close: "I *feel* I'd get well if I was in the country with you. I'm desperately lonely for you and I want you to be *careful* above all else. Wire me before you leave, All my love Louise."

4. JR to LB, December 13, 1916. JR Coll.

5. JR to LB, telegram, December 13, 1916. JR Coll.

6. JR to E.E. Hunt, January 4, 1917. JR Coll.

7. Doris Alexander, *The Tempering of Eugene O'Neill*, 235–36.

8. Louis Sheaffer, *O'Neill: Son and Artist*, 275.

9. Mrs. Marion Bryant, the second wife and widow of Floyd Sherman Bryant, of Burlingame, Ca., was interviewed June 24, 1970; Bryant had told her the story of his visit to the Village.

10. JR to LB, May 18, 1917, telegram, JR Coll.

11. Conrad Aiken interview.

12. Louise Bryant memoir, Granville Hicks Collection.

13. Alexander, *Tempering of Eugene O'Neill*, 242.

14. Andrew Dasburg interviews.

15. LB to JR, headed "The sixth night at sea" (June 1917); JR Coll.

16. JR to E.E. Hunt, May 26, 1917. JR Coll.

17. "Almost Thirty," the first of two installments published posthumorously in *The New Republic*, April 15 and 29, 1936.

CHAPTER 6. PARIS WITHOUT REED

1. Louise Bryant memoir, Granville Hicks Collection.

2. Louise Bryant to John Reed; headed "Saturday morning in town" and

apparently written while the ship lay at anchor or before she boarded it. John Reed Collection.

3. JR to LB, June 9 and 11, 1917. JR Coll. Reed addressed her letters, "Miss Louise Bryant, % American Express, 11 rue Scribe, Paris, France." He was receiving his mail at the Harvard Club.

4. Floyd Dell, *Homecoming*, 282–83.

5. When Colum was queried about this, he had forgotten the incident but said that of course his friends would have been underground so soon after the 1916 insurrection. (Colum interview, 1969.) A list of Irish leaders in Louise Bryant's hand was among the Reed papers at the Houghton Library.

6. JR to LB, n.d. JR Coll.

7. Excerpts quoted from John Reed's "Almost Thirty" are from the two installments in *The New Republic*, which published it posthumously April 15 and 29, 1936.

8. "This Unpopular War," by John Reed, appeared in the August 1917 issue of *Seven Arts*. Brief-lived, the *Seven Arts* lost its subsidy not long after, and "the courageous voices of James Oppenheim, Waldo Frank, and Randolph Bourne were silenced." Albert Parry, *Garrets and Pretenders*, 292.

9. JR to LB, "Saturday," June 16, 1917. JR Coll.

10. JR to LB, June 19, 1917. JR Coll.

11. LB to JR, n.d. Presumably it was written June 14. JR Coll.

12. JR to LB. n.d. JR Coll. The story appeared under her by-line in the *Sunday New York American* July 8, page 3 of Section LII. It carried a headline, WOMAN TELLS LINER'S FIGHT WITH U-BOAT

13. JR to LB, n.d. JR Coll.

14. LB to JR, June 22, 1917. JR Coll.

15. LB to JR. n.d. JR Coll. The incident about Rainey's note also is told in LB memoir, Hicks Coll.

16. LB to JR, "July 1917." JR Coll.

17. LB to JR, dated June 22, 1917. JR Coll.

18. LB to JR, July 2, 1917. JR Coll. This letter from Bryant to Reed was written after she had been entertained at the home of John Storrs, the Chicago-born sculptor who lived in Paris. His papers are in the Archives of American Art at the Smithsonian Institution and include more than 20 letters from Bryant to John Storrs and his wife, Marguerite, from 1917 to 1930 and one from Reed written on their way to Russia in 1917.

19. "News From France," by Louise Bryant and John Reed, *The Masses*, October 1917, Vol. IX, No. 12, Issue No. 76, pp. 5, 6, 8. It was the second to the final issue of the magazine. With the November-December issue, the long fight against its suppression was lost.

20. LB to JR, "July 4," addressed to Reed at the Harvard Club. JR Coll.

21. This probably was Esther Andrews, who worked on *Women's Wear*, lived with Canby Chambers in the Village and then on Chambers Street; see *The Best Times*, John Dos Passos, 82, 135–36. She became a good friend to Bryant and had known Reed and Max Eastman.

22. LB to JR, Sunday morning, July 15, 1917. JR Coll.

23. JR to LB, June 28, 1917. JR Coll. It began, "My dearest little lover."

24. Hutchins Hapgood, *A Victorian in the Modern World*, 352.

25. Believed to be the wife of a newspaper correspondent, Isaac McBride.

26. JR to LB, July 5, 1917. JR Coll.

27. Max Eastman, *Love and Revolution*, 251, quoting the "no one I love" passage (slightly truncated) with the natural sympathy of a womanizer for the sentiment, adds: "If Louise learned to do it, Jack was lucky, for he was a truth-teller by nature, and truth does not often mix in a perfect emulsion with love."

But nowhere in the letter does Reed even imply a hope that Louise would "learn to do it."

28. Hicks's treatment of the letter is unfathomable until it is recalled that he makes a mystery of the quarrel between Reed and Bryant: "Whatever the cause, they had separated. . . ." In quoting part of the letter he never reveals that Reed is being self-critical over his sexual activity. He says Reed said, "No one I love," etc., and follows it (without any ellipses) with part of the sentence occurring several paragraphs later: "You've got to recognize that I am defective (if that is what it is). . . ." Granville Hicks, *John Reed*, 239. Hicks gives no explanation for what he has done. Thus his effort to conceal Reed's sexuality (perhaps he thought it unbecoming in a revolutionary?) results in the unfortunate impression that Reed was impotent.

29. Robert A. Rosenstone, *Romantic Revolutionary*, 241, inspired by the letter, envisions a scene in Louise's Portland studio in which "Jack confessed weaknesses usually concealed . . . he felt weak, at the limit of 'fighting strength'." Whatever Rosenstone's interpretation was is unclear except that it is one of sad disapproval: "All this was difficult for Louise to believe. Blinded by the image, she could not take such words seriously." But it wasn't any image but the reality of his lovemaking recalled specifically and rapturously in her first letter to Reed.

30. LB to JR, n.d., from Paris. JR Coll.

31. JR to LB, July 8, 1917. JR Coll.

32. JR to LB, n.d. JR Coll.

33. LB memoir, Hicks Coll.

CHAPTER 7. INTO THE WHIRLWIND

1. Louise Bryant memoir, Granville Hicks Collection.

2. "Everything was falling apart. . . . The government was obviously unable either to wage war or avert revolution."—Joshua Kunitz on the February revolution, *Russia: The Giant That Came Last*, 348–56. Petrograd was exploding by mid-February, 30,000 workers struck the Putilov works on the 18th and five days later marched in the streets, joined by huge crowds, "mostly women from bread lines. On the same day, the Petrograd Committee of the Bolshevik Party called out into the streets 90,000 more workers to mark International Woman's Day. The next day strikers in the capital rose to 200,000 in number. On February 25 the city was in the grip of a general strike." Next day Petrograd workers were in control of the Viborg district and elections of Soviets of workers and soldiers began. Tsar Nicholas II abdicated in favor of his brother Michael on March 2; on March 3 Michael abdicated. On March 2 the Petrograd Soviet was in the ascendancy but declared its allegiance to the Provisional Government.

3. "Russia," by John Reed, *The Masses*, May 1917, quoted in Granville Hicks, *John Reed*, 249.

4. Louise Bryant, *Six Red Months in Russia*, 20. All citations from Bryant in this and the following two chapters unless otherwise stated are from this source. The book was based in part on newspaper stories she wrote on her return, distributed by the Philadelphia *Public Ledger* syndicate.

5. *Ibid.*, 23.

6. *Ibid.*, 35.

7. *Ibid.*, 259.

8. *Ibid.*, 39.

9. Interview with Manuel Komroff in his Woodstock, N.Y. home, August 31, 1973. Komroff said he went to Russia for *The World* but on arrival found the cables down and went to work as editor of a British-subsidized newspaper, *The Moscow*

Daily News. A Kropotkin man and not sympathetic with Lenin, Komroff confessed, "In afterlife when I meet St. Peter he will say he has two things against me, and that the whoring wasn't important, but what about the other? And I will admit it lay on my conscience. I didn't know it then but we printed a lot of stories that weren't true—the kind of thing that appeared so generally over here." Komroff died in December 1974 at 84 before he could complete an autobiography which would include, he said, his first account of his Russian experiences.

10. Bryant, *Six Red Months*, 44. Writing in a less hopeful period in 1922, after her third sojourn in the land of Soviets, Bryant notes: "A curiously touching . . . phase of the revolution was the Soviet Government's sincere attempt to wipe out prostitution . . . it appeared then as if the whole idea of traffic in women had forever ended. But even after the economic pressure was removed the curse returned." She quotes Kollontai as blaming insufficient pay for women as a main factor. Kollontai told her: "Under the law the earnings of men and women are equal, but the great majority of women are unskilled laborers. It resolves itself into a question of how to make female labor skilled labor. And the second cause is the political backwardness of women. It is not the woman who is inspired . . . by the idea of the revolution . . . who falls into this pool of degradation." *Mirrors of Moscow*, 124, 127.

11. Aleksandr Ulianov had not even come of age; Lenin was 17. Aleksandr was a member of the illegal *Narodnaya Volya* (People's Will) sponsored by the *narodnik* revolutionaries, who took part in the attempt on the life of Aleksandr III in 1887. N. K. Krupskaya, *Reminiscences of Lenin*, 14–15, writes that Lenin's brother was a naturalist. On his last summer vacation at home he used to get up at daybreak to get all the light possible as he pored over his microscope, preparing a dissertation. Vladimir Ilyich watched him and thought, "No, my brother won't make a revolutionary. . . . A revolutionary can't give so much time to the study of worms." Krupskaya adds, "It was not long before he saw his mistake." His brother's fate "undoubtedly influenced Vladimir Ilyich profoundly . . . gave his mind a keener edge, developed in him an extraordinary soberness of thought, an ability to face the truth without . . . illusions. It developed in him a scrupulously honest approach in all questions."

12. Georgi Valentinovich Plekhanov, foremost Russian Marxist theoretician when Lenin was a youth. He had first embraced populism but became a Marxist as a political exile. After the split in the Russian Social Democratic Party in 1903 into Bolsheviks (majority) and Mensheviks (minority) he supported Lenin for a time, but then cast his lot with the Mensheviks. In 1917 he still held that not until capitalism and industrialization were more advanced would Russia be capable of instituting a socialist revolution. He died in 1918.

13. Bryant, *Six Red Months*, 46–47.

14. *Ibid.*, 48–49.

15. Louise Bryant to Stella Ballantine, niece of Emma Goldman, January 25, 1919, asking that the letter be sent to Goldman, in prison in Jefferson City, Mo., after she and Alexander Berkman were convicted of conspiracy to induce persons not to register for the draft. A copy, typed and unsigned, is in the JR Coll.

16. Bryant, *Six Red Months*, 111.

17. *Ibid.*, 144. In the West the spelling of Lenin's name generally was presented as "Lenine" at that time.

18. The *narodniks* were not an organized party but members of the radical intelligentsia whose beliefs, spawned in the 1850s, centered about the Slavophile concept of Russia's destiny as one that would bring the true light to the West—by means of devising modifications to Western socialist theory. Their "going to the people" involved a utopian concept that they could lead "the dark people"

(peasants) to revolt against the feudal landlords, i.e., that the Russian peasant commune could lead directly to a socialist order. The emancipation of the serfs in 1861 broke up the landowner-serf relationship but failed to shake the *narodnik* abstraction. Their activities reached their height in the 1870s.

19. The Bolshevik program for sending teams of outstanding city workers armed with supplies to exchange for grain, and to help poor peasants organize into committees, got started six months too late—due to the Bolsheviks' weak hold on the countryside. After the humiliating peace with Germany at Brest-Litovsk and the consequent loss of the Left Social Revolutionary support, their hold was even weaker.

20. In April 1917 Lenin had impressively written: "The commune, i.e., the Soviet, does not 'introduce,' does not propose to 'introduce,' and must not 'introduce,' any transformations which have not matured both absolutely and in economic reality, and in the consciousness of the overwhelming majority of the people." E. H. Carr cites this as consistent with Lenin's principle of learning from the masses and adds: "Lenin emphatically did not believe in revolution from above." See E. H. Carr, *The October Revolution*, 21–22. Lacking the patience or capacity to evoke the measure of mass consciousness and support Lenin had, his successors "took the short cut. . . . Stalin's once famous short history of the Communist Party called the collectivization of agriculture 'a revolution from above . . . with direct support from below'; and, though the phrase 'revolution from above' has since been condemned as heretical, it was symptomatic of the Stalinist epoch."

21. Bryant, *Six Red Months*, 164–65.

22. Two days before the assassination of Count Mirbach, Spiridonova mounted the platform at the fifth Congress of Soviets, accused Lenin and Trotsky of treason, and warned, "I shall grasp in my hand the revolver and the bomb, as I once used to do." The two assassins Blumkin and Andreev, Left Social Revolutionaries and high officials in the *Cheka*, "acted on Spiridonova's order." Isaac Deutscher in his biography of Trotsky, vol. I, *The Prophet Armed* 403. Louis Fischer, *The Life of Lenin*, 244, 242, relates that "Maria Spiridonova stayed in the Bolshoi Theater [at the time of the insurrection by the Social Revolutionaries] and calmly submitted to arrest by the Cheka." She also told the *Cheka*, "I organized the Mirbach affair from the beginning to the end . . . as part of a plan we had accepted of annulling the Brest treaty of peace."

23. U.S., Congress, Senate, Subcommittee of the Judiciary Committee, *Bolshevik Propaganda: Hearings*, 551. Louise Bryant's testimony, Feb. 20 and 21, 1919.

24. Krupskaya uses the same figure but denies that peasant delegates were more than a dream at the time. "Inessa Armand, Samoilova, Kollontai, Stael, and A. D. Kalinina worked hard on the organization of this congress." N. K. Krupskaya, *Reminiscences of Lenin*, 492.

25. Bryant, *Six Red Months*, 128.

26. Kollontai, *The Autobiography of a Sexually Emancipated Communist Woman*, 36, 7. The original edition, *Autobiographie einer sexuell emanzipierten Kommunistin*, claimed to be the first publication of the autobiography as written in 1926; a "Prefatory Note" explains that matter killed in galley proofs by Kollontai was restored, set in italics. The two quotes cited here were not deleted by Kollontai.

27. Bryant, *Six Red Months*, 129.

28. *Ibid.*, 128–29.

29. Bryant, *Mirrors of Moscow*, 114–15. Bryant spelled his name "Dubenko" and gave him a first name of "Fedore"; I have substituted the later spelling, Pavel Dybenko.

30. John Reed Collection. Also see *Six Red Months*, opp. 130, photograph of Kollontai inscribed "To dear comrada Louise Bryant from her friend Alexandra Kollontay," and below that, "Petrograd l/4/18."

CHAPTER 8. RED PETROGRAD

1. Louise Bryant, *Six Red Months in Russia*, 39–40, 259.

2. On the day before the tsar signed his own abdication papers, the loyal troops, ordered to Petrograd by the tsar, were stopped at Tsarskoe Selo where they immediately began to fraternize with the already revolutionized troops. On the same day the famous Order Number One was contained in an extraordinary decree issued by the Petrograd Soviet that called for strict execution by the military of all Soviet orders even if they conflicted with orders issued by the Provisional Committee of the Duma.

3. Bryant, *Six Red Months*, 259.

4. Isaac Deutscher, *The Prophet Armed*, 283.

5. Bryant, *Six Red Months*, 59–60.

6. *Ibid.*, 67, 61–62.

7. *Ibid.*, 63.

8. Albert Rhys Williams, *Journey Into Revolution*, 82–83.

9. From "Marxism and Insurrection," a letter to the Central Committee of the Russian Social Democratic Labor Party (Bolshevik) written September 13–14/26–27, 1917, first published in 1921 in the magazine *Proletarskaya Revolutsia* No. 2. V. I. Lenin, *Selected Works in Three Volumes* (New York: International Publishers, 1967), vol. 2, 365–70.

10. Williams, *Journey Into Revolution*, 82–83.

11. Deutscher, *Prophet Armed*, 287.

12. Bryant, *Six Red Months*, 66–67.

13. Williams, *Journey Into Revolution*, 87.

14. Deutscher, *Prophet Armed*, quoting from Sukhanov, N. N., *Zapiski o Revolutsii (Notes on the Revolution)*, vol. v., 125–26. See also Leon Trotsky, *History of the Russian Revolution*, vol. II, 333–37.

15. Bryant, *Six Red Months*, 68–70.

16. From "The Crisis Has Matured," letter to the Central Committee and the Petrograd and Moscow Committees of the Russian Social Democratic Labor Party (Bolshevik) written September 12–14/25–27, 1917. Sections I–III and V published October 20/November 2, 1917 in the newspaper *Rabochy put* No. 30; section VI first published in 1924, section IV still unpublished. Lenin, *Selected Works*, vol. 2, 362–4 (quotation from 363).

17. Williams, *Journey Into Revolution*, 90.

18. *Ibid.*, 41.

19. The question here is not a quote; the reader wishing to understand Reed should read "Almost Thirty" in its entirety—published in two sections, *The New Republic*, April 15 and 29, 1936. When he wrote it he was "not sure any more that the working class is capable of revolution, peaceful or otherwise. . . . The War has been a terrible shatterer of faith."

20. Interview with Andrew Dasburg by telephone, May 11, 1975.

21. Bryant, *Six Red Months*, 73–74.

22. Deutscher, *Prophet Armed*, 290.

23. V. I. Lenin, *Collected Works*, vol. 26, *September 1917–February 1918* (Moscow: Progress Publishers, 1964), 57; written September 23/October 6, 1917. Noting that the boycott was defeated among the Bolshevik group at the Democratic Conference, he added: "Long live the boycott!!"

24. Bryant, *Six Red Months*, 74–75.

CHAPTER 9. A STRANGE REVOLUTION

1. Written October 8/21, 1917, it was first published November 7, 1920, in *Pravda*, signed "An Onlooker." V. I. Lenin, *Selected Works in Three Volumes* (New York: International Publishers, 1967), vol. 2, 426–27.

2. This is Rakhya's story, for which see V. N. Astrov, A. N. Slepkov, and J. Thomas, eds., *Illustrated History of the Russian Revolution*, trans. Freda Utley (New York: 1928), vol. II, 347–48. Rakhya observes, "I had two revolvers in my pocket."

3. N[adezhda] K[onstantinovna] Krupskaya, *Reminiscences of Lenin*, 387.

4. Louise Bryant, *Six Red Months in Russia*, 225.

5. U.S., Congress, Senate, Subcommittee of the Judiciary Committee, *Bolshevik Propaganda: Hearings*, 494. Louise Bryant testified Feb. 20 and 21, 1919.

6. Even the Cossacks deserted Kerensky. See A. F. Kerensky, *The Catastrophe* (New York, 1927), 328–31. On the night of October 24/November 6 he summoned three regiments of Cossacks to defend the government, but a delegation from the regiments called on him and asked what other forces he could count on. By 1 a.m. he thought he had persuaded them to act "on my personal orders," and informed the garrison commander they "could be relied on fully." By 2 a.m. he planned to use all available forces to capture the Smolny Institute. But "endless telephone negotiations" with the Cossack regiments brought the same answer: in 15 or 20 minutes they would begin to saddle their horses. The Council of Cossack Troops, meeting throughout the night, proclaimed their neutrality in the conflict—Kerensky learned later.

7. Apparently this was the only machine gun then in possession of the Red Guard. V. Nevsky, a member of the Military Revolutionary Committee, in "October in 1917," in R. MacIlhone, ed., *Petrograd, October 1917: Reminiscences*, trans. G. Hanna and L. Lempert from Russian text prepared by S.Knyazev and A. Konstantinov (Moscow, 1957), 239, lists Red Guard weapons: ". . . at the Obhukov Factory there were 500 rifles; in the Lesnoi sub-district there were 84, and in the City District there were factories which had 100 rifles and others with only 20. The Red Guards owned a machine-gun and even an armored car (at the same Obukhov Factory). At the best we had a thousand or two thousand rifles at our disposal while the enemy had all types of weapons."

8. Ambassador David R. Francis had secret agents deliver reports to him on Reed's talks at meetings in the Cirque Moderne and elsewhere. "Francis' agents stole Reed's wallet, in which they found a letter from Morris Hillquit to Camille Huysmans, and one from Huysmans to the Scandinavian Socialist Committee," Granville Hicks reports in *John Reed*, 260–61. From that time on, Reed was followed by Secret Service men.

9. Bryant was so described by the late George Biddle, painter; six interviews with Biddle from September 1969 through 1972.

10. The story about Gumberg derived from Albert Rhys Williams, *Journey Into Revolution*, 106–9. The quote from Bryant on the Kronstadt men is from *Six Red Months*, 157. Gumberg happened to be right. Contrary to Lenin's expectations, the Centrobalt could send only a few destroyers to support the uprising, and the units assigned to rush the Winter Palace were late in arriving.

11. Bryant, *Six Red Months*, 81.

12. Victor Serge and Natalia Sedova Trotsky, *The Life and Death of Leon Trotsky*, 63.

13. Gorky's newspaper, *Novaya Zhizn (New Life)*.

14. Bryant, *Six Red Months*, 46–47, speaks of watching "the leaders once accused, hunted and imprisoned raised by the mass of the people of all Russia to

the highest places in the nation. They were borne along on the whirlwind of radicalism that swept and is still sweeping Russia and they themselves did not know how long or how well they would be able to ride that whirlwind." The Kamenev-Steffens comparison is on page 67.

15. *Ibid.*, 66.

16. Yuri Ossipovich Martov was a co-founder with Plekhanov and Lenin of Russian Social-Democracy; at the time of the Revolution he was the leader of the Menshevist Internationalists. Victor Serge in *Memoirs of a Revolutionary 1901–1941*, 110–11, describes Martov as "a man of scruple and scholarship, lacking the tough and robust revolutionary will that sweeps obstacles aside." Sharply critical of the Bolsheviks, "his general solutions verged on the Utopian."

17. Bryant, *Six Red Months*, 82–83.

18. *Ibid.*, 83–84.

19. *Ibid.*, 84–86.

20. *Ibid.*, 86–87.

21. *Ibid.*, 137.

22. John Reed, *Ten Days That Shook the World* (New York: International, 1967), 126.

23. Serge and Trotsky, *Leon Trotsky*, 66.

24. Bryant, *Six Red Months*, 137–40, 136.

25. Lenin, *Selected Works in Three Volumes*, "Report on Peace," vol. 2, 459–63. His concluding speech following discussion on "Report on Peace," 464–66.

26. N. N. Himmer, alias N. N. Sukhanov, *The Russian Revolution 1917: A Personal Record*, ed., abr. and trans. Joel Carmichael (New York: Oxford University Press, 1955), from *Zapiski O Revolutsii* (London: Oxford University Press, 1955), 644–45. Himmer was a well-known editor of Gorky's newspaper.

27. Serge, *Memoirs*, 248–49, declares that Sukhanov, imprisoned at Verkhne-Uralsk, "undertook lengthy hunger-strikes to obtain the liberty he had been promised [by the G.P.U. for confessing according to their dictation]; he disappeared in 1934." Also see 251–52: Sukhanov (Himmer) had been won over to the Party and worked in the Planning Commission with his fellow-defendants Groman, Ginsberg, and Rubin.

28. Albert Rhys Williams, *Journey Into Revolution*, 135.

29. Lenin, *Selected Works in Three Volumes*, vol. 2, 467–70.

30. The desirability of large-scale collective agriculture and the use of machinery was recognized since the time of Marx. After his death Engels dealt with the problem of just how small peasants should be enlisted in collective efforts: "not . . . by forcible means, but by example and by offering social aid for this purpose." Quoted by E. H. Carr, *The Bolshevic Revolution 1917–1923*, vol. 2, 390, note C, "Marx, Engels and the Peasant."

31. A resolution written by Lenin and passed by the Party congress of March 1919 declared that while middle peasants were to be encouraged to enter agricultural communes and associations of all kinds, "not the smallest compulsion" was to be applied for this purpose. Carr, *Bolshevik Revolution*, vol. 2, 167. At the Party conference of May 1921, called to expound N.E.P. (New Economic Policy) to activists, Lenin said: "The proletariat is the leader of the peasantry, but that class cannot be driven out as we drove out and annihilated the landowners and the capitalists. It must be transformed with great labor and great privations." *Ibid.*, 278.

32. Bryant, *Six Red Months*, 166–67.

33. *Ibid.*, 178–80.

34. *Ibid.*, ch. 18, 186-89.

35. *Ibid.*, 203.

36. *Ibid.* They left their place on Troiska Ulitsa, she explains, and moved to the Astoria Hotel, the official war hotel. "There I was not molested as it was impossible to go in and out without a pass unless one was known. Husky [Kronstadt] sailors guarded the entrance."

37. *Ibid.*

38. Williams, *Journey Into Revolution,* 178.

39. The poem was found in Louise Bryant's memoir, Hicks Collection. In a part called "Christmas in Petrograd 1917" she described a Christmas Eve she, Reed, Bessie Beatty, and Albert Rhys Williams spent as guests of Col. Raymond Robins. They had turkey and exchanged trinkets, but her real present to Reed was the poem.

CHAPTER 10. "BOHEMIA IN RETREAT"

1. Madeleine Z. Doty, "Women of the Future," *Good Housekeeping,* August 1918, 32–34. As "Around-the-World Traveler for *Good Housekeeping,*" Doty wrote a series on women of various countries. "Russia and Her Women" appeared in the issue of July 1918.

2. John Reed Collection. Robins misspelled the name of Breckinridge and used no initials or given name. His letter explained that Mrs. John Reed, a correspondent, left Petrograd without the assurance of transportation on the first boat leaving Christiania. He said moreover: "She and her husband have been helpful in the work we have been doing in Petrograd and I commend her to such special consideration as may be possible for you." He closed with "kindest regards and best wishes, Faithfully yours."

3. Personal communications. His father was Clifton R. Breckinridge, a former Congressman from Arkansas, appointed ambassador to Russia by President Cleveland.

4. The wire read: "Department informed that Consul Petrograd has visaed passports of John Reed and his wife alias Louise Bryant. Latter is said to have engaged passage on the BERGENSFJORD.

"Do not verify passports without authorization from the Department.

"Please inform Consul General and Consuls.

"Repeat to Legations Stockholm and Copenhagen for similar action."

5. The American Legation wired the State Department: "Your telegram 227, February 7, 7 p.m., received February 8th, 7 p.m. Louise Bryant left on steamer BERGENSFJORD February 7th, with a Miss Beatty. Reed did not go." F.O.I.A. records.

6. Edgar Sisson, newly arrived in Petrograd and at the time of the Judson interview siding with Robins, wired his chief, George Creel of the Public Information Bureau, that he approved—as if it were a feather in his cap. "But not long after," Reed told Albert Rhys Williams and Louise Bryant, "the boom falls, and old Judson, stunned, is recalled." Williams, *Journey Into Revolution,* 197.

7. William V. Judson to Louise Bryant, March 20, 1918, referring to his weeks in Washington after landing, "I accomplished a part . . . I set out to do." But "Russia had run her course . . . as far as I could influence it and I came down here [Camp Shelby] to command the 78th Brigade.

"I wish you could go back as you propose, & I wish it were so I could go too, if any thing were on the carpet." JR Coll.

Further light on Judson's attempts in Washington is provided by a letter in the Robins papers from Lincoln Colcord, then a correspondent for a Philadelphia newspaper, later a Secretary of State, to Robins, enclosing excerpts from Colcord's diary of March 1918. A March 10 entry noted that the President refused to see General Judson, who had then been in Washington three weeks.

8. A February 12 entry in General Judson's diary: "News by wireless that Russians have refused to sign peace treaty but declared peace exists on all fronts and army ordered demobilized. Is this true? Couldn't we have prevented it?"

On February 17 he noted: "Off Long Island—due in N.Y. tomorrow morning. Our propaganda in Russia is rotten. Vide the . . . film about Uncle Sam patronizing Ivan, which our Y.M.C.A. workers say disgusts . . . the real Ivan, who is not so unsophisticated as people think. We need real radicals in Russia for propaganda work with the Bolshevicks against our Enemies—along lines when the said radicals' honest purposes would run parallel to the purposes of our government." Judson MSS., Newberry Library, Chicago.

9. Kitty Cannell interviews, 1971–72. An attempt to interview Djuna Barnes failed: she wrote that she did not "trust the memory."

10. Albert Parry, *Garrets and Pretenders*, 314.

11. The *Liberator* would feature in its first issue, March 1918, the first half of Reed's article as "Red Russia—The Triumph of the Bolsheviki."

12. Hutchins Hapgood, *A Victorian in the Modern World*, 377.

13. Dasburg and Robert Edmond Jones the stage designer had been summoned to Taos to help enliven her menage. They had been living rent free in her servants' quarters on Ninth Street and were glad to oblige, unaware that she was about to send away her spouse, Dasburg's friend Maurice Sterne, to take on another, the Indian Tony Luhan (to whom she would cling fast until death parted them). Sterne it was who on a trip to the West had discovered the nobility of the Indians and wrote her pleading that she join him in New Mexico and devote her life to the Indians' welfare. Dasburg interviews.

14. Interviews with Dorothy Day 1969–78. A Communist at one time, as she has written, Day became a convert to Catholicism, founded *The Catholic Worker* with the help of Peter Maurin, and devoted her life to the Catholic Worker movement, to feeding and caring for the poor on New York's Lower East Side and sharing their life. Long a leader in battles for social justice, Dorothy Day died November 29, 1980 at the age of 83.

15. Agnes Boulton, *Part of a Long Story*, 46–47, 60, 119–20. Also see Arthur and Barbara Gelb, *O'Neill*, 370–72: "(In her memoir Agnes has placed the time when Louise came back into O'Neill's life somewhat later—after her marriage to O'Neill, in fact—but actually Louise reappeared soon after O'Neill and Agnes arrived in Provincetown.)"

16. Louis Sheaffer, *O'Neill: Son and Playwright*, 432.

17. LB to Granville Hicks. Hicks collection. In the same note she said that she knew "his whole family, Jim and his father and his mother who used to pray for me every night."

18. Louise Bryant, *Six Red Months in Russia*, Introduction, x–xi.

19. Philip S. Foner, *The Bolshevik Revolution*, 74–77, "Radicals Here Offer Lives to Russia," based on *New York Call* of February 28, 1918.

20. Bryant, *Six Red Months*, 141–42.

21. Louis Untermeyer, "Battle Hymn of the Russian Republic," in *The Ladies' Garment Worker*, February 1918, 12, quoted by Foner, *Bolshevik Revolution*, 81. The poem urged, "Friends in all lands, arise. . . . "

22. *Ibid*. 87–89.

23. LB to Granville Hicks, n.d. Hicks Coll. After she was informed that Hicks was on a trip to the West—a dodge—Bryant sent many of her letters to him to Corliss Lamont for forwarding.

24. The cables are in John Reed Collection.

25. *Ibid.*

26. Roger Baldwin interviews.

27. When Baldwin was shown a copy of this note from Bryant and told it was written when she was said to be "falling apart," he commented: "She wasn't falling apart when she wrote *this.*"

In 1910 when the *Los Angeles Times* was leading a fight against the efforts of trade unions to change the open shop face of Los Angeles, a small charge of dynamite exploded in an alley beneath the press room of the newspaper. It went off at a time when ordinarily no one was working, but the printers were getting out an extra edition and 20 lives were lost. Maj. Gen. Harrison Gray Otis, publisher of the *Times*, editorialized that "Unionite murderers" should hang and the union movement as a whole be held responsible. In 1911 John J. McNamara, secretary of the International Association of Bridge and Structural Iron Workers, and his younger brother James, active in the Typographical Union, were arrested; the American Federation of Labor stood by the brothers, Gompers visited them in jail, and a quarter of a million dollar defense fund was raised. Clarence Darrow defended them. See Hapgood, *Victorian in the Modern World*, 287 ff.: "Steffens . . . thought he could secure an easier verdict by getting the men to plead guilty." The world of labor was shocked: "For some time after that case he was known in labor circles by the bitter name of 'Golden Rule' Steffens."

For a fuller account see Justin Kaplan, *Lincoln Steffens*, ch. 10, " 'Somewhat like handling dynamite' ".

28. Crystal Eastman to LB, no date. JR Coll.

29. Testimony in a test case of former radium dial painters in Ottawa, Illinois, February 11, 1938, came from nine women who worked for the Radium Dial company. Mrs. Marie Rossiter, 32, testified that after the publicity given to cases of industrial radium poisoning in New Jersey in 1928, she asked Rufus L. Reed, assistant superintendent of the Ottawa plant, if the workers were in danger. "Mr. Reed said we didn't have anything to worry about," said Mrs. Rossiter, her sallow face unsmiling. "He said radium would put rosy cheeks on us—that it was good for us."

Another former worker, Miss Marguerite Glacinski, 29, then was questioned by the attorney for the nine, Leonard Grossman.

"Q.—What did Mr. Reed say about radium dial paint and its effect on girls? A.—He told us it would make us good looking.

"Q. [with heavy chivalry]—And is that why you're so good looking? A. [her mouth drawn down in bitter lines]—Hardly." From a by-line story in the February 12, 1938, *Chicago Tribune* by Virginia Gardner.

30. JR to LB, March 27, 1918, from Christiania. JR Coll.

31. Edgar Sissons, *One Hundred Days* (New Haven: Yale University Press, 1931), 259.

32. See Williams, *Journey Into Revolution*, 220–27, on George F. Kennan, *Russia Leaves the War*, 405–11, and the revocation of Reed's consul appointment. " . . . he finds that two documents were involved, of such an incriminating nature that 'they were shocking to Lenin'." Reinstein had told Williams that Gumberg put "the newspaper thing" in Lenin's hands and that Lenin asked Trotsky, "Why do you trust a man like this, who works one day for the capitalists and the next day for the Revolution?" Williams replied, "Too bad someone couldn't have let Lenin know that there's bad blood between Reed and Gumberg." It was at a time, before the Bolshevik victory and after *The Masses* was shut down, "when the Reeds were broke." Robins was exploring a possible English-language newspaper in Petrograd and asked Reed to draw up what he called a "prospectus." In the long run it would help U.S. businessmen sell products to democratic Russia; mean-

while it might create a friendly attitude toward the United States and help keep Russia in the war. Reed had scruples; Williams, tired of hearing him grumble and fret—such a paper would mislead the masses, and so on—told him, "I thought better of the masses, and so should he." One day Reed said Robins had come by their hotel room and he had turned over the thing to him. " 'Anyway,' he said triumphantly, 'I dummied in a line under the masthead: "This paper is devoted to promoting the interests of American capital"!' " Williams also remembered "the embarrassment of Louise Bryant when she later found that Robins had tucked a thousand-ruble note under some object . . . in their hotel room; but they took it because they were broke." The document in question (in the Robins papers, Wisconsin Historical Society) is not a dummy, and is not in Reed's typing. The other document Williams considers even more innocuous, although Kennan said it "must have made Lenin jump." Reed's name is on this one, and it is in his typing, distinct because to cross out a word he used the dollar symbol instead of xxx. Headed "Skeleton Report," it is a compilation of interviews Reed had with government people on what Russia needed. To refute Kennan, who he says seemed saddened to find such a betrayal of socialism in Reed's "curious proposals," Williams quoted from Louise Bryant's interview with Lenin, who said he told Americans, Robins for one, early in 1918 that it was to the interest of both countries to have commercial relations. But Lenin said, "We offered concessions to foreign capital," and those Reed interviewed did not go that far!

33. Max Eastman, Merrill Rogers, business manager, and Floyd Dell, Art Young and certain contributors to *The Masses* were indicted, along with the absent John Reed, on a charge of conspiracy to obstruct the operation of the military laws. The jury could not agree. Max Eastman testified the first day of the trial on April 22, 1918, that he had changed some of his views. "I believe now," he said, "that this is a war for liberty and freedom, which I did not believe then." In a park outside the courtroom a band played the national anthem to advertise a Liberty Loan drive. Eastman declared, "My feelings were sad as I stood up and listened to the anthem, for I was thinking of the thousands of our boys who are destined to die 'over there' fighting for liberty." A second trial was held in which both John Reed and Louise Bryant testified in October.

CHAPTER 11. IN SEARCH OF REVOLUTION

1. From "Part of a Letter from Jack Reed," Lincoln Steffens, *The Autobiography of Lincoln Steffens*, vol. II, opposite 771.

2. Lincoln Steffens, *Letters of Lincoln Steffens*, vol. I, 428–29.

3. Steffens, *Autobiography*, vol. II, 799.

4. Albert Rhys Williams, *Journey Into Revolution*. 41. Along the same theme, Williams observes, 42: "It was Reed's curse to have this contradiction in his personality—a buoyant, light-hearted spirit, a creative talent, and at the same time a mocking self-judge within him. It had driven him into many unexplored channels in which he found success too easily; the judge was not satisfied. What he now struggled with—his own relation to the events seething in Petrograd, where his sense of history told him mankind had reached a turning point—would challenge all his forces. Would he find himself wanting? The moods were but the natural waverings of a very human young American before he set himself a goal more difficult than any he had yet picked."

5. Granville Hicks, *John Reed*, 313, 342.

6. William Carlos Williams, *The Autobiography of William Carlos Williams*, 142.

7. Roger Baldwin interviews.

8. As quoted in Louis Waldman, *Labor Lawyer* (New York: Dutton, 1944), 72–73.

9. Interview with Waldman, September 2, 1972, in his Croton, N.Y., home.

10. Hicks, *John Reed,* 329–30.

11. Interview with Conrad Aiken in his home in Brewster, Mass., July 20, 1971. He died in August, 1973, at the age of 84.

12. Interview with S. D. Levine by telephone, December 15, 1971. For many years on the *Daily Freiheit,* Levine in 1972 published his memoirs, *Chapters of My Life,* in the Yiddish language.

13. Interview with Nearing in New York, 1972. "Both Louise and Jack were intellectuals; neither was anywhere near as great as the labor orators of the day." He conceded that because of their subject they were in demand as speakers. A Marxist, Nearing became a counterculture hero when he was dismissed from the faculty of the University of Pennsylvania. It was the theme of a masque in verse "Education: A Community Masque," in the September 1916 *Masses,* by Seymour Barnard. Reprinted in William L. O'Neill, ed., *Echoes of Revolt: THE MASSES 1911–17* (Chicago: Quadrangle Books, 1966), 90, 93-94.

14. Elizabeth Gurley Flynn, *I Speak My Own Piece,* 270–71.

15. Mabel Dodge Luhan, *Movers and Shakers,* 143–44.

16. Hicks, *John Reed,* 308.

17. *Ibid.,* 346. Hicks declared that Reed was hurt, but Sinclair had carried little weight with American Socialists since he took a pro-war position in 1917. See James Weinstein, *The Decline of Socialism in America 1912–1925,* 119.

18. Interview with Isobel Walker Soule, writer, editor, and labor activist, in her rooms at Stonington, Conn., in May 1972. She died July 31, 1972, at the age of 74.

19. Hazel Hunkins-Hallinan to author, letter of October 2, 1972, from her home in London, followed by interview in New York, January 25, 1975. She was in love with Charles T. Hallinan, a Washington newspaperman who organized the Union Against Militarism, and later married him. She is the editor of and a contributor to *In Her Own Right: A Discussion Conducted by The Six Point Group* (London: George C. Harrap, 1968). At the time of the interview she was 85.

20. James Gilbert, *Writers and Partisans: A History of Literary Radicalism in America* (New York: John Wiley, 1968), 40–41, declares: "The war and the Russian Revolution inserted a quality of seriousness into the Bohemianism and radicalism of the New York intellectuals that had heretofore been missing. It forced choices on them. . . . The community of young intellectuals would ultimately split apart." In his opinion only Randolph Bourne and John Reed were capable of holding it together. By the end of 1918 Bourne would be dead.

21. The house belonged to Grace Mott Johnson, sculptor, whose insistence on working as a full-time artist and on an absolute division of work, even as to caring for the child, made for domestic difficulties. The trial separation with Dasburg began in 1913, and she let him live in the house, while he improved the grounds. "From 1913 to 1922, when they divorced, Andrew and Johnson were often together with or without me in Woodstock, Wurtsboro [Andrew's mother's farm], or Yonkers," said Alfred Dasburg, their son. "Both were interested in other people at various times and were open about it."

22. See Louise Bryant's *Six Red Months in Russia,* "The Decline of the Church," 260–61. The ikon is now in the Wurlitzer Foundation's museum in Taos, where when seen in 1972 it was labeled as a gift to Dasburg from John Reed!

23. Andrew Dasburg interviews in Taos, N. Mex., March 22–24, 1972, August 1978, and by telephone between 1972 and 1978.

24. *Ibid.*

25. New York *Tribune,* October 4, 1918, page 14. The story was headed "John Reed, Editor, War Correspondent, Consul, Testifies/Bolshevik Emissary Takes Stand."

26. "News from France," *The Masses,* October, 1917, 1 and 6.

27. "About the Second *Masses* Trial," by John Reed, *Liberator,* December 1918.

28. Joseph Freeman, *An American Testament,* 243.

29. Floyd Dell, *Homecoming,* 327–28.

30. Interview with Floyd Dell, October 31, 1968, in his home in Bethesda, Md. Dell died July 23, 1969 at the age of 82.

31. Unsent letter Dell addressed to Edmund Wilson, February 13, 1959. Dell papers.

32. Josephine Herbst, novelist, to author, November 7, 1968, from Erwinna, Pa.: "Dell became a bore, more or less, after Vincent, was analzyed, became a propagandist for *monogamy!* A fine sensitive critic once, he buried himself in the bureaucracy of Washington."

33. Interview with Louis Waldman. Waldman said he got the story from the man from whom he bought his house at Croton. The enormous tree was destroyed in a storm.

34. Quoted in *The Book Review Digest,* Fourteenth Annual Cumulation, *Reviews of 1918 Books,* ed. Mary Katharine Reely assisted by Alice Sterling and Pauline H. Rich (H. H. Wilson, 1919), are *the Nation* of November 10, 1918, 107:591, and *the Dial* of December 30, 1918, 65:504. *Pearson's Weekly* reviewed the book in December 1918, 90.

In 1970 a reprint of Louise Bryant's *Six Red Months in Russia* was issued by Arno Press, with illustrations.

35. *Liberator,* vol. 1, no. 11, January 1919, 42–43.

CHAPTER 12. A NEW VOICE

1. Sponsoring the meeting was the Know the Truth About Russia Committee, headed by publisher Albert Boni; its members included such eminent names as Jane Addams, Frank P. Walsh, Gilson Gardner, Lincoln Colcord, and Albert J. Nock. But Senator Thomas of Colorado at the height of the Senate oratory characterized them in these words: "Every murderer: every criminal who hopes to prosper politically or materially, or both, on the overthrow of the Social state by violence, massacre of men, the ravishing of women and the destruction of liberty by robbery, arson and all the other known social crimes, are not only members but are enthusiastic members of this so-called organization."

2. The witness was a Roger T. Simmons, who represented the United States Department of Commerce in Russia.

3. Hazel Hunkins, then on the staff of *The Suffragist,* issued by the National Woman's Party. As Hazel Hunkins-Hallinan, veteran of the first suffragists' march from the Mall along Pennsylvania Avenue to the White House in 1913, she led 3,500 women on the same route on August 26, 1977, and was photographed with President Carter as he signed the proclamation making it the first Women's Equality Day. In her day she chained herself to the White House fence and was trundled off to jail by the police, only to return to repeat the act. When feminist Lucy Burns stood by and proffered one bent knee, she was boosted up over the fence and remained long enough to light a fire on the front lawn of President Wilson. The 1977 march was in commemoration of Alice Paul and in anger that fifty-seven years after the Nineteenth Amendment women are still fighting to obtain the Equal Rights Amendment. She also marched in 1917.

4. Millie Morris was described in a letter from Hazel Hunkins-Hallinan to the author from London, October 23, 1972, as "thin and wiry, her hair red with streaks of white as it stood out in all directions. . . . She was the best newspaper woman in the country. She would stop at nothing to get a story and she would write it at top speed and usually got front page coverage. . . . She slept wherever she happened to be when she got sleepy; she ate whenever she had enough money or when her friends would give her a meal. She drew good money when she was in employment but never had any left by the end of the day. She drank too much and smoked endlessly. But she could sum up a situation in a few unforgettable words and her prose was rushing like a river and very cynical. And the young John D. Rockefeller was one of her firm friends! She used to take off with my clothes and sometimes I connived at it so that she would be decently dressed. I would leave money in pockets so that she would have her car fares and her salary was twice mine. . . . As a person I loved her and was secretly proud of her but almost ashamed to be seen with her."

5. Louise Bryant to John Reed, n.d., from Washington. John Reed Collection.

6. *Die Fackel* became *Der Völkerfriede* December 19/January 1, 1918, and with the temporary armistice, distribution was easier than before. The paper was thrown over into the German trenches or handed to German and Austro-Hungarian soldiers at appointed fraternization points. It ended when the Brest-Litovsk peace treaty was signed. Albert Rhys Williams, *Journey Into Revolution*, 176–77: "As for General Hoffmann's often quoted statement that 'Immediately after conquering those Bolsheviks, we were conquered by them. Our victorious army on the Eastern front became rotten with Bolshevism,' perhaps . . . we played a minor role there."

7. U.S., Congress, Senate, Subcommittee of the Judiciary Committee, *Bolshevik Propaganda: Hearings*, Bryant testimony, 465–561.

8. *Ibid.*, John Reed testimony, 561–593. On March 5 Bessie Beatty, editor of *McCall's* magazine, testified, confirming Bryant's testimony on the "nationalization of women," and was also bullied by committee members.

9. JR to LB, n.d., from New York. Mention is made of the McCall's check. JR Coll.

10. A. M. Goldberg replied to Bryant, August 16, 1918, on a letterhead of the Philadelphia *Press*, in part: "My suspicions are that Schenck, the local secretary, who developed a prejudice against Jack, told Nelson not to do the work for the local; therefore the $250 letter. Of course Schenck had no right to do this. Schenck flew into a rage because Jack got himself arrested after he had been requested to remain away from the meeting and he evidently regards Jack's actions as inexcusable blundering. But Schenck is in the courts for somethng so outrageously witless that if you say so I'll stir up a storm against him." JR Coll.

11. This indictment was later dropped.

12. *Pearson's*, "Louise Bryant Before the Elders," with a half-column drawing of her, April 1919, 246–47. The *Liberator* piece appeared April 1919, 20–21.

13. "I can't seem to get up any very wild enthusiasm about having a pension under *soviet* rule!" she told her son, March 11, 1919. JR Coll.

14. Philip Jaffe, "The Strange Case of Anna Louise Strong," *Survey* No. 53, October 1964 (a British publication). Jaffe, former editor and publisher of *Amerasia*, said Strong went from militant pacifism in World War I to "an emotional socialism," and maintained: "Although a prolific writer . . . especially on Russia and China, she never really understood socialism or Marxism." After Jaffe published her long article, "The Thought of Mao Tse-tung," asserting Mao had transformed Marxism to an Asiatic form—followed by a book weaving in the same material—Strong was arrested in 1949 in Moscow, held in Lubianka Prison

a few days, and accused as a spy for the United States. Jaffe declares that Stalin "decided to strike at the ideological rival in China by depicting his American political Boswell and the carrier of Mao's heresy as a 'capitalist spy.' "

Although not formally exonerated in Russia until two years after Stalin's death, she wrote a book in his defense late in 1956. Strong had been waiting for months for an exit visa for China when she was arrested. Nym Wales in "Anna Louise Strong: The Classic Fellow-Traveler," *New Republic*, April 25, 1970, said Strong was "even more angry about missing the victory celebrations in Peking than about her unjust arrest." Strong died at 84 in Peking in 1970. "Anna Louise always envied John Reed's being buried in the Kremlin wall," Wales said.

15. This report by a confidential source was verified by Roger Baldwin. Baldwin interviews.

16. Anna Louise Strong to LB, February 14, 1919. JR Coll.

17. Anna Louise Strong, then in Moscow on the *Moscow News* she had founded in 1930, wrote to Louise Bryant on the anniversary of John Reed's death and told her of the ceremony in Moscow. See LB to Corliss Lamont, October 30, 1935. JR Coll.

18. LB to JR, n.d., on Hull House letterhead. JR Coll.

19. LB to JR, March 13, 1919. JR Coll.

20. LB to JR, headed "Saturday on the Train" (date unknown). Louise Bryant memoir, Granville Hicks Collection.

21. Phillip Knightley, *The First Casualty—From the Crimea to Vietnam*, ch. 7, "The Remedy for Bolshevism Is Bullets 1917–1919," 138–70. Phillips Price of the *Manchester Guardian* and John Reed, he declares, stand "head and shoulders above any other war correspondent of the time." 141. He also names Arthur Ransome of the London *Daily News* as "one of the few voices of accuracy and reason in the hysteria." 149. Reed's description of events in Petrograd in November, 1917, "is unequalled." 147. "The insistent theme of Russian news in the *New York Times* was that the Bolsheviks could last for only a moment." 149.

22. See James Weinstein, *Decline of Socialism in America 1912–1925*, 172.

23. Elmer Rice, *Minority Report*, 167–68.

24. Max Eastman, *Love and Revolution*, 144.

25. Interview with Andrew Dasburg in his home in Taos, N. Mex., July 1978, when he was 91.

26. The Strong February 14 letter: see note 16.

27. Anna Louise Strong, *I Change Worlds: The Remaking of an American* (New York: Henry Holt, 1935), 70–71.

28. LB to JR, March 21, 1919. From Seattle. JR Coll.

29. LB to JR, March 23, 1919. From Seattle. JR Coll.

30. *Tacoma Labor Advocate*, Vol. 10, Number 47, Friday, March 28, 1919, 1, 2 and 3, six columns in all. Regarding Bryant's answer to the last cited question, on Lenin's readiness to extend concessions, especially to trade unions in America, see Robert W. Dunn, "Labor Helped Russian Reconstruction," *New World Review*, Winter 1970, 153–58. Dunn relates how the then unaffiliated Amalgamated Clothing Workers sent its president, Sidney Hillman, to Russia: after visiting textile plants and clothing factories and conferring with Lenin he proposed to his union, May 11, 1922, that it form the Russian-American Industrial Corporation to aid Russia's clothing industry. The convention agreed and on June 2 RAIC was incorporated and in business. By the time it was liquidated its loan of $300,000 for the project was entirely repaid by the Soviets. Every penny of the stockholders' investment was paid back at 8 percent interest.

31. Inez Milholland, on a tour of the West for the National Woman's Party in 1916 to urge the enfranchised women to vote Republican because of the Demo-

crats' failure to act for suffrage, collapsed as she spoke in Los Angeles. After a ten-week illness during which she often rallied after blood transfusions, her condition reported daily in the press as the entire Village and radicals everywhere longed for her recovery, she died in a Los Angeles hospital, November 25, 1916. Her husband, Jan Boissevain, aware that she had pernicious anemia, had begged her not to go. Rice, *Minority Report,* 135, recalled that he was "one of a small male contingent that had marched up Fifth Avenue in a woman-suffrage parade headed by the beautiful Inez Milholland astride a white horse."

32. JR to LB, March 18, 1919, from Croton. JR Coll.

33. JR to LB, March 16, from Croton. JR Coll.

34. LB to JR, March 24, 1919, from Seattle. JR Coll.

35. Strong, *I Change Worlds,* 70.

36. LB to JR, "12:30 Monday night, March 24." JR Coll.

37. JR to LB, March 21, (1919), from Croton. JR Coll.

38. LB to JR, March 29. JR Coll.

39. LB to JR, "Sunday, March 30, Seattle." JR Coll.

40. Hartwig interview, April 19, 1970; he was then 80. The Portland *Telegram,* now extinct, March 25, 1919, page one, said the executive board, Portland Labor Council, "without endorsing the purpose of Miss Bryant's speech," saw no reason why the Auditorium should not be available, and March 28, page one, reported permission granted by City Council to a committee from Central Labor Council "for the use of the Auditorium for Louise Bryant"; also see *Oregon Labor Press,* March 29, page one.

41. Interview with Ruth Trullinger, widow of Paul, October 30, 1970. Dr. Trullinger died of cancer in 1957. Ruth Trullinger said Paul had told her of hearing his former wife speak in Portland. He was "interested and sympathetic, as he did not believe in violence," she said. The marriage took place in 1929, after which they moved to Waldport, Ore. She returned to Portland after his death.

42. LB to JR, April 4, from San Francisco. JR Coll.

43. Horton W. Nicholas to author, July, 1970. Nicholas was then 83, and operated the Nicholas Sales Company of San Jose, Ca.

44. Interview with Ethel Bernard Myers, of Sierra Madre, in Pasadena, Ca., where she was visiting, in April 1970. She was the widow of Albert S. Myers, for many years the city manager of Sierra Madre.

45. Mabel K. Strong, widow of Robert H. Strong, interviewed in Portland by telephone, August 24, 1970. Mrs. Strong died at the age of 102 in January 1979.

46. LB to JR, April 4 (1919), from San Francisco. JR Coll.

47. The startlingly beautiful Sara Bard Field was weeping not only for the very rough time the Soviets were having, but for her 17-year-old son Albert Field Ehrgott, killed the previous October in a car accident in which she was the driver. Unmentioned in press reports of the accident, Wood was along, and was briefly hospitalized as a result. The accident occurred October 12, 1918; young Ehrgott was killed almost instantly. His sister Katherine, 12, and their mother were hospitalized. Coroner's inquest at San Rafael January 30, 1919, testimony of Sara Bard Field and C. E. S. Wood, copy of which was certified by Marin County Coroner Donovan G. Cooke, M.D., December 13, 1971.

Other facts set forth in a letter from Edwin R. Bingham, professor of history, University of Oregon at Eugene, to author August 21, 1970 follow: Field was divorced from Albert Ehrgott in Goldfield, Nev., in 1914. Wood's first wife, Nanny Moale Smith Wood, died December 18, 1933. Col. Wood and Field were married in a secret ceremony performed by Rabbi Jacob Weinstein of Chicago at Los Gatos, California, their home, probably in 1935. Professor Bingham was writing a biography of Col. Wood.

In a moving letter to Louise a few years later, Sara Bard Field mentioned "that passing through of my girl on her mission of telling the truth about Russia when I hobbled out on crutches, my first attempt to go into public since the accident that took my darling boy from me for a time. How proud I was of you that night in your slender strength. It was as if I had borne you myself—my little girl!" January 26, 1922, from her home, 1601 Taylor Street, San Francisco. JR Coll.

48. LB to JR, "Sunday night April 6 [1919]," from San Francisco. A postscript to an earlier letter. In the latter she complained, "They work me to death!" She had spoken twice that day in Oakland. She was glad he had thought of "the Chinese stuff for curtains" (apparently a suggestion that she could hunt for it) but pointed out she had "not *even* a minute to myself." She had been explaining that "the *Unions* are now outlawed in Siberia" and "the Unions are aghast and are passing resolutions." JR Coll.

49. LB to JR, April 16 (1919). JR Coll.

50. JR to LB, April 1, (1919). JR Coll.

CHAPTER 13. ANOTHER FAREWELL

1. Louise Bryant memoir, Granville Hicks Collection.

2. *Ibid.*, 43.

3. *Ibid.*

4. *Ibid.*, 44.

5. *Ibid.*

6. Mabel Dodge Luhan, *Movers and Shakers*, 189.

7. LB memoir, Hicks Coll. 42.

8. LB memoir, Hicks Coll. She adds that when she next saw it, after Reed's death, the woodbine covered the "studio." The little building in the yard behind the house is still there.

9. Louise Bryant to an editor of *Soviet Russia*, July 19, from Truro. John Reed Collection.

10. Louise Bryant, *Mirrors of Moscow*, "Anatol Vassilievitch Lunacharsky and Russian Culture," 71–84.

11. Susan Glaspell, *The Road to the Temple* (New York: Stokes, 1927), 302.

12. Of course it must be a socialist future, but Lunacharsky, at a time "when a revolution was only a vague goal," had foreseen a future he saluted in these dream-like terms: "Oh, happy earth! Out of the blood of generations/ Life yet will blossom, innocent and wise,/ And thou, my planet, shall be cleansed of lamentations,/ A jade-green star in the moon-silvered skies." The Lunacharsky poem is quoted in Bryant, *Mirrors*, 71.

13. Reed and his remaining cohorts now faced a much more significant group than the one that had opposed the Reed-Gitlow position at the June 21 National Left Wing Conference. The Reed tactic, of opposing an immediate split in Socialist Party ranks while working to capture the party from entrenched bureaucracy, had prevailed, although 31 delegates led by Nicholas Hourwich of the powerful Russian federation walked out and soon thereafter issued a call for convening a Communist party in Chicago September 1. Reed's argument that it was possible to win over many Socialists who were not declared followers of the Left but were outraged by the party's National Executive Committee's flagrant abrogation of the membership's mandate in the spring elections, was upheld in the vote of 55 to 38 against the proposal to organize a new party at once. What had sent Reed hurrying away from Truro was word that some of his trusted fellow members of the National Left Wing Council of nine had been meeting behind the scenes with the Slavic Federation and swung a majority vote in the Council to

support the call for a Communist party convention. Now Reed and his minority group faced not only the entrenched Socialist Party bureaucracy (which had summarily declared the elections illegal, as 12 of 15 seats on its National Executive Committee and four out of five International Delegate positions had gone to the Left Wing), but a fragmented Left Wing.

14. Interview with Ben Legere of San Francisco June 12, 1970. Legere had lived with Jim Larkin just steps away from Patchin Place.

15. See R. M. Fox, *Jim Larkin: Irish Labor Leader* (New York: International, 1957), 136–37. Larkin would be convicted in 1920 on criminal anarchy charges in connection with the Left Wing manifesto published in *Revolutionary Age*. "But the *Revolutionary Age* document," Fox declares, "was framed in heavy Continental jargon, the kind of theoretical exposition and analysis that was entirely foreign to Larkin's outlook and temperament." "Larkin declared that there were many parts of it both in thought and in phrase with which he personally disagreed."

16. James Weinstein, *The Decline of Socialism in America 1912–1925*, 180. The Soviet republic, he added, "has lived one year in spite of the hatred of every other government in the world," and its survival "in the face of all attacks" proved that "it had satisfied its own people."

17. E. H. Carr, *The Bolshevik Revolution 1917–1923*, vol. 3, 130, says it "resulted from lack of serious competition rather than any conscious Russian design."

18. From Debs's farewell speech in Cleveland two days after the Supreme Court affirmed his conviction under the Espionage Act: *The World* of Oakland, Ca., March 28, 1919. " . . . the springtime of revolution. I have faith in it and in humanity; I have faith in the Man of Galilee [of whom they] said 'He is preaching dangerous doctrine. He is a Bolshevist.' "

19. Victor Serge, *Memoirs of a Revolutionary 1901–1941*, 83. Arriving in Russia in the spring of 1919, he found that even the fall of Munich "seemed rather unimportant by comparison with the revolutionary victories now expected to follow in Central Europe, Bohemia, Italy, and Bulgaria."

20. LB to JR, n.d. JR Coll.

21. A letter to Louise Bryant from Santeri Nuorteva, secretary of the Russian Soviet Government Bureau, with offices in the *World*'s Tower Building, New York, of October 18, 1919 (JR Coll.) appears to be a reply to a query from her regarding the Russian Committee of the American Friends Service Committee. He informs her that if the A.F.S.C. wants to get supplies into Russia, "we could give them an opportunity to send medicines and milk, and I am sure it would also be possible to procure passage to Russia for representatives of the American Friends on such ships." He would like to meet with her on details of the plan. Nuorteva had been designated as an official representative of the Soviets, assisting Ludwig C. A. K. Martens, Soviet envoy. Nuorteva had been editor of *Toveri (Comrade)*, daily newspaper in the Finnish language, in Astoria, Ore.

22. JR Coll.

23. Interview with James H. Dolsen in his Philadelphia home in 1970. At 85 Dolsen, tall, straight, with match-like thinness, still wore a look of guileless candor and innocence. Dolsen was arrested in the aftermath of the 1920 Palmer Raids with C.L.P. leader Anita Whitney and three others and charged with violating the California Criminal Syndicalist Act. Acting as counsel for himself and others, he obtained not one but two hung juries. In the second trial young Earl Warren was the prosecutor. Dolsen for many years covered Pennsylvania for the *Daily Worker*.

24. Granville Hicks, *John Reed*, 366.

25. As it happened, Fraina would not arrive in Russia until June 1920. After

Reed's departure he was held up by a charge as a police spy. The Communist Party of America conducted a trial and he was cleared of any taint. But time was consumed in contending with competitors who were eager to go in his stead. See Theodore Draper, *The Roots of American Communism*, ch. 17, "The Revolution Devours Its Children." Stopping off for a meeting in Amsterdam, and with serious delays due to the blockade, he was four months in getting to Moscow. Once there he was subjected again to examination on the old spy charge; a committee named by the Comintern heard witnesses, including Reed; he was unanimously acquitted and a CI resolution exonerated him completely.

26. Robert A. Rosenstone, *Romantic Revolutionary*, 360.

27. "Certainly he dearly loved women," said Dasburg's oldest living friend, Lila Wheelock Howard, sculptor, interviewed in her home at Westport, Conn., August 18, 1976, "but if he's not painting life isn't worth living." Although he pursued and was pursued by women throughout his life, they formed "a procession of singular women, all talented, and not one of them who would make a home for him and be content to blend in with the background," she said, laughing. Howard once shared a studio in the Village with Johnson, Dasburg's first wife, also a sculptor. "On principle, Johnson never made a pot of tea, although she enjoyed the tea I made. She used to say she wished I could be her wife."

28. Dasburg interviews.

CHAPTER 14. THE TERROR

1. Robert W. Dunn, ed., *The Palmer Raids*, 26.

2. John Reed to Louise Bryant, October 21, 1919, from Christiania (Oslo), sent by courier. John Reed Collection.

3. Secret instructions had been sent out by Attorney General Palmer, which read in part: "If possible you should arrange with your undercover informants to have meetings of the Communist Party and Communist Labor Party held on the night set. I have been informed by some of the bureau officers that such arrangements will be made." See Dunn, *Palmer Raids*, 30–31.

4. *Ibid*.

5. *Ibid*., 33, quoting from *The Deportation Delirium of Nineteen-Twenty*, by Assistant Secretary of Labor Louis F. Post (Chicago: 1923), 97. Judge Anderson presided over habeas corpus proceedings brought by 18 Communists suing for their freedom from Deer Island. So widespread was the use of provocateurs and spies in the two Communist parties in the cases before him that Judge Anderson suggested that the Secretary of Labor review his proscription of the then Communist Party, Dunn, 47, quoting from the Senate Judiciary Committee *Hearings* of January 19–March 13, 1921, 74–75, quotes Judge Anderson as declaring that "it appears that government spies constituted in December, 1919, an active and efficient part of the Communist Party."

6. Wearing the army uniform he had worn overseas, Wesley Everest, a crack shot, was waiting for them when the American Legion gang broke down the door and rushed the I.W.W. hall in Centralia, Wa., on Armistice Day 1919. He fired his rifle into the marauding crowd and fled to the woods, the mob at his heels. He tried to swim the River Skookumchuck but the current was too strong. He told the oncoming mob, "If there's bulls in the crowd I'll submit to arrest." On came the mob. He shot Dale Hubbard, nephew of a lumber boss, dead before his gun jammed; he threw it away and fought with his fists. "You haven't the guts to hang a man in daylight," he said. They hadn't. They dragged him to jail, returned after the city's lights were doused and threw him into a waiting taxi. As he left the jail he said to other prisoners, "Tell the boys I died for my class." He was castrated

and hanged and his body riddled with bullets by a mob of 100 at the Chehalis River bridge. From the affidavit of a coal miner, Claude Clifford, a witness to all he recites, in the files of the University of Washington, supplied by Archivist Richard C. Berner and quoted in Patrick Renshaw, *The Wobblies*, 164.

7. See Dorothy Day, *The Long Loneliness*, 97–100. In the women's section of the city jail they were stripped and searched for drugs and locked in cells. Before her release on bail and later dismissal of the case there were "new indignities" but she "did not want to be spared one of them," for "I was sharing, as I never had before, the life of the poorest of the poor, the guilty, the dispossessed." The Chicago experience was a sample of "the ugliness of men's justice, which set me more squarely on the side of the revolution." Also Day interviews.

8. The Haymarket martyrs, Albert Parsons and August Spies, who helped organize the International Working People's Association which fought for the eight-hour day, and Adolph Fischer and George Engel were hanged November 11, 1887. Fielden and Schwab the day before the execution had their death sentences commuted to life imprisonment by Illinois Governor Oglesby, and the same day 22-year-old Louis Lingg, who spoke no English, either committed suicide or was murdered in his cell. William Dean Howells, America's leading man of letters, wrote while the tragedy was impending: "This case constitutes the greatest wrong that ever threatened our fame as a nation." Two days before the scheduled hangings letters to the governor from Spies and Parsons were read aloud to him by Joe Buchanan, a Denver labor editor. Parsons had written, "If I am guilty and must be hanged because of my presence at the Haymarket meeting, then I hope a reprieve will be granted in my case until my wife and two children, who were also at the meeting, can be convicted and hanged with me." See Richard O. Boyer and Herbert M. Morais, *Labor's Untold Story*, 84–104, and Sender Garlin, *William Dean Howells and the Haymarket Era*, Occasional Paper No. 33, American Institute for Marxist Studies, 1979.

9. Louise Bryant, "Out of the Sunset," *Voice of Labor*, Vol. I, No. 6, November 1, 1919, 4.

10. Under the by-line of Louise Bryant, the article appeared in the *Voice of Labor* for November 15, 1919, 1–2.

11. JR to LB, November 9 (1919), from Helsingfors. JR Coll.

12. Louise Bryant, *Voice of Labor*, December 15, 1919, page one.

13. Louise Bryant, "How the Revolution Began in America," *The Revolutionary Age*, January 25, 1919, 6. (A letter from S. D. Levine of Brooklyn, N.Y., to author, January 10, 1972, first described the fable and said he was sure it appeared in January 1919 and thought it might have been in *Voice of Labor*. When the only known file of the publication showed January and February 1920 issues missing—the *Voice of Labor* was initiated only in the summer of 1919—the search continued. By the time it was found Levine, long on the staff of *The Morning Freiheit*, was dead.)

14. Hella Wuolijoki, a Finnish writer, to Granville Hicks, January 15, 1935, from Helsingfors. Hicks Collection. Reed came to her with a letter from a friend in Stockholm "who did *not* know that my house was surrounded by the Finnish *ochrana* both day and night—except during an almost Siberian snowstorm . . . I nursed him for a fortnight and he left—during another snowstorm." To her John Reed was "one of the most genial boys of our time." Like Lenin, she wrote, "He had no hatred . . . and he was tremendously *free*, but not an adventurer—of course Marxists cannot be adventurers." Of his wife, she wrote, "John . . . told me tremendous things about her courage."

She had had to delay answering his letter, she told Hicks. She had sustained a fractured skull in a motor crash. This Finnish writer, who in later years kept

Bertolt Brecht during his Finnish exile on fleeing the Nazis before he came to the United States, asked Hicks if a short book about "this 'mysterious' period in [Reed's] life" might be published anonymously in America.

She knew all about what happened to Reed in Finland "but it is still a rather dangerous knowledge in this country. Besides it is a long, romantic detective story with coalboxes and disguises and terrible dangers [in which he rejoiced] both for him and his friends." Reed, wrote Wuolijoki, "was a revolutionary thinking scientifically . . . listening, looking and acting with his heartblood."

15. Louise Bryant, "Russian Memories," *The Dial*, Vol. 68: 565–6 (May 1920).

16. Then newly arrived in the Village from Minnesota, the poet Meridel Le Sueuer was staying with M. Eleanor Fitzgerald ("Fitzi") of the Provincetown Players staff and recalled how "Fitzi and I just moved in with Louise Bryant somewhere on Washington Square to help, as others were doing" and remembers the crisis atmosphere that gripped the Village. (Le Sueuer to author, in New York City, in 1977.)

17. On April 14 Bryant wired Secretary of State Colby, received a reply April 16, and after other telegrams wrote him April 23 enclosing $40 for cable expenses asking that an inquiry be made on legal aid. The next day the department cabled the legation at Helsingfors saying if no counsel had been retained for Reed, his wife requested that one be engaged at her expense. (Documents obtained from National Archives and Record Service through Freedom of Information Act.)

18. Hays had given Reed the title for his book *Ten Days That Shook the World*.

19. Gilson Gardner to LB, May 5, 1920. JR Coll.

20. Eadmonn MacAlpine to LB, December 27, 1932, Paris. JR Coll. He enclosed "the facts—as told me by Jack in Moscow—of his arrest in Finland."

21. Granville Hicks, *John Reed*, 379, declared Reed suggested to Mme. Malmberg "that she should announce his death." But MacAlpine's account that Reed wrote the story is more convincing than otherwise. At the same time, MacAlpine's saying that he gave it to a jailor to hand to a news agency is less plausible than Hicks's version that he left it to her to make it public.

22. Victor Hugo's novel of the French revolution, *Ninety-three*, appeared in 1884 and was translated into English the same year. A translation by Helen B. Dole was issued by Thomas Y. Crowell in New York in 1888.

23. "Jim Larkin Goes to Jail," by Louise Bryant, *Liberator* for June, 1920, illustrated with drawings of the trial by F. Wilson, 13–16.

24. Bryant did go to the pawnbroker, J.E. Simon & Co., 470 Sixth Avenue, New York, about the gold repeater Swiss watch, and obtained an extension of time until January 1921 by paying the interest; she arranged with her friend Esther Andrews to redeem it by then, after getting a letter from Reed to the pawnbroker authorizing her as agent.

25. JR to LB, May 3, 1920, from Abo, Finland. JR Coll.

26. Dasburg interviews.

27. JR to LB, last letter from the Abo jail, June 2, 1920. All letters and telegrams from JR on prevous pages in JR Coll.

28. State Department documents obtained through Freedom of Information Act.

29. Eadmonn MacAlpine to LB, December 27, 1932, Paris. A penciled notation by LB relates he gave it to her.

CHAPTER 15. PERILOUS JOURNEY

1. Hazel Hunkins-Hallinan of London, to author, September 9, 1972, and April 13, 1974, and interview with her in New York City, January 25, 1975.

2. It may well have been one of the three editors to whom Bryant dedicates

Mirrors of Moscow. Or she may have dealt with Marlen E. Pew, general manager of International News Service, who later in 1920 offered to forward letters to her. Margaret Reed to Mrs. Fred G. Bursch, December 7, 1920. John Reed Collection.

3. Margaret Reed to LB, June 17, 1920, JR Coll. She enclosed letter to her son, which Bryant delivered to him in Moscow.

4. JR to LB, June 16, 1920, from Moscow. JR Coll.

5. JR to LB, June 23. JR Coll. The letter, in Reed's handwriting, was in an envelope addressed in another hand, with Russian words at the top, to Professor R. E. Rogers, Massachusetts Institute of Technology, Boston, U.S.A. (Reed's classmate Bobby Rogers). Across the top of the letter Reed wrote, "Please give to Louise Bryant."

6. Horace B. Liveright to LB, March 15, 1920. JR Coll. In an interview with Albert Boni he was asked if Reed submitted any of his planned second book on Russia, "Kornilov to Brest-Litovsk," before he sailed in 1919. Boni said that he had arranged to have *Ten Days* published before he left the firm but knew nothing about subsequent events there. Boni said he found Liveright "untrustworthy and irresponsible" and told him they would have to split: "We drew straws and I won, so Liveright bought me out." Interview in his office in New York, May 10, 1973. In a review of Walker Gilmer's *Horace Liveright: Publisher of the Twenties,* David Dempsey termed *Ten Days That Shook the World* Boni & Liveright's "first major success." *New York Times Book Review,* May 31, 1970, 4-5.

7. She had moved to 72 Washington Square South after Reed was in jail at Abo, Finland.

8. JR to LB, June 26, 1920, from Moscow. JR Coll.

9. It was published in the *New Republic* in 1936 in two installments, April 15 and April 29, under the title "Almost Thirty."

10. Bryant's visit to Woodstock is based on extensive interviews with the noted artist, Andrew Dasburg, in his Taos, N. Mex., home in March 1972 and July 1978, and by telephone, 1972-77. His son, Alfred V. Dasburg, retired engineer, provided rich background material in frequent letters, 1975–78, and interviews in New York July 19, 1976, and July 1978. A copy of a letter Andrew wrote his son, aged 9, from Woodstock, said in part: "A friend of mine will send stamps from Russia and other[s] of the Baltic states—I'll ask for uncancelled ones. . . . Miss Bryant, a friend of mine who was here last Sunday gave me a turtle named Sappho—I put it in your pond where it seems content with a few frogs and sunfish for company."

11. "Kornilov to Brest-Litovsk" is spoken of by Reed in his Preface to *Ten Days* as the second of three books he planned on the Bolshevik Revolution, and already under way.

12. Dasburg when visited in Taos in 1972 still had the little snapshot, as well as a little black box of the lacquerware made famous by the Palekh peasants in Russia (this one plain, without figures) that she brought him. He kept stamps in the box and used it daily.

13. In Paris in 1914 Dasburg saw Reed, who was determined to see the results of the German bombing of the Reims cathedral. "Jack had wanted me to go with him behind the German lines but fortunately I had too much good sense for that," said Dasburg. "Paul Rohland and I went with him to Reims—a tremendously impressive sight. But as we wandered around later Jack was hungry and opened the door of a little restaurant. Inside all the tables had been shoved together to make one long table, and there sat the whole French staff of commanders and officers. Of course we were escorted out and put under arrest. We were allowed to stay the night at a little hotel and next day were put on an Army train to return to Paris."

14. "Even as an undergraduate he betrayed what many people believe to be the central passion of his life, an inordinate desire to be arrested," wrote his classmate Walter Lippmann in "The Legendary John Reed" (*The New Republic*, December 26, 1914). "He spent a brief vacation in Europe and experimented with the jails of England, France and Spain. In one Spanish village he was locked up on general principles, because the King happened to be passing through town that day."

15. The entire account of Bryant's visit to Woodstock and Dasburg's trip with her to the pier and putting her on the tramp steamer is based on extensive interviews with Andrew Dasburg in Taos and by telephone. Both he and his son, Alfred Dasburg, approved the chapter on its completion. She did not set out dressed as a boy, but in ordinary clothes.

It was the last weekend that Louise ever visited Andrew. When he finally saw her again, Reed's death had altered everything. "It wasn't only Louise who was affectecd by it. We all were. And in the letter she wrote me from Moscow afterward it was obvious that his death had given her a new awareness of how greatly she had loved him." Dasburg interviews.

16. The cases of those indicted with Reed in Illinois after the formation of two Communist parties in 1919.

17. Esther Andrews, a writer for *Women's Wear*, whom Louise Bryant is believed to have known in Paris in 1917, had agreed to take care of her mail while she was away. See John Dos Passos, *The Best Times*, 135–36. Some saw in Esther Andrews a potential for self-sacrifice. She and Canby Chambers reportedly had agreed to part, and Chambers was in Europe when he was stricken with infantile paralysis. Andrews went to his resuce—taking care of him during his years in a wheelchair—and never left him. Virginia Dehn, widow of Adolph Dehn, to author, March 3, 1977. (The Dehns knew Chambers and Andrews in Key West in 1948.)

18. LB to Andrew Dasburg, letter undated, postmarked Goteborg, Sweden, August 11, 1920. Andrew Dasburg papers. All the letters to Dasburg from LB quoted here are from this source. Dasburg to his regret destroyed letters from Reed and others from LB but felt that these, and one in a forthcoming chapter, "belonged to history."

19. Dasburg interviews.

20. The letter from LB to Dasburg was written in pencil on a letterhead of the Grand Hotel & Grand Hotel Royal, Stockholm, dated August 20, 1920. The postcard was postmarked Narvik, the date indecipherable except for the year: 1920. Dasburg Papers.

21. Because of its ports, Vardö and Vadsen, and its geographical position, Finnmark County in World War II was the scene of severe fighting between the Russians and the Germans in 1944–45.

22. See the *Liberator*, February 1921, Vol. 4, No. 2, 11.

23. LB to AD, n.d., postmarked Vardö, Norway, August 19, 1920. Dasburg papers.

24. Interview at Norwegian Embassy's Information Division.

25. In the civil war Murmansk was occupied by Allied intervention forces 1918–20.

CHAPTER 16. THE DEATH OF JOHN REED

1. "The 'first congress of peoples of the east' (as it was officially called) met in Baku 1 September 1920." E. H. Carr, *The Bolshevik Revolution 1917–1923*, vol. 3, 262.

2. In view of Balabanov's vaunted intimacy with Reed at this time, it is of

interest that he did not know just where she was to be found or even if she was in Moscow.

3. Within a few years V. Vorovsky, while ambassador to Switzerland, would die in Lausanne, "riddled with bullets by a young White Russian émigré." Victor Serge, *Memoirs*, 167.

4. After the Bolshevik seizure of power, a radical captain in the French military mission was the first Allied official to try to establish friendly relations with the new regime. He was Jacques Sadoul, whom Reed and Bryant knew in 1917.

5. This is important in view of the things that would be said about Reed after Louise's death. It shows him essentially optimistic about conditions in Russia, and leery of Petrovsky's approach. Petrovsky was an anarchist from home who on his return after the February revolution worked in the Obukhovsky munitions plant and was later a member of the Military Revolutionary Committee.

6. John Reed to Louise Bryant, August 26, 1920. John Reed Collection.

7. Carr, *Bolshevik Revolution*, vol. 3, 253.

Reed explained just what the "Jim Crow" system meant in the South: separate and inferior schools; in industry only unskilled jobs for blacks; the ministers of white churches preaching a segregated heaven. The old Socialist Party had separate branches for blacks in the South, and in some states not even that. He told the Comintern: "Negroes can be killed by white men with impunity. The great institution of the Southern white men is the lynching of Negroes. . . . The entire population of the town, men, women, and children, come out to see the show."

Until recently, he said, in the North as well as the South "they were excluded from most unions of the American Federation of Labor. The I.W.W. of course, organized the Negroes." American Communists, he declared, should stress organization of all blacks, North and South, in labor unions with white workers. Agrarian workers and tenant farmers of the South "present problems identical to those of the white agrarian proletariat." He warned that Communists, while working to organize workers, "must not stand aloof from the Negro movement for social and political equality, which in the present growth of racial consciousness enlists the Negro masses." *The Second Congress of the Communist International: Proceedings of Petrograd Session of July 17th, of Moscow Sessions of July 19th-August 7, 1920* (Publishing Office of the Communist International, America, 1921), 123–26.

Four pages of Reed's rough pencil jottings and some typed ones, possibly from which he spoke, are in the JR Coll.

8. Letter of Louise Bryant to Max Eastman, who headed the *Liberator* staff, dated Moscow, November 14, 1920. The letter, "Dear Max," was reproduced in the February 1921 *Liberator*, Vol. 4, No. 2, Serial No. 35, 11, 14, under the title "Last Days With John Reed: A Letter from Louise Bryant." All quotations and indirect quotations in this chapter are from this letter unless otherwise stated, including the short poem "Thinking and dreaming" Reed tells her about. Even when quoting her indirectly the language is hers essentially. It and a letter to Margaret Reed are both in the JR Coll.; the quotes from the latter are noted separately.

9. *Ibid.*

10. "Letter to Louise" appears in Granville Hicks's *John Reed* as having been written in the Finnish jail, 384–85. The Bryant memoir, Hicks Collection, declares it was written when he was detained in 1918 in Christiania.

11. LB to Margaret Reed, October 20, 1920. JR Coll.

12. Louise Bryant, in *Mirrors of Moscow*, 21–22, wrote of Lenin's interest in the United States, adding unhesitatingly, "John Reed was as near to his heart as

any Russian." She also wrote, "No wonder he dominates his Cabinet! When he narrows his small Tartar eyes, looks at one with such understanding and intimacy, one feels he is the best friend in the world."

13. "Last Days With John Reed": see note 8. Reed was at all times the reporter, gathering information where and how he could, for his next two books on the Revolution. Before going to Finland he had done all sorts of poking around villages up and down the Volga, he talked to hospital workers in Moscow not only to note the tragic shortages in medicines, modern instruments and common supplies but in personnel, talking to some who were organizing, learning about working conditions. After his painful idleness at the Abo jail, he doubtless found it more interesting to hunt around and explore other things than to lie and rest and demand enough food. All his reporter's notes are at Harvard in the John Reed Collection. One wry note, entered on a page filled with data and quotes on one hospital, reads: "For doctors there is even yet good private practise among speculators." (Reed wasn't his best at spelling. In an album drawn up by delegates at the Second Congress, July 1920, he wrote: "Lenin, Simplest, most human, and yet most far-seeing and immovable. John Reed." Reproduced in N. K. Krupskaya, *Reminiscences of Lenin,* 376.)

14. Victor Serge, *Memoirs of a Revolutionary 1901–1941,* 102–3.

15. Later Lenin would admit it had been a serious mistake to carry the war into Poland. Louis Fischer, *The Life of Lenin,* 397: "Lenin . . . looked for the political error. He named it: 'our political miscalculation—the hope of a revolution in Poland.' " Serge, *Memoirs,* 108–9, admits Lenin forced the attack somewhat by sending Rakovsky and Smilga as political commissars to accompany Tukhachevsky: ". . . it would, despite everything, have succeeded if Stalin and Budyenny had provided support instead of marching on Lvov to assure themselves of a personal victory." But Serge admitted that only students and a few workers, not the peasants or proletarian masses, favored embracing their liberators.

16. Carr, *Bolshevik Revolution,* vol. 3, 200: "The Second Congress marked the crowning moment in the history of Comintern as an international force, the moment when the Russian revolution seemed most certainly on the point of transforming itself into the European revolution, with the destinies of the RFSFR merged in those of some broader European unit. No one was more interested in this consummation than the Russian Bolsheviks, who still implicitly believed that their own salvation depended on it." Nevertheless, 201, "Russian leadership throughout the congress was absolute and unchallenged." Serge, *Memoirs,* 107, put it: "The Russians led the dance. . . . The only figure in Western Socialism that was capable of equalling them, or even perhaps of surpassing them so far as intelligence and the spirit of freedom were concerned, was Rosa Luxemburg, and she had been battered to death with a revolver-butt in January 1919 by German officers."

17. JR to LB, his first letter on his 1919 journey to Russia, sent from Christiana by courier. JR Coll.

18. Only after 1920 would the region be named Azerbaijan, with Baku as its capital; it joined the U.S.S.R. officially in 1922 and became its constituted republic in 1936.

19. Michael Gold in his column, "Change the World!" in the *Daily Worker,* October 14, 1935, 5, told of Reed's pursuit of the bandits with a contingent of the Red Army attached to the train bringing delegates from Baku.

20. See Carr, *Bolshevik Revolution,* vol. 3, 267.

See also Bryant, *Mirrors of Moscow,* 157–58, on Enver Pasha, in which she heaps scorn on Zinoviev: "When Enver turned to Moscow he had no other place to turn to and when Zinoviev took him to Baku, Zinoviev knew no other means of effectively threatening the English in order to change their attitude on the blockade. Zinoviev could not complain about Enver's shallow attitude towards Socialism since there was hardly anything Socialistic about Zinoviev's appeal for a 'holy war.' " In 1923, the Eastern bubble had burst.

But Reed, writing in his report for *The Communist*, was, in contrast, all for the holy war: "The interest taken in these revolutionary nationalist movements is emphasized by the . . . great congress of Oriental peoples . . . meeting on the seashore of the Caspian, planning the new Holy War of the Eastern proletarians for freedom." (Manuscript in Hicks Collection.)

21. Robert A. Rosenstone, *Romantic Revolutionary*, 379–80, regarding Reed's confessing there had been a Russian lover. Within a few lines, on 380, Rosenstone reports: "Feeling abandoned when he had departed for Russia a year before, Louise had turned to other men for comfort." No source is cited for that. Louise turned to Andrew Dasburg, as Rosenstone knew (and indeed I am indebted to Mr. Rosenstone for that information). But Rosenstone adds, same paragraph, "In the spring and summer she had lived with Andrew Dasburg in Woodstock." As Dasburg shared the care of his young son he had a right to be upset about this mistake, especially "when I carefully specified no visit was for more than a weekend." Dasburg interviews.

22. "Last Days With John Reed," 11: see note 8.

23. JR to J. E. Simon & Co., 478 Sixth Avenue, New York, September 28, 1920, informs the pawnshop that the bearer of this, Miss Esther Andrews, is authorized to act as his agent in redeeming "my gold repeater Swiss watch, with the initials J. G. engraved in monogram on the case." The watch was first pledged by Simon & Co. the summer of 1918, repledged in the summer of 1919 and the ticket mislaid. "In the summer of 1920 my wife came to your establishment; you promised to extend the time of collection until January, 1921, and to allow the redemption of the watch upon receipt of this letter from me." The letter is in Reed's hand and signed by him. JR Coll.

The watch had been his great-uncle John Green's, one of the utility magnates of Portland. Arthur Garfield Hays reportedly attempted to obtain the watch for Miss Andrews to give to Reed's widow, but what the result was is unknown.

24. Serge, *Memoirs*, 109, provides a plausible history for the particular microorganism which bit Reed. Writing of what he terms the Congress of Oppressed Nationalities of the East at Baku, he relates: "Returning home from this remarkable trip, John Reed took a great bite out of a water-melon he had bought in a picturesque Daghestan market." Serge was not present but heard about it from his good friend Yakov Blumkin who had been entrusted with the care of the travelers through "perilous country." This crazy act was typical of Reed, who, having overcome a sickly childhood, always laughed at Americans' fear of infectious diseases and himself had never known the meaning of caution.

25. Clare Sheridan, *Mayfair to Moscow: Clare Sheridan's Diary* (New York: Boni & Liveright, 1921), 160–64, wrote of Reed in part: "Everything possible was done for him, but of course there are no medicaments here; the hospitals are cruelly short of necessities. He should not have died."

26. LB to Reed's mother, October 20, 1920. JR Coll.

27. Reed's birthday had been thought by Granville Hicks and others to be October 20. Arthur C. Spencer III of the Oregon Historical Society supplied a copy of a record from the Trinity Episcopal Church of Portland (from the desk of the Rev. William B. McKenzie) showing that John Silas Reed when 4 months old was baptized Sunday, February 12, 1888, and that his birth was recorded as taking place in Portland October 22, 1887. Interestingly, one of his godfathers at the baptism was his great-uncle John Green, from whom he received the cherished watch.

28. "Last Days With John Reed": see note 8.

29. LB to Margaret Reed, October 20, 1920. JR Coll. This is a copy, typed and signed "Yours, Louise" in typing. It appears to have been dictated and proofed by Louise. For example, the last line is: ". . . [her ellipsis] And be brave, little dear mother. Jack was a beautiful and wonderful person and his memory demands that at least of us," with the last two words written in ink. The letter was among the 1962 accessions to the John Reed Collection, given by Virginia Hunt, widow of E. E. Hunt, a classmate of Reed's. Granville Hicks, *John Reed*, 423, said a copy was lent him by Hunt, when he was preparing his biography of Reed.

30. John Reed, *Ten Days That Shook the World*, International Publishers edition of 1967, 132–23: It is the night of October 26/November 8. Reed says: "The *Internationale* is an alien air, after all. The Funeral March seemed the very soul of those dark masses whose delegates sat in this hall, building from their obscure visions a new Russia—and perhaps more." He gives as the words (the ellipses are his):

> You fell in the fatal fight
> For the liberty of the people, for the honour of the people . . .
> You gave up your lives and everything dear to you,
> You suffered in horrible prisons,
> You went to exile in chains. . . .
>
> Without a word you carried your chains because you
> could not ignore your brothers,
> Because you believed that justice is stronger than the sword. . . .
> The time will come when your surrendered life will count.
> That time is near; when tyranny falls the people
> will rise, great and free!
>
> Farewell, brothers, you chose a noble path,
> You are followed by the new and fresh army ready to
> die and suffer. . . .
>
> Farewell, brothers, you chose a noble path,
> At your grave we swear to fight, to work for
> freedom and the people's happiness. . . .

31. Albert Rhys Williams, *Journey Into Revolution*, 320, after recounting the unbelievably brutal deaths of many Vladivostok comrades in the civil war involving Japanese, declares: "Along with all these and with Yanishev and Voskov and Volodarsky, I think of John Reed. Only Reed is well known around the world. Of all the others, only Volodarsky is mentioned in Western histories. Only Yanishev and Reed are buried by the Kremlin's massive wall in Red Square. Heroism was so ordinary in those days and the Bolsheviks were used so unsparingly in the key areas of fighting that most Russian histories, so far as I know, say nothing of Yanishev or Voskov."

32. Alexander Berkman, *The Bolshevik Myth* (New York: Boni & Liveright, 1925), 277–78.

33. But she fainted while the speeches were in progress, said Clare Sheridan, *Mayfair to Moscow*, 162–63. "Although the poor widow fainted, her friends did not take her away. It was extremely painful to see this white-faced unconscious woman lying back on the supporting arm of a Foreign Office official, more interested in the speeches than in the human agony . . . I could not get to her, as I was outside the ring of soldiers who stood guard nearly shoulder to shoulder."

That account seems to negate at least in part Alexander Berkman's in *The*

Bolshevik Myth, 277–78, that, seeing Louise had fallen to the wet ground, he almost forcibly held her up, and would indicate he did not reach her until the end of the ceremony. Most certainly it contradicts Mabel Dodge Luhan's most inaccurate, vindictive, and unnecessary of remarks about Louise. John Reed was dead now, why should she continue her vendetta? But she wrote, in *Movers and Shakers*, 421–22: "Louise, draped in crêpe, the wife of a hero, threw herself on his bier long enough to be photographed for the New York papers."

CHAPTER 17. ALONE AGAIN

1. Louise Bryant, *Mirrors of Moscow*, 10–11.
2. J.R. Coll.
3. "To collect stories during the day and sit up all night to get them off is not a correspondent's paradise," wrote Louise Bryant in one of a 1921 series of by-line stories copyrighted by Universal Service that appeared in the *New York American* August 27, 1921, 2, under the headline "Tchitcherin 'Oddest Politician in the World.' " (Before the year was out the western spelling of his name would become Chicherin.) Correspondents were not to submit stories until shortly before midnight, for the Commissar for Foreign Affairs did not like the daylight. "Tchitcherin had to read every wire himself and he sometimes did not find time until 5 o'clock in the morning. . . . The plain truth is that correspondents are far from welcome. And those that ever do penetrate as far as Moscow are treated with suspicion or ignored. In any case . . . the reporter usually departs in anger and writes all sorts of scathing things against the Soviets after he gets out because he feels personally insulted. The Soviets on their side feel that they have been very badly treated by our reporters."
4. In 1919 both the Committee of Forty-eight, largely intellectuals of a radical bent, and a National Labor Party, soon to become the Farmer-Labor Party, were organized. The former attended the latter's convention in the hope of achieving a platform on which Senator Robert La Follette would run. But the labor people proved too radical for the Forty-eighters and La Follette. James Weinstein, *The Decline of Socialism in America 1912–1925*, ch. 7.
5. *Washington Times*, October 14, 1920, 1–2.
6. Bryant, *Mirrors*, 11.
7. In New York, where the series ran in the *New York American*, a morning paper, the first story appeared on August 16, 1921. In *The San Francisco Examiner*, Bryant's first article on conditions in Russia four years after the October Revolution ran on August 17, 1921. The *Examiner* is an afternoon newspaper. The articles were copyrighted by Universal Service, one of the Hearst wire services.
8. LB to Andrew Dasburg, headed "Nov. 1920," was postmarked Moscow December 11, 1920. Dasburg Papers.
9. Bryant, "In Memory." *Liberator*, July 1921.
10. Bryant, "Aftermath." *Liberator*, November 1921, 21. It was reprinted with creditation in *Current Opinion*, July 1922, 110.
11. In the sixteenth in her series of 1921, headed, in the *New York American* of September 3, 1921, 3, "Strangers Like Old Friends on Russian Trains." She wrote: "The trains running out of Riga and Reval to Petrograd and Moscow are quite clean and one runs small risk travelling, but to go to the Caucasus or to Turkestan means to take a tremendous chance of contracting typhus. It is impossible to escape the vermin, especially in the fourth-class carriages." But democracy was inescapable in packed fourth-class cars. In one diary note quoted she "felt myself lucky to find a bench to sleep on."
12. *Ibid.*

13. *New York American*, August 20, 1921, 2.

14. *New York American*, August 26, 1921, 3, with allusion to her second story in *The San Francisco Examiner* of August 18, 1921 (page number illegible).

15. *New York American*, August 26, 1921.

16. *Ibid*. In this connection Louis Fischer, *The Life of Lenin*, 384, says Lenin warned Soviet agents going into Turkestan that the goal was "the overthrow of feudalism, not communism." As Fischer adds, "The nationalities had a long row to hoe to democracy."

17. *New York American*, August 26, 1921, 3, under headline, "Lenin Restores Sacred Koran to Samarkand."

18. *New York American*, Sunday, August 21, 1921, 4–L. In one minor reference to the main Soviet foreign affairs official, we can see that the Western spelling of Tchitcherin has dropped its two "t"s by then.

CHAPTER 18. BRYANT WRITES UNSPARINGLY OF REVOLUTION'S "GRAY DAYS"

1. From records of State Department obtained through the Freedom of Information Act.

2. Interview with the late Dorothy Day of April 12, 1978. Of her brother she said: "Donald quit a job he had in order to go to Russia. He went over with Martens [Ludwig C.A.K., representative of the Soviet government], who was being deported; Martens had told Donald he could get him into Russia. But the Russians would not let him enter. He was in Riga, almost starving, when Floyd Gibbons of the *Chicago Tribune* came through, bound for Russia. Gibbons got Donald a job on the *Tribune*, for which, with Riga as headquarters, he covered northern Europe and the Balkans."

When American forces entered Berlin in 1945 Donald Day was placed under arrest on a charge of collaborating with the Nazis.

3. All State Department and Division of Passport Control documents obtained through the Freedom of Information Act.

4. The last two lines of this missive, which had made the rounds like others concerning Bryant, were marked and questioned in the margin, but there is no record that the Riga Consul ever was corrected in his misunderstanding. Doubtless Mr. Hurley, who seems to have been J. Edgar's watchdog at State, saw to that. At times a Mr. Keel of Department of Justice was informed and he informed Hoover.

5. This was among documents received from the Federal Bureau of Investigation under the Freedom of Information Act. Hoover referred to "the probability of a connection between her and Mrs. Charles Carver, alias Margaret Berry" but information as to her identity was denied by the F.B.I.

The Bureau of Investigation's dossier on Bryant is full of wildly inaccurate statements, such as: "October, 1921: Subject, who recently arrived from Russia was a delegate to the Red Trades Union International Committee (Justice says this is a very radical organization)." But Louise Bryant was on the S. S. *Latvia* headed for the United States when, in July 1921, the first congress of the Red International of Labor Unions was held.

Included in her file was this anticlimactic statement: "Letter dated June, 1921, from Military Intelligence Dept. states it was reported that subject seemed to be entirely in sympathy with the Russian revolution, as she saw in it a means by which the Russian people might obtain something better"—as read on phone to State May 24, 1922, it was noted. Obtained through the Freedom of Information Act.

In 1918, when Bryant also failed to obtain a passport, one item of information the authorities were asked to consider admits to some recent activity by the State Department in filching mail. W.A. Newcome, passport agent, New York City, noted that "Miss Clarke," apparently a local employee, "furnishes me with the following relative to the applicant:

"Mrs. John S. Reed is the wife of the correspondent John S. Reed and both she and her husband are decidedly *Bolsheviki*. The Department seized the keys to his luggage upon his return to this country and intercepted her letters to him."

6. Bryant was given an appointment with the new Secretary of State, Bainbridge Colby, to present letters from two men who knew him, Philip Francis, I.N.S. executive and editor, and Gilson Gardner of the Scripps organization; and in addition Frederic C. Howe, known for many things, not least as the husband of Jenney C. Howe, president of Heterodoxy. Howe wrote that Bryant was long an "intimate friend of mine and of Mrs. Howe," that she had been given "a most important and highly lucrative assignment" by I.N.S., and that "anyone as talented as she is should not have their means of livelihood . . . interfered with." Francis claimed that "she will be useful not only to us, but to the country, if she works for us in Russia." When all else failed, William A. De Ford, as attorney for I.N.S. (he was also attorney for William Randolph Hearst Sr.), wrote that his client was "quite anxious to know the grounds upon which the refusal of the Department to issue a passport" to Louise Bryant was based. He asked if there were anything his client, I.N.S., or Miss Bryant could do "to overcome the objections which the Department has interposed to her visit to Russia, whatever they may be." But all was to no avail.

7. Ralph Mahoney, former national editor of the Hearst Newspapers, who retired in 1976, to author, letters of May 26, June 15, and September 23, 1977. He based his impression on talk with a newspaperman uncle but, he said, it is clearly supported in W. A. Swanberg's *Citizen Hearst* (New York: Charles Scribner's Sons, 1961). At one time William Randolph Hearst Sr. hoped to make the *New York American* competitive with the *Herald Tribune* and *The World*, initiating an op-ed page patterned after *The World's*. This was always referred to by the staff as "the highbrow page."

8. *The San Francisco Examiner*, August 17, 1921, page 4 CC, under by-line of Louise Bryant.

9. E. H. Carr, *The Bolshevik Revolution, 1917–1923*, vol. 2, 271.

10. *The San Francisco Examiner*, August 18, 1921.

See also on the Tenth Party Congress where Lenin presented N.E.P., E.H. Carr, *The Russian Revolution, From Lenin to Stalin*, "The Breathing-Space of NEP," 30–37. A.G. Shlyapnikov and Kollontai were the leaders of a "Workers' Opposition." But while Carr put Kollontai's prestige in the past and found the leadership of the group "not very impressive," he makes it clear that "it enjoyed wide sympathy and support in the party ranks." According to Carr the congress accepted N.E.P., although without enthusiasm, but argument over trade union policy was bitter, and the final resolution offered by Lenin "skirted the crucial issues without solving them." At one end Trotsky and Bukharin proposed making the trade unions "production unions" and part of the state apparatus. At the other end, the Workers' Opposition wanted the organization and control of production in the hands of the workers as represented in unions. For the first time "the complete abolition of all fractionalism" was agreed on and the rule put in effect that although disputed issues could be discussed by all, formation of groups with platforms was banned. Authority at the Tenth Congress was put in "the central organs of the state," said Carr.

11. *The San Francisco Examiner*, August 18, 1921.

12. This was the lead paragraph in Louise Bryant's September 12, 1921, story

in the *New York American*. But Kollontai went on to speak with pride of how at the beginning of the October Revolution "we wrote into the laws better conditions for mothers than were ever written . . . in any other country."

13. Leon Trotsky, *My Life*, 462, admits that this issue of the trade unions over a two-months discussion clouded his close relationship with Lenin. He points out that it also gave Stalin and Zinoviev a chance "to bring their struggle against me out into the open. . . . It was for them a rehearsal of their future campaign against 'Trotskyism.' But it was just this aspect of the thing that disturbed Lenin most, and he tried in every way to paralyze it."

14. *New York American*, August 23, 1921, by Louise Bryant, under the main headline, "United Russia Living in Peace, Aim of Trotsky."

15. Louise Bryant and Emma Goldman met in Portland, Ore. The widow of Bryant's first husband, Dr. Paul Trullinger, recalled that Paul had told her he and Louise entertained Goldman in their home on one occasion.

16. Charles A. Madison, *Critics & Crusaders*, "Emma Goldman, Anarchist Rebel," 231.

17. Louise Bryant's story on Emma Goldman appeared in the *New York American*, August 22, 1921, the seventh in her series.

18. No government offered asylum to the two refugees, Goldman and Berkman; it was only with difficulty that their friends wrested from Sweden permission for them to stay in Stockholm long enough to obtain visas for a visit to Germany. In 1924 she was permitted to enter England; to secure citizenship and a passport, she married James Colton, a friend and supporter. In 1928 she retired to a cottage given her by friends at St. Tropez, France. Berkman moved to Paris in 1925 and then to Nice in 1929. Not until 1934 was Goldman allowed to enter the U.S. for a 90–day visit.

19. Madison, *Critics*, 233.

20. Letter of Willard R. Trask to author, May 1, 1977. Trask was a noted translator, also known as editor of *The Unwritten Song, Peotry of the Primitive and Traditional Peoples of the World* and compiler of *Joan of Arc: Self Portrait*. Franzen, he said, was visiting Llewellyn Powys and his wife Alyse Gregory in Owemoigne, Dorset, England, when he was killed in an accidental fall from a chalk cliff there in May 1927. Willard Trask, after many honors, including the award of its initial gold medal from the Translation Center at Columbia University when he was 78, died at the age of 80 in New York University, August 10, 1980.

21. Letter of Vincent Sheean to author September 8, 1971, from Leggiuno-Arolo, his home in the northern Italian lake country around Lago Maggiore.

22. Vincent Sheean, *Personal History* (first published in 1934), 24–26. A best-seller, it was reissued in 1969, when Harrison E. Salisbury wrote of it: "Certainly those of us who first read it in the thirties have never forgotten the world of revolutionary events, the fresh, bright words of the young American who lived through them all, and his quicksilver gift for capturing the drama of his day." (Quoted in Sheean's obituary in *The New York Times* March 17, 1975; Sheean died March 15 at his home in Arolo at the age of 75.)

23. Claude McKay, *A Long Way from Home*, 253–54. The poem was Louise Bryant's "Aftermath," which he mentions more than once in this volume.

24. *Ibid*.

25. *Ibid*., 254.

26. This statement by Bryant is borne out by Louis Fischer, *The Life of Lenin*, 337–38: ". . . when the enemy breached the line, communists were hurled in to hold or die. No soldier could say the communists merely used him as cannon fodder; they were the cannon's first meal. Every battlefield has seen the contagion of fear. If an officer falters, the unit may run. Courage too is contagious.

When communists stood, or advanced under fire, those behind were sometimes too human to retreat.

"The communist party was the Soviet spearhead in the civil war. Lenin toughened, tempered, and honed it. . . . Communists were taught to talk politics in the army during noncombat hours. But their chief contribution, a major one, was exemplary heroism in combat. A party member whose valor failed faced a firing squad."

27. The *New York Call*, October 18, 1921, 4.

28. All documents from State Department or Justice Department Bureau of Investigation files obtained through Freedom of Information Act. Hurley's May 22 letter was to a Mr. Adams. Hurley's inspiration as to her speaking tour was headed "SUPPLEMENTAL MEMORANDUM re Louise Bryant (Mrs. John Reed)."

CHAPTER 19. "FAMOUS CORRESPONDENT"

1. Moshe Lewin, *Lenin's Last Struggle*, 33. "He fell seriously ill towards the end of 1921 and was forced to rest for several weeks. During the first half of the following year, his capacity for work was reduced and was constantly deteriorating. Then suddenly, on May 25, 1922, catastrophe struck: his right hand and leg became paralyzed and his speech was impaired, sometimes completely so. His convalescence was slow and tedious." Louis Fischer, *The Life of Lenin*, 600, fixes the date of Lenin's first stroke as May 26, 1922.

Few knew how grave Lenin's illness was. "It seemed that no one thought that Lenin could ever be taken ill . . . was immune to disease." Natalia Ivanovna Sedova, Trotsky's wife, quoted by Leon Trotsky, *My Life*, 472.

2. June 4, 1922. An editorial note said in part: " 'Mirrors of Moscow' reveals as never before the individuality of the men who have maintained the Soviet Government intact against the onslaught of the great Powers of Europe. Whether it is the most beneficial government for Russia is beside the question. The thing is that these men have been successful in carrying on the most amazing experiment in political history, affecting hundreds of millions of people.

"None is better qualified than Miss Bryant to reveal to the world at this time the personality of the great Soviet leaders."

In the *New York American* this appeared in the Sunday "March of Events" section LII, 1 and 2.

3. June 11, 1922, *New York American*, "March of Events" section, 1.

4. According to Vincent Sheean, who said she had told him neither she nor Reed knew Stalin. Sheean and his wife, Diana Forbes-Robertson, author and youngest daughter of the British actor Sir Johnston Forbes-Robertson, were interviewed in New York on January 25, 1975. Sheean had come to New York for treatment for lung cancer; they were to return shortly to Italy.

5. This was her final story of the series. An editorial introduction to her third story, June 18, 1922, declared: "Information from Moscow indicates that Nikolai Lenin, the Russian Premier, will be compelled to give up the reins of government for at least six months. The recent stroke suffered by Lenin has caused specialists to order him to the country for a long rest and doubt is expressed that he can ever resume active control of affairs."

6. Louise Bryant's *Mirrors of Moscow* was dedicated "To Three Wise Editors—M. Koenigsberg, Bradford Merrill, Phillip Francis." Koenigsberg's first name was Moses.

7. State Department records obtained through the Freedom of Information Act.

8. Taped interview with Floyd Ramp obtained in behalf of author, April 24,

1970. He had shipped out to Reval, Esthonia, where he jumped ship and went to Petrograd; he was on his way to work on a collective farm and help get it started. He was for years a farmer and rancher at Roseburg, Ore. The interview was by Julia Ruuttila in Ramp's home in Eugene, Ore.

9. *Augur* of Eugene, Ore., January 21, 1972. Ramp was then 89. In the same interview, Ramp, asked if it were true that he had met Lenin, was quoted as replying: "Yes I saw Lenin and shook hands with him at the meeting of the Third International in the Kremlin in 1922." He remained in Russia for eight months on that trip, his second after the Revolution, and returned with his wife, Vera, in 1966, according to *Augur*.

10. Walsh was head of the U.S. Industrial Relations Commission until its end in 1916. He held a joint chairmanship of the War Labor Board with William H. Taft. He was among the lawyers who signed the *Report Upon Illegal Practices of the Department of Justice* on the subject of the Palmer Raids. Walsh's correspondence in the New York Public Library includes a number of letters sent to Irish revolutionary figures introducing Bryant, who apparently had planned to go there in 1922.

11. Frank Walsh to Louise Bryant, September 30, 1922, from New York. John Reed Collection.

12. The story under Mussolini's by-line appeared in the *New York American* January 21, 1923, Section LII, 1.

13. The Steffens story, datelined Lausanne, December 15, ran for more than five columns and in the *New York American* ran under the headline, "Mussolini, the Dictator, Something New in World Politics / Lincoln Steffens Gives Vivid Pen Picture of Great Italian Leader at Lausanne," on Sunday, December 24, 1922, LII, 3.

14. Although her article speaks of spending a month in the Milan area on the Mussolini story, apparently she was there longer. A letter from Frank P. Walsh to Rebecca Hourwich, November 3, 1922, acknowledges receipt of keys to Bryant's apartment at 1 Patchin Place and states: "She has written me from Rome to look after some of her affairs here, which makes it necessary for me to call at the apartment." Walsh papers, New York Public Library.

15. Louise Bryant's story on Mussolini, copyrighted by International News Service, appeared in the *New York American* Sunday, January 28, 1923, on page one of the "March of Events" section, (beneath a by-line story by Senator William E. Borah of Idaho on the Ruhr crisis). The Bryant story was one of many of her articles obtained through the courtesy of the University of Texas Humanities Research Center library.

16. Clare Sheridan, *Mayfair to Moscow: Clare Sheridan's Diary*.

17. *The New York Times Book Review*, March 11, 1923, 3, under the headline, "Machievellian Muzhiks."

18. *The World*, April 1, 1923, (650 words), quoted by *Book Review Digest* for the year.

19. *Freeman*, 7:237, May 16, 1923, quoted in *Book Review Digest*.

20. *The Nation*, 116:548, May 9, 1923 (1050 words), quoted in *Book Review Digest*.

21. *Times Literary Supplement* of London, April 26, 1923, 279, 1050 words. Quoted in the *Book Review Digest*.

22. *Bookman*, 57:464, June 1923 (100 w.), quoted by *Book Review Digest*.

23. *Time* magazine, March 3, 1923. Bryant's calendar age then was 37, her eyes were blue, but the description otherwise is convincing.

24. *Mirrors of Moscow*, 115, in the chapter, "Madame Alexandra Kollontai and the Woman's Movement," 111–26.

CHAPTER 20. PALACE ON THE BOSPORUS

1. From Aleksandra Kollontai's *Love and Freedom*, quoted by Isabel de Palencia in *Alexandra Kollontay, Ambassadress from Russia* (London: Longmans, Green, 1947), 137. Palencia, a Spanish feminist, is also the author of *Smouldering Freedom: the Story of Spanish Republicans in Exile*.

2. Ralph E. Mahoney, national editor of the Hearst Newspapers before his retirement in 1976, to author by telephone in 1977 after receiving some copies of stories by Louise Bryant.

3. News item in *The San Francisco Examiner*, February 1, 1923, 4CC. It spoke of Bryant's "difficult and dangerous mission that enabled her to send some of the finest newspaper 'beats' since the war." It mentioned her travels throughout Russia and "the uncertain Caucasus," her reports of the war between Greeks and Turks in Asia Minor. She was, it said, the only woman reporter to have visited Kemal Pasha, ruler of Turkey, in his home in Angora (now Ankara).

4. From an associate and confidant of Bullitt's who requested anonymity.

5. When the new marriage laws were passed in mid-December 1917 Kollontai's companion Dybenko, the sailor now head of the Red Fleet since the Revolution, urged marriage. As she was considering the matter, her son Misha and her friend Soja were horrified. "Will you really put down our flag of freedom for his sake?" Soja asked. Misha said stoutly, "You must remain Kollontay and nothing else." A high school student, he went on: "You have always . . . paid no attention to what people say [because] you yourself know that you are right." [Palencia, *Alexandra Kollontay*, 162–64, quoted "from Alexandra's own writings," without specifying which. In earlier years the name was universally spelled Kollontay.]

6. Grace Mott Johnson owned the house but in 1922, when she obtained a divorce from Dasburg (as Rauh had from Max Eastman), Johnson released the house to Dasburg for this new experiment in conjugality. (Later she sold it to him at cost.) The boys were thrilled and for a time Rauh played at housewifery but, like Johnson, was a determined feminist and she and Andrew never married. A trained lawyer, she never practiced law but became a sculptor, painter and poet. Rauh and Dasburg parted in 1927 or 1928; Alfred and Danny remained friends for life. "Dan, a psychologist, was talking to his mother by long distance when he collapsed with a fatal heart attack. I went to see Ida. She no longer wanted to live—and did die a few months afterward, in February 1970, at the age of 92," said Alfred. (Dasburg interviews.) *The New York Times* obituary of Rauh on March 13, 1970 called her "an outspoken feminist" and "a beautiful woman."

7. Louise Bryant to Anne Dennis Bursch, February 13, 1922. John Reed Collection. Bursch's husband, Frederick Bursch, had been Reed's friend and publisher of many of his poems. She was helping Bryant obtain copies of all his works. The letter was written from 1 Patchin Place.

8. Kenneth S. Davis, author of *F.D.R.: The Beckoning of Destiny* and other books, in a major review of the Orville Bullitt book on his brother's correspondence with F.D.R., *The New York Times Book Review* of December 17, 1972, 4, 5, 10, 12 and 14. The quotation is on page 4.

9. Strikes in Glasgow and Belfast in January 1919 were publicly greeted by some British politicians as a prelude to Bolshevism, and a demand for the arrest of the strike committee in each city. Arno J. Mayer, *Politics and Diplomacy of Peacemaking: Containment and Counterrevolution at Versailles, 1918–1919* (New York: Knopf, 1967), 608.

So concerned was President Wilson about labor unrest in the United States that he issued a call for a National Industrial Conference on September 3, 1919, to convene in Washington October 6 and to be made up of spokesmen for labor, the public, and the employers. But before the meeting could be held the storm broke. On September 22, 365,000 steel workers struck. Refusal of the October 6 conference to deal with the strike led to the withdrawal of the labor delegates and the break-up of the meeting. The class war was on in earnest, initiating the greatest labor struggles in U.S. history.

10. William C. Bullitt, *The Bullitt Mission to Russia* (New York: B. W. Huebsch, 1919), 4.

11. Lincoln Steffens, *The Autobiography of Lincoln Steffens*, Ch. XVIII, "The Bullitt Mission to Moscow," 792–3.

12. Quoted by Orville Bullitt, *For the President*, 9, citing as his source John Silverlight in *The Observer*, October 25, 1970.

13. Bullitt, *Mission to Russia*, 94.

14. *Ibid.*, 96.

15. Mayer, *Peacemaking*, 468.

16. *Ibid*.

17. George Biddle the painter, in interviews 1969–71 in his Croton, N.Y., home.

18. H. G. Dwight, *Constantinople Old and New* (New York: Charles Scribner's Sons, 1915), 251–54.

19. Vincent Sheean to author, April 13, 1973, from Leggiuno-per-Arolo, Italy. "I never knew anybody," he added, "so conscious of social and economic privilege even while pretending to make fun of it."

20. Interview with William C. Bullitt's associate and intimate.

21. Orville Bullitt, ed., *For the President*, 16.

22. Gussie Burgess Nobbes, bound for Europe to confront Lincoln Steffens, who had just married Ella Winter and had written to end a long-standing sexual relationship with Nobbes, wrote his sister Laura Suggett from her ship before sailing for France and, mentioning the coming child, declared: "I told you, didn't I, that this Bullitt who fell in love with Louise Bryant was crazy for a child, and I really think L. took on some of his obsession. I have learned that so much L. does are mere gestures." Quoted by Justin Kaplan, *Lincoln Steffens*, 268.

23. Datelined Paris, December 5, it appeared December 23, 1923, in the *New York American's* "March of Events" or world events section, LII, 1 and 4, copyrighted by the *New York American*, headlined: "The Most Unhappy King in Europe Was George of Greece, Now in Exile," and includes an interview with Dictator Nicolas Plasteras. An editorial note preceding Louise Bryant's by-line declares:

"This article, written before the exile of the King and Queen of Greece, turns out to be a remarkably accurate forecast. It gives a valuable insight into the real facts and personalities behind the present upheaval. While Admiral Condouriotos has been made Regent, the real ruler of Greece is Colonel Plasteras, who could easily become President of a Greek Republic, but who has no personal ambition for office."

24. Bullitt-Bryant divorce record of 1930. William C. Bullitt's long suppressed testimony was made available to the writer. (In Philadelphia uncontested divorce cases are assigned to a Master, who hears the plaintiff's testimony and makes his recommendation to a Court of Common Pleas, and the record is withheld from the press, not by law but as policy.)

25. According to Andrew Dasburg. However, this applied alone to events in which Bryant herself was running the risk. In those that Reed alone undertook, usually with her intense disapproval, such as his last trip to Russia in 1919, she was apprehensive and constantly feared the worst.

CHAPTER 21. FROM PARIS TO VIENNA

1. See Orville Bullitt, ed., *For the President Personal and Secret,* Biographical Foreword, xliv–xlv. As the editor is describing how "Bill was always given headlines, and whether the story was accurate did not seem to make any difference," it is unclear how accurate his relationship to all these people was. "Some articles told of the kinship Bill felt with William Christian. . . ." and "Bill would talk of his relationship with 'Grandma' Pocahontas. . . ." are examples of this seeming confusion, but Orville Bullitt goes on to say: "Most of these families had opposed oppression and Bill identified himself with them."

2. *Ibid.,* 15. "She used the pen name of Louise Bryant," Orville Bullitt reports, and was "extremely talented, and striking-looking." But it was not a pen name, it was her stepfather's name, which all the Mohan children took on their mother's marriage to Bryant.

3. *Ibid.,* xli.

4. Interview with Padraic Colum.

5. Interviews with George Biddle, October 1 and October 27, 1969, February 23, 1971, and February 5, 1973.

6. Vincent Sheean to author, from Arolo, Italy, January 31, 1973, and interview with Sheean and his wife, Diana Sheean, in the Adams Hotel, New York, January 24, 1975. He had undergone treatment for lung cancer, from which he died in his home in Italy, March 15, 1975. Mrs. Sheean in permitting the interview explained, "He did want to see you before we left, he feels so deeply about Louise."

7. Excerpt of a letter from William C. Bullitt to anonymous confidant and associate.

8. Lincoln Steffens to Laura Suggett, Paris, February 26, 1924, *The Letters of Lincoln Steffens,* vol. II, 638. The letter alludes to the birth as of "last Sunday." February 26, 1924 was a Tuesday.

9. Ella Winter (Mrs. Donald Ogden Stewart) to author, April 19, 1971.

10. Interview with Charmion von Wiegand and her mother, Inez von Wiegand, then in her nineties, March 10, 1972; interviews with Charmion von Wiegand August 8, 1972 and October 7, 1973.

11. Interview with Prof. Katherine Caldwell, the former Kay Ehrgott, of Mills College, August 10, 1970, in her home in Berkeley, Ca. An authority on Chinese and Japanese art, she was to retire the following year.

12. Interview with Sara Bard Field Wood in her home in Berkeley, Ca., March 26, 1970. Mrs. Wood died June 15, 1974 at the age of 91. She was the author of several books of poetry: *The Pale Woman, Barabbas,* and *The Darkling Plain.*

13. Letter of Hazel Hunkins-Hallinan to author from London, September 9, 1972. She had searched unsuccessfully for the letter from Louise Bryant.

14. Bullitt divorce testimony of 1929. The divorce was granted to him in 1930.

15. But there is evidence that he did fall off his horse once. Among the Louise Bryant letters in the John Storrs Papers at the Smithsonian Institution is one dated only Conway, Mass., October 12, containing this paragraph: "We have been having unpleasant excitement. Bill broke a leg and almost a head. First just walking out a door and the latter a bad fall from his horse. He is hobbling about now."

16. George Biddle interviews.

17. See Vincent Sheean, *Personal History,* 63–66. The telegram from Sheean to Louise Bryant Bullitt was: "Vivent la France et les patates frites!" and "was signed (grave, suspicious circumstance!) with my nickname instead of my professional name." When Sheean insisted that the telegram was a joke, the Colonel

read it again and said: "I see, a joke. An American joke. It was not so regarded at the Censura."

18. Vincent Sheean to author from Arolo, Italy, letters of April 6, 1973 and January 31, 1973. The neighborhoods of the Bullitt residences were provided by Sheean.

19. *Ibid.*, April 13, 1973.

20. The *New York American,* March 9, 1924, "March of Events" section, 1, 7 and 8; March 16, 1924, 2, and March 30, 3, each in "March of Events," or LII. The book was never published and the chapters published in this newspaper are, insofar as is known, the only ones to survive. All of these 1924 stories were obtained from the William Randolph Hearst archives at the Humanities Research Center, The University of Texas at Austin.

21. Latife Hanoum was the daughter of Muammer Usaki (also spelled "Ouchaki"). "Hanoum" is a title of respect, meaning "lady."

22. Louise Bryant, "A Turkish Divorce," *The Nation,* August 26, 1925, Vol. 121, 231-32.

23. Kemal Pasha, or Kemal Ataturk, the name taken in 1934, died in 1938; the cause of death was cirrhosis of the liver. Fifty years after their divorce Latife Usaki, daughter of a wealthy cotton merchant of Smyrna and formerly Kemal Pasha's wife, died at the age of 77. Neither had remarried.

24. Padraic Colum interview.

CHAPTER 22. LOUISE AND CLAUDE McKAY

1. Janet Flanner, "Mr. Ambassador—II," the second of a two-part profile on William C. Bullitt, *The New Yorker,* December 17, 1936, 25.

2. Correspondence between Evelyn Averbuck of Oakland, representing the author, and Juliette L. George of Stanford, Ca., in 1970. With her husband, Alexander L. George, Juliette George is the author of *Woodrow Wilson and Colonel House: A Personality Study* (New York: Dover, 1964; first published by John Day, 1956). In 1970 Mrs. Averbuck advertised for contact with persons who had known Louise Bryant, in behalf of the author. Mrs. George, like many still interested in the published Bullitt study of Wilson, allegedly with the collaboration of Dr. Freud, replied in the hope of learning more, convinced—as others apparently were—that Louise Bryant had been Freud's patient. She cited the Steffens letter as the basis for her assumption.

Erik H. Erikson, in "The Strange Case of Freud, Bullitt, and Woodrow Wilson," *The New York Review of Books,* February 9, 1967, 3–6, 8, felt the collaboration "dubious," adding: "Nor can I see how this book reveals anything about Wilson that has not been described and analyzed better by the Georges in their pioneering study *President Wilson and Colonel House.*"

3. Lincoln Steffens, *The Letters of Lincoln Steffens,* vol. II, 745.

4. Vincent Sheean to author, from Arolo, Italy, February 25, 1973.

5. A query was sent to Dr. Anna Freud, who wrote that she had received it. "And I can answer your question very easily.

"It was certainly Mr. William C. Bullitt who was in analysis with my father in Vienna and I think that fact is rather well known in many circles." Dr. Freud to author, March 27, 1973. (The query to Dr. Freud was addressed to a third party, Peter Lambda, of London, March 1, 1973, by the author, having learned through the kindness of Diana Forbes-Robertson Sheean that Mr. Lambda often saw Dr. Freud.)

6. Quoted by Erikson in "The Strange Case of Freud, Bullitt, and Woodrow Wilson."

7. Sigmund Freud and William C. Bullitt, *Thomas Woodrow Wilson, Twenty-eighth President of the United States: A Psychological Study*. In his Foreword, Bullitt said that in 1932 Freud made textual changes he did not accept and they agreed to put the book aside. In 1938 when he met Dr. Freud at the railway station in Paris after "the Nazis permitted Freud to leave Vienna," Bullitt suggested that after he was settled in London they discuss the book again. He visited him with the manuscript in London and Freud agreed to omit the disputed passages. They decided to postpone publication until after Mrs. Wilson's death. The Foreword does not say so, but Bullitt's obituary in *The New York Times* of February 16, 1967, declares that Bullitt helped Freud to leave Vienna after the Nazi takeover. Freud died in 1939.

8. Interviews with Mura Dehn in her home in New York City September 4 and December 13, 1976, and a later taped interview. She and Adolph Dehn were married in 1926 and although they were later divorced and she was married to Herman Thomas, she is known professionally as Mura Dehn. Herman Thomas died in March 1982.

9. Vincent Sheean to author from Arolo, Italy, April 6, 1973.

10. Sheean letter to author, March 27, 1973.

11. Although his name was James Vincent Sheean, a Paris editor on *The Chicago Tribune* made his first by-line read "Vincent Sheean," and it stuck. His friends and, after he was married, his wife continued to call him "Jimmy."

12. Interviews with Kitty Cannell at the old Sheraton-Plaza Hotel in Boston, October 26, 1971, and January 11, 1972, and numerous long telephone interviews and letters since then. Kathleen Eaton Cannell died May 19, 1974. She was long divorced from the poet Skipwith Cannell. After years of writing on fashions for *The New York Times* she became dance critic of *The Christian Science Monitor*. She also reviewed books for the *Monitor* and wrote many feature stories reminiscing about the famous artists and writers she knew in Paris.

13. Claude McKay, *A Long Way from Home*, 254.

14. Louise Bryant to Claude McKay, from 11 rue Montalivet, Paris, March 30, (1926), one of 20 letters she wrote McKay that he kept. James Weldon Johnson Collection.

15. LB to CM, May 18, (1926): Johnson Coll.

16. Floyd Dell interview. The Dells believed that Bullitt had taken Louise Bryant to leading doctors in various countries when her illness had not yet been determined.

17. LB to CM, June 20, (1926). Johnson Coll. In a postscript she wrote, "I hate your sense of 'hurry' about writing but I think it is only because you find living conditions so hard and difficult to find time to write. L." This June 20 letter from LB to CM is on a letterhead with the Bullitt address presumably, 11 rue Las-Cases VII.

18. Claude McKay to Louise Bryant from Marseilles, June 24, 1926. Johnson Coll.

19. McKay's devoted, long-suffering literary agent, Carl Cowl, now literary executor of the McKay estate, said he had received more than one letter similar to that McKay sent Louise Bryant. Cowl when he was a copyboy for the *Liberator* knew Bryant slightly and said she was "an extremely generous and warm-hearted person. There's no question she was very helpful to Claude." Claude "had a genius for making enemies. He broke with almost every black writer of his time and with one group after another. But he is revered by his people as a whole. He wrote superbly, but had a very hard time." Interview with Carl Cowl in his apartment, Brooklyn, N.Y., July 21, 1976.

20. LB to CM, July 2 (1926), from 11 rue Las-Cases, Paris. Johnson Coll.

21. LB to CM, July 26, from Paris. Johnson Coll.

22. McKay in his autobiography, *A Long Way*, 281, wrote: "My stories finished, I mailed them to Louise Bryant who received them on the very morning she was leaving for America."

23. *Sunday New York American*, September 12, 1926, Section L, 4.

24. In addition to the 50 francs she had in her purse she was enclosing, she said, "10 —" but whether the symbol was for dollars or pounds was unclear.

25. LB to CM, September 26, (1926), from New York, on a letterhead, "The Plaza." Johnson Coll. Whether McKay received "Jack's typewriter" is unknown.

26. These four letters from LB to CM were dated October 8, 1926, from Conway, Mass., where Bullitt had a country home; December 18, on a letterhead, "12 East Eighty-second Street," where Bullitt had rented an apartment; December 26, and January 4 (1927), from same address. Johnson Coll.

27. Interview with F. H. Elwyn, a scientific artist, widow of Dr. Adolph Elwyn, professor of neuroanatomy, College of Physicians and Surgeons, Columbia University. She used to illustrate his books among others. They bought the old Boardman Robinson house in Croton, N.Y.

28. George Biddle interviews.

29. Floyd Dell interview.

30. Dasburg and Ida Rauh were together, either in her Santa Fe home or in Woodstock, N.Y. for six years, beginning in October 1921. She was the daughter of wealthy, indulgent New York parents.

31. Andrew Dasburg, in a telephone call to author amplifying an earlier interview on the evening with the Bullitts.

32. Last interview with Andrew Dasburg, in Taos in 1978. He died there on August 13, 1979 at the age of 92. His work in his late life was his strongest, according to Van Deren Coke, former director of the University of New Mexico Art Museum at Albuquerque, presently a curator of the Museum of Fine Arts, San Francisco, author of *Andrew Dasburg* (Albuquerque: University of New Mexico Press, 1979), a grant from the National Endowment for the Arts providing some of the funding for its color plates. His late drawings, said Coke, combine "the world of the spirit with the world of Euclid and Einstein." He also assessed him as "a worthy descendant of . . . Cézanne and Picasso."

A retrospective of his work from 1909 to 1979, put together by Coke, after opening in the museum at Albuquerque in October 1979 and traveling through the West, made its last stop in Santa Fe in 1981. The 94 paintings, drawings and lithographs included three works made when he was 92. Another grant made the retrospective possible.

Alfred Van Cleve Dasburg, engineer, who on his retirement built a house in Santa Fe to be near his father, died of cancer at 69 on June 3, 1980.

34. Willard Trask interview.

35. Louise Bryant to Claude McKay, undated. Postmark obscured. On reverse of envelope is stamped "Antibes 23/3/27." The play she expresses such hope for apparently was rejected.

CHAPTER 23. THE DESPERATE YEARS

1. Bullitt so testified in a preliminary hearing in 1929 of his divorce suit against Louise Bryant. He was granted a divorce March 24, 1930. In Philadelphia uncontested divorces are decided by one of the Common Pleas courts, but only after testimony is presented to a Master and he has made his recommendation. It is a matter of policy of the prothonotary, or chief clerk, not to release the record of the testimony to the press, but it is not a matter of law. The record in Bullitt's uncontested divorce was made available to the author.

2. See Vincent Sheean, *Personal History*, "Revolution," 182–302. *The New*

York Times in its obituary on Vincent Sheean, March 17, 1975, 32, said: "In 'Personal History,' Mr. Sheean said the most important influence on his life was the red-haired American Communist, Rayna Prohme, whom he met in China in 1927. It was Mrs. Prohme, he said, who persuaded him to broaden the objective concern of a newspaper reporter to include a subjective judgment on the larger issues involved."

3. It was a period when Sheean was convalescing from the experience of witnessing Rayna Prohme's tragic death in Moscow, movingly described in *Personal History*. He sought out a refuge—work on the small newspaper in English, the Paris *Times*. "Its staff was tiny and yet none of its members seemed to see much of anybody else in Paris." Such a restricted life was suited to "the defeated and battered mood" in which he had returned. *Ibid.*, 303–7. (He could not recall when he had last seen Louise Bryant.) Sheean interview, 1975.

4. The review, by Malcolm Cowley, appeared in *The New Republic* of December 25, 1971, 27–8; the book was *Memoirs of Montparnasse*, by John Glassco, published by the Oxford University Press in 1970. Cowley wrote that he was reviewing it as it had received "very little notice in this country." It presented "the most accurate picture of Montparnasse that I have seen; this is the way it was." Glassco was a Canadian.

5. Kitty Cannell interviews.

6. Louise Bryant to Claude McKay, December 2, 1927, from 44 avenue Victor Hugo, Paris. James Weldon Johnson Collection.

7. When McKay's novel *Home to Harlem* was issued early in 1928 it did bear the dedication "To my friend Louise Bryant." See letter of LB to CM, December 16 (1927). Johnson Coll.

8. LB to CM, January 3 (1928). Johnson Coll.

9. LB to CM, January 18 (1928). Johnson Coll.

10. *Home to Harlem,* by Claude McKay, was published by Harper, 1928. There was a paperback edition by Avon, 1951, and the Cardinal paperback edition by Pocket Books, 1965.

11. LB to CM, n.d. Johnson Coll. Envelope shows it was sent to McKay at Marseille and postmarked March 21, 1928. Unlike most of her letters to McKay, it was typewritten, headed "Paris, Monday."

12. This old associate of Bullitt's, who never broke with him, asked that his name not appear.

13. Dr. F. X. Dercum, "Three Cases of a Hitherto Unclassified Affection Resembling in its Grosser Aspects Obesity, But Associated with Special Nervous Symptoms—Adiposis Dolorosa," read before the American Neurological Association, New York, June, 1892. *American Journal of Medical Science* (November 1892), 104: 521535.

14. In 1952 four authors, William A. Steiger, M.D., Henry Litvin, M.D., E.M. Lasché, M.D., and Thomas M. Durant, M.D., say that although many cases of adiposis dolorosa have been described in the literature, little has been added in clinical description or etiologic definition since Dercum's original findings. "It is our purpose to report, from the birthplace of this disease, another case of adiposis dolorosa in which special studies were performed." They note a weight loss of from 225 to 130 pounds, shedding of head hair, and marked fatigue and weakness. An endocrine survey, believed to be the first made on such patients with modern technique, gave no conclusive evidence that the disease results from a primary disturbance of the endocrine function. In the report of the patient it was noted that she "was at all times unhappy, tearful and complaining." *The New England Journal of Medicine* (September 11, 1952), Vol. 247, No. 11, 393–6.

15. Janet Flanner in a postcard to the author of December 20, 1971, described the symptoms of Bryant's malady so exactly that an internist, shown the card, at once said the name Flanner couldn't remember: Dercum's disease.

16. LB to CM, April 16 (1928), from Baden-Baden, Germany. Johnson Coll.

17. Desiree Liven was described by Dehn as "a writer of left sympathies."

18. Mura Dehn interviews.

19. Dell interview.

20. The physician requested anonymity.

21. LB to CM, September 15 (1928), from Conway, Mass.

22. After Steffens and others were guests of Louise Bryant at lunch in the Bullitt home, he wrote his son Pete, an infant, that he should tell "Peter" (Ella Winter) she "must call on Bullitt with you when you return to Paris. The house alone is worth seeing: it is old and grand"—June 12 1926(?). A second letter, to Ella Winter, June 12, 1926, reads in part: "I guess Bullitt has been having some more aunts and uncles dying. He is rich, richer than ever, and their apartment is gorgeous, the lower floor of a house in a court with a picture garden in the rear." Lincoln Steffens, *The Letters of Lincoln Steffens*, vol. II, 744–47.

23. Kitty Cannell said that Peggy Marquis, the unidentified "Mrs. Marquis" of Bullitt's testimony, was heiress to a chocolate fortune and a great friend of Bullitt's. Of two apartments in Paris owned by Cannell, she rented one to Marquis, who used to confide in Cannell that she would like to marry Bullitt. It was Peggy Marquis, said Cannell, who actually introduced Bryant to the lesbian community—and at Bullitt's request. Cannell insisted: "Bill Bullitt did this with deliberate intent. He wanted to destroy Louise. He always had his spies, and Peggy was a chief spy of his." Kitty Cannell interviews.

24. George Biddle was told of this testimony and asked if Louise ever sculpted. "Never," he replied. "Impossible. She was a very competent journalist, not an artist." When Bullitt's confidant was told that Bullitt made the statement somewhere that Louise was a sculptor as well as a writer, he laughed. "Bill had a lively imagination," he said indulgently. "If Louise ever drew or painted, then he could imagine her a sculptor with great ease." Of course, her counterpart in his novel *It's Not Done*, dedicated to Louise Bryant, was a sculptor.

25. Orville Bullitt, ed., *For the President, Secret and Confidential*, 16.

26. To two friends of Louise, Kitty Cannell and Mura Dehn, it plainly was immaterial whether she was a lesbian but they believed she was not. An acquaintance who wished to remain anonymous, one of the many talented members of the lesbian community in Paris, said she never considered Louise Bryant a lesbian, although she understood that at one time after the divorce Bryant returned to the Village and was seen with Gwen Le Gallienne in such Village landmarks as Romany Marie's. (Kitty Cannell added: "Louise was seen around with the lesbian girls in Paris. I myself knew all of them; many were interesting persons; that did not make me a lesbian.")

27. The widow of Floyd Sherman Bryant, of Burlingame, Ca., expressed doubts that Louise Bryant ever made the proposed visit to her brothers.

28. Bullitt testimony, from the record of his divorce suit.

29. William C. Bullitt, *It's Not Done*, 324.

30. Cannell interviews.

31. The historian Kenneth S. Davis, author of *F.D.R.: The Beckoning of Destiny*, in a review of *For the President*, the book of the William C. Bullitt–F.D.R. correspondence edited by Orville Bullitt, describing Bullitt's personality, declares: "As his editor-brother remarks in this book, 'Bill had very little use for compromise in his character.' He *did* have in his character, as his brother does not remark but the record shows, a streak of vindictive malice which contradicted the

warm, spontaneous generosity of his nature. When it surfaced in utterly ruthless expression, it resulted in grievous injury—on occasion, to historic persons and causes, including himself." *The New York Times Book Review,* December 17, 1972, 4, 5, 10, 12 (quotation is from 4, 5).

When the peace proposal he brought back from Lenin was officially ignored by Wilson and Bullitt personally humiliated by the President's refusal to see him, his letter of resignation to Wilson, when the Versailles terms became known to him, was hugely publicized; his appearance before a Senate committee later helped defeat the entrance of the United States to the League of Nations. Even more indicative of Bullitt's never-dying hatred was the book on Woodrow Wilson, purporting to be by Bullitt and Sigmund Freud (Wilson was long dead and Bullitt died shortly after it was issued in 1967). To Erik H. Erikson it is inconceivable that Freud would "knowingly collaborate in a pschoanalytic belittling of any person, great or small," and he speaks of "Freud's revolutionary and abiding respect for his patients." The *New York Review of Books,* February 9, 1967, 3, 4, 5, 6–8.

32. When he broke with President Roosevelt, his ban on all who had been associated with Roosevelt was complete, I was told, with the exception of Loy Henderson. After Elbridge Durbrow, one of Bullitt's warm (although not uncritical) admirers who had been put on ice by Bullitt, insisted an interview with Henderson might be advantageous, Henderson said he was too ill to be interviewed, but added: "I think Anne had great sympathy for her mother." He was writing his memoirs, he said.

33. Orville Bullitt, ed., *For the President,* xl–xli.

34. Bullitt, *For the President,* 448, quotes William L. Shirer's criticisms of several dispatches of Ambassador Bullitt to F.D.R. in a period after Bullitt had given up on the idea of a Franco-Nazi rapprochement and was reporting on the battle of France. " 'Bullitt's hysteria about Communism . . . led to some fanciful reporting,' " he quoted.

Shirer quoted a dispatch of May 17, 1940, on two "serious 'fifth column' operations" that ended, "Please for the sake of the future, nail every Communist or Communist sympathizer in our Army, Navy and Air Force." One operation involved French heavy tanks manned as Bullitt said "by Communist workmen from the Renault works" who refused to advance against the Germans. Another, "in cooperation with the Germans on orders of the Soviet government," involved one regiment of Chasseurs "composed of Communists from the Paris industrial suburbs" who revolted and seized Compiègne. Shirer said: "These two horrendous tales appear to have been made up out of the whole cloth by Bullitt's informants . . . and swallowed by the Ambassador, who was prone to believe any tall tale about Communists. . . . The detailed testimony of the commanders of all four armored divisions, and even of the two Inspectors General of the Tanks Generals Buffieux and Keller, both . . . extreme Rightists and as anti-Communist as Bullitt, is unanimous that the French tank crews fought magnificently before they were wiped out. As to the 'regiment' of 18,000 Communist Chasseurs taking over Compiègne . . . this was pure fantasy." William L. Shirer, *The Collapse of the Third Republic,* 681 n2.

Other correspondents not cited by Orville Bullitt included Vincent Sheean, who in a letter to the author from Arolo, Italy, April 13, 1973, just "trusted that FDR didn't pay too much attention to [the Ambassador]" and George Seldes. Seldes in a letter to the author August 23, 1971, from Windsor, Vt., wrote:

"I always thought Bill Bullitt (whom I knew at the Versailles Treaty when he worked with Lincoln Steffens) had become a dirty bastard, and he was worse than that when I came to see him in 1937, after covering the War in Spain for the N Y Post. I found that Bullitt had been lying to F D R in his official reports on 'communist control of Spain.' I had a 2-hour talk with him, I told him the facts, he told me what he had sent to FDR, I practically told him he was a liar, and he threw me out of the embassy."

35. Bohlen interview.

36. Dean Acheson, *Present at the Creation* (New York: W. W. Norton, 1969), 46. "For some time rumors of a personal nature about Welles had been circulating in Washington, assiduously furthered by his malign enemy, William Christian Bullitt, a singularly ironic middle name."

37. Interviews with George Biddle.

38. Janet Flanner, "Mr. Ambassador–I," the first of a two-part profile of Bullitt in *The New Yorker*, Vol. XIV, December 10, 1938, 30–33.

CHAPTER 24. FINAL DAYS

1. Louise Bryant to Arthur Garfield Hays, May 18, 1935, from Hotel Raspail, Paris. From Corliss Lamont archives.

2. Ernesta Bullitt in her sprightly diary of their European honeymoon notes that they put up at Hamburg's greatest hotel, but "We feared to go to sleep lest we talk indiscreetly. That a dictograph was hidden in the heater was a certainty, in Billy's mind." Ernesta Drinker Bullitt, *An Uncensored Diary from the Central Empires* (Garden City, N.Y.: Doubleday, Page & Co., 1917), 4.

3. Louise Bryant to Claude McKay, May 11, 1930, from Les Rosaires, Brittany, France. Addressed to McKay in Barcelona, it was forwarded to him in Paris. James Weldon Johnson Collection.

4. Garnett McCoy, Senior Curator, Archives of American Art, Smithsonian Institution, to author, September 19, 1980. He had recently called on Anne Dasburg, widow of Alfred Dasburg, in Santa Fe to pick up the Andrew Dasburg––Grace Mott Dasburg Papers, "and she told me of your work on Louise Bryant. I wondered if you knew about the Louise Bryant letters to the sculptor John Storrs."

5. Louise Bryant's youngest half-brother, William Philip Bryant, who had wanted to be an architect. Drafted, he came home from the war shattered. He lived with his parents for a time, then married and when he died March 29, 1944, was 47 years old. On his death certificate his occupation is listed as "Disabled War Veteran." He and his wife, Marion Jessie Bryant, lived in North Hollywood, Ca.

6. Louise Bryant to Marguerite and John Storrs, July 20, 1930. John Storrs Papers, Archives of American Art, Smithsonian Institution, Washington, D.C.

7. Drs. Steiger, Litvin, Lasché and Durant, *op. cit.*, 395, agreed that "those who have claimed efficacious results from various therapeutic agents have neglected the one factor that is common to patients who have survived and improved—namely, weight reduction."

8. Claude McKay, *A Long Way from Home*, 309–10.

9. See Wayne F. Cooper, ed., *The Passion of Claude McKay*, 21. See also n. 51, 321–22: "Some of his friends remember him as primarily, if not totally, homosexual; others knew nothing of his homosexuality and regarded him as heterosexual, while some who knew him best maintain he was bisexual."

10. McKay, *A Long Way*, 310–11, 324–25.

11. Margaret Reed to Louise Bryant Bullitt, June 19, (1930), from Portland, Ore. John Reed Collection.

12. Margaret Reed to LB, August 1, (1930). JR Coll.

13. Charles E. ("Chip") Bohlen, speaking of Bullitt: "Bill kept a watchful eye over Anne. Perhaps too much so. Anne became an obsession with him." Bohen interview.

George Biddle, Anne's godfather, said, "Bill's attempts to control her life resulted in a love-hate relationship." Biddle interviews.

14. Margaret Reed to LB, whom she addressed as Mrs. W. C. Bullitt, August 1, (1930). JR Coll.

15. Mura Dehn interviews.

16. Margaret Reed to LB, September 22, (1930), from Portland, Ore. JR Coll.

17. Margaret Reed to LB, October 6, (1930). JR Coll.

18. George Biddle interviews.

19. Interview with the Dells.

20. Joe Pass interviews, November 16, 1971 and July 27, 1973.

21. Interview with Martin Kamin at home of Ethel Ellis, New York, April 1974.

22. Margaret Reed to LB, December 22, 1931. It was addressed to her at the 44th Street Hotel, then forwarded to her at 118 West Eleventh Street, New York, N.Y. JR Coll.

23. Margaret Reed to LB, May 27, 1932. Written on a letterhead of The Shoreham, Los Angeles, it said that she was living there and giving bridge lessons to make a little money. She had received some money from the bank that closed, but not all. Harry and family were in Pasadena. She addressed Bryant at 3 Weehawken Street, New York, N.Y. JR Coll.

24. Orville H. Bullitt, ed., For the President, Secret and Confidential, 17.

25. Sherwood Anderson to LB, September 19, 1932. It was addressed to her at the Murray Hill Hotel, 40th Street and Park Avenue, New York, from Marion, Va., where Anderson was associate editor of two weeklies, The Marion Democrat and the Smyth County News. JR Coll.

26. Records obtained through the Freedom of Information Act.

27. Gellert hoped to have his book Karl Marx' 'Capital' in Lithographs published in Moscow. "I had the plates of the lithographs. But I found that there was a serious shortage of paper in the Soviet Union, and the handmade paper I wanted was out of the question." The book was published in 1934 in New York by R. Long & R. R. Smith. It was a condensation, compiled (from Eden and Cedar Paul's and Ernest Untermann's translation of the original text) by Gellert and interpreted by him in 60 lithographs.

28. Interview with Hugo Gellert in his home in Freehold, N.J., November 21, 1971. Youngest of the artists on The Masses, in 1981 his ninetieth birthday was celebrated by admirers at a large gathering.

29. Kitty Cannell interviews.

30. Mura Dehn interviews.

31. Letter of Professor George Kennan to author, March 25, 1977.

32. New York Daily News, June 3, 1934.

33. Sunday Mirror Magazine Section, June 24, 1934, 5, 18.

34. In 1934–35 Francis Biddle, brother of George Biddle, was chairman of the National Labor Relations Board, but maintained his law practice in Philadelphia. The firm was Barnes, Biddle and Myers. Later he became Attorney General under Roosevelt.

35. Floyd Dell interview.

36. Granville Hicks to Robert Hallowell, October 11, 1934, from Troy, N.Y. Corliss Lamont archives on John Reed.

37. LB to Robert Hallowell, November 18, 1934, from 50 rue Vavin, Paris. Typed copy, Granville Hicks Collection.

38. LB to Robert Hallowell, n.d. From content it was written in the Christmas season, and after the other letter she wrote him. Typed copy, Hicks Coll. Original in pencil, Lamont archives.

39. Alan Cheuse, "Portrait of Mrs. Reed's Husband," *The Nation*, February 16, 1974, 215–16; a review of Barbara Gelb's *So Short A Time: A Biography of John Reed and Louise Bryant*. Cheuse adds that "Bertram Wolfe, in his widely circulated introduction to the Vintage Russian Library edition of *Ten Days That Shook the World*, leads the ranks of this rather ghoulish company, and Sidney Hook plays the fife and beats the drum." He regrets that Gelb "has aligned herself with this odd band." (Sidney Hook reviewed the Gelb book favorably in *The New Republic*, September 29, 1973.)

40. LB to Robert Hallowell, n.d. Lamont archives.

41. LB to Corliss Lamont, May 30, 1935, from Paris. Hicks Coll.

42. LB to Corliss Lamont, to be forwarded to Granville Hicks, n.d. Hicks Coll.

43. LB "Notes to Corliss Lamont, or John Stuart or Hicks," May 30, 1935. JR Coll.

44. Interview with Granville Hicks, January 27, 1977, in an apartment where he and Mrs. Hicks were spending the winter, Barrett Gardens, Kendall Park, N.J.

45. LB to Robert Hallowell, Typed copy, n.d. Hicks Coll.

46. Barbara Gelb, *So Short A Time*, 292, indirectly quoting Janet Flanner: "Louise's drinking, Miss Flanner said, had been a terrible embarrassment to Bullitt. He had tried to have her committed to a nursing home."

47. LB to Corliss Lamont, March 5, 1935. Lamont archives.

48. Arthur Garfield Hays to Corliss Lamont, June 7, 1935. The letter from LB to Hays, enclosed, was written May 18, 1935. Lamont archives.

49. Bryant does not explain "my $300," treating it as a matter familiar to Attorney Hays. If it was the stipend allowed her by Bullitt's lawyers after paying her rent direct it can only be a matter of speculation as to how often she received it.

50. LB "Notes to Corliss Lamont or John Stuart or Hicks," May 30, 1935, cited in note 43. Also in Hicks papers.

51. Jack Carney, close to Reed when he edited a labor paper in Duluth, Minn. When Padraic Colum was told about this passage in her letter and asked to comment, he said, "Probably true," and implied they were overshadowed by Michael Collins, "who was serious about the revolution." Colum interview by telephone, following earlier interview.

52. LB to John Stuart, September 2, 1935, by way of the United States Lines, from Dublin to Paris, JR Coll.

53. LB to Corliss Lamont, October 30, 1935. Lamont archives. This was among letters from Bryant turned over to the John Reed Collection by Lamont in 1967.

The Lenin note with Bryant's incorrect translation and portions of this letter were reproduced in "John Reed and Lenin: Some Insights Based on Mss. Collection at Harvard," by Virginia Gardner, in *Science and Society*, Fall 1967, 388–403. The next issue carried a correction of the translation of the Lenin note.

54. *One of Us: The Story of John Reed*, lithographs by Lynd Ward, narrative by Granville Hicks (New York: Equinox Cooperative Press, 1935).

55. LB to Corliss Lamont, December 2, 1935. Lamont archives.

56. Samuel Putnam, *Paris Was Our Mistress*, 86–88.

57. Art Young, *Art Young—His Life and Times*, 389.

CHAPTER 25. THE DEATH OF LOUISE BRYANT

1. Her mother, Louisa Bryant, also died of a cerebral hemorrhage, in Roseville, Ca., on May 9, 1924. She was buried in the Odd Fellows Lawn Cemetery.

Louisa's husband, Sheridan D. Bryant, the stepfather of Louise Bryant, outlived his wife by 33 years, dying at the age of 93 in Roseville.

2. Alice Bretherton Powell of Salem, Ore., interviewed at her home, June 9, 1970. She died December 18, 1971.

3. George Seldes to author, writing from Windsor, Vt., August 23, 1971, and September 9, 1971. He did not recall the years that he saw Bryant, but when he was Berlin correspondent of the *Chicago Tribune* he visited Paris about three times a year, staying at the Hotel Liberia; from 1928, when he moved to France, until 1932 he lived at the Liberia, off and on. Louise lived at the Liberia then, and at the time of her death. Seldes wrote that Varèse, Kathe Kollwitz, and other notables stayed at the Liberia, "the room price being $2 a day or less, depending on the rate of exchange."

"The talk was that Bullitt refused to help her in any way. When Louise died it was said that she 'died in the gutter' and that the Ambassador refused to give her a funeral. All this is mostly hearsay," Seldes wrote in the August 23 letter.

4. Richard and Anna Maria Drinnan, eds., *Nowhere At Home: Letters from Exile of Emma Goldman and Alexander Berkman*, 192.

5. *Ibid.*, Index. Apparently the editors took the remark Goldman attributes to Steffens in a curiously literal fashion, for the Index lists: "Bryant, Louise (John Reed's companion), 23, 191, 192." To allude to Bullitt, 191, as Arthur Bullitt, and to list him in the Index as "Bullitt, Arthur (U.S. expatriate)" can be explained by sloppiness, but not the former.

6. Mura Dehn interviews.

7. Diana Sheean to author, February 18, 1975, from Arolo, Italy. Vincent Sheean died of cancer March 15, 1975.

8. Vincent Sheean, on a visit to Mexico in 1939, got word that Josephus Daniels, ambassador to Mexico and a power in Democratic politics, wanted to see him. He presented himself and Daniels asked what he thought of Bullitt's performance as ambassador to France. Sheean "tried desperately to think of something good to say about Bill, and finally came up with 'I think he speaks excellent French.' 'Oh, you do, do you?' Daniels growled. 'Well, what do you think of his *judgment?*'" Interview with Vincent Sheean, January 24, 1975.

9. Asked about reports that Bullitt was the first envoy ever to be granted an interview by Stalin, Charles E. Bohlen replied: "He never interviewed Stalin. In December 1933 when he went to Russia to present his letter, he was given a dinner by Voroshilov, and Stalin just dropped in."—Bohlen interview, January 22, 1973.

Orville Bullitt, ed., *For the President, Secret and Confidential*, 69, shows Bullitt as telling Stalin on that occasion that he would like to have a bluff overlooking the Moscow River (in a part of a city park) for "an American embassy modelled on the home of the author of the Declaration of Independence," and reporting to FDR that Stalin replied, "You shall have it." It never eventuated, to Bullitt's deep disappointment and fury. According to Charles Bohlen it was fortunate, for to have erected another Monticello with its flat roof, so inviting to Moscow's heavy snows, would have been inauspicious. Also see Bohlen's *Witness to History 1929–1969*, 32.

10. Interview with Elbridge Durbrow in his home, 3505 Porter Street, Washington, January 23, 1973. In his student days in Paris where he attended the École Libre des Sciences Politiques from 1927 to 1929, he met Louise Bryant several times at the Dôme, near which he lived, on the Left Bank. At the time he had no idea he would be working for her husband—who by March 1930 would be her former husband. "Louise was going down the chute. However, she had lucid moments. She was kind of pitiful. And fairly bitter."

11. Bohlen, *Witness*, 34.

12. Vincent Sheean to author, April 13, 1973, from Arolo, Italy.

13. *New York Herald Tribune*, January 10, 1936, 16. A favorable story, it declares, "She became a close friend of Lenin. . . ." This is an exaggeration. Lenin regarded Reed highly and after his death was very kind to Louise Bryant. Of course when Reed went to Russia in 1917 it was not as "official envoy of the American Communist Party" which had not been organized then but as a reporter, and she went with him. Nor did she meet William C. Bullitt during his mission to Moscow for the American government; she was not in Russia in 1919.

14. *The New York Times*, January 10, 1936, 19. It speaks of "The death of the well-known Communist. . . ." and one bank of the headline over the story states "WAS A COMMUNIST LEADER." Louise Bryant was "a champion of the Bolsheviki," as the story says, but has written she was never a member of any party, Communist or Socialist. The *Times* likewise had her meeting Bullitt in Moscow. Her age was given as 41; she was 50 at the time of her death.

15. *New Masses*, January 21, 1936, 4.

APPENDIX I: A NOTE ON HISTORICAL QUESTIONS

1. Theodore Draper, *The Roots of American Communism*, 286–87. Goldman's first version is in *My Further Disillusionment in Russia*, p. 26; the second is in *Living My Life*, vol. II, p. 851. Draper cites also *My Disillusionment in Russia*, p. 16.

2. Agnes Smedley wrote Goldman that in her years in China she became convinced that the Communists were "the only ones who offer any hope for the peasants." She did not want to see Emma again, for "I do not want to think of you with bitterness." Richard Drinnan, *Rebel in Paradise;* 312. Drinnan also reveals that Goldman's former manager and lover, Dr. Ben Reitman, expressed his sympathy for the Communists and let her know he thought she had been unfair in her criticism of the New Order in Russia.

3. A typed copy of the letter, unsigned, is in the John Reed Collection. It was dated January 25, 1919, and was from 1 Patchin Place, New York City. The practice of using all letters without alterations in spelling has been ignored here, the original being unavailable. Bryant was far from being always accurate but the serious mistakes in this copy were not typical.

4. A Preface accompanies Max Eastman's first article attacking Granville Hicks and his biography of John Reed in *Modern Monthly*, October 1936, 19–20, reproducing a short letter to Eastman from Hicks asking to see him and offering to let him read his first draft, dated November 9, 1935, and Eastman's refusal, dated November 23, 1935. Eastman wrote in part: "Does the fact appear in your book that John Reed . . . denounced Zinoviev and resigned from the Executive Committee of the International on the day he went to his death bed?"

By the time he wrote the article he was less sure of the day. It became: "In my memory of what Louise told me, Reed's final interview with Radek and Zinoviev occurred after the Baku conference and a very short time before he went to his death-bed. Indeed it stayed in my imagination, perhaps because dramatically it belonged there, as occurring on the same day."

5. Max Eastman, *Heroes I Have Known*, 228–29. His quotation from Hicks appears in *John Reed*, 395.

6. Hicks, "A Letter from Granville Hicks." *Modern Monthly*, December, 1936, 29.

7. Lewis Corey to Granville Hicks, December 30, 1935. Granville Hicks Collection. Hicks's biography of Reed was issued in 1936. Corey had objected to

Hicks's stating in a first draft, "When Zinoviev refused to recognize him, Reed peremptorily offered his resignation."

8. Louis Corey to Granville Hicks, January 9, 1936. Hicks Coll.

9. Hicks, "A Letter from Granville Hicks." He adds that Louis C. Fraina (Corey) "says the resignation took place before Reed went to Baku." It had nothing to do with Baku.

10. Draper does not give the date on which two F.B.I. men interviewed Corey. But in describing Fraina's activities in 1922, when he went to Germany to break with the Comintern and resign his job in Mexico which he'd found impossible, at a time when he was "still a Communist at heart"—Draper declares that "thirty years later" he talked to the F.B.I. (By that time he had become anti-Communist.) On Christmas eve 1952 the government served him with a writ of deportation. At a hearing in early 1953 he finds as the government witness, brought in to confront him with his Communist activities of the early twenties, his old opponent Ben Gitlow (who was in prison 1920–22). Gitlow had nothing to say about Corey's recent activity as a prominent anti-Communist. Six months later Corey, formerly Fraina, suffered a cerebral hemorrhage, dying the next day, September 16, 1953. He was 59 years old, the author of numerous widely read books written from a Marxist viewpoint. A visa the government consented to, that he might leave the country, arrived two months after his death. See Draper, *Roots,* 295–302.

11. Draper, *Roots,* 289. A note explains that Draper obtained a copy of the Corey letter to Hicks of December 30, 1935, from Mrs. Esther Corey. It is in the Hicks Collection, possibly added by Hicks at a later time.

12. Draper, *Roots,* 289. Hicks included the quote in his *Modern Monthly* letter of May 1937.

13. Lewis Corey to Granville Hicks, December 30, 1935. Hicks Coll.

14. *Ibid.* Corey wrote in part: "Reed was absolutely wrong in his report that the Congress theses made it possible to work 'for the destruction of the reactionary AFL.' The theses rejected the idea of destruction and urged working from within and capture. You are wrong in saying that 'the theses did recognize that dual unionism might in some circumstances be necessary.' . . . the concession about organizing new unions among the unorganized did not mean dual unionism . . . where unions existed the communists should work through them."

15. Draper, *Roots,* 291.

16. Robert A. Rosenstone, *Romantic Revolutionary,* 379n.

17. Draper, *Roots,* 292.

18. *Ibid.,* 293.

19. Max Eastman, *Love and Revolution,* 259–60.

20. Eastman, *Heroes,* 234.

21. Draper, *Roots,* 285.

22. See David Caute, *The Great Fear,* 79, 126, on the government's use of Benjamin Gitlow as a paid informer in the 1950s. In the 1950s he was also one of seven "nationally prominent ex-Communist professional witnesses" hired by the Canwell State Fact-Finding Committee on Un-American Activities—"all men who knew a Communist when they saw one, even if they had never seen him before"—in Washington State.

23. Richard O'Connor and Dale L. Walker, *The Lost Revolutionary,* 285–86; and much more from Gitlow, Balabanov, Eastman et al., and even Jacob H. Rubin, 270–91. The authors do admit, however, 281, "Some doubt has been cast on the accuracy of Rubin's account, because he also claimed that Reed referred to Joseph Stalin as his best friend. . . ." But they insist that "Rubin's quotations, whether accurate or not, expressed Reed's mood during the Second Congress and after."

24. Barbara Gelb, *So Short A Time,* 275.

25. Souvenir Program of the John Reed Memorial Meeting of October 17, 1921. John Reed Collection. No citation was given for "John Reed, Poet and Revolutionist," from which the extract was taken. Perhaps if Draper had known of this writing, he would have withheld credence from "the rest of Mme. Balabanoff's recollections."

26. Bertram D. Wolfe, Introduction to John Reed's *Ten Days That Shook the World,* Vintage Russian Library edition, Random House, and the Modern Library edition. The Wolfe 44 page Introduction replaced the eight-page Introduction by Granville Hicks of the 1935 Modern Library reprint.

27. Granville Hicks, Introduction to *Ten Days That Shook the World,* by John Reed (New York: Signet, New American Library, 1967), xiii.

28. The text is reproduced from the first edition as published by Boni & Liveright in March 1919 (by July of that year it went into its fourth printing). Not only Lenin's Introduction, first published in the Boni & Liveright edition of 1922, but N.K. Krupskaya's preface for the 1923 Russian edition, are included, and an Index and Biographical Notes were added. Lawson's Introduction declares of *Ten Days,* "As a historical document, a work of art, it looms larger in the sixties than it did in the twenties."

29. "The Living John Reed," *Masses & Mainstream,* November 1950, 24. The article (pp. 13–25) was abridged from a 31-page Introduction by John Stuart to *The Education of John Reed,* a volume of selected writings by Reed, published by International Publishers, New York, in 1955.

APPENDIX II: REGARDING WILLIAM C. BULLITT

1. Thomas Raeburn White, Jr., to author, March 28, 1977.

2. Orville Bullitt, editor, *For the President Personal and Secret: Correspondence Between Franklin D. Roosevelt and William C. Bullitt,* With an Introduction by George F. Kennan (Boston: Houghton Mifflin, 1972), 16.

3. Justin Kaplan, *Lincoln Steffens, A Biography* (New York: Simon and Schuster, 1974), 254–55.

4. *Ibid.,* xli.

5. William C. Bullitt, *It's Not Done* (New York: Harcourt, Brace, 1926) 324-25, 326.

6. Orville Bullitt, ed., *For the President,* 14. "Most historians of this period now agree on the importance of the treaty with Lenin that Bullitt brought to Paris. His action in presenting all the details to the Senate committee was in keeping with his idealistic approach as to what would make a better world."

7. Jonathan Daniels, *White House Witness 1942–45* (Garden City, N. Y.: Doubleday, 1975), from the chapter, "Diary 1943," 193. Daniels was the son of Josephus Daniels, former secretary of the Navy and ambassador to Mexico 1933–42. Jonathan in WWII was assistant director, Office of Civilian Defense, and administrative assistant to President Roosevelt 1943–45. In 1925 he had joined the staff of the Raleigh *News and Observer* and on his father's death in 1948 became editor.

8. Interviews with George Biddle.

9. Kenneth S. Davis, author of *F.D.R.: The Beckoning of Destiny,* reviewing *For the President, New York Times Book Review,* December 17, 1972, 4, 5, 10, 12. Quote is from page 12.

10. Orville Bullitt, ed., *For the President,* 173–74.

11. *Ibid.,* 62.

12. *Ibid.,* 173–76. Quote is from 176.

13. Elbridge Durbrow interview.

14. Kenneth Davis, *New York Times Book Review* December 17, 1972, 12.

15. Erik H. Erikson, "The Strange Case of Freud, Bullitt, and Woodrow Wilson," *The New York Review of Books,* February 9, 1967, 3, 4, 5, 6–8. The quote is from page 4.

16. Ernst L. Freud, editor, *The Letters of Sigmund Freud and Arnold Zweig,* translated by Elaine and William Robson-Scott (New York: Harcourt Brace Jovanovich, 1970), 25, and n. 25.

17. Beatrice Farnsworth, *William C. Bullitt and the Soviet Union* (Bloomington, Ind.: University of Indiana Press, 1967), 176.

18. Orville Bullitt, *For the President,* xlv.

19. *Ibid.,* Bullitt to the Secretary of State, 154–167. Quote is from 155.

20. Daniel Yergin, *Shattered Peace, The Conquest of the Cold War and the National Security State* (Boston: Houghton Mifflin, 1977), n. 24.

21. Kitty Cannell interviews.

Bibliography

Manuscript Sources

Bessie Beatty Collection, New York Public Library, New York.

Andrew Dasburg Papers, George Arents Research Library, Syracuse University, Syracuse, New York.

Floyd Dell–Arthur Davison Ficke letters, Newberry Library, Chicago.

Floyd Dell–Joseph Freeman correspondence, Newberry Library, Chicago.

Alex Gumberg Collection, Wisconsin Historical Society, Madison, Wisconsin.

Granville Hicks Collection, George Arents Research Library, Syracuse University, Syracuse, New York: Louise Bryant memoir.

James Weldon Johnson Collection, Beinecke Rare Book and Manuscript Library, Yale University, New Haven, Connecticut: letters of Louise Bryant to Claude McKay (and one from McKay to Bryant).

General W. V. Judson Papers, Newberry Library, Chicago.

Corliss Lamont Archives.

Mabel Dodge Luhan Collection, Beinecke Rare Book and Manuscript Library, Yale University, New Haven, Connecticut: letters of Andrew Dasburg.

Eugene O'Neill–Agnes Boulton letters (portion), Rare Manuscripts Division, Princeton College Library, Princeton, New Jersey

John Reed Collection, Houghton Library, Harvard University, Cambridge, Massachusetts: all the letters exchanged between John Reed (JR) and Louise Bryant (LB) quoted in this book, except for one from the L.B. memoir.

Raymond Robins Papers, Wisconsin Historical Society, Madison, Wisconsin.

John Storrs Papers, Archives of American Art, Smithsonian Institution, Washington, D.C.: letters of Louise Bryant.

Theatre Collection, Lamont Library, Harvard University, Cambridge, Massachusetts.

Frank Walsh letters of 1922, New York Public Library, New York.

Newspaper and Periodical Sources

Labor and Socialist newspapers of 1919, Bancroft Library, University of California, Berkeley, California.

Early 20th century labor papers, Tamiment Library, New York University, New York.

Early city directories of San Francisco predating San Francisco fire and earthquake, Oakland Public Library.

William Randolph Hearst archives, Humanities Research Center, The University of Texas at Austin.

Library of Congress, for the only known copy—and it partial—of *Voice of Labor*. Early research into Bryant's stories for Hearst publications also done at Library of Congress.

New York Public Library, Newspaper Annex, for a large part of the *New York American* publication of Louise Bryant's stories.

Theatre Arts Library at Lincoln Center, New York, part of New York Public Library: material on Provincetown Players.

Books and Articles:

Alexander, Doris. *The Tempering of Eugene O'Neill*. New York: Harcourt, Brace, 1962.

Anthony, Katharine. "Alexandra Kollontay," *North American Review*, September 1930, 77–82.

Beatty, Bessie. *The Red Heart of Russia*. New York: Century, 1918.

Bebel, August. *Woman and Socialism*. Authorized translation by Meta L. Stern (Hebe). Jubilee 50th edition. New York: Socialist Literature, 1910.

Bimba, Anthony. *The Molly Maguires*. New York: International Publishers, 1932.

Bohlen, Charles E. *Witness to History 1929–1969*. With the editorial assistance of Robert H. Phelps. New York: Norton, 1973.

Boulton, Agnes. *Part of a Long Story*. Garden City, N.Y.: Doubleday, 1958.

Bowen, Catherine Drinker. *Family Portrait*. Boston: Little, Brown, Atlantic Monthly Press, 1970.

Boyer, Richard O., and Morais, Herbert M. *Labor's Untold Story*. 1955. Reprint. New York: United Electrical, Radio & Machine Workers, 1970.

Boylan, James, ed. *The World and the Twenties*. New York: Dial Press, 1973.

Bryant, Louise. *Six Red Months in Russia: An Observer's Account of Russia Before and During the Proletarian Dictatorship*. Illustrated. New York: George H. Doran, 1918.

———. *Mirrors of Moscow*. Illustrated by Césare. New York: Thomas Seltzer, 1923.

———. "The Poets' Revolution," *The Masses*, July 1919.

———. "Jim Larkin Goes to Jail," *Liberator*, June 1920.

———. "A Turkish Divorce," *The Nation*, August 26, 1925.

———. "Russian Memories," *The Dial*, May 1920.

———. "Six Poems," *The Masses*, October 1916.

Bullitt, Ernesta Drinker. *An Uncensored Diary from the Central Empires*. Garden City, N.Y.: Doubleday, Page, 1917.

Bullitt, Orville, ed. *For the President, Personal and Secret: Correspondence between Franklin D. Roosevelt and William C. Bullitt*. Boston: Houghton Mifflin, 1972.

Bullitt, William C. *It's Not Done*, a novel. New York: Harcourt, Brace, 1926.

Carr, E.H. *The Bolshevik Revolution 1917–1923*, 3 vols. 1952. Reprint. London: Penguin Books, 1971.

———. *The Interregnum 1923-1924*. London: Macmillan, 1954.

———. *The Russian Revolution, From Lenin to Stalin*. New York: Macmillan, Free Press, 1979.

————. *Socialism in One Country*, vol. 2. Reprint. Baltimore, Md.: Penguin Books, 1970.

————. *Studies in Revolution*. New York: Grosset & Dunlap, by arrangement with Macmillan, 1964.

————. *What Is History?* The George Macaulay Trevelyan Lectures delivered in the University of Cambridge, January–March 1961. New York: Knopf, 1966.

————. *The October Revolution Before and After*. New York: Random House, Vintage Books, 1971.

————. "Revolution from Above," *New Left Review*, November–December 1967, 17–26.

Caute, David. *The Great Fear: The Anti-Communist Purge Under Truman and Eisenhower*. New York: Simon & Schuster, 1978.

Chernyshevsky, N.G. *What Is To Be Done? Tales about New People*. Introduction by E. H. Carr. Translated by Benjamin R. Tucker. Revised and abridged by Ludmilla B. Turkevich. New York: Random House, Vintage Books, 1961.

Cheuse, Alan. *The Bohemians: John Reed & His Friends Who Shook the World*, a novel. Cambridge, Mass.: Applewood Books, 1982.

Churchill, Allen. *The Improper Bohemians*. New York: Ace Star, reprinted by arrangement with Dutton, 1959.

Cohen, Stephen F. *Bukharin and the Bolshevik Revolution: A Political Biography 1888–1938*. New York: Random House, Vintage Books, 1975.

Cook, Blanche Wiesen. *Crystal Eastman on Women and Revolution*. New York: Oxford University Press, 1978.

Cooper, Wayne, ed. *The Passion of Claude McKay: Selected Poetry and Prose, 1912–1948*. New York: Schocken, 1973.

Cowley, Malcolm. *Exile's Return: A Literary Odyssey of the Twenties*. 1934. Reprint. New York: Viking, 1970.

Day, Dorothy. *The Eleventh Virgin*. New York: Albert and Charles Boni, 1924.

————. *Loaves and Fishes*. New York: Harper & Row, 1963.

————. *The Long Loneliness*. 1952. Reprint. New York: Harper & Row, 1980.

Dell, Floyd. *Homecoming: An Autobiography*. New York: Farrar & Rinehart, 1933.

de Palencia, Isabel. *Alexandra Kollontay, Ambassadress from Russia*. London: Longmans, Green, 1947.

Deutscher, Isaac. *The Prophet Armed: Trotsky, 1879-1921*, vol. I. 1954. Reprint. New York: Random House, Vintage Books, 1965.

————. *The Unfinished Revolution: Russia 1917–1967*. The George Macaulay Trevelyan Lectures delivered in the University of Cambridge, January–March 1967. London, New York: Oxford University Press.

Dos Passos, John. *1919*. 1932. Reprint. New York: Washington Square Press, 1961.

————. *The Best Times: An Informal Memoir*. New York: New American Library, 1966.

Draper, Theodore. *The Roots of American Communism*. New York: Viking, 1957.

Drinnan, Richard. *Rebel in Paradise: A Biography of Emma Goldman*. 1961. New York: Bantam, by arrangement with Beacon Press, 1973.

————, and Drinnan, Anna Maria, eds. *Nowhere at Home: Letters from Exile of Emma Goldman and Alexander Berkman*. New York: Schocken, 1975.

Duncan, Isadora. *My Life*. New York: Boni & Liveright, 1927.

Duniway, Abigail Scott. *Path Breaking: An Autobiographical History of the Equal Suffrage Movement in Pacific Coast States*. New York: Collectors Editions Ltd., Source Book Press, 1970.

Dunn, Robert W. *The Palmer Raids*. New York: International, 1948.

Eastman, Max. *Love and Revolution: My Journey Through an Epoch*. New York: Random House, 1964.

———. *Enjoyment of Living*. New York: Harper & Row, 1948.

———. *Heroes I Have Known*. New York: Books for Libraries, 1942.

Engels, Friedrich. *The Origin of the Family, Private Property and the State, In the Light of the Researches of Lewis H. Morgan*. New York: International, n.d.

Farnsworth, Beatrice. *Aleksandra Kollontai: Socialism, Feminism and the Bolshevik Revolution*. Stanford, Ca.: Stanford University Press, 1980.

———. *William C. Bullitt and the Soviet Union*. Bloomington, Ind.: Indiana University Press, 1967.

Fischer, Louis. *The Life of Lenin*. New York: Harper & Row, 1964.

———. *Men and Politics: An Autobiography*. New York: Duell, Sloan and Pearce, 1941.

Flynn, Elizabeth Gurley. *I Speak My Own Piece: Autobiography of "The Rebel Girl."* New York: Masses & Mainstream, 1955.

Foner, Philip S. *The Bolshevik Revolution: Its Impact on American Radicals, Liberals, and Labor*. New York: International, 1967.

Foster, William Z. *American Trade Unionism: Principles and Organization, Strategy and Tactics*. New York: International, 1947.

———. *Pages from a Worker's Life*. New York: International, 1939.

Fox, R.M. *Jim Larkin: Irish Labor Leader*. New York: International, 1957.

Freeman, Joseph. *An American Testament: A Narrative of Rebels and Romantics*. New York: Farrar & Rinehart, 1936.

Freud, Ernst. L., ed. *The Letters of Sigmund Freud & Arnold Zweig*. Translated by Elaine and William Robson-Scott. New York: Harcourt Brace Jovanovich, 1970.

Freud, Sigmund, and Bullitt, William C. *Thomas Woodrow Wilson, Twenty-eighth President of the United States: A Psychological Study*. Boston: Houghton Mifflin, 1967.

Gardner, Virginia. "John Reed and Lenin: Some Insights Based on MSS. Collection at Harvard," *Science & Society*, Fall 1967, 388–403.

Gelb, Arthur, and Gelb, Barbara. *O'Neill*. New York: Harper & Row, 1962.

Gelb, Barbara. *So Short A Time: A Biography of John Reed and Louise Bryant*. New York: Norton, 1973.

Ginger, Ray. *Eugene V. Debs: A Biography*. New York: Macmillan, Collier Books, by arrangement with Rutgers University Press, 1970. (Original title, *The Bending Cross, A Biography of Eugene Debs*.)

Goldman, Emma. *My Disillusionment in Russia*. Garden City, N.Y.: Doubleday, Page, 1923.

———. *Living My Life*, New York: Knopf, 1931.

———. *My Further Disillusionment in Russia, Being a Continuation of Miss Goldman's Experiences in Russia as Given in "My Disillusionment in Russia."* Garden City, N.Y.: Doubleday, Page, 1924.

———. *Red Emma Speaks: Selected Writings and Speeches by Emma Goldman*. Compiled and edited by Alix Kates Shulman. London: Wildwood House, 1979.

———. "Love Among the Free," in *The Anarchists*, edited, with an Introduction, by Irving L. Horowitz. New York: Dell, 1964.

Greer, Germaine. *The Female Eunuch*. New York: McGraw-Hill, 1971.

Gregory, Horace. *The House on Jefferson Street: A Cycle of Memories*. New York: Holt, Rinehart and Winston, 1971.

Halliday, E. M. *The Ignorant Armies: The Anglo-American Archangel Expedition 1918–1919*. London: Weidenfeld and Nicolson, 1961.

Hapgood, Hutchins. *A Victorian in the Modern World*. New York: Harcourt, Brace, 1939.

Hastings, Donald W., M.D. *Impotence and Frigidity*. Boston: Little, Brown, 1963.

Haywood, William D. *Bill Haywood's Book: The Autobiography of William D. Haywood*. New York: International, 1929.

Hicks, Granville, with the assistance of John Stuart. *John Reed: The Making of a Revolutionary*. New York: Macmillan, 1936.

————. Introduction to *Ten Days That Shook the World*, by John Reed. New York: Signet Books, 1967.

————. *Part of the Truth*. New York: Harcourt, Brace & World, 1965.

————. "A Letter from Granville Hicks," *The Modern Monthly*, December, 1936, 29, and May 1937, 15–16.

Hill, Christopher. *Lenin and the Russian Revolution*. London: Hodder & Stroughton English Universities Press, 1949.

Howe, Marie Jenney. *George Sand: The Search for Love*. New York: John Day, 1927.

Hull, Cordell. *The Memoirs of Cordell Hull*, 2 vols. New York: Macmillan, 1948.

Humphrey, Robert E. *Children of Fantasy: The First Rebels of Greenwich Village*. New York: John Wiley & Sons, 1978.

Hunkins-Hallinan, Hazel. "A Revolution Unfinished," in *In Her Own Right*, a discussion conducted by The Six Point Group. London: George C. Harrap & Co., 1968.

Kaplan, Justin. *Lincoln Steffens: A Biography*. New York: Simon & Schuster, 1974.

Kennan, George F. *Russia and the West Under Lenin and Stalin*. New York: New American Library by arrangement with Little, Brown, 1961.

————. *Russia Leaves the War*. Princeton, N.J.: Princeton University Press, 1956.

————. Introduction to *For the President, Personal & Secret: Correspondence Between Franklin D. Roosevelt and William C. Bullitt*, Orville H. Bullitt, ed. Boston: Houghton Mifflin, 1972.

Knightley, Phillip. *The First Casualty—From the Crimea to Vietnam: The War Correspondent as Hero, Propagandist, and Myth Maker*. New York: Harcourt Brace Jovanovich, 1975.

Kollontai, Alexandra. *The Autobiography of a Sexually Emancipated Communist Woman*. Edited with an Afterword by Iring Fetscher. Translated by Salvator Attanasio. Foreword by Germaine Greer. New York: Herder and Herder, 1971. Original edition: *Autobiographie einer sexuell emanzipierten Kommunistin*. Munich: Verlag Rogner & Bernhard, 1970.

————. *Communisn and the Family*. New York: Literature Department, Workers Party of America, n.d. (Said to have been written in 1920.)

————. *A Great Love*. New York: Vanguard, 1929. (Includes her controversial—in the U.S.S.R.—"The Loves of Three Generations.")

————. *Love of Worker Bees*. Translated by Cathy Porter. Afterword by Sheila Rowbotham. Chicago: Cassandra Editions, 1978.

————. "Sexual Relations and the Class Struggle," and "Love and the New Morality," translated by Alix Holt. Bristol, England: Falling Wall Press, 1972.

Kreymborg, Alfred. *Troubadour*. New York: Boni & Liveright, 1925.

Krupskaya, N. K. *Reminiscences of Lenin*. Translated by Bernard Isaacs. 1960. Reprint. New York: International, 1970.

Kunitz, Joshua. *Russia: The Giant That Came Last*. New York: Dodd, Mead, 1947.

Lasch, Christopher. *The New Radicalism in America 1889–1963: The Intellectual as a Social Type*. New York: Random House, Vintage Books, 1965.

Lenin, V. I., *Selected Works in Three Volumes*, Vol. 2. New York: International Publishers.

Lerner, Gerda. *The Grimke Sisters from South Carolina: Pioneers for Woman's Rights and Abolition*. New York: Schocken, by arrangement with Houghton Mifflin, 1971.

Lewin, Moshe. *Lenin's Last Struggle*. Translated from the French by A. M. Sheridan Smith. New York: Pantheon Books, 1968.

Luhan, Mabel Dodge. *Movers and Shakers*. vol. 3, *Intimate Memories*. New York: Harcourt, Brace, 1936.

———. *Edge of Taos Desert*. New York: Harcourt, Brace, 1937.

Lukacs, Georg. *Lenin: A Study on the Unity of His Thought*. Translated by Nicholas Jacobs. Cambridge, Mass,: MIT Press, 1971. (This translation was first published by New Left Books, London, 1970.)

Luxemburg, Rosa. *Selected Political Writings*. Edited with an Introduction by Robert Looker. Translated from the German, unless otherwise indicated, by William D. Graf. New York: Grove Press, 1974.

McAlmon, Robert. *Being Geniuses Together 1920–30*. Revised, with supplementary chapters, by Kay Boyle. Garden City, N.Y.: Doubleday, 1968.

McCoy, Garnett. "An Archivist's Choice: Ten of the Best," *Archives of American Art Journal*, Vol. 19, No. 2, 1979.

McKay, Claude. *A Long Way from Home*. 1937. Reprint. Introduction by St. Clair Drake. New York: Harcourt Brace & World, 1970.

———. *Home to Harlem*. New York: Harper, 1928.

Madison, Charles A. *Critics & Crusaders*. New York: Henry Holt, 1948.

May, Henry F. *The End of American Innocence: A Study of the First Years of Our Own Time 1912–1917*. 1959. Reprint. Chicago: Quadrangle Books, 1964.

Mayer, Arno J. *Politics and Diplomacy of Peacemaking: Containment and Counterrevolution at Versailles 1918-1919*. New York: Knopf, 1968.

Millett, Kate. *Sexual Politics*. Garden City, N.Y.: Doubleday, 1970.

Murray, George. *The Madhouse on Madison Street*. Chicago: Follett, 1965.

O'Connor, Richard, and Walker, Dale L. *The Lost Revolutionary: A Biography of John Reed*. New York: Harcourt, Brace & World, 1967.

O'Neill, Eugene. *Nine Plays Selected by Author*. Introduction by Joseph Wood Krutch. New York: Liveright, Inc., 1932.

O'Neill, William L., ed. *Echoes of Revolt:* THE MASSES *1911–1917*. Introduction by Irving Howe. Afterword by Max Eastman. Chicago: Quadrangle Books, 1966.

Pares, Bernard. *Russia*. With "An Appreciation" by Richard Pares. New York: New American Library, 1949.

Parry, Albert. *Garrets and Pretenders: A History of Bohemianism in America*. New York: Covici-Friede, 1933.

Porter, Cathy. *Alexandra Kollontai, A Biography*. London: Virago, 1980.

Putnam, Samuel. *Paris Was Our Mistress*. New York: Viking, 1947.

Raeburn, Antonia. *Militant Suffragettes*. With an Introduction by J. B. Priestley. London: New English Library, 1973.

Reed, John. *Insurgent Mexico*. 1914. Reprint. New York: International Publishers, 1969.

———. *Ten Days That Shook the World*. New York: Boni & Liveright, 1919; International, 1926; Modern Library, 1935. New edition with foreword by V. I. Lenin, preface by N. K. Krupskaya, introduction by John Howard Lawson: International, 1967, reprinted with introduction by A.J.P. Taylor, Penguin Books, 1981.

———. *The War in Eastern Europe*. New York: Charles Scribner's Sons, 1916.

——. *"The Eternal Quadrangle: A Farce Adapted from the Wiener-schnitzler,"* a play. Unpublished manuscript, John Reed Collection.

——. "Moondown," a play, *The Masses*, September 1913.

——. "Freedom," a play, *The Provincetown Plays Second Series*. New York: 1916.

Poetry

——. "Fog," *Scribner's*, August 1919. Reprinted in the *Liberator*, December 1920.

——. "America, 1918," *New Masses*, October 15, 1935.

——. "Proud New York," *Poetry*, April 1919.

——. "Sangar," *Poetry*, December 1912.

——. "Tamburlaine," *American Magazine*, January 1913.

——. "A Letter to Louise." In *John Reed: I Saw the New World Born*, an anthology of Reed's writings issued in the U.S.S.R., 1976.

Short Stories

——. *Adventures of a Young Man: Short Stories from Life*. Berlin: Seven Seas Publishers, 1963, 1966. An approximate reprint of the short stories and excerpts from his reportage gathered together with the consent of Louise Bryant by Floyd Dell in 1927 by the Vanguard Press.

——. *Adventures of a Young Man: Short Stories from Life*. Introduction by Lawrence Ferlinghetti. Reprint with the addition of "Almost Thirty." San Francisco: City Lights, 1975.

——. *Daughter of the Revolution*. Edited with an introduction by Floyd Dell. New York: Vanguard Press, 1927.

Renshaw, Patrick. *The Wobblies: The Story of Syndicalism in the United States*. Garden City, N.Y.: Doubleday Anchor Books, 1968.

Rice, Elmer. *Minority Report: An Autobiography*. New York: Simon & Schuster, 1963.

Rosenstone, Robert A. *Romantic Revolutionary: A Biography of John Reed*. New York: Knopf, 1975.

Russell, Dora. *The Tamarisk Tree: My Quest for Liberty and Love*. 1975. Reprint. London: Virago, 1977.

Salaff, Janet Weitzner, and Merkle, Judith. "Women and Revolution: The Lessons of the Soviet Union and China." *Socialist Revolution*, Vol. 1, No. 4 (July–August 1970).

Schneir, Miriam, ed. *Feminism: The Essential Historical Writings*. With an introduction and commentaries by Schneir. New York: Random House, Vintage Books, 1972.

Seldes, George. *Never Tire of Protesting*. New York: Lyle Stuart, 1968.

——. *Tell the Truth and Run: My 44-Year Fight for a Free Press*. New York: Greenberg, 1953.

Serge, Victor. *Memoirs of a Revolutionary 1901–1941*. Translated by Peter Sedgwick. London: Oxford University Press Paperback, 1967.

——, and Trotsky, Natalia Sedova. *The Life and Death of Leon Trotsky*. Translated by Arnold J. Pomerans. New York: Basic Books, 1975. Originally published in France as *Vie et mort de Leon Trotsky*. Amoit-Dumont, 1951.

Seroff, Victor. *The Real Isadora, The Life of Isadora Duncan*. New York: Avon, by arrangement with Dial Press, 1972.

Sheaffer, Louis. *O'Neill: Son and Playwright*. Boston: Little, Brown, 1968.

———. *O'Neill: Son and Artist*. Boston: Little, Brown, 1973.

Sheean, Vincent. *Personal History*, 1934. Boston: Houghton Mifflin, Sentry edition, 1969.

Shirer, William L. *The Collapse of the Third Republic*. New York: Simon & Schuster, 1969.

Smedley, Agnes. *Daughter of Earth*. Afterword by Paul Lauter. Old Westbury, N.Y.: The Feminist Press, 1973.

Smith, Jessica. *Woman in Soviet Russia*. Edited by Jerome Davis. New York: Vanguard, 1928.

Sochen, June. *The New Woman: Feminism in Greenwich Village, 1910–1920*. New York: Quadrangle, 1972.

Stearns, Harold E., ed. *Civilization in the United States: An Inquiry by Thirty Americans*. New York: Harcourt, Brace, 1922.

Steffens, Lincoln. Autobiography of Lincoln Steffens. New York: Harcourt, Brace, 1931.

———. *Letters of Lincoln Steffens*. Edited by Ella Winter and Granville Hicks, with introductory notes; memorandum by Carl Sandburg. Vol. I. New York: Harcourt, Brace, 1938.

N. N. Sukhanov. *The Russian Revolution 1917: A Personal Record*. Edited, abridged and translated by Joel Carmichael. New York: 1962, Harper & Row. From *Zapiski O Revolutsii*, London: 1955.

Swanberg, W. A. *Luce and His Empire*. New York: Charles Scribner's Sons, 1972.

Tomkins, Calvin. *Living Well Is The Best Revenge*. New York: Viking, 1971.

Trotsky, Leon. *History of the Russian Revolution*. 3 vols. Translated by Max Eastman. New York: Simon & Schuster, 1932; London: Victor Gollancz, 1933.

———. *Lenin*. New York: Minton, Balch, 1925.

———. *My Life*. 1930. Reprint. New York: Grosset & Dunlap, 1973.

———. *The Age of Permanent Revolution: A Trotsky Anthology*. Edited with an Introduction by Isaac Deutscher, with the assistance of George Novack. New York: Dell 1973.

Ulam, Adam B. *The Bolsheviks: The Intellectual, Personal and Political History of the Triumph of Communism in Russia*. New York: Macmillan Collier Books, 1965.

U.S., Congress, Senate, Subcommittee of the Committee on the Judiciary. *German Propaganda and the Brewing and Liquor Industries and Bolshevik Propaganda: Hearings and Report*. 66th Cong., 1st sess. Washington, D.C.: Government Printing Office, 1919.

Vorse, Mary Heaton. *A Footnote to Folly*. New York: Farrar & Rinehart, 1935.

———. *Time and the Town: A Provincetown Chronicle*. New York: Dial Press, 1942.

Weinstein, James. *The Decline of Socialism in America 1912–1925*. New York: Random House, Vintage Books, 1969.

Williams, Albert Rhys. *Journey Into Revolution: Petrograd 1917–1918*, published posthumously. Edited by Lucita Williams, with Foreword by Josephine Herbst. Chicago: Quadrangle Books, 1969.

———. *Lenin The Man and His Work*. New York: Scott and Seltzer, 1919.

———. *The Russian Land*. New York: New Republic Inc., 1927.

———. *Through the Russian Revolution*. Illustrated with photographs and Russian posters in colors. New York: Boni and Liveright, 1921.

Williams, William Carlos. *The Autobiography of William Carlos Williams*. New York: New Directions, 1948, 1951.

Wilson, Edmund. *To the Finland Station: A Study in the Writing and Acting of History*. Garden City, N.Y.: Doubleday Anchor Books, 1953.

Winter, Ella. *I Saw the Russian People*. Boston: Little, Brown, 1945.

———, and Shapiro, Herbert, eds. *The World of Lincoln Steffens*. Introduction by Barrows Dunham. New York: Hill and Wang, 1962.

Wolfe, Bertram D. "The Harvard Man in the Kremlin Wall," *American Heritage*, February 1960, 6–9, 94–103.

Young, Art. *Art Young His Life and Times*. Edited by John Nicholas Beffel. New York: Sheridan House, 1939.

Zaturenska, Marya (Mrs. Horace V. Gregory). "They Bury Him in the Kremlin"—which won for her the first John Reed Memorial Prize from *Poetry* (awarded annually from 1924 to 1930, financed by Louise Bryant, discontinued in 1931 when she was financially unable to continue it.)

———. *Selected Poems*. Grove Press, 1954.

Zetkin, Clara. Appendix, "My Recollections of Lenin," *The Emancipation of Women: From the Writings of V.I. Lenin*, with Preface by Nadezhda K. Krupskaya. New York: International, 1966.

Index